Praise for No One Must Know

'…set in the wonderful scene of Devon at the time of Edward III the reader is drawn easily into that time with the atmosphere captured beautifully in the writer's description of life in the 1330s. One of the best books I've read for a while. Susan has captured the feel of the time almost as well asa Ken Follett in Pilars of the Earth.'

Laura White, The Moorlander

'No One Must Know is a great read…captivating…the author manages to keep the reader in suspense throughout the book.'

NC Kennedy, OnlineBookClub

'…is a read page-turner…a must read…well written and entertaining…I cannot recommend enough.'

Evelyn Hadley, Reedsy Discovery

Praise for No Going Back

'…is a fantastic read. Thomas was a uniquely, fully and exceptionally well-developed character…is a wonderful and captivating read…I would read the novel over and over, and I highly recommend it. It is a captivating exploration of love, loss and the pursuit of destiny.'

Jon Owen, Onlinebookclub

The unforgettable cast of characters, lively dialogues, unpredictable twists, and an honest picture of life make this a must-read…the characters are so perfectly portrayed and stay with you long after closing the book…the author explored topics rarely broached in the historical fiction genre – physical and intellectual disabilities, homosexuality, family violence, and singlehood…No Going Back has a special relevance after the Covid pandemic…

The Chrsalis BREW Project

…once again, Susan Frances shows an incommensurable talent in bringing to life the realistic picture of a time that we often picture just with stereotypes…holds a special significance after the recent pandemic…make sure not to miss this saga.

Maria Andrea, Goodreads

…couldn't put it down…Her characters are so well-developed that you feel you know them…I loved this book and would highly recommend both No One Must Know and No Going Back to anyone who enjoys a good historical tale with various twists and turns, and a few surprises!…it's loved by so many that it won an award…

Laura White, The Moorlander

Susan Frances was born in Surrey, England where she went to Godalming Grammar School. As a child, she was fascinated by her grandfather's stories of their Devon family which later inspired her to research her family history and write *No One Must Know*, Book 1 of the Chiddleigh Saga. She lives in Devon with her husband and their golden retriever dog, Monty.

www.susanfrances.co.uk

NO GOING BACK

BOOK 2

OF THE CHIDDLEIGH SAGA

Susan Frances

This novel is entirely a work of fiction. The names, characters and incidents portrayed in it are the work of the author's imagination. Any resemblance to actual persons, living or dead, events or localities is entirely coincidental.
First edition 2024

First published in Great Britain by Susan Frances Wheeler
Copyright © Susan Frances 2024

Susan Frances asserts the moral right to be identified as the author of this work.
A catalogue record for this book is available from the British Library.
ISBN: 9798873700967
Independently published

Cover Design: William Michael
Typesetting: Bill Wheeler

All rights reserved. No part of this publication may be reproduced, stored or transmitted in any form or by any means, electronic, mechanical, photocopying, recording, scanning, or otherwise without written permission from the publisher. It is illegal to copy this book, post it to a website, or distribute it by any other means without permission.

This book is sold subject to the condition that it shall not, by way of trade or otherwise, be lent, re-sold, hired out or otherwise circulated without the publisher's prior consent in any form of binding or cover other than that in which it is published and without a similar condition including this condition being imposed on the subsequent purchaser.

Thanks to Kylie Fitzpatrick for her help in the early stages of this book. Invaluable, as ever.

I also owe thanks to my friend and fellow author, Jude Austin, for her hard work and for giving me the benefit of her literary experience.

Finally, but not least, my husband, Bill, for his support, encouragement, and typesetting skills.

CHAPTER 1

Devonshire, England: August 1348

Thomas dropped the cloth bag at his feet and slouched against the familiar grey stone wall of the cloisters.

It wasn't fair. He didn't want to go home. He liked being a scholar in the monastery with its regular bells and prayers, and he was the favourite to win top scholar. He'd never get that now.

The once welcoming quadrant was deserted and as grey as the clouded sky. In his memory, he could see a line of brothers crossing the cobbles on their way to the chapel, faces hidden within their cowls and hands tucked away in their wide sleeves. He could hear their melodious chants and the crunching of their steps keeping time as clearly as if they were there.

When would he see them again? Would he ever race across those same cobbles in the pouring rain, holding his hood over his head with one hand and clutching his precious parchments under his surcoat with the other, knowing he was late for his lesson again? Despite the monks' best efforts, punctuality was a virtue that he still struggled with. Many was the time he thought he'd been on time, only to burst through the door to find Brother Luke seated behind a neatly lined row of sharpened quills, his fingers drumming on the waxed oak table and lips pursed in disapproval.

A few days ago, everything had changed. Lessons had been cancelled, and the monks had huddled in dark corners and spoke in hushed whispers. Yesterday, Abbot Bartholomew had gathered the scholars in the refectory and broken the news to them that the Pestilence was sweeping the town, and they had to go home. Most had left as soon as their belongings could be gathered, and now he was the only student remaining.

The townspeople of Tavistoke were beyond the walls; he could hear their screams loud and desperate as their fists hammering on the doors demanding sanctuary. The noise had started before sunrise and been growing steadily ever since then. Crossing himself, he prayed the doors would hold.

Above the din, the midday bell tolled, its solemn notes an ugly counterpoint to the commotion outside. Thomas counted the strikes and kicked the cloth bag at his feet.

'Thomas!' Brother Luke's voice pulled him out of his mood, and he turned, hope fluttering in his chest. Was Brother Luke about to tell him things had changed and that he could stay after all?

Brother Luke's leather sandals slapped on the flagstones as he hurried towards him, the rope cord around his habit swinging back and forth with every step. Hopes of a reprieve faded with the echoes of the midday bell as Thomas saw the agitated look on the monk's face.

'What are you still doing here?' Brother Luke demanded. 'The last of the other scholars left before prime bells.'

'I couldn't find my almanac, and I had to say farewell to the bees and tell them I'd be back.' Thomas's chin wobbled, and he bit his lip, furious at his weakness. At fifteen summers, he was too old to cry. 'I will be back, won't I?'

Brother Luke placed his hands on the boy's shoulders. 'Do you not hear the sound of the townsfolk pounding on our doors? As God's servants, they believe we can save them from His wrath.' He squeezed Thomas's shoulders hard, bony fingers digging into the flesh. 'They are wrong. When they hear the door bolts grate and the bars slam shut, they'll be angry, and angry folks are dangerous. You must go home, Thomas. Go, while you still can.'

Thomas looked into Brother Luke's eyes and asked the question he'd been too frightened to ask before. 'What is this deadly Pestilence that sweeps our lands?'

Brother Luke released him with a sigh, looking older and more tired than Thomas had ever seen him. 'Truthfully, we don't know for certain. Some, like myself, believe that it's sent by God to cleanse the world of all sinners. Our physician, Brother Leviticus, says it was predicted in the stars and is being spread by people's bad humours. Maybe it's both, but whatever it is, it sweeps through the land leaving nothing but death in its path, and we are powerless against it. We must pray for God's mercy and do what we can to save ourselves.'

Fear seeped through Thomas's body at the monk's words, turning him cold. If the holy men were powerless, what hope could there be for ordinary people like him?

A metallic clanging added to the hammering outside, suggesting that some of the mob had weapons or even simple farming implements. Thomas shivered; he would have to pass the crowd if he was to go home.

'Must I go?' he said.

Brother Luke nodded. 'Yes, you must.'

'But...I can come back, can't I?' he persisted. 'I haven't finished my Greek transcription yet. I...I took my writing quills and ink and some parchment; I hope you don't mind.'

Brother Luke smiled. 'Of course I don't mind, and you will always be welcome. You're the best pupil I've ever taught. I pray that one day you'll take your place at the University of Oxford, but maybe God has other plans for you first. You have to be a man now, Lord Thomas de Chiddleigh, and as such, you have responsibilities to your family and your people. In these troubled times, they need you and your duty is with them.'

He didn't feel like a lord, and the thought of responsibilities scared him. His Mama, Lady Joan, had run the estate ever since the death of his father, Sir John. She was the one their people needed, not him.

'But I want to stay here and go to Oxford and learn to be a physician, like Brother Leviticus.' He could hear the whine in his voice and looked down, biting his lip as he scraped the stones with the side of his boot.

'Thomas, we can't wait. The hordes grow as we speak, and I must bar the gates and doors. Your horse is ready and waiting. Leave by the back way – it's safer – but keep your wits about you. Remember, people are desperate; don't stop for anyone. Take this.' The monk held out a dagger. 'It's dangerous to travel alone, now more than ever. Come.'

Brother Luke picked up Thomas's bag and strode across the quadrant, ducked under a low stone arch and led the way along a gravelled path through the herb gardens. He stopped before a small faded wooden door in the wall. 'Godspeed,' he said, his face grim.

Thomas ducked through the door and found his horse saddled and waiting, just like Brother Luke had said. He secured the bag to the saddle and mounted, He glanced back for a final farewell, but Brother Luke was gone and the door already firmly barred.

The journey was twelve miles across the moor, and he wasn't looking forward to it. Alone, outside the safety of the monastery's walls, the world was a large and scary place. Grey clouds were scudding across a wide and darkening sky, bringing the smell of rain.

He was no longer a boy scholar. He was a lord, and his first task was to get home safely to Mama and his people. With his jaw set, he gathered his rains and turned his horse for home.

With the cries of the mob fading behind him, he trotted past the pillory on the town green and turned into Tavistoke's main street where he brought his horse to a walk. The shops were shuttered and barred with red crosses painted on most of the doors. He had no idea what the crosses meant but they added a sinister feel to the eerie silence.

On his right, above the cordwainer's shop, the wooden shoe swung above the boarded door. He had been in there only last week to collect his brand-new boots. Back then, it had been bustling and full of life, like the street itself. Now both were deserted.

Passing a narrow alley, he sniffed for the waft of fresh bread from the ovens but he smelt nothing. It seemed the entire town was abandoned, and with a shiver, he kicked his horse into a trot, tension churning in his stomach.

As he approached a line of tall narrow merchants' houses, a stench spread through the air like a blanket. He reined in his horse and grappled inside his surcoat for his kerchief. It wasn't the open sewer – he was used to that smell – but something else, something vile and evil that made him want to heave.

Despite the kerchief held to his nose, the stench grew stronger as he rode forward. His muscles tensed and with growing trepidation, he reluctantly continued. Ahead, on the side of the road was what looked to him like a pile of discarded rags.

He was almost on top of it when it moved, causing his horse to shy. Thomas stared down, tilting his head one way and then the other. He couldn't make it out. Rats, perhaps? But rats wouldn't be interested in discarded rags.

The stink was making his eyes water, and he nudged his horse forward, intending to ride on when a head lolled out from the pile of filthy rags. The man's eyes were a bloodied mess and the white cheek bones were exposed where the crows had feasted. Grotesque black pustules bulged from his neck.

Thomas stared in fear, his heart pounding in his chest.

The Pestilence.

Quickly, he crossed himself. No wonder folks were scared. Maybe Brother Luke was right, and this was God's vengeance. An overwhelming sense of panic surged through him. He had to get out. Get away from this evil before it touched him.

Ahead of him, the east gateway loomed high and grey. It was the only way out of town, but hordes of townsfolk blocked the street, pushing and shoving trying to squeeze through the narrow archway. Babies wailed, women screamed, and men shouted. Thomas watched with horror as an ox lunged, and escaping the hands of its owner, trampled a crippled man on crutches as it charged through the crowd.

Dear God, he wanted no part in this. Brother Luke had said *get out, and stop for no one*. Gripping his reins, Thomas took a deep breath, rammed his heels into his horse's sides and raced for the arch.

Galloping as though the Devil was behind him and scattering people to right and left, he ignored the guard's shouts to stop. Skidding on the cobbles, he swung sharp right over the river bridge and was still galloping two miles on as he passed the boundary stone to Tavistoke.

The road forked around a triangle of grass where the gallows stood empty. In a cloud of dust, Thomas went right onto a wide track heading straight across the high Forest of Dartmoor. He cast a glance over his shoulder, saw that there was no one chasing him and slowed his blowing horse to a walk. Heart pounding, he wiped his shaking hands on his hose.

Miles of open moor stretched to the horizon. Creamy white sheep grazed contentedly amongst the heather, whilst brown wild ponies lifted their heads as he passed, entirely ignorant of what was happening only a few miles away. A few late skylarks trilled so high above his head that, no matter how hard he tried, he couldn't see them.

He inhaled deeply. The air was filled with the sweet peaty smell of drying grass, hinting at autumn to come.

Everything was normal as though he'd ridden through a bad dream. Maybe the Pestilence wasn't God's work after all, but the Devil's. Either way, he was glad to be out of it.

A mile on, the track curved back on itself and wound steeply into a narrow valley. If there were any waiting road thieves, this was a likely spot. Trembling, Thomas checked the dagger on his belt. It was still there.

His father, Sir John, had died at the hands of such men eight months ago. He had been a large, forbidding man, so what chance did he have in a fight? He wasn't good at wrestling. He wasn't good at any sport, unlike his older brother. Richard, who had died at the Battle of Crecy. For his entire life, he couldn't remember a time when he hadn't been unfavourably compared to Richard; brave, strong Richard, who had fought and died in a blaze of honour and glory.

Mama liked Thomas, but she'd been the only one, and you could argue that it was a mother's duty to like her sons. Even some of the scholars at the monastery had teased him, calling him Delicate Thomas, and saying he fought like a maid.

The path descended, and the trees closed in around him as though he'd just ridden into the mouth of a huge, wooden beast. Goosebumps crept up his arms sending the hairs to rise on the back of his neck.

There! Was that a shadow? His heart hammered and his pulse drummed in his ears. Fumbling for the dagger, he dug in his heels. The trees towered thickly overhead, making it difficult to see. The path twisted and turned steeply to a stream at the bottom. The horse took a huge leap over the water, his hooves slipping as he landed. Struggling for a foothold, he began sliding back into the stream.

The shadows were closing in. Thomas could feel them stretching out long, black fingers to pluck him off his horse, black like the pustules on the dying man's neck.

'Get up, you muxy nag!' he yelled and, fearing for his life, whipped his horse hard with the end of the reins. His hand white on the dagger, he braced for figures to loom alongside and pull him down.

His horse scrabbled his way to the top where the trees thinned and the path opened out. Gasping and sweating and not daring to look back, Thomas kicked his horse on, driving the exhausted beast into a stumbling canter until the wood was far behind him

All was quiet. There were no demonic shadows, no bandits running after him. He pulled his horse to a stop and shook his head, wiping the sweat from his brow. What a cloth head he was. There was no one there, only harmless shadows in the trees. He sheathed his knife, gave his horse a grateful pat and with a relieved laugh, continued across the moor at a sedate walk.

The worst of his journey was over. Soon, he'd be home with Mama. He couldn't wait to see the look on her face when he arrived.

After six miles, he left the moor behind and with the sun on his face, he breathed in the smell of the gorse and ling as he crossed the rough grazings. He passed Ellyn and Annie-healer's cottage on his left but there was no one home. Their cottage was typical of the peasants' homes on the estate: a poor squat cruck house put together from sticks and mud with bracken thatch for a roof, a tiny door at one end and sacking nailed over a small opening on one side. A hazel wattle fence surrounded a small front garden, well-tended with herbs, flowers and vegetables. Annie had been as busy as usual. She must be out tending to some of the peasants on the estate.

He was nearly home. Standing in his stirrups, Thomas punched the air and let out a whoop of joy, startling a few fowl scratching the dirt. Laughing, he cantered along the familiar path to Court Barton, his manorial seat.

His manorial seat. How strange that sounded. People would call him Lord Thomas and doff their caps or curtsy to him. He wasn't sure he'd like that. It would make him feel too responsible.

He hadn't seen Mama since Papa's funeral, eight months ago. Even then, he'd only been home two days; Mama had sent him back to school as soon as the service and the feast were over. He'd missed her, but tonight they'd sit down to a hearty meal in the grand hall, and he'd tell her that he had been the favourite to win top scholar. She was always proud of his achievements and didn't mind that he couldn't string a bow or fly a hawk. He smiled. Mama would help him be a lord, she always knew what to — God's teeth!

He yanked the reins and skidded to a stop inches before crashing into a barricade. It towered above him, taller than even the monastery walls, and spanned the entire lane. It looked like it had been thrown together with everything from stones and logs to upturned wagons and anything else the builders could lay their hands on. There was no way around it.

'Turn away, stranger!' The deep voice from above made Thomas jump. 'You're not welcome here.'

A man with a thick dark beard to his chest and dressed in a brown tunic with the hood pushed back, stood on the top. He held a longbow with the arrow nocked and aimed straight at Thomas's chest.

Thomas swallowed and looked up; his eyes fixed on the arrow. 'I'm no stranger. I'm Thomas. Lord Thomas de Chiddleigh. I've come home to see Mam — Lady Joan.' He hoped the man didn't notice the tremor in his voice.

The man peered forward, his arm steady on the bow. Thomas put a hand to his dagger, although it would be useless against such a weapon.

The guard lowered his bow. 'Prithee, my lord, you've been away, and I didn't recognise you. Lady Joan said as how I was to let no one in. I'll tell her you're here.'

'What's happened?' Thomas called out but the man had already gone.

Had a mob from the village come to the house as they had the monastery? Was that why the barricade was there? But—no, that couldn't be it. Any mob would have reached the house long before a barricade of this size could have been built.

Nervously, he glanced around. He could try and climb over, but he couldn't leave his horse to wander off and what about his bag? Mama would soon be here and explain.

He tapped his fingers on his thigh, his mouth bone-dry. What he'd give for a cup of ale or mead.

Hurried footsteps stopped on the other side of the barricade and his mother's welcome voice reached him. 'Thomas! I'm so glad you've come! I thought my message hadn't got through, or maybe—but praise God you're safe.'

It was good to hear her again. 'I received no message, Mama, but when the Pestilence reached Tavistoke, the crowds were trying to get into the monastery and the monks sent us home. I came as fast as I could. What's this wall for?'

'Simon said we needed it to keep people out and stay safe from the Pestilence, but it doesn't matter now.'

At least, he thought that was what she'd said. The barricade wasn't helping, and her voice was quieter than usual. 'Mama, I can hardly hear you. Wait and I'll climb over.'

'No!' The fear in her voice brought him up short. He couldn't remember ever hearing his mama sound so frightened. 'Stay there!'

'I'll be alright. I'm sure I can do it.'

'Thomas, you don't understand.' Lady Joan's voice cracked a little. 'The Pestilence is already come.'

An image of the hideous head in the street loomed in his mind. 'It can't have. We're too far from the town.'

'I prayed for that to be true, but this evil knows no boundaries. Our stableman, Mark, died of it two days ago. There was nothing I could do. I tried to comfort him, but he sent me away. He knew he had it and wanted me to save myself.' Her words broke with sobs. 'May God forgive me, but I was afraid, so I did as he asked and left him to die alone. I should have stayed with him.'

He'd never heard Mama weep before. It was unnerving and he wasn't sure what to say.

'Now one of the stable lads has black lumps on his neck and under his arms,' Lady Joan continued. 'He's in such agony, it's hard to hear it. If God is merciful, He'll take him soon.' Her voice now barely a whisper

'Mama, you must leave before this evil takes you too.'

'It's too late for me, Thomas, but you can still save yourself. You must go.'

Too late? Did that mean — *That head in the street* — no, God wouldn't do that to her, he couldn't. Tears pricked the backs of Thomas's eyes, and he wiped at them with the back of his sleeve.

'But as the new lord, my duty is here. Brother Luke said so.' He forced out the words.

'Brother Luke was right but you're no good to your people if you die, and I couldn't bear it.' He heard her sobs muffled in a kerchief.

'I can't be a lord without you. I don't know how.' A tear tricked down his cheek

'You will. My cousin Eleanor and your sister Maria are with Simon. Pray God they escaped this evil. You must make haste and go to them, and I must stay here.'

Thomas shook his head. 'I can't ride away and leave you here.'

'You must.' Now she sounded more like his mama; the strength back in her voice. 'I have peasants and their families living in the house with me. Each man has his job, we guard the barricades and have provisions. The women and children exercise daily, going no further than the orchard. All is as well as can be. With God's blessing, we shall be saved.' She was trying to be brave, but she didn't fool him, she was as scared as he was.

'Mama, the people can manage. You must come —'

'My place is here, Thomas. No one knows why one person gets this and another doesn't, but I won't risk you or the girls. If God is cleansing the lands of sinners, as the priests say, then I shall accept His judgement. The Lord knows that I have sinned more than most,' she added in a quieter tone.

His mother, a sinner? That couldn't be right. She was the most kind-hearted person he knew. 'You're no sinner. God will spare you. I know he will.'

She tried to laugh. 'I pray you're right.'

'When will it be over?' he asked.

'I don't know. We're all in God's hands, now. Thomas, listen to me. You must stay safe. Do whatever you can. You are the lord, and when God sees fit to end this Pestilence, I know you will return.'

Her words hung in the air. For a second time, he didn't know what to say. 'Mama, I shouldn't be the lord. Richard was the firstborn; he was the one whom Papa was training to take over.'

The silence from the barricade lasted so long this time that he started to wonder if his mother had walked away.

'Thomas…' Her voice shook a little. 'Thomas, before you go, I want to tell you something. Something I should have told you years ago, but…' She broke off, a sob choking in her throat.

'Mama? What is it? What do you want to tell me?'

This was feeling so final and she was weeping in a way that suggested her heart was being torn out of its chest and he could feel his own sobs wrenching with her.

'God, I'm so weak but I can't, not like this. May God in His mercy forgive me, but I can't. When this is over, if He spares us, we'll talk then.'

'And if God doesn't spare us?'

'If God takes me, and if certain…knowledge should come your way — Thomas, promise me you will remember that it wasn't her fault. We did what we thought was best. I have begged for God's forgiveness ever since that day. If we are spared to each other, I pray for the chance to beg yours as well.'

Thomas frowned. 'What wasn't her fault? Mama, I don't understand.'

'Pray God you never do.' Her voice was so soft he had to strain to hear it.

'Mama—'

'And in the dark times to come, think of the fun we had. Do you remember our picnics by the river and the day you showed us how to, what was it? Tickl—'

'Tickle for trout, but tell me what you meant—'

'That's it, tickle for trout. I slipped on a rock and got soaked. Didn't we laugh?'

He heard her strained laugh and forced a smile onto his face. 'I remember we used to play bears around the trees with Eleanor and Maria. They never growled as well as me.'

She laughed a little. 'No, they didn't, did they? When all this is over, we shall have the biggest picnic ever. I'll get Cook to make your favourite oatie cakes and we'll laugh and dance.'

It was a nice picture, but he wasn't sure he believed it any more than she did.

'And pray, my son, as I shall pray that we'll survive this. Promise me you'll look after your people and be a fair and just lord. Swear on your soul.'

The colour had gone; they were back in the grey of the moment.

It was so adult, so final, so surreal, like a dream that he would wake from and look around to see the bare walls of his chamber at the monastery.

'I swear on my soul I will be a good and fair lord.'

'Thank you, I know you won't let me down and now I'll rest easy in my mind. God spare you and never forget that I love you, Thomas. Now make speed.' He heard her voice break and then the sound of her steps as she hurried away.

'I promise, Mama, and I love you too,' he called after her.

Staring at the wall, he strained his ears, hoping to hear her run back and say she'd changed her mind, but her steps grew faint until there was nothing but silence.

She'd gone. Turned him away, just as Brother Luke had. He reached up and caressed a stone on the barricade as though it had been his Mama's face.

'I love you and may God be with you,' he whispered.

He stood for a few moments, wiped a final tear from his eye and slowly turned away.

He gazed across the fields to the high hills and beyond, to the moor and then up to the vastness of the sky. The world was a large and forbidding place and he had never felt so frightened or alone.

CHAPTER 2

In the short space between day and night when the sun was a thin streak of orange, Thomas turned off High Drovers Road onto a rutted track which led to the house of the bailiff, Simon de Perceux.

He shifted in his saddle, wincing. He'd been riding for over six hours and every bone in his body ached.

Mama was scared. It hardly seemed real. Even his father had never been able to frighten Mama. She'd always stood tall and strong, like the rocky tors that dotted the moor. If she was afraid, he was terrified. More than that, he was upset. It wasn't fair of Mama to make him promise to be a fair and just lord, only to abandon him without telling him how he was supposed to do that.

But she had faith in him. Apart from the monks and Annie-healer, she was the only person who ever had, so he would try. Maybe he'd even succeed. He would be strong like a knight. Like Richard.

Following the track around a bend, he saw a stone longhouse sitting neatly behind two large oak trees. Swallows' nests clustered in a row below the bowed beams of the thatched roof, as though huddling together for warmth. As always, a welcoming glow of candles flickered through the shutters. Approaching the hurdle gate, Thomas breathed in the familiar sweet scent of rambling honeysuckle around the door. There was something solid and reassuring about the place. In many ways, it was more like a home than the grandeur of Court Barton.

Before Thomas had reached his seventh summer, he'd known that his father only had eyes for Richard. Perfect Richard; his strong son and heir. As the second son, Thomas had been of no consequence and this place had become his refuge.

Seeing it again lifted his spirits. He wouldn't be alone in this. He had Simon.

A large shadowed figure opened the door, holding a flaming torch in one hand.

'Hail, stranger.' The man raised the torch, moving it slowly from side to side. 'State your business.'

'Simon, hail! It's me, Thomas,' he said, slipping his feet from his stirrups.

'Thomas?' Simon lowered the torch a little. 'Praise God, you're safe. You gave me a scare; these are strange times, and one can't be too careful.'

Thomas slid from his horse and staggered on his aching legs, grateful for the feel of the ground. 'Have you ale? I've been on this muxy horse since Tavistoke, and I swear I could drink a whole barrel!'

'You look as though you need it.' Simon looked over his shoulder and shouted towards the stables. 'Boy! Rouse yourself from your sack and come see to Lord Thomas's horse! Come in and sit down, Thomas; you look ready to drop.'

Gratefully, Thomas threw his reins to the sleepy-looking boy then followed Simon through the low door into the house.

Inside, it was the same as he remembered. Thomas glanced over to the solid oak table placed squarely under the window. He half-expected to see old Carac, Simon's father, bent over his parchments, goose quill in hand as he attended to his figures. The Lord had taken him one night in the dark months, leaving Simon to take up his father's job as bailiff.

Thomas stared at the empty chair, then jumped as Simon put a warm hand on his shoulder.

'I miss him too. But come; sit by the hearth and take off your boots while I fetch the cups.'

Settled in a warm house with good ale sliding down his throat, Thomas relaxed for the first time that day. At least here nothing had changed. Simon was still tall and broad with a brown beard that bushed to about a hand below his chin. The same silk tapestries hung on the walls, the torches flamed in their sconces, and Carac's quills were in their precise line on the table just as he would have left them. It was a nice tribute and presumably something Simon liked to do.

Simon relaxed in his chair, his legs outstretched. 'So, tell me what has happened,' he said, his fingers touching, as though in prayer.

Thomas poured another cup of ale and leaned forward, his arms resting on his knees. 'The townsfolk were mobbing the monastery, seeking refuge from the Pestilence. The monks bolted their doors and sent us home. Did you know the Pestilence has reached the manor?'

'I heard about Mark. God rest his soul.' Simon crossed himself.

'Mama wouldn't let me in. She told me to come here, but she refused to come with me. I'm afraid for her but what can I do to make her change her mind?'

Simon shook his head. 'There's nothing you can do. Take heart, your mother's a brave and good woman. God will spare her, I'm sure of it.'

Thomas stared into the warm fire as though searching for an answer in the flames. 'Pray God you're right, but He has taken other people who were just as brave and good.' He swallowed the rest of his ale in a single gulp, feeling it tingle all the way down. 'She said something else. She spoke of *knowledge that might come my way* and said that *it wasn't her fault* and *we did what we thought was best*. She wouldn't tell me any more but asked me to forgive her. Do you know what she meant?'

Simon shifted in his seat. 'No; why should I? But she was right to protect you by not letting you in. It's bad out there, and it's getting worse. A few weeks ago I rode to Exeter with samples of your Mama's scarlet cloth to present to the guild. It was my first visit to the city, and I was looking forward to it. I'd hoped to meet up with other travellers at the inn at Okewolde, but when I arrived the shutters were closed and the town was deserted. I thought it odd but decided to take my chances and rode on.'

'Tavistoke was like that.'

Simon nodded. 'I hadn't heard of the Pestilence then, but I saw many barricades blocking routes through villages. At the time, I didn't understand. I assumed there was a local feud or something. Later, after what I saw in the city, I understood.'

'Okewolde and Exeter have the Pestilence? Is nowhere safe?' said Thomas.

'It seems not, but let me finish. As I approached from the west road, I saw the cathedral they're building. It's huge, bigger than anything you can imagine.

'Two furlongs from the gatehouse, I crossed a brook overflowing with refuse, animal bones, and human waste. It hadn't been dug for a long time. The smell was so bad I gagged and had to cover my face.

'The city walls are so high it makes your neck ache and on either side of the gatehouse are two enormous round towers. They must have been forty feet or more; much bigger than Okewolde castle.

'I was expecting a guard to stop me, but there was no one about except for a few travellers. It was early, so I thought nothing of it.'

'No guards? Even Tavistoke has a guard, and that's only a small market town.' Thomas finished his ale, poured another and settled back to hear the rest. He was beginning to feel better than he had all day.

Simon nodded. 'I made my way along a wide street. Every inn, shop and house I saw was barred and the shutters closed tight. Folks were travelling towards me, heading out of the city, with their belongings piled on wagons or strapped to their backs. The street was crammed, and they were like animals; men shouting for others to move on while tight-faced women held onto their children's hands. I couldn't understand it. I thought maybe there was a fire, only the bells weren't ringing and there was no smoke or smell of burning timbers.' Simon paused and topped up his cup. 'I tried asking but no one would stop. They just pulled their hoods further down and kept moving, refusing to even look at me. By then the hairs were pricking on the back of my neck, I can tell you.

'I came to a crossroads where a priest was standing beside a stone cross. He was naked to the waist, his arms stretched wide to the heavens. His face was twisted in torment and when he turned, I saw his back was a mass of bleeding cuts. I thought he'd been whipped on the wheel but he held a bunch of bloodied birch twigs. He kept wailing how God was cleansing the land of all sinners, and shouted for passers-by to beat out their sins and repent.'

'And did they?' Thomas asked.

Simon shook his head. 'Some people crossed themselves and skirted around, but most scurried past. Others dipped rags or the hems of their clothes in his blood and wiped their eyes with it, praying for God to protect them from the Pestilence with the blood of one in His favour.

'It was the first time I'd heard the word *Pestilence* and I couldn't believe what I was seeing. I asked the priest what it was. He stepped forward, grabbed my horse's reins and brought his head so close I could see the lice in his hair. He hissed that God's wrath was upon us, and He had sent terrible black buboes to rack sinners with pain before they died. God's blood, he scared me! I wondered if he was mad, but the people were fleeing the city, even the priests.' Simon drained his cup, poured another and sat forward.

'What did you do?'

'Before I could think, a man grabbed my boot and pulled at my legs. As I looked down at him, I saw hideous black lumps on his neck, just as the priest had described. I kicked out and got him on the jaw. He staggered back, falling into the path of the oncoming hordes. Some stepped over him, but most kept moving as though he didn't exist.'

'God's teeth, the people were acting as a mob,' said Thomas. 'It was the same in Tavistoke.'

Simon nodded. 'By then, I was too scared to go to the Guild Hall, so I made for the north gate as quickly as I could. I had to force my way through, and as I left the gate, I noticed the crowds were keeping to one side of the road, and the *stench*. Dear God, the stench. I'd never smelled anything like it. It burned my throat and made my eyes sting. It was worse than all the channels in the towns.'

Thomas knew that smell and guessed what was coming.

'As I neared the place, the horror of what I saw will stay with me for the rest of my days.'

'A body?' said Thomas.

'Worse than that.' A haunted look came into Simon's eyes, he leaned further forward and lowered his voice. 'There were men with their faces covered with thick sacks and their hands swathed in cloths. They were digging pits, hundreds of paces long and deeper than a carp pond.' Simon ran a hand roughly through his hair and shook his head.

'What for?'

'For the dead, Thomas. For the cartloads of rotting dead.'

Cartloads? No wonder Mama had feared for his safety. What Simon was describing sounded like the Devil's own land.

'By the side of the pit was a grotesque heap of bodies piled high as a haystack,' Simon continued. 'They'd been tossed there like discarded poppet dolls. Arms and legs stuck out in all directions through the clouds of black flies. Folks were leaving their dead nearby.' He swallowed, staring into his mug. At last, he continued. 'There was a pack of dogs scavenging and fighting over the bodies. Literally pulling them apart, tearing the dead limb from limb. I had to lean over and bring up my dinner, and I wasn't the only one.' Simon gulped back his drink and flopped back, his face ashen.

'God save us.' Thomas shivered and crossed himself. 'Brother Luke also said it was God's wrath, but Brother Leviticus thinks it spreads from bad humours in the air.'

'Who knows? But whatever this Pestilence is, it's deadly. And it touches everyone.'

They sat there in silence, staring into the dying embers. It was all so surreal, or at least, it seemed that way to Thomas. Last week, he'd nothing more to worry about than his Greek translation, and now he was swept up in the midst of evil carnage.

'Drink up.' Simon refilled their cups. 'Let us speak of more pleasant matters. Tell me, how does it feel to be Lord de Chiddleigh?'

That was hardly a pleasant matter for him. Thomas rubbed the back of his neck and frowned.

'I'm not sure. I vowed to Mama to do my duty and be a good lord, but...I don't know how.' He sighed. 'In truth, I wish everything was as it was. It's my last year as a scholar and in January I was to take my place at the University of Oxford to study as a physician but now...' He dropped his head and stared at the floor.

'There are times when we all wish things were otherwise but we have to accept God's will. You never expected to be the lord. I can understand that it must be hard, but you're clever. You'll find the way. And I can help.' Simon emptied the last of the ale into their cups.

Could he? Could he truly? Simon had always been a good friend, but he was a bailiff, not a lord. What did he really know of such matters?

'Are we safe here?' Thomas asked. 'I mean, we're close to High Drovers Road. What if travellers from Exeter or further come this way?'

Simon let out a long breath. 'You're right. I thought of barricades, like the ones at the manor, but I've only the stable boy, and I couldn't build them on my own. Now you're here, we could do it, but it would still leave only the three of us to guard, and Jake's but a lad.'

Thomas thought of the longbow that he'd seen pointing at his heart earlier. He wasn't sure he was the guarding type.

'In truth, I'm not sure what to do for the best. I have Maria and Eleanor under my care as well. I don't think they have any idea of what's happening,' said Simon.

'Lucky them. How are they?' Thomas had never been particularly close to his little sister – Maria had always been too haughty for his liking – but his mother's cousin, Eleanor, was nice enough, in her odd, childlike way.

'Fine. They're asleep in the bedchamber upstairs.' Simon spread his hands on his knees. 'So, what are we going to do?'

Thomas considered their choices for a moment, even though he knew they only really had one. 'Before we were sent home, Abbott Bartholomew got all the scholars together in the refectory. He said that we should *go quickly, go far and be slow to return.*'

'Where would we go? Your Ashetyne lands are too close to Exeter, so they're no good.'

'Somewhere remote. The north Chiddleigh lands, perhaps?' said Thomas.

Simon ran his fingers through his hair and shook his head. 'That's wild and barren country, no good for anything but sheep. The only dwelling I know of is Combe Hide near the eastern border of your lands, out Holdesworthe way. It might serve us for a short while, but we don't know how long this Pestilence is going to last.'

'It sounds perfect!' Thomas exclaimed.

'No, it's not; it's been abandoned for years. I can't vouch for its state, but I expect it's little more than a ruin by now. You'd be wise to ride over and investigate before you rush into any decisions. The last thing we need is to get there and find out that it's no good.'

Thomas shook his head. 'We don't have time for that. The Pestilence is coming too fast.'

'Hm.' Simon drew his brows together in a frown. 'Maybe so, but wherever we go, we'll have to hide there for the dark months at least. We'd not survive on our own; we'll need others to come with us if we're to eke out a living. More ale?' He picked up the flagon and went to the barrel at the end of the hall.

Thomas stared into the flames and twisted the empty cup in his hands. Too many changes were happening too fast, and he'd been thrust into the middle of the storm with his people to think of. Already, the weight of responsibility hung heavily on his shoulders.

He had to do something. They couldn't go back to the manor, and it wasn't safe here.

That left what Abbott Bartholomew had said, but *that* brought him back to Simon's objections: where could they go, and how would they survive when they got there?

CHAPTER 3

Rose ambled downstream from her father's mill to the village of Ashetyne. Lifting her face, she let the sun wash over her, warming her skin. It was good to get away from the drudgery of the mill, where the dust was so thick on some days that she could hardly see her hand.

She switched her basket to her other hip, the clay jars of whortleberries clinking together as she did so. She was taking them to the forge in payment for the nails Peter had made last week for her Pa.

Humming to herself, she breathed in deeply, taking in the smell of the meadowsweet that grew in high, creamy tufts along the river's edge. She'd pick some on her way back. Her mother used them to sweeten berries and frumenty pudding.

Rose licked her lips at the thought of her favourite treat. It was a shame that it was only served on special occasions like May Day and Christmas.

Lifting her skirts, she picked her way across the ford and turned left just as the bell in the square, stone church on her right tolled the first quarter. That was fine. It was still early, and she was in no hurry.

Fowl scratched in the dirt and a cur stretched lazily in the side of the lane. A peasant strolled ahead of her with a shovel casually balanced on his shoulder, and two ploughmen leaned against the wall of the inn, ale cups in their hands.

The village was unusually quiet – on a normal day, you couldn't move for folks blocking the lane – but Rose didn't think much about it, apart from being disappointed that she wouldn't be able to pick up any choice pieces of gossip to take back to her mother.

Well, it probably didn't matter. Rose sauntered past a row of cob cottages, their thick walls made from mud and straw and their steep thatched roofs almost touching the ground. She glanced hopefully at the doorways, where she'd often see women sitting and working their drop spindles, their fingers a blur as they teased the wool from the fleece to spin into thread.

Nobody was there. Cecily's door was still barred. They'd been the first to flee, and as news of barricades and Pestilence at the manor had reached the village, others soon packed up and followed. Pa had said he wasn't going anywhere. Rose hoped there were some other folks who felt like he did, or they'd be left on their own.

She glanced at the village green. At least the stocks were empty today. She didn't like to see some poor wretch with his arms fixed in the wooden bars and left, sometimes for hours, sometimes days. She hated it, even though she had thrown that egg at the innkeeper last Michaelmas after the weights inspector had caught him watering his ale.

That wasn't why she had thrown it, though. Ma was always complaining that the innkeeper never paid for his flour on time, and so Rose had thrown the egg at him and laughed as the raw yolk slid down the side of his nose and stuck to his lips. It hadn't taken long for the flies to settle. She'd felt guilty then and had never thrown anything since.

She was nearly at the forge and could hear the hiss of a hot shoe on a horse's hoof followed by smoke billowing out of the doors. Closing her eyes, she breathed in, relishing the acrid aroma.

When she opened them again, two riders were coming down the hill into the village. The one on the left was Simon the bailiff, and the other looked like Lord Thomas. What was he doing here? He never came home from school until the harvest.

Rose stayed where she was and fiddled with the jars, hoping to see where they went and, with luck, hear something interesting. They were stopping at the forge. Maybe they needed their horses shod.

'No sign of the Pestilence,' said Thomas, glancing around.

'Not yet but we're only a mile from the manor. I'll wager it won't be long,' said Simon as he dismounted.

'Do you think my plan will work?' said Thomas.

Plan? What plan? Rose poked around in her basket and kept listening.

'Of course, it'll work. You were sure this morning, and I can't think what else we can do,' said Simon, tying his horse to the iron ring on the wall.

'That was this morning. Now we're here—you are coming in with me, aren't you?' Thomas dismounted and tied his horse alongside Simon's. 'It's just—you know what Peter's like.'

Rose smiled. So, the new young lord was scared of the smithy. She didn't blame him; a lot of folks were. Her Pa said Peter was as blunt as his hammer.

'Peter will do as he's told,' said Simon, striding into the forge.

It sounded as though Peter was in trouble. Rose waited until they were inside, then crept closer. Willing the jars not to chink, she put down her basket, stood behind the doorway and peered around.

The forge was dark and smoky with a wide stone hearth glowing red at one end. Out of the red and grey shadows, a ghostly figure emerged.

'Thomas! Prithee, my lord.' William, Peter's son, let the bellows die with a slow sigh and bowed low sweeping his arm in a dramatic gesture. He was the same age as Thomas but a head taller, and as broad and muscular as Thomas was fair and lean. That was what an easy noble's life did for you, Rose thought with a twinge of envy.

William grinned as the two friends exchanged boyish punches on each other's shoulders. 'Hail, what brings ye here?' said William. 'If it's shoeing ye want, I'll give Pa a call.'

'No, it's not shoeing.' Thomas swallowed. 'The Pestilence has reached the manor.'

'I'd heard.' William crossed himself.

'M'lord.' Peter came through from the back of the forge, wiping his hands on his leather apron, and removed his cap in respect. He was as broad as he was high, his arms bulging from years of hammering, his face embedded with the very heat and glow of his embers. 'What can I do for ye?'

Thomas ran a hand around the inside of his collar and glanced at Simon.

The lord's nervous. This should be interesting. Rose edged closer.

'The Pestilence has reached Tavistoke and is already at the manor. I came to say that I think you should leave,' said Thomas.

As a lord, he didn't sound very commanding and kept fiddling with his hat as though he wasn't sure. Well, he was new to the job, and Rose supposed that even lords had to learn.

'So, the rumours are true,' said Peter. 'Folks are saying the roads are full of travellers, many dying in the ditches. We'd not be any safer on the roads than if we stayed put.'

'Tis true, a lot of folks have gone and some have come back,' said William.

'They're wrong,' Simon said sharply, his voice echoing in the semi-darkness of the forge. 'I've been to Exeter and seen what the Pestilence can do. We can't stop travellers from coming and they'll be here soon enough bringing the death humours with them, but we can try to save ourselves while we can.'

'What about Lady Joan?' said William. 'Is she leaving?'

Thomas shook his head, staring at his boots. 'No, she's staying at the manor. I've been staying with Simon, Maria and Eleanor.'

No wonder Thomas was so quiet. He must be worried sick knowing his Ma was trapped in the manor with the Pestilence.

'Lord Thomas has a plan, and I think it's our only chance,' said Simon.

Rose dared another step forward, her curiosity soaring.

'Janet! Ye'd better come and hear this,' Peter called over his shoulder into the dark recess of the forge.

His wife, Janet, a small mouse of a woman, crept through from the back, dipped a silent curtsy and stood in the shadows.

'So, what's this plan, m'young lord?' Peter asked, making himself comfortable on his anvil.

Thomas glanced anxiously at Simon and cleared his throat. 'The monks at the monastery had word from a sage, I can't remember his name, but he said the only way to save ourselves was to go quickly, go far and return slowly. I think he's right. My idea is to take a small group where travellers won't find us. I can't take too many, since we won't have enough supplies and I need people with skills. We'll be safe, and it'll only be for the dark months until this evil has passed. We can come home in the spring.'

Rose leaned back against the wall, her heart racing. Imagine leaving the village and going somewhere new! She'd never been further than the market at Okewolde. Might she have one of the skills Lord Thomas was looking for?

'Some say 'tis God's will, cleansing the world of sinners,' Peter said brusquely. 'If that's true, it doesn't matter where we go; He'll find us. Where ye planning to go, anyway, m'lord?'

Thomas looked crestfallen and said nothing.

'There's an abandoned farmstead called Combe Hide on the east of the estate,' Simon answered. 'It has a house and barns, but we have to keep the numbers small. As Thomas said, we don't have enough supplies for too many.'

They were going to a proper farmhouse built with oak timbers, as the tenant farmers had! It wouldn't be as grand as the lord's house, of course, but better that than the mill cottage with its draughty doors and shutters that didn't close properly. It might even have horn-glass windows and a proper hearth and chimney. Rose could see herself curled up on sheep skins, all warm and cosy by a roaring fire while the winter storms raged outside.

Please God, let Lord Thomas take her Pa with him and let her have one adventure before she was married off.

She was fifteen summers and as Pa often reminded her, old enough to be wed. He kept talking of William for a husband, and there was nothing *wrong* with William, except for his missing limb that made her recoil whenever she laid eyes on it. It wasn't William's fault he'd lost his arm in the battle of Crecy two years ago, but that didn't make it easier to look upon.

Even if he hadn't lost an arm, Rose doubted things would be different between them. She didn't want to marry at all. Why should she wed a lad of her father's choosing and spend the rest of her life obeying him, having his babies and working from dawn to dusk? Why couldn't she choose who to wed or not to wed at all? Lads could, so why not lasses?

She'd said as much to her Ma and Pa. Ma had looked horrified and Pa had got riled and told her she was stubborn and lasses should do as they were told. If she could just have this one chance of freedom before all that, it would be something to cherish and think back on.

'Leaving like this is a bit sudden. What do you think, Peter, should we pack up and go?' said Janet fiddling with her hands.

'I'm thinking we'll stay and take our chances here.'

Simon stood tall and with his shoulders squared looking every inch the authoritative bailiff he was. 'No, you won't. Your lord needs a smithy and is ordering you to come. You'll abide by his wishes.'

Thomas straightened his back and lifted his chin. 'I'd like you to come too, Will.'

Peter sighed and addressed his remark to Simon. 'I don't like it. 'Tisn't right to let a forge go cold but if the young lord here says we're to leave, I'll have to go, won't I?'

'Yes, you will. Pack as many tools and materials from the forge as you can. Janet, bring household pots, bed covers, food stores and cage the fowl. Will, round up any stock; you'll have to play drover and herd them. Load a wagon and we'll meet tomorrow at sunrise on High Drovers Road by the ancient stone circle – you know the one? If anyone asks, say you're going north to Janet's folks.' Simon stood head and shoulders above the other men. It was obvious to Rose who was in charge, and it wasn't the new lord.

'I speak me mind, folks knows that, and I say we'd be better staying put. But—' Peter spread his hands in a hopeless gesture— 'if it's what m'lord wants…we'd best pray he's right.' He stood up from his anvil very slowly, as though every part of him was weary. 'Well, get going, woman, ye heard what the bailiff said. Boy, fetch the ox. Can we take the village ox, m'lord? Only we don't have a beast to pull the cart and if we don't have a cart, I can't bring me tools.'

'Yes, take him and the pony too,' said Thomas.

William hovered in the doorway, and Rose's eyes went straight to the empty sleeve tucked into his belt. She couldn't take her eyes off it even though the sight repulsed her.

'What ye waiting for, boy?' demanded Peter.

'Is Geoffrey-miller coming?' said William.

Peter laughed. 'Ye still soft on the miller's maid, boy? I keep saying, she's not the right one for ye.'

Not the right one! What was wrong with her? She might not be the prettiest lass in the village, being short and stocky with a mass of fair curls that refused to be tamed, but she was strong, and she knew her numbers up to twenty which was more than most lasses could say.

On the other hand, if Peter didn't want her for William, maybe her Pa would look elsewhere. Dear God, she hoped so. She couldn't wed William, not with that arm.

'I'm not a boy, Pa. I like Rose and a miller would be useful. Wouldn't he, Thom — my lord?'

'Only if there's a mill and grain to grind,' Peter muttered into his beard.

'We're going to see Geoffrey-miller now,' said Thomas, straightening his cotehardie.

'Tomorrow at sunrise by the stone circle, be there,' said Simon, turning on his heels and heading outside.

They were going to see Pa! She'd soon be out of here and living in a grand house. She'd often wondered what it was like beyond the moor, and now she was going to have the chance to find out. Stifling a whoop of joy, Rose flattened herself behind the door as Simon and Thomas strolled out.

'Glad you were there,' said Thomas. 'For a moment, I thought we'd have trouble.'

Simon shook his head. 'Peter moans about everything, but he's no fool. He knows he has to do his lord's bidding.'

Rose waited until they turned to mount their horses, then leaving the basket by the door; picked up her skirts and ran for home. She couldn't wait to tell Ma.

Arriving at the mill, she ripped off her coif and raced in through the back door. 'Ma! Ma! Lord Thomas is coming with Simon. They want us to go with them and live in a huge farmhouse. Say we can, Ma, *please*!'

Her mother, Mary, tightened the knot of nettle twine around the neck of a sack of flour and heaved it across the floor to join others in the corner of the store room. 'What are you talking about? And look at you! Where's your coif? I hope you didn't go outside looking like that! Did you give Janet the berries?'

'Of course I didn't, and yes I did, well, sort of, but Ma, *listen!* Thomas has this plan, and Peter's closing the forge, and Simon wants—oh Lord, they're here.'

'I've no idea what you're talking about, but they'll want to speak to your father. We'll stay here and let the men talk,' said Mary.

Damn! She'd hoped to get her Ma on her side before they arrived. Now all they could do was watch from the doorway and listen.

As Thomas and Simon entered the mill and began speaking with Geoffrey, Rose strained to hear, her heart pounding with excitement. 'It's our chance to escape the Pestilence,' she whispered to her Ma, as Thomas outlined his plan.

'Shhh, I'm trying to listen.'

'I hear what you're saying but with due respect, my lord, I'm not leaving my mill,' said Geoffrey, standing over an empty sack by the chute, waiting for ground flour to pour down from the grinding stones above. 'I'm a free man and pay my dues every Michaelmas. You can't force me to go.' He wiped his flour-white hands through his already white hair, creating a shower of dust.

'We must go.' Rose bit her lip. 'Make him, Ma.'

'Your Pa doesn't have to and I don't know…'

'You'd be safer with us than waiting for the Pestilence to strike,' said Thomas brushing the dust from his sleeves.

'You're a miller, a respected man. There's a mill where we're going and we need you. Your lord needs you,' Simon added.

'I told you, Pestilence or no Pestilence, me and mine are staying put,' said Geoffrey, dragging a filled sack out of the way and hooking an empty sack in its place.

Mary straightened her headdress. 'You wait here, Rose. I need to know more about this.' Wiping her hands on her apron, she stepped through the narrow doorway.

Rose dug her nails into the palms of her hands. Maybe Ma could persuade him.

'My lord.' Mary nodded respectfully. 'It's coming, isn't it?' she said.

'Yes, it is,' said Thomas. 'And many will die, so save yourselves and come with us.'

Geoffrey heaved the sack into a corner. 'I'm too old to pack up and go. We'll be fine tucked up the river here. No Pestilence or travellers will bother us. Someone has to stay and feed those who survive.'

'Lord Thomas says we'll be safer if we leave, and if it's God's will—' said Mary.

'If God deems us sinners, He'll take us wherever we are,' Geoffrey said, resuming his post at the bottom of the chute.

'I've heard it's a horrible death. Think on it, Geoffrey. Folks will manage without us.' Mary gripped his arm, forcing him to look at her.

Rose felt her stomach tighten. It sounded like Ma wanted to go. *Please, God, let her persuade him.*

Geoffrey scratched his head sending another fine shower of dust to settle on his shoulders. 'And where will folks get their flour or bake their bread? I've not let them down yet, nor my father before me, and I'll not do it now.' He turned his back and picked up the filled sack.

Rose bit her lip. Pa was as stubborn as a mule. Couldn't he see the adventure they could have?

'Mary's right, it is a horrible death. Ugly black buboes grow out of your neck and armpits, your throat chokes and you stink as you rot inside. It's a certain and painful death.' Simon warned.

Rose swallowed. No one had mentioned *how* people died. Now she definitely wanted to leave.

'We need a miller and we won't be gone forever. We'll sit out the dark months and return in the spring,' said Thomas.

'For Rose's sake, we should go,' said Mary.

Rose bit her lip harder. *Go on, Ma, make him see sense.*

'We need you, Geoffrey, or there'll be only four men. Hardly enough to cope with the heavy labouring peasants usually do,' said Simon, stepping further back as the number of filled sacks crept over the floor towards him.

'I told you; we're staying here.' Geoffrey glared at Simon as the grinding stones groaned above them.

Mary was right behind him. 'God's bones, you're a stubborn old fool when you want to be. At least let Rose go and give her a chance.'

Geoffrey shook his head. 'I've made my decision and that's an end to it.'

Ma was losing. She had to do something. She was too young to die of black buboes and she only wanted a little taste of freedom.

Crossing herself, Rose marched into the mill. 'Let me go, Pa. I'm as strong as any lad and as useful. I can use a hammer, work a plough and I know how to run a mill, you know I do. They need me, *please* let me go,' she begged.

'You're my little girl, Rose. I couldn't.' Geoffrey turned away, his face set.

'She's not so little, she's nearly fifteen summers,' said Mary.

'I've said my piece. The lass can't work a mill and she's to wed in the spring. I'll hear no more. We're staying.'

Rose fought her tears as she saw her opportunity slipping away and her life with William stretching before her.

Mary strode forward, her face black as thunder. Coming only to her husband's shoulders, she jabbed her finger into his chest.

'Now you listen to me, Geoffrey-miller! I've been a good wife to you all these years. I've never questioned or disobeyed you, but I'm doing it now. Forget your damn mill for once and think of your family!'

She'd never heard Ma speak like that before or look so fierce and, judging by the look of shock on her Pa's face, neither had he.

'I do think of you and Rose,' he said, the edge gone from his voice. 'You know that.'

Mary put her hand on his arm. 'I know you do, and you're a good man. But you heard what Lord Thomas said; it's only until the spring.'

Geoffrey stared at his boots and shook his head. 'I can't. I won't let folks down. I have to stay.'

Mary sighed. 'Then let Rose go and give her a chance.' She glanced at Thomas. 'Is Annie-healer going with you?'

'We saw Annie on our way to the village. She said her duty is here, but Peter, Janet and William are coming. Janet will look out for her,' said Simon.

Mary gripped Geoffrey's arm tighter and looked deeply into his eyes. 'Do you hear that? Rose knows Janet, and you like Peter. I'd never forgive myself if the Pestilence comes and anything happened to her. Would you?'

Her Pa's face creased with indecision, and his eyes flicked in her direction. Above her, the wooden cogs creaked with monotonous regularity as they struggled to turn the giant grinding stones around and around. Outside, the water wheel tipped splashes of water into the pool below.

They were familiar, everyday sounds that Rose had grown up with, but she'd be back in the spring. Lord Thomas had said so.

Please Lord, if you let me go I'll never ask for anything again.

Geoffrey lifted his head. 'Can you swear on your soul, my lord, that you'll look after my Rose?'

'I swear,' said Thomas swallowing.

God had heard her prayers! Pa was relenting.

Geoffrey nodded and turned back to Mary, with warmth on his face. 'You're a good wife and if it's what you want.' He turned to Rose and sighed the sigh of a defeated man. 'Best get your things together then before I change my mind. And—' he faced Mary— 'you can go with her if you've a mind.'

Mary's eyes glistened. 'God bless you, but my duty is with you. If you're staying, then my place is here. Whatever happens, we'll face it together.'

She was going! She could hardly believe it. And on her own too, just like a proper grown lass. Rose flung her arms around her Ma and hugged her in pure joy.

'I take it you'll be needing grain and flour, my lord? We're at the end of the supplies until harvest and my stocks are low but I can spare a few sacks.' Geoffrey nodded to the corner.

'Anything you have—' Thomas began.

'Yes, and other supplies, like tools and food.' Simon cut in. 'Load a cart.'

'Rose...' Geoffrey gave her the same soft look he'd given her mother. 'You don't have to go. You know that, don't you?'

Rose nodded seriously. 'I know, but Ma thinks it's for the best. Besides, I'll have Janet.' Seeing the sadness in her Pa's eyes, she bit back the excitement that was bubbling up inside her.

Geoffrey wiped a tear with his sleeve and opened his arms. He'd never embraced her before, and when she felt his big rough hands gently stroking her hair, she felt like crying.

'God be with you, child,' he whispered, so low only she could hear.

'And with you,' she whispered back.

Slowly, he loosened his hands and smiled down at her, his eyes wet. Her big bear of a Pa was almost weeping. Rose didn't know what to say, so she stood on the tips of her toes and kissed his cheek. For a moment, they looked at each other and then he coughed and stood tall.

'Dawn tomorrow at the stone circle on High Drovers Road, you say? Rose'll be there. And I'm trusting you, m'lord. You gave me your word to care for her. If anything happens, it's you I'll be coming to, lord or no lord.'

'I'll look after her. I promise,' said Thomas.

Fighting to keep the grin off her face, Rose discreetly followed Thomas and Simon outside.

'Shame Geoffrey and Mary aren't coming,' Simon said as he mounted his horse and gathered his reins. 'We really needed the miller, Rose is only a lass. Still, I suppose she can help in the mill, sweep up, that sort of thing.'

'I know,' Thomas agreed. 'I'm wondering about how I'm going to look after her.'

Rose smiled; she didn't need looking after. She'd show them.

Clenching her fists, she silently shouted for joy. She was about to begin the first real adventure of her life.

CHAPTER 4

The shadows of the long stones stretched towards him, and Thomas cast his eyes to the horizon for the third time. The dark orange band in the sky had changed to a pale yellow ribbon, against which the silhouettes of ragged tors on the moor stood out sharp and black. It was a view he'd grown up with and one he was going to miss.

He glanced down High Drovers Road, his stomach twisting in knots as he waited for the first of his people to arrive. His eyes were stinging with lack of sleep; he'd barely rested at all last night. Doubt and excitement battled for supremacy within him, just like they had ever since he and Simon had come up with their plan. Right now, doubt was winning.

He turned to Simon next to him. 'They are coming, aren't they?'

'They'd better be,' muttered Maria, from where she sat slumped and half-asleep in her saddle. 'You rushed us out of the house this morning like a storm. I had no time to pack properly; three kirtles are all I've got with me. Three! How am I supposed to cope with that?' She yawned, flexing her back to work out the kinks. 'I still don't see why we couldn't have stayed with Simon.'

Thomas sighed. Smithies were terrifying, but annoying younger sisters could be easily dealt with. Maria was thirteen summers and, as Mama kept saying, at *a difficult age*. It seemed to him Maria had always been at a difficult age. 'Maria, you knew we were leaving, so you had plenty of time to pack. You've done nothing but complain since you got up.' He shifted in his saddle, shading his eyes even though he could see well enough already. Still no sign of anyone.

'They'll come,' said Simon.

He wished he could be so certain. What would he do if they didn't? Go alone? Slink back to Simon's house with his tail between his legs like a whipped cur? What would the villagers think of him then?

'And look at my hair. Eleanor didn't have time to do it properly. The braids are uneven and this loop—' Maria held out a curled braid pinned behind one ear— 'is longer than this one.' She held out the other.

Thomas sighed, thinking wistfully of the monastery and the books there. One of his favourite non-scholarly texts had been Joseph of Exeter's *Daretis Phrygii Ilias*. He couldn't remember whether the poet had mentioned Herakles having any sisters or not. If he had, Thomas doubted he'd have completed even a quarter of what he was reputed to have done.

'Pin your headdress down, then no one will see it, will they?' he said sharply. 'God's teeth, I've got more to worry about than muxy braids!'

'They look very p-pretty, but I c-can do them again for you if you want,' said Eleanor, her apple-round face smiling.

Dear Eleanor, always cheerful with a kind word, always trying to pour oil on troubled waters. She was his mother's cousin and had come to live with them years before he was born, and the only one who didn't seem to mind Maria's moods. She was old enough to be his mother but somehow had never grown up.

His mother. He'd like to have asked Mama about his plan, but there hadn't been time. Who knew when he'd see her again?

Where were they? They should be here by now. The knot in his belly tightened, and he felt a little sick.

'I am doing the right thing, aren't I?' he said, more to himself than to anyone in particular.

Maria scowled at him. 'You mean you've got us here and you're not sure?'

'Of course I am! I checked my star charts last night and the alignments are good. It's just that...' Thomas broke off abruptly. If he was wrong, he'd have failed at being a lord before he even started. If he was right, he didn't have the least notion of how he was supposed to be a lord to those people.

'Good.' Simon stood in his stirrups, peering down the track. 'Because unless my eyes are playing tricks, here comes Rose and Peter's not far behind her.' He waved. 'Make haste!'

Thomas's stomach twisted a notch tighter. Pray God Peter wouldn't be difficult.

Rose stopped the wagon a few feet away, her face shining. 'I'm packed and ready. I can't wait to see this place,' she said with a bright grin. 'Pa's put three sacks of flour in the wagon along with some other bits and pieces he thought might be useful.'

The knot loosened a tiny amount. At least Rose was keen, which was more than Peter was. The smithy was striding towards Thomas, a dour look on his face as Janet brought their wagon to a stop a few paces behind Rose's.

'Tis dawn, like ye said, m'lord, but I'll say now—' he wagged his finger towards Thomas— 'I'd rather be back in me forge. Ye are sure, aren't ye? Only we could turn back now before it's too late?' He stood with his legs firmly apart, his arms tightly crossed.

Thomas swallowed. Peter had always scared him, ever since he'd been five summers and Mama had taken him to the forge to have new shoes put on his pony. It had been Thomas's first visit, and he'd been so excited he'd bounced in the saddle all the way to the village. Outside the forge, the sound of hammering and the smell of burning embers had enticed him through the huge door towering above him like he was a knight entering a mighty castle.

That had lasted until he'd seen an enormous black monster with a fiery mouth – Peter – reach out for him with glowing red claws. Thomas had screamed and hidden behind his mother's skirts.

He felt like hiding now, but his mother was barricaded in the manor and besides, he wasn't five anymore. He was a lord.

Taking a deep breath, he raised his chin. 'I've made my decision,' he announced in a voice that sounded lordly to him, at least.

Peter didn't move. 'How far is this place, m'lord? Ox isn't as young as he was, and one of the wagon wheels is wobbling.'

Thomas had no idea how far it was. He'd only been to Combe Hide once when he visited with Simon. He couldn't have been more than six summers then.

'Twelve, maybe fifteen miles,' Simon answered for him. 'I'll ride at the back with Will and help herd the stock. Thomas, you lead the way and stay on High Drovers

Road to the second crossroads where we turn off. I'll show you.'

'Glad someone knows where we're going,' Peter muttered, stamping back to his wagon and hauling himself onto it next to Janet. 'Shift over, woman, I'll take the reins from 'ere.'

'Can we go now?' Maria demanded.

Thomas walked his horse forward, glad to be moving at last and alone with his thoughts. He had no idea how he was going to cope with Peter. A smithy should be scared of his lord, not the other way around. And folks had always called him Master Thomas up until now. *M'lord* hung on his shoulders like a shroud.

The sun beat down on the road for mile after dusty mile, making heat shimmers dance before his eyes. The road was wide with ditches on either side and ran in a straight line twenty miles to Holdesworthe and, if travellers were to be believed, as far as Salisbury and the giant stone circle. Brother Luke had told him the road was built by the ancients hundreds of years ago and the giant circle thousands of years before that, but nobody had yet been able to explain why. Right now, Thomas was much too hot and tired to care.

A trickle of sweat ran down the back of his neck. He should have worn a tunic instead of his cotehardie. The laces were strangling him, but he thought it made him look more lordly. He loosened the laces a little and wiped a kerchief over his face.

The moor was far away to his right and the grain fields on either side of the road were brown and parched. If it didn't rain soon, the seeds would shrivel and folks would starve. He hoped Peter and Rose had grain on the wagons and cursed himself for not thinking to check before they'd set off.

When the sun reached midday, Simon stopped beside a small copse of hawthorn trees. Little was said as they huddled under the shade and greedily quenched their thirst from flagons of cider. Janet produced a basket of cheese and apples from the back of the wagon and passed it around. As soon as it was empty, they resumed their journey.

Riding on, Thomas wondered how Mama was. He prayed she didn't have the black buboes. He couldn't bear to think of her looking like the body he'd seen lying on the road. No, he mustn't think like that. His mother was a good woman; the best of women. God would save her. He had to.

Hot and tired, he lost count of the miles and often felt his head droop and his eyes close. Every time, he jolted himself awake. Lords didn't fall asleep on their horses. At least, he didn't think they did.

Simon trotted up beside him. 'We turn left here. It's not far now, just a mile or so along the valley. You lead the way, and I'll help Will with the livestock at the rear.' He stood up in his stirrups and shouted over his shoulder to the others behind. 'It's steep going down, so be careful with the wagons!'

He turned back in his saddle long enough to grin at Thomas, then kicked his horse into a canter and went to join William at the rear.

This was it. Burning with anticipation, Thomas turned his horse into the wide straight valley. To the left of the river, marshland and rough grazing came down to the water's edge. On the right bank, a rutted track followed the river upstream with grassy wasteland giving way to a rising field that ran the length of the valley and was topped with woods. That would be a good source of fuel for the hearth, he thought, and was quite proud of having noticed it.

If he remembered correctly, at the end of the valley, the track bent sharp right and led to the farmhouse. Just a little further now. His first decision as lord, and it had worked. They'd followed him just as they should, and now everything would be fine until they could go back home in the spring.

The wagons moved far too slowly for his liking, and Thomas urged his horse forward. He wanted to be the first to arrive so he could face his people with pride and welcome them to their new home. He couldn't wait to see the scowl drop from Peter's face. He might even demand Peter beg pardon for his lack of trust in his lord.

Cantering along the valley, he slapped his horse's neck, ignoring an indignant moorhen who took flight with a high-pitched trill. He was smiling broadly in anticipation as he splashed across the ford and rounded the bend that led to Combe Hide farmhouse.

He pulled his horse to a sudden stop and in one swift thud, his heart fell to the bottom of his boots.

No. No, it wasn't possible!

The farmhouse squatted long and low within the dark shadows of the steeply wooded slopes that rose behind. Gaping holes in the grey stone walls grinned at him like a row of missing teeth beneath a sagging roof. Fallen beams lay broken on the ground, and what was left of the thatch hung dismally between dark holes which stared at him like dead, accusing eyes. One of the window shutters dangled on a single nail, and the other was a pile of rotting wood on the ground. The door sagged on one wooden peg, half twisting around as though ashamed of its condition.

This was supposed to be their place of refuge. The new home where he, the great Lord Thomas, had brought them. He'd boasted about having a plan, of knowing a place where they could live in comfort and hide from the Pestilence, certain that travellers would pass them by. He'd been right about that - no travellers in their right minds would want to come here.

He glanced back, shame and fear raging within him. Dear Lord, what was he going to do?

Simon rounded the corner at a canter and reined in his horse alongside him, looking at the ruins of the homestead.

Thomas glared at him, only too glad to have someone to vent his wrath on. 'Why didn't you tell me it was like this? You're my bailiff, aren't you?'

'I did tell you. I distinctly remember saying you should come and investigate before rushing into things, but you wouldn't listen,' Simon answered. 'The place was abandoned by your great-uncle Boren nearly twenty years ago. What did you think you were going to find?'

'Not this. What am I going to say?'

Simon let out a long breath and raised his eyebrows. 'I don't know but you'd better think of something quick because they're nearly here.'

Thomas turned in his saddle. Already, he could hear the rumble of solid wooden wheels on the track. The first wagon would soon be splashing its way across the ford. He ran a finger around the inside of his collar.

This wasn't how it was supposed to be. Any moment his people, the ones he was supposed to be looking after, the ones who had followed him blindly to this ruin would see what he was seeing.

The rumble of the wagons grew louder.

'There's no hiding it,' Simon remarked. 'You've got to face them, although I dread to think what Peter's going to say.'

Thomas swallowed. He could make a run for it, but there was nowhere to go. He turned his horse to face his people, his mind a complete blank.

Rose stopped her wagon a few paces in front of him, the enthusiastic light dying from her eyes. Dropping the reins, she tilted her head. 'I thought you said we were going to a farmhouse. This is a ruin! I don't know what Will or his Pa will make of it.'

Neither did he, and he wished he didn't have to look at the disappointment on her face. Simon glanced at him and raised his eyebrows as if to say *that's just the start*, which didn't help.

They waited in silence, Thomas's heart sinking lower and lower with every clop of the approaching hooves and rumble of the wheels. At last, William came around the bend on a small shaggy grey pony, his thick legs dangling, his boots nearly scraping the ground and a smile on his face. 'I've put the sheep in the orchards and—' He broke off and reined to a halt, his face paling.

'Don't say anything,' Thomas pleaded. 'Will, I swear I didn't know it was like this, or I'd never have brought you.'

'And there's me thinking we was coming to live in a castle.' William removed his cap and scratched his head. 'Don't know what Pa'll say.'

If one more person wondered what Peter was going to say, he would scream. Feeling like a naughty schoolboy awaiting the wrath of Abbot Bartholomew, he wiped his sweaty hands on his hose.

Peter or the abbot? For choice, he'd take the abbot.

Maria and Eleanor arrived next. Maria took one look at their new home and went pale with shock or rage, or both. She opened her mouth to speak, but Peter came up alongside and drew his ox and cart to a steady halt alongside Rose before she could get the words out.

Thomas braced himself.

'I knew it.' Peter's rough voice hit his ears. 'Ye've brought us all these miles for nothing. This hovel won't protect us from the rain, let alone the Pestilence.' He folded his thick muscular arms across his broad chest. 'Some lord. Ye're no more than my Will's age and I were a fool to believe ye.'

Thomas winced, but it could have been worse. He'd half-expected Peter to knock him to the ground, but folks didn't do that to their lord unless they wanted to swing for it.

''Tis all your fault we're here, woman!' Peter turned and bellowed at Janet, who was perched next to him and shrinking with every word.

'Sorry, I only thought—'

'Well, don't! God never meant for women to think. You were a cloth head when I wed ye and a cloth head you'll be to the day the good Lord takes ye. And *you*, me lad!' He pointed an angry finger at William. 'You're just as bad! *Thomas is clever, be a good idea,* ye said, and between you and your Ma twittering on, I closed the door to me forge, hung up me hammer and put out me cinders for the first and last time, muxy fool that I was.'

Thomas didn't think it would be a good idea to remind Peter that he'd had no choice in the matter. Janet shot him an embarrassed look and put a nervous hand on Peter's arm.

'No good getting vexed. I'm sure it's not as bad as it looks—'

He threw off her hand. '*Not as bad as it looks*? It's a wreck!'

'Sorry, I was just saying…' She twisted her hands nervously in her lap and stared at her feet.

Peter was right. The place was a wreck. Thomas bit his lip. He had been so sure that he was saving his people. He'd imagined their approving faces and how they'd all say what a good lord he was, when the truth was that he was nothing but an ass. Thank God Mama wasn't here to see his shame.

'Well, I think it's p-pretty,' Eleanor piped up.

'Ye would. You're like her.' Peter jerked his thumb towards Janet.

Rose leaned forward. 'Don't you pick on El. It's not her fault she's…a bit young.'

Peter snorted. 'That's one way of putting it. She's old enough to be ye Ma and still plays with poppet dolls.'

Rose tore off her coif and stood up with her fists on her hips, her thick mop of wiry curls bouncing up and down on her head. 'You're nothing but a bully, Peter-forge! Pa always said—'

'Your Pa always thought himself above the likes of us, up in his precious mill while the rest of us slaved for Sir John.' Peter bellowed. 'And you're no better. Should have taken his belt to ye long ago!'

'Rose isn't like that!' William protested.

Peter barely spared him a glance. 'What do ye know, boy?'

William shot a look at Rose and flamed deep red. 'I'm not your boy. See this beard?' He tugged proudly at the few wispy beginnings of growth on his chin.

Thomas stroked his chin, checking it like he did every morning. Still smooth. Maybe if he could grow a beard like William, his people would treat him more like a lord.

'Thomas's idea was good. He didn't know the place was...well, like this.' William's voice trailed off a little.

'Might have known you'd side with your old pal,' Peter growled. 'But he's a noble. Ye'll learn that soon enough.'

William glanced apologetically at Thomas, who shrugged. He wasn't surprised at Peter's hostility. His Papa had had nothing but contempt for his workers. He knew how heartless Sir John could be; he'd experienced the man's callousness himself often enough.

Peter wasn't finished, gesturing at William. 'And look at ye, boy, with your one arm. Sir John had no right sending a boy to a man's war.'

William turned an even deeper red as he pulled down his left sleeve and self-consciously held the stump of his arm.

'He wasn't the only one that went.' Rose said stridently. 'You should count yourself lucky Will came back at all. Most of our young men didn't.'

Simon leaned over to Thomas. 'You'd better do something or we'll have a fight on our hands,'

'Me?' Thomas turned pale. 'What can I do?'

Simon gathered his reins and inched his horse between Peter and William. 'Both of you, be silent!' he commanded, his authoritative voice making Thomas feel small. 'Your lord did what he thought was right. We're here now, and the sun's nearly at third quarter; we need to unload, see to the stock, get a fire lit, mattresses laid out and sort something to eat before nightfall. Now stop arguing and get started.'

'Then I'll look to me and mine. We'll 'ave that barn. Come on, boy.' With a final hard stare at Thomas, Peter flicked the whip over the ox and headed for a tumbledown barn in the corner of the yard.

Janet turned in her seat. 'Sorry,' she said in a squeak of a voice to no one in particular.

Rose blew out her cheeks. 'Good. I'm glad he's gone, the miserable old coot. El, Maria, we can put the horses in with the sheep and take care of the fowl. Come on, staring at the place won't change things.' She scrambled off the wagon and glanced at Thomas. 'My lord?'

Thomas shrugged. Why not? She seemed to know what she was doing, which was more than he did.

Maria narrowed her eyes, flicked her hair behind her ears and tilted her chin, crossing her arms tightly over her chest. 'I'm not taking orders from a peasant, and I have never taken care of fowl or handled livestock. I don't know why you've brought us here, and I demand to go home.'

'You can't go home; Court Barton has the Pestilence,' Rose said. 'Things are different now and we all have to help, no matter who we are. Isn't that right, m'lord?'

Why hadn't he thought to say that? 'Yes, it is. Maria, get off that horse and help unless you want to stay up there all night.' That sounded authoritative enough, but it was easy to order his sister around.

With a huff, Maria slid to the ground. 'Only until we're sorted, and I'm *not* doing the fowl. Filthy, smelly creatures. Come on, El.'

'I made a right ox-tail of that, didn't I?' Thomas said as he and Simon watched Rose organising the girls.

'You weren't to know —'

'But I should have known. I'm supposed to be their leader. Right now, Rose has more about her than I have. Peter hates all nobles, including me, and I should have stood up to him but instead, I sat there with my tongue between my teeth.'

'He'll come round.' Simon slapped him on the back. 'Now, stop feeling sorry for yourself and help me unload.'

Thomas sighed, biting his lip. He'd failed. Worse, he'd failed in front of his people. His first day as lord was one he would rather forget.

CHAPTER 5

Thomas lay wide awake on his straw mattress, his hands behind his head as he stared through a hole in the roof. It was dark, but if he moved his head a little to the right, he could see the stars. He couldn't make out which ones. Brother Leviticus would have known.

His thoughts drifted back to the monastery. It must be nearly time for the prime bell. The brothers would be stirring and sleepily making their way to the chapel for the first prayers of the day before starting work. He wished he was with them.

He gazed around the room, although it was too dark to see much. Years of stale rat droppings had left a musty, acrid smell that pricked his nose and made him feel ill. He reached out and ran a hand down the damp wall, then grimaced and wiped the slime off his fingers on the woollen cover.

How long would it be until everyone woke up? Habit had roused Thomas at the same time as he'd been accustomed to getting up in the monastery, but the girls were still asleep on their mattresses around the hearth, and Simon was snoring in the corner.

His stomach growled and he lay down again irritably, shifting onto his side. God's teeth, how much longer?

Three days ago he'd been perfectly happy learning his

Latin and Greek and now look at him; trying to be a lord he didn't want to be and living in a ruin of a house surrounded by people who all resented him.

How had it come to this? His path in life had been so certain: finish school, then go to Oxford to study for his degree and become a physician. He had been looking forward to learning more about astronomy, for that was a large part of a physician's life and a fascinating subject.

Then Richard had stupidly got himself killed on the battlefields of Crecy and left him as heir. That was when Papa had started drinking, leaving Mama to run the estate with Simon. Sir John had supposedly died at the hands of road thieves, but he had always had his doubts about that. His father had been a knight and a capable fighter, and his family's horses of the best quality. He could have outrun his attackers even if he couldn't have beaten them in a fight. More likely, Papa had fallen drunk off his horse. It wouldn't have been the first time.

Sir John's death had made him lord earlier than expected, but even that wouldn't have mattered; Mama had been determined that he should finish his studies and be a physician if he wanted. Then God sent the Pestilence and here he was.

If he could make a success of this and keep his promise to Mama, he could go home in the spring with his head held high and still go to Oxford next Michaelmas. That dream was all he had to cling to right now.

He ran Mama's words over in his head again.

It wasn't her fault. Try to understand and forgive me. Who was she talking about? Maria? No; Mama would have said. Besides, Maria was shrewish, but she lacked the imagination to do anything truly reprehensible.

Eleanor? Unlikely, but who knew how someone like

her really thought? Maybe she'd done something terrible without understanding.

There was only one other possibility, and that was Annie-healer. She and Mama were very good friends, which had always struck him as odd because Annie was low-born.

Why couldn't Mama have just told him instead of leaving him to work it out?

Thomas rolled onto his back and put his hands behind his head again. The star he'd been watching had slipped out of sight. Pray God dawn would come soon, although that would mean dealing with his people again. Peter had made his contempt quite clear. Simon indulged him; he didn't respect him. And Rose...Rose wasn't what he had expected at all. She was feisty, and she'd taken care of the horses and fowl and helped unload the wagon and organised the mattresses while Maria just stood and complained there were no furs to sit on. Rose wasn't the fragile maid her Pa thought she was. Despite his promise to Geoffrey, it seemed to him that Rose was quite capable of taking care of herself, which was a relief for he had no experience of maids.

Did William see him as a failure? He hoped not. Before Thomas went to school, they were friends and spent many days fishing together. William had been fun until he came back from the battlefields. He hadn't laughed much after that.

The sky was changing from night blue to pale lilac. The straw mattress scratched Thomas's back, and he threw back his covers irritably. He needed to clear his head, and the best way to do that was to take a walk and look at the stars before they disappeared.

Outside, it was already warm and the smell of dewy

grass came fresh to his nose as he sauntered along the path listening to an early robin and watching the moorhens scurrying among the reeds. He was halfway along the valley before the mists began to lift and the first rays of the sun appeared over the hills. There were no clouds, which meant it was going to be another hot dry day.

He scuffed his boots through the dirt. The problem was that most of his life had been spent in a monastery. He'd spent some time with Simon on the estate but he was young and it felt like a game. This was no game. There were only eight of them, all looking to him and he had no clue what needed to be done. He should have brought more people, but it was too late now; he couldn't very well go back.

He gazed around. It wasn't all bad. The long field on his left stretched the whole length of the valley with plenty of grass for livestock. The ancient earth boundaries dividing the field into strips were still there from years of tilling, which meant they could move the sheep from strip to strip providing they checked the boundaries for gaps in the hedges.

He glanced at the river. Most of the shallows were choked with reeds, but if they cleared them and the girls made nets, they could catch fish. In the orchards next to the house, the branches of the fruit trees bowed almost to the ground with the weight of ripening apples, pears and damsons which meant fresh fruit and cider. They would need a screw press to make the pulp and squeeze out the juice. He made a mental note to look around and see if there was one rusting in a corner somewhere because, without it, they'd be crushing the apples with their feet.

There were plenty of flowers in the hedgerows, which

led his thoughts down a pleasanter track: where you found flowers, you often found wild bees, which meant wax for candles and honey for mead. His stomach growled softly at the thought. Maybe he could do this after all, just until he went to Oxford. Thinking about it, a plan started forming in his mind and the more he thought about it, the better it seemed. It would be perfect, something he understood and like a little piece of home. Feeling brighter, he returned to the house.

Rose was awake and stacking baskets in a corner of the room. Eleanor knelt over the hearth blowing life into reluctant embers while Maria sat on her mattress, dragging a white bone comb through her hair. Simon was stretching and yawning on the edge of his mattress.

'Instead of standing there idle, take these.' Rose thrust an assortment of baskets into his arms so hard she knocked him back a step. 'And we need to get these sacks of flour off the floor before the damp gets in and they go mouldy. It would be a lot easier if there were flagstones instead of *this*.' She dug a toe into the dirt floor, wrinkling her nose.

'I don't know about making flagstones,' Simon said, 'but shelves might be possible.' He caught sight of Thomas. 'You can make shelves, can't you?'

'Yes, of course,' he said, not paying much attention. 'Listen, I've had an idea. What do you think about setting this place up to run like the monastery in Tavistoke?'

Simon dropped the tottering pile of baskets against the wall with the others. 'I think you'll have a job getting folks to pray God knows how many times a day, that's what I think.'

'That's not quite what I meant. Anyway, we haven't got a bell. At the monastery, every monk was responsible for his own task, and I was thinking that we could do the same.'

When Simon didn't answer, being far more occupied with catching another pile of baskets that Rose had pushed into his arms, he tried again.

'Should we ask Peter and the others to come over and talk about it? I'll help Rose if you go and see him.'

Simon raised his eyebrows, shoved the baskets into Thomas's hands and swiped his cap off the bench on his way out.

Thomas smiled to himself. There were some advantages to being the lord.

Maria put down her comb and sat for Eleanor to do her braids and as he handed the last basket to Rose, heavy footsteps drew his attention to the door.

Peter strode in, dragged a stool to the hearth and sat down. 'Right, m'lord, Simon says ye wants us together for summat.' He raised his voice and bellowed at the open door. 'Don't stand useless; bring in the vittles, woman! We're starving!'

Janet edged her way inside, clutching a large willow basket, long wisps of brown hair poking in apologetic strands from under her headdress.

Eleanor's eyes lit up. 'Is that food? I'm hungry.'

'Yes, I thought we could do with something. I've got some bread from yesterday and cheese and apples, but I'm afraid they're a bit wrinkled,' Janet said as she unpacked the basket and placed the contents in piles near the hearth.

As they gathered around, William sat on the floor next to Rose, who shuffled away from him. Thomas went to join them, but changed his mind. Standing would be far more lordly.

'Right, everyone get stuck in, and young lord 'ere can

speak.' Peter broke off a large chunk of bread and stuffed it into his mouth.

Swallowing his nerves, he stood a little straighter and put his hands behind his back in his best imitation of Brother Luke addressing the class. 'I've been thinking, and I have an idea—'

'Hope it's better'n the last one,' Peter mumbled through a mouthful of bread.

Maria giggled, but Thomas pretended not to hear. He cleared his throat. 'We've come here to sit out the Pestilence until we can go home in the spring. We can't travel, there are no markets and no traders bringing goods to us, and we don't have enough stores to last. We've got to be self-sufficient—'

'What d-does suf-suffiant, mean?' said Eleanor.

'It means we've got to stay here and fend for ourselves or we'll run out of food,' said Rose rather tartly, taking the knife from her belt and slicing an apple. Next to her, Peter swallowed his last mouthful of bread and wiped the crumbs from his beard.

'I know this place isn't what we expected,' he admitted. 'I believe we need to think a bit like the monks at Tavistoke. They were self-sufficient.' Now he'd started, he was feeling more confident. At least they were listening to him.

'I'm not on getting' on me knees praying all day if that's what ye're getting at.' Peter bit into one of the old apples and spat out a bad piece.

He sighed. Did folks think that was all monks did? 'What I mean is, everyone at the monastery had their own jobs to do at set times, and I think that's what we should do here. Simon's the bailiff, so he can manage who does what. Simon?'

Simon gave Thomas a rather irritated look and tossed his apple core onto the hearth. 'Alright, well, the first thing we need to do is get this roof mended. If it rains and the stores get wet, we'll starve. You lasses can make a start by cutting reeds from the river for thatch, lots of them.'

Peter nodded. 'He's not wrong there. First things first, though; me and my boy will build a hearth for the embers. A place don't feel right without embers. And —' Peter looked at Thomas — 'no embers, no nails and no stakes for the roof.' He wiped his mouth with the back of his hand and stood up.

'Yes, but we still have to discuss —' Thomas began, but Peter was already putting his knife back on his belt and turning to leave. 'Peter, if I can just explain —'

'Nothing to explain. You've brought us to a right wasps nest, m'lord. I said we shouldn't come, but you didn't listen, and we're 'ere now; God help us. Get the basket, woman.'

Janet gave a thin smile to the room, and William shot a hopeful glance at Rose, who looked away.

It was humiliating. None of them was taking him seriously. He tried raising his voice. 'What I thought was...' but Peter was already outside. Helpless, he turned to Simon. 'Can you get him back?'

'No, I can't. He's right, Thomas. Can't you see that? We've no roof, no sticks for the fire, no hay for the sheep and not enough food to last. If we're to survive until the spring, we need to get to work, not sit around discussing monasteries.' Simon stood and rammed his cap on his head. 'We should never have come.'

'But you *knew* the place was a ruin!'

'I didn't know it was as bad as this. I'm going to ride out and see what's here, and pray God I find something worth coming for.'

He watched the door close behind Simon. So much for being authoritative. Maybe he just didn't have it in him. Janet had taken the basket, so there was nothing to eat, and his feet hurt. He sat by the hearth, rubbing his toes tenderly.

'Something up with your boots?' said Rose staring at them.

'They look new,' said Maria, twisting a curl around her fingers.

'They are new.' Thomas squirmed a little. 'They pinch my toes if you must know.'

'They're too tight. New boots always need stretching—' said Rose.

'It's *my lord* when you speak to my brother.' Maria tilted her chin and smiled sweetly.

Rose raised her eyebrows. 'Take 'em off and I'll see to 'em for you, *my lord*.' She held out her hand, glaring at Maria.

Dear God, he didn't care what they called him. 'What are you going to do to them?' The boots had come from the best cordwainer in Tavistoke and had cost most of his savings. If she ruined them, he only had his old ones with holes in the bottom.

'Rub the leather with goose fat to soften 'em, then stuff 'em with grass or rags to make 'em stretch. It's what Ma used to do to my shoes to make them last longer. Come on, you can't go around like that. Get 'em off.' She stood in front of him, her hand held out, waiting.

His throbbing toes told him he wasn't going very far as things were, and Rose was still standing there in a manner that said she expected to be obeyed, lord or no lord. Thomas pulled off his boots, breathing a short sigh of relief as his toes popped out of their confinement, and handed them over.

'Leave these to me.' Rose looked at Maria and Eleanor.

'Don't just sit there. You two, can start cutting reeds for the roof as Simon said. I'll join you once I've done his boots.'

'I'm not cutting reeds,' Maria sat on her mattress examining her pale, long-fingered hands. 'That's peasant's work. Besides, the water's filthy, and there are *things* in there.'

'I don't m-mind, Rose. I'll help you,' said Eleanor.

'Thanks, El. Then that's what we'll do. Maria, if you won't cut reeds, then you can collect sticks for the hearth. We'll need a good fire, or there'll be no meal tonight,' said Rose, pinning her white linen coif to her head.

Maria snorted. 'I'm not taking orders from you. You're nothing but a miller's maid. Tell her, Thomas.'

God's bones, did his sister always have to make things so difficult? What was the correct, lordly response here?

'Thomas?' said Rose as three pairs of eyes stared at him waiting for an answer.

Thomas's empty stomach growled again. That settled it; he wanted a good, hearty meal that night. 'You should help, Maria. Collect sticks, as Rose said.'

Rose smiled and, with a firm nod in Maria's direction and a swish of skirts, bustled out the door with Eleanor in tow and his precious boots in her hand. Maria stuck out her tongue at Rose's back and with a dramatic sigh, hauled herself off her mattress and scowled at him on her way out.

It seemed no one liked him at the moment. He rubbed his toes. He'd thought of cutting reeds and gathering wood, only he hadn't had a chance to say so before Simon had spoken up. Picking up a stick by the hearth, he scratched an isosceles triangle in the dirt.

Rose was a summer younger than him and only a maid, but they listened to her. Thomas didn't know whether to admire or hate her.

Damn the Pestilence. If God was angry with folks, why couldn't He have chosen some other way to express His displeasure and left him alone to study? Or at the very least, waited until he was safely ensconced at Oxford. Irritably, he scrubbed out the triangle with his foot and stared around the empty room. For all his grand talk about everyone having their own jobs, he wasn't entirely sure what his job was supposed to be.

He pulled on his old boots with the hole and praised God it wasn't raining. While the others were working on the roof, he'd look for a wild bees' nest and poke around in the barns for a cider press. If he found either of those things, maybe he could prove he was fit to lead his people.

The sun was past the third quarter when Thomas returned from his search, arriving at the same time as Simon. Good. He could talk to him about what he'd found. Leaning on the wattle fence, he waited for Simon to finish unsaddling his horse in the orchard. A horsefly landed on his arm, and he slapped it hard, watching it fall to the ground with grim satisfaction. They had a bite like an angry cur, and there was no Annie-healer with one of her lotions.

'What did you find?' he said, as Simon came to join him.

'Well, it's not as bad as I feared. The fencing and hedging are quite good. I rode beyond the valley field and the land's poor, mostly wet grass, but there's better grazing beyond the trees that'll do for the sheep. I also went into the woods and marked some straight oaks to cut for new roof beams. The quicker we get that roof fixed, the happier I shall be. What have you been doing?'

'Looking for wild bees, but all I found were patches of nettles that stung through my hose,' he said ruefully. 'I found a rusty cider press behind the linhay that might serve if it could be mended. There's also a mill further upstream that's little more than a ruin, but I spotted brown trout in the river, so we can fish.'

Simon nodded. 'I don't suppose the mill has been used for years, but we may be able to rebuild it. At least then we could grind flour. I was thinking we could also improve the lands by digging ditches to drain for crops.' He started to say something else, then looked down with a frown. 'Something wrong with your feet?'

He sighed. 'Rose is stretching my new boots. These have holes, and I have a thorn in my toe.' He pulled off the boot and started poking around, trying to get a grip on the end of the thorn. 'That's got it! Blackthorn; it must be half an inch long.' He tossed it over the wattle fence. 'What were you saying about crops?'

'I was saying that we could dig drainage ditches.'

'Whatever for? We're going home in the spring.'

Simon kept his hand on the gate. 'We don't know when the Pestilence will end. We could be here longer than you think.'

'No, we won't. My charts say we'll be out of here in the spring, and anyway, I have to go home.' He pulled on his boot and tested his foot on the ground. 'That's better.'

Simon paused in the middle of securing the gate with nettle twine. 'Your...charts?'

He nodded eagerly as they started to amble back towards the house. 'Everything is foretold in the stars and by how the planets move and align. The ancient Greeks and Arabs have known about it for centuries. The future is all in the charts if you know how to read them. I was studying it with Brother Leviticus. I'll show you if you like.'

'I have more important things on my mind. What in

God's name is this?' Simon kicked a sodden brown pile of reeds with his boot. 'It wasn't here when I left this morning.'

'They're the reeds Rose and El gathered as you asked.'

'These — but they're useless!'

'What's wrong with them? They look alright to me.'

'They're too short, that's what's wrong. And they should be spread out to dry, not left in a clump to rot. We can't use any of these for thatch. Didn't you check what they were doing?'

'I didn't know any of that! If you'd stayed long enough to listen to me, I was going to suggest Peter and William cut the reeds.'

Simon sighed. 'Well, I suppose we can always cut more and use these for twine but we don't have time to waste like this. Anyway, it's done. I also found a couple of linhays behind the forge that only need a few nails to patch them up, and there's a barn that's just about usable, so it's not all bad news.' He laid a hand on Thomas's shoulder. 'Let's go back. God's bones, I hope the girls have sorted some food. My belly's empty as a dry well.'

As they entered the house, Eleanor was stirring a large iron pot hanging over the hearth, and two oat cakes sat on the hot stones. The smell of herbs filled the room, a painful reminder to Thomas that he'd only eaten a sour apple all day.

'Rose showed m-me how to m-make it. It's got c-corn, beans, c-carrots, herbs and wild garlic. I found the garlic.' Eleanor put down her stirring stick for a moment and beamed.

'Had to do something, I couldn't go another night with nothing inside,' Rose said. 'Did you see the reeds we cut? We worked hard, didn't we, El?'

'Yes, I saw them, but they should be—' Simon began.

Janet crept in carrying a large iron pot, sending tantalising smells of oat potage with rosemary, thyme and carrots wafting around the room.

'I made this for tonight,' she said.

'Wonderful! That was good of you, Janet. We're all hungry,' said Rose. She took the pot and placed it in the embers to keep it hot.

Simon raised his eyebrows. 'Yes, but one meal would have been enough. We can't waste what few supplies we have. Like Thomas said this morning, we need to sit down and work out a plan to organise who's doing what.'

Rose nodded. 'I agree.'

Oh, *now* they agreed. Thomas felt resentment bubble up inside him. Why couldn't they have been this cooperative in the morning when *he'd* put the idea forward?

He choked back a sigh and sat down next to Simon. Brother Luke had once told him that it didn't matter which physician cured a disease, only that the disease was cured. He supposed the same thing could apply here – the idea was good whether it came from Simon or himself – but it still rankled; after all, he was the lord.

Maybe tomorrow he could find a way to prove himself.

CHAPTER 6

For the second night, Rose didn't sleep a wink. The rats scurrying around didn't bother her – there had been plenty of those in the mill – but the night air kept whistling through the gaps in the roof like an evil ghost, and the damp stink of the place was making her nose hurt.

She let out a long sigh. Some adventure this was turning out to be.

Early light slid through the broken shutters making stripes across the floor. It was nearly dawn. Back home, Pa would already be up and baking bread for the village while Ma swept the cottage floor.

Rose had prayed for their safety from the Pestilence, but if she was honest, she was glad they hadn't come. For the first time in her life, she was free. How many maids could say that? How many went from obeying their parents straight to obeying their husband with no chance to live for themselves?

Husbands. Rose thought of William and felt a shiver run down her spine. Folks always assumed that she and William would marry one day, even though she'd never heard of any formal agreement between their fathers. Before the war, William had been the proud son of a smithy who'd boasted that he would one day own the forge. That would have made him almost as respectable as a miller. He was handsome, always ready with a jest, and she'd been the envy of many lasses.

Unfortunately, the old, cheerful William had been lost on the battlefields, replaced by a dour, moody man with only one arm. He couldn't possibly take over the forge like that, so where would that leave her? Wed to a dullard who was capable of no more than doing odd jobs for pennies, living in a cruck house amongst the poorest of the poor.

She shuddered. She was better than that.

Turning over, she snuggled the woollen blanket up to her chin. Someone was stirring in the shadows. It couldn't be Simon, he was lying on his back with his fingers laced behind his head and snoring like a hog.

She glanced across the room at the two mattresses close to the hearth. Maria lay on her side with one arm stretched on the floor, the outline of her body gently rising and falling. Next to her, Eleanor was curled in a ball, her head tucked close to her chest like a puppy. That only left Thomas. Rose lay completely still, watching him get to his feet and tiptoe out. Poor Thomas. He'd been excited as a ram in a field of ewes when they'd first set out, but when they'd arrived, he'd looked as though he wanted to cry. What use was a lord that cried?

She could see Thomas was trying hard to be a lord, but the tremble in his voice when he spoke to Peter gave away his uncertainty. She'd wager Thomas would much rather be safely hidden inside his monastery walls than here with the rest of them.

God's bones, she was tired, but there was still so much to do: make shelves to get the flour and food off the damp floor, wash down the walls, fix the shutters and make some rushlights and tapers – the house was as gloomy as a wet day in January – then there was still twine and rope to braid, and that was without the huge tasks of repairing barns and putting a roof over their heads. Pray God it wouldn't rain before they fixed the roof. Rain would destroy their remaining stores of food.

Things needed organising, and from what she could see, the house and the girls were going to be down to her. She sighed. Eleanor was willing enough, but still a child in her mind, and Maria was a lazy creature and about as much use as a pail with a hole. Just the sight of her made Rose prickle like a hedgehog.

Maria's hands were milky white and smooth, the sign of a lady, and her hair was long and shining. Rose examined her coarse hands in the dim light and pulled her fingers through her hatefully short wiry curls. Why couldn't she look like Maria?

Wearily, she reached for the same woollen kirtle she'd worn yesterday and for weeks before that. She only had two and this one had the smallest hole. She ran her hand over the coarse cloth that her Ma had made by pounding wool in water until it matted, or *fulled* as the millers' called it.

What was it like to wear a fitted silk kirtle instead of this baggy old thing that was hot in summer and heavy and wet in winter? She scrunched it up in disgust. She'd wager Maria's kirtle wouldn't itch when she sweated. Then again, Maria didn't work hard enough to sweat, so she'd never know.

Slipping the garment over her head, she gathered the folds with a leather belt and tied on her purse, eating knife and drop spindle, although when she'd have time to use that again, Lord alone knew. She slipped on her over-tunic, making sure the loose folds covered her purse, and tied her apron. Sitting on the floor, she wrestled her foot into a woollen stocking, pulling it hard to her knee. No matter how tight she tied the ribbons, the muxy things would be around her ankles by the time the sun reached the first quarter.

Having cleaned the bowls and pots, fetched pails of water from the river and checked the baskets for a meal, Rose was back working amongst the reeds with Eleanor. The sun blazed down, burning her face and making diamonds of light dance on the water.

For the umpteenth time, she pushed up her sleeves and wiped her brow with a hand that was covered in scratches. The water had seeped into her boots, making her stockings cling to her legs, sweat stuck her kirtle to her back, and her stomach was demanding something to eat.

She straightened up and adjusted her coif, leaving muddy brown smudges on the linen. Lord, how she hated this. It felt like she and Eleanor had been cutting reeds forever, but when she looked at the sky, the sun was only a little way past the first quarter. Eleanor was humming to herself, always happy in her own little world. How Rose envied her.

A trickle of sweat ran down the side of her nose. She wiped it away and glanced at the grass bank, where Maria was sitting picking daisies.

'You could help us,' Rose said, pushing her sleeves further up her arms.

'I've already gathered the sticks and seen to the wretched fowl. Simon said that those were my tasks, and I've finished them.' Maria tilted her nose and carefully threaded a wilting daisy onto her chain.

Jealously crawled up Rose's throat and into her mouth.

'That must have taken you to the first quarter. I hope the sticks are dry this time, otherwise, the fire'll be all smoke like last night.'

'They are, and I had to walk up the hill to find them, and now I'm tired. I'm not used to working. Unlike some people I could name,' Maria added as she twirled a curl of hair around her fingers, a small smile on her lips.

Rose gritted her teeth. 'We're all tired and having to walk miles last night rounding up sheep didn't help. All because someone left the orchard gate open.'

'That wasn't my fault. If the gate wasn't so rotten, I could have closed it. Besides, I didn't know the stupid sheep would walk out, did I?' Maria tilted her head to one side. 'I don't know what you and Eleanor have been doing all this time. I thought you'd have finished the reeds by now.'

'We would have done if we'd had some help. God's feet, El and I haven't stopped, and if we don't get enough reeds cut and dried, we'll have no roof. You heard what Simon said. How would you like that with the rain soaking your pretty kirtle?'

Maria stood up and held out her skirts, swirling the exquisitely gold embroidered blue silk folds from one side to the other. 'This old thing? I've much nicer ones.' She lifted her chin. 'I don't suppose you've ever worn a silk kirtle, have you?'

No, she hadn't, and how pretty Maria looked with her heart-shaped face, huge doe-like eyes and beautiful long hair. And damn her, she was as lithe as a willow.

'No, and if you had any sense, you wouldn't either. Why don't you wear something sensible like the rest of us? Then you could help instead of playing the high and mighty lady.' She had never dared to speak to a noble in such a way, but the words were out before she could stop them.

Maria drew herself up, regarding her like a piece of dirt. 'How dare you speak to your betters like that? *I* am the lord's sister and *you* are a common miller's daughter. You'd do well to remember that.'

There was nothing common about her Pa. He was the best and most respected miller in Devonshire. The breadweighers would find no grit in his flour.

Maria smirked and Rose's temper snapped. She waded out of the river, dripping water in her path, and lunged for Maria, seizing a good double-handful of hair and yanked hard. Maria screamed and kicked out, clawing at Rose's face. Rose released her hair long enough to try and catch hold of her wrists, but Maria twisted out of the way and grabbed her arm. Seconds later, Rose felt a ragged pain shoot up from her hand like an arrow.

'You bit me!' The reaction was as much shock as pain. Noble girls didn't bite. They shrieked and wailed and flapped their hands, but they didn't *bite*.

'So I did!' Maria shoved her hard in the chest, and Rose felt her feet slip from under her on the edge of the bank. She flailed her arms but there was nothing she could do, and the next thing she felt was the shock of cold water as she landed in the river.

Spluttering, she struggled to her feet and stood waist-deep in brackish water that stank like rotting cabbage. Her hair hung in rats' tails and the thick wool sleeves sagged off her arms like overweight curtains. Humiliated, she spat out the gritty water and saw Maria on the bank, holding her sides and laughing.

'I hate you!' Rose screamed.

'Help! S-someone help! Rose is d-drowning!' Eleanor shouted at the top of her voice.

'I'm not drowning!' Rose yelled back and holding out her arms like a scarecrow, she waded through the reeds, the mud sucking and oozing between her toes. Cold, wet and filthy, she scrambled onto the bank.

Maria stopped laughing and backed away fast. 'Keep away! Don't you come near me!'

Eleanor stopped shouting and her eyes went as wide as pewter plates as she stared at her.

'What?' Rose demanded.

Wrinkling her face, Eleanor raised her hand and pointed.

She looked down and felt hot bile rise in her throat. Her arms were crawling with black slug-like leeches.

'Get off! Get them off!' She swiped, slapped and shook her arms but nothing she did removed the disgusting creatures. 'They're sucking my blood!'

'At least they'll suck the bad humours out of you,' said Maria, flouncing away. 'Maybe they'll suck out some of your temper, too.'

'What's going on?' Thomas's voice silenced her reply as he scramble over the wattle fence. 'I could hear screaming from the other side of the orchard.'

'Rose and M-Maria had a fight. Rose said M-Maria was lazy and p-pulled her hair so M-Maria pushed her in the river and Rose came out c-covered in leeches,' said Eleanor, bouncing with excitement.

'*She* attacked me like the peasant maid she is and pulled my hair! Look!' Maria bent forward, holding out her hair. 'She should be put in the stocks for that! Isn't that right, Thomas?'

She thought that Maria could do with a spell in the stocks herself, but such a punishment was unthinkable for a noble. She bit her tongue. The stocks wouldn't be quite so bad, considering that she'd attacked the lord's sister. Thomas could have her whipped if he chose.

'Thomas? Did you hear what I said?' Maria demanded, her hands on her hips.

Thomas stared at the leeches. 'We've got to get them off or they'll suck too much blood and the humours will be out of balance. Rose, sit down and hold out your arm.'

She did so, too scared to even rejoice at Maria stamping past in a huff. Thomas took hold of her arm and began removing the leeches one by one with his knife.

'How do you know how to do that?' she said, to take her mind off the unpleasant procedure. She kept her gaze fixed firmly away from her arm, flinching every time he dug the tip of his knife into the skin and took off another leech.

Thomas looked at her through the fair fringe flopping over his eyes and grinned. 'Brother Leviticus showed me. He was always careful about the number of leeches he used to bleed someone. Too many, he said, and they would suck out the good humours as well as the bad. That's why I must get as many off as I can.'

He had a nice smile and a kind face. His touch was soft, not unlike a maid, and his manner far more refined than William's. She hadn't noticed before, but he was quite handsome in a boyish sort of way.

'The Lord help us if Rose loses her good humours. She hasn't got many to spare,' Maria quipped from the bank.

She glanced over to her adversary, who sat primly on the grass with her fine kirtle spread around her as though nothing had happened, delicately examining her daisy chain. Even the way she held her head said *noble*. A week ago, she would have called her Mistress Maria and curtsied to her.

She shouldn't have lost her temper. Wasn't Ma always

telling her to keep her tongue between her teeth or the good Lord would cut it off?

'I think Rose has m-many good humours,' said Eleanor, picking daisies for her own chain.

'Yes, well, you would,' Maria snapped back.

'Stop it you two, I'm trying to concentrate,' said Thomas bending to his task.

As he held her arm, a flush spread to her cheeks. Embarrassed, she looked away. A groan burst from her as she saw William striding down the path towards them. That was all she needed.

'William!' Eleanor jumped to her feet, her daisy chain forgotten in her excitement. 'M-Maria p-pushed Rose in the water and now she's got leeches all over her and T-Thomas is t-taking them off!'

William took in the scene with one swift glance and put a firm hand on Thomas's shoulder.

'I'll do that.'

Thomas glanced up at him. 'It's no trouble. Brother Leviticus showed me how to do it. I've already finished one arm.'

William's face hardened. 'Rose is my lass. We've an understanding to get wed. If anyone's going to be holding her arm, it's me.' He elbowed his way between them.

Typical! She couldn't so much as stand next to a lad without William butting in, claiming her as his own. He was doing that now, gripping her arm in a rough hand and pushing so close to her that she could feel the coarse cloth of his tunic and smell the sweat on him. Thomas didn't smell like that.

'Will, you can't hold her arm and take off the leeches with only one hand,' Thomas pointed out. 'I—'

'She'll keep it still for me. Won't you, Rose?' William

pulled off a leech and she winced. He wasn't nearly as gentle as Thomas.

'Simon's c-coming!' Eleanor shouted.

Wonderful. Someone else coming to take charge.

'What's going on?' said Simon, as he climbed over the fence. 'I could hear the commotion from the high fields. I thought there'd been an accident or something.'

'Rose and M-Maria had a fight,' Eleanor announced. 'Rose p-pulled Maria's hair so Maria p-pushed her in the river and Rose c-came out covered in leeches. T-Thomas was taking them off but William got angry and now he's doing it.'

Simon looked from one to the other, his mantle hanging in authoritative folds to his knees. 'Thomas? What's your dealing in this?'

'I was taking a walk over the orchards looking for bees when I heard screams and came to see what had happened. I didn't see the fight; I was just removing the leeches when Will turned up and took over.'

He would be more useful making shelves for the food instead of wandering around looking for bees, in her opinion, but she kept that to herself.

Simon stared at them in disbelief. 'I don't believe this. Don't any of you understand the situation we're in? There are eight of us, that's all, and with only the food we brought with us. We've no harvest to reap and no roof on the house. Instead of helping to get us out of this mess, you're squabbling amongst yourselves or wandering around idle!' He looked hard at the group. 'Don't you understand? If we're to survive, we must work together. I thought I'd already made that clear.'

Eleanor looked away suddenly, pointing up the valley. 'Who's that?'

Will ripped the last leech off Rose's arm and scrambled to his feet to join Eleanor. 'Looks like travellers.' He glanced at Thomas. 'Thought ye said no travellers would come here.'

'I didn't think they would.'

Maria drew back a little, clutching her kirtle close about her. 'I hope they haven't got the Pestilence.'

'So do I,' said Simon. 'Will? Thomas? With me.'

He unsheathed his knife and stood square in the middle of the track, waiting, as William and Thomas took up positions on either side.

Rose rubbed her sore arms and watched the wagon creak its way slowly towards them. It was an odd-looking group; the driver was an old man, with a young lad sitting next to him. Walking alongside was a priest wearing long black robes and the rope belt of his office with his hood up.

'Who are you, and where are you from?' Simon demanded.

'You won't be needing that.' The old man brought the wagon to a stop and nodded to Simon's knife. 'We mean no trouble.'

This close, Rose thought he looked rather like an old billy goat. His long pointed chin was covered in spiky grey whiskers, and his head almost bald save for a few strands of white hair.

'God's blessing.' The priest stepped forward, making the sign of the cross. 'I am Father Rulf.'

'Hail,' Thomas answered, nodding respectfully to the priest. 'I'm Lord Thomas de Chiddleigh, and you are on my land.'

Father Rulf lowered his hood, bowing his head slightly in response. 'We wish you no harm, my lord. We have travelled from the southern and eastern shires.'

'Don't come any closer,' said Simon. 'I've heard the Pestilence came from the ports in those shires.'

She had heard that too. Cecily had said that foreign sailors had brought forbidden idols and angered the Lord into sending the Pestilence, and of all the women in the village, Cecily ought to know; her son had been sent to the harbours to buy salted fish for the manor. The quicker Simon sent these three on their way, the better.

Father Rulf opened his arms and spoke in the placid tones of all priests. 'I've heard the same tales, and I understand your fears. We stayed away from the ports and the main routes as much as we could. We've seen no death if that's what you're afraid of.'

The old man nodded, peering at them through grey, rheumy eyes. 'The name's Gee, my lord. This here's my son, Jarin.'

Jarin's grey tunic strained across a barrel chest. He snatched his cap from his head with small, thick hands and held it awkwardly in his lap. 'My lord.'

'Me and the lad are from no place in particular, but we've not been near ships and we've no buboes, look.' Gee held out his thin arms and pulled down the neck of his brown tunic to expose a black dirt line around his neck. 'Truth is, I'm too old for travelling. I'm looking for a place to settle. You'll have no trouble from us, and my boy's strong and a good worker.'

Jarin's plump cheeks flushed, making her wonder how old he was. He didn't look more than twelve summers.

Simon half-turned his back and lowered his voice. 'What do you think? The priest said they've not been to the ports, but how do we know he's not lying?'

'Priests don't lie,' said Thomas.

'They're not sick, and a priest would be a comfort to us

all,' William added. He glanced at Jarin. 'We could use another pair of hands, too. What do ye say, Thomas?'

'We do need all the help we can get,' Thomas agreed. 'That Gee's got a wagon and a horse, and if the priest wants to stay, we can't very well turn him away unless we want to risk God's wrath.'

She shivered at that. There was rather too much of God's wrath being visited upon His people these days.

'They're waiting for an answer, and someone had better say summat.' William looked at Thomas. 'Go on; you're the lord.'

Thomas bit his lip before turning back to the group. 'You're welcome to stay. The dark months are coming, and that's not a good time to be travelling.'

'God bless you for your kindness,' Father Rulf said. 'I know my companions are grateful. For myself, I am passing through and wish no more than to stay the night. Tomorrow I shall be on my way.'

'A shame he's not staying,' William said in an undertone. 'I could do with cleansing me soul.'

If the way Thomas was looking at Father Rulf was any indication, she thought that William wasn't the only one who was disappointed.

Simon stepped forward and pointed to a patch of land about a hundred yards behind the wagon. 'Old man, do you see that may tree and the rowan beyond? You can pitch up there for a week. If you're still well by the end of that time, you can make it your plot, from the track back to the ancients' stones. You'll provide for yourselves, and Lord Thomas will settle wages later.'

'I can't. I've no money,' Thomas hissed.

Simon leaned close. 'They don't know that.' He raised his voice again. 'If that's not to your liking, you can stay the night and move on tomorrow.'

'I'm grateful to you, my lord. We'll stay, and you'll not regret it.' Gee nodded to Thomas. 'Jarin, get off the wagon and turn the horse.'

'God will bless you, good people.' Father Rulf bowed.

Thomas stepped forward. 'Are you sure you won't stay too, Father? You'd be most welcome. You wouldn't have to sleep in the house; we could find you somewhere of your own.'

'Don't know where apart from that shack of a linhay,' Rose muttered. 'Besides, we've enough trouble without another mouth to feed.'

'Rose! Father Rulf's a man of God!' Thomas looked at her, appalled, then turned to Father Rulf with a pleading expression. 'Prithee, Father, it's just—'

Father Rulf held up his hand and smiled. 'I understand, and I shall remember your kindness in my prayers. I am sorely tempted, but I must go north.' Sedately, he followed Gee along the track.

'If you're ever this way again, do come and see us, Father!' Thomas called after him. 'We're here until the spring! Then we return to Ashetyne.'

Father Rulf raised his hand in acknowledgement and kept walking.

'You're desperate for him to stay,' said Rose.

'No, I'm not. It would be good for us to have a priest here, that's all. And you should be ashamed of yourself, speaking so about him!'

She was, and she would be sure to ask God's forgiveness in her prayers that night, but – priest or no priest – he still needed feeding. God would understand.

'Right, you two,' Simon pointed at her and Maria. 'You have been scratching at each other since we arrived.

Maids shouldn't fight. Now beg pardon to each other.'

'I'm the lord's sister. I don't need to beg pardon to a miller's daughter.'

'I'm not asking you, Maria; I'm telling you. And find yourself a tunic. You can't work dressed like that.' Simon scowled at Maria's fine kirtle.

Rose smiled smugly. It was about time someone put Maria in her place, and now she'd have no fine kirtles to flaunt.

'That's not fair!' Maria protested. 'Thomas, tell him I can wear what I like!'

Thomas shrugged and kept his head down. Rose frowned. Surely, Thomas wasn't afraid of his little sister?

'Just do it, Maria,' said Simon, who looked as fed up with her as she was. 'Rose, get back to the house and organise the work there. Make sure jobs get done and keep an eye on the stores and the fowl, that sort of thing. I'm relying on you.'

'God help us. I'm not being bossed around by her.' Maria looked her up and down.

If Maria was trying to make her feel inferior, she was going to be disappointed. She could lift her chin in the air as well as any noble, and she did.

'You'll do as Rose says!' Simon snapped. 'Now get back to the house. El, you go with them.'

Fancy that! She was in charge now, and her just a miller's lass. She smiled. A chance like this would never have come her way in the village. She'd get things organised, and even if she wasn't as pretty or refined as Maria, she'd show her that she was as good as her any day.

Simon turned to William. 'You need to go back to the forge and help Peter. We need nails and iron bands, lots of them. It's no use cutting reeds to thatch the roof if we've nothing to fix them with.'

'Fine. Rose, if ye need help again, ask *me*. Understand?' William glared at her and Thomas as he sloped off.

Anger surged through her, burning away her elation. William had no right to treat her this way. He didn't own her, and he wasn't her husband, although he was behaving as though he was. If this was going to work, she had to make him see sense.

The problem was, she had no idea how.

CHAPTER 7

Rose picked up two apples and a hunk of cheese from the table and wrapped them in a piece of sacking. Humming to herself, she reached for her cloth shoes. She had been in charge for two weeks and loved making decisions with no one peering over her shoulder to tell her what to do. This was the freedom she had dreamed of.

She rammed a stubborn curl under her coif and pinned it in place, William. Had been getting more and more persistent lately, acting as though their marriage was a natural occurrence that wanted nothing but time to make complete. She would have asked Ma for advice, but Ma was miles away and would probably tell her to accept her lot and that, she thrust another pin savagely into her coif, was something she was determined not to do. She wanted independence, well she'd got it. It was up to her to find a solution.

Grabbing a flagon of cider, she tucked the food parcel under her arm and opened the door with a twinge of pride. She'd made a good job of repairing that; it had only needed a few nails. Stepping outside, the heat hit her like a wet curtain. A little way off, she could see Peter and Jarin splitting a large oak trunk to make beams for the roof. How Peter could do such heavy work in the heat, was beyond her, although being a smithy probably helped.

She watched as he axed slits along the length of the trunk. Jarin followed behind, inserting timber wedges into the gaps and hammering them fast. After they'd worked their way down the whole length, Peter pounded the wedges in deeper and deeper, until the trunk began to split in half. When the gap was two fingers wide, he swung his hammer high above his head and brought it down in the middle with a final crack.

'Mind yer feet!' he yelled as one half toppled towards her.

She leapt back as the trunk crashed down three feet away from where she'd been standing.

'I'd often wondered how that was done,' she said.

Peter wiped his brow and let out a long breath of air. 'Well, now ye knows.'

'It was easy.' Jarin swung his hammer through the air with a proud grin, his dark button eyes shining out from his jovial face.

She raised her eyebrows; if he was trying to impress her, he'd failed, but—'What's that?' she crossed herself.

Jarin frowned a little. 'What?'

'*That!*' Staring, her heart pounding, she backed off, pointing to a black swelling under Jarin's left eye.

'This?' he grinned. 'Oh, that's nothing. I tripped over my own feet. I'm always doing it.' He touched it and winced. 'It's a bit sore, though.'

It looked like a bruise. She took another step back just in case. 'Are you sure? Only folks say that's how it starts.'

'Oh, you think it's a buboe! I swear on my soul, it's only a bruise. See for yourself.' He came towards her.

'Don't come near me!' she shrieked but now she looked closer, it wasn't a raised lump, and there was yellow around the edges. No one had ever said anything about yellow buboes.

Peter snorted a laugh. ''Tis only a bruise, lass, or I wouldn't be standing 'ere!'

A little embarrassed, she laughed nervously 'For a moment I thought…'

Peter nodded. 'Aye, I see that.' He clapped Jarin on the shoulder. 'Come on, lad, line up the poles, let's get these timbers rolled over to the others. The sooner we get this finished the quicker we'll have a roof and we can all rest easy.'

Now the fear of the Pestilence had settled, she moved closer, intrigued. She'd never seen how large timbers were moved.

Jarin lined five poles in front of one half of the trunk. He and Peter slowly pushed the trunk across the poles. When it reached the last one, Jarin grabbed a pole from the back, ran to the front and put it on the ground. It was a slow procedure but pole by pole, they moved the trunk across the yard to join the growing pile.

'That was a heavy one.' Jarin wiped his face and sat down on the log, sweat glistening on his round cheeks. 'Reckon it'll do for the main beam down the centre.'

'Are Simon and Will felling in the woods?' she asked.

'Aye. The old 'orse only has two more trees to drag down 'ere and I reckon we'll have enough. And right glad I am too. I'm a smithy, not a sawyer and 'tis too hot for this work.' Peter mopped his brow with a filthy rag that was the same colour as his embers.

'It's even hotter in the forge,' Jarin pointed out.

Peter gave him a withering look. 'Tis a different kind of hot. Embers heat's nothing like this blazing sun, making the sweat run down me face worse than a waterfall. Could do with a swig of that cider,' he added, eyeing Rose's flagon.

'I'm taking this to Simon, but there's a barrel indoors. Help yourself. I'd best be going.'

As she crossed the yard, Maria was coming towards her dressed in a loose grey kirtle and an apron. Judging by the patch that was covering another patch and the tacked-on hem, it was one of Janet's.

Maria marched passed. 'Before you ask, I've cleaned out the fowl and collected the eggs,' she said, holding up a bowl. 'And yes, I'm going to collect the firewood and after that, I shall pick meadowsweet for Janet to put with the berries.'

Surprisingly, Maria hadn't argued when given her tasks. Instead, she put on a grand show every time she did them, making sure everyone knew she was working. Rose smiled to herself. She wasn't fooled; Maria was only obeying because of Simon. He was probably the only person who had stood up to her in her entire life.

'Gather as much firewood as you can!' she called after Maria's retreating back.

'Arse to you!' Maria shouted over her shoulder and kept walking.

Well! Ladies swore too. Who'd have thought it? Chuckling to herself, Rose went to see how Janet and Eleanor were getting on with the reeds.

It was cooler by the river. The water sparkled like diamonds, and the willows hung over the opposite bank in swathes of green silk. She felt a sudden urge to plunge in and feel the refreshing water on her face. Then she remembered the leeches and rubbed her arms. She wouldn't want that again.

Walking on, she found Eleanor and Janet around the next bend where they were turning a pile of cut reeds.

'Rose!' Eleanor ran to meet her. 'C-come and see what

we've d-done.' Grabbing Rose's hand, she pulled her along.

Janet leaned on her fork. She had smudges on her cheek and her thin hair hung lank beneath her headdress. 'God's feet, I'm tired. This heat drains me, but praise God, this is the last turn, and the reeds should be dry and ready for thatching.'

'Then we'll have a roof and we won't get wet when it rains,' said Eleanor.

'That's right, we won't.' Janet laughed.

Rose couldn't help noticing how much more relaxed Janet was away from Peter. If he'd been her husband, she would never have let him speak to her the way he did to Janet. It was shameful how some husbands dominated their women into snivelling wrecks, often by the use of their belts. All the more reason not to be wed off. William probably wouldn't be that sort, but a lass never knew until the ring was on her finger, and then it was too late.

'I've sorted all the food into one store and put it in the corner of the house as you asked,' Janet went on. 'There's not much of it, though. Beans, carrots, and we've two hunks of cheese, but the sheep won't give milk now the lambs are grown. What are we going to do when the food runs out?'

A good question. Janet's words had given voice to a fear that had kept her awake at night. Even if they cut back, she doubted their stores would last the dark months. They still had the three sacks of flour her Pa had given them, but when those were gone, they'd have no bread. Many poor folks died in the cold months from starvation. Pray God, she wouldn't be one of them.

'We'll do what common folks always do, We'll water the potage, eat less, tighten our belts and pray we don't starve. And,' she added as she caught sight of a rabbit scurrying into the hedge. 'We'll poach.'

'Hardly poaching, Thomas will be as hungry as the rest of us. I can't see him hanging any of us, can you?'

'No, I can't.'

For a moment they laughed but the laughter soon died.

'I'll share my bowl with you.' Eleanor wrapped an arm around Janet and squeezed her.

Janet smiled at her. 'You're very kind, El.' The smile trembled as she looked at Rose. Both of them knew that it wouldn't be enough.

Sometimes, Rose envied Eleanor her innocence. Trapped as she was in her childish world, she only saw good in folks and was always happy. She was such a dear creature.

'I miss the village and my friends,' said Janet staring to the moor. 'Do you think coming here was such a good idea? I know Peter would leave tomorrow if he could, and God forgive me, but some days, I feel like packing everything up and leaving too.'

'You can't! We need you, and anyway, we can't go back until the spring. Things will get better, you'll see.' She wished she could feel as confident as she sounded.

'I like it here although I m-miss Lady Joan,' Eleanor said. 'There're fish in the river. I saw them. Great big brown ones. I could make t-twine if someone knows how to m-make nets.' Her eyes shone at the prospect.

'Good idea, El,' Rose agreed. 'You could use those short reeds we cut by mistake.'

'Oh, T-Thomas is using those for his shelves,' said Eleanor.

Rose laughed in delight. 'Praise God, don't tell me he's finally started making the shelves for the food! I've been reminding him for over a week.'

'He was going to the woods to cut hazel poles, so he is

doing it,' said Janet.

'T-Thomas has found a bees nest and I've made a skep for them,' said Eleanor proudly.

'Good Lord, has he found one at last? He's spent days wandering those fields looking,' said Rose. Just hearing the word *bees* gave her the shivers. She loved the honey, but the bees themselves; nasty, buzzing things with a sting sharp as a needle and a temper to match! What God had been thinking of when He'd created them, she couldn't fathom.

'We'll have honey and m-mead again. I like honey.' Eleanor rubbed her hands together at the idea.

'And wax for candles. That's something else we're short of. Can you braid grass wicks for rushlights, El?' Rose asked.

'Yes, they're easy,' Eleanor answered. 'Just keep c-coating the grasses in the m-melted wax or swine fat. I've done it hundreds of times.'

'El, you've just got yourself another job. Make as many as you can and get Maria to help you. After I've taken this food to Simon, I'm washing the walls inside the house; I can't live with that slime any longer. Janet, you can help and El, you can pick grasses and nettles for tapers and twine.' Satisfied things were running smoothly, she picked up the flagon. 'I'll leave you to it and get this cider to the men. They'll be parched by now.'

The walk up the hill was blissfully quiet, the well-trodden path soft with centuries of fallen leaves. Above and in front of her, the sunlight broke through the thick green canopy into welcoming dappled shade. It wouldn't be long before the leaves turned yellow, heralding the shortening of the days and the cooling of the nights. Pray God they'd manage to get some more stores in and the roof fixed by then.

Following the sound of chunking axes. Rose found Simon and William halfway up the hill. Stripped down to their hose, the sweat glistened on their muscular shoulders as they took turns swinging their axes into the base of an ancient oak.

The oak tree was known as the King of the Woods, and many folks believed it held power over the fairy folk, who would wreak havoc on those they disliked. Some oaks were thought to be hundreds of years old. She wondered what it had seen and what stories it could tell, if it had been able to speak. It seemed a shame to cut it down, but they needed the wood.

'Stay there, lass, we're nearly through,' said Simon.

William swung the axe, revealing the puckered stump of his left arm hanging uselessly below his elbow. Shuddering, Rose turned her head away. She would ignore him. She'd give the food to Simon and then leave.

Simon spat on his hands, swung the axe high over his shoulder and brought it down with a loud thud.

Creaking and groaning in protest, the old tree teetered as though struggling to cling to life in its final moments, then it surrendered with a dying groan and crashed to the ground in a storm of broken branches and flying leaves, sending a flock of indignant crows whirling and screeching above their heads.

The forest fell silent. William and Simon laughed and slapped each other on the back.

'He put up a fight,' said William, wiping his brow.

She thought the remains of the tree looked rather sad but kept quiet. The men would only think her silly.

'He certainly did. Praise God it's the last.' Simon slumped on the trunk, slapping it hard.

'I've brought you something to eat,' she said offering

the parcel to Simon.

'If that's a flagon of cider, then God bless you!' said Simon. Picking up his discarded tunic, he wiped the sweat from his chest, then accepted the flagon and took a long gulp before passing it to William.

She was going to ignore him, and she didn't mean to stare, but William's stump fascinated her as much as it revolted her, like the deformed freaks caged for show in the markets. Seeing her gaze, William hastily thrust the flagon back at Simon and pulled his tunic over his head.

'There's apples and cheese,' she said awkwardly, aiming the comment somewhere between Simon and William.

William grinned at her. 'Bringing us vittels, eh? Just a like a proper little wife.'

She stiffened. Little wife indeed! He could get that idea straight out of his head. 'Any of us could have brought it,' she said in a voice as cold as her stare. 'Me or one of the others.' Damn! She meant to ignore him.

William's grin broadened, became more subtly knowing. 'Aye, but it *wasn't* one of the others, was it?'

Lord, he was arrogant. Hadn't it occurred to him that she might not want to be his *little wife*? Next time, she'd send Janet; William could hardly misconstrue the intentions of his own mother.

'Stay and sit yerself down 'ere next to me.' William shifted up and patted the trunk.

She would rather die. 'I can't. I've things to do and Janet's waiting for me.' She turned and hurried back down the path before he could protest.

The sun had passed the third quarter, and a low shaft of light shone through the openings into the house. The green walls were now back to their original grey stone, apart from in the corners where the slime refused to budge no matter how hard she scrubbed. An enticing smell of mint and herbs came from the pot bubbling over the hearth.

'That smells good. I'm so tired, I could eat a horse.' She threw what was left of the twig brush into the pail of green water. She'd empty it later.

'It's bean potage,' said Janet, stirring it as though her life depended on it. 'I held back on the peas, as you said. I hope the others won't be long.'

'Done!' Thomas stood back from the corner. 'Rose, come and look. I've finished your shelves.'

The shelves stood four feet high and three feet wide. Instead of solid shelves made from wood like they needed, Thomas had lashed hazel poles together with twine and secured each corner to an upright pole.

'What do you think?' he said, beaming proudly.

She had no idea how to answer without risking the stocks. The upright poles weren't upright, the shelves sloped and the whole thing didn't look strong enough to hold a candle, let alone clay jars and baskets of food.

Thomas stood back, nodding with the satisfaction of a job well done. 'I've given you three shelves and a low one off the floor for the flour as you asked, and I could add another one on top if you want.' He tilted his head on one side and turned to face her, pride shining from every inch of his face. 'I'm pleased with that. I've never made shelves before.'

She swallowed her laughter. 'Is it strong enough?'

'Of course it is! Look.' He shook the top shelf, which promptly fell down. Blushing, he picked it up and set it back in place. 'It just needs a little adjusting, that's all.'

It needed more than that.

'It's all wonky!' Eleanor piped up from her mattress. 'Everything will slide off the end.' She giggled, setting Rose off into gales of laughter.

'Why are you laughing? There's nothing wrong with it,' he said.

'We're not laughing at you,' she said wiping her eyes. 'Really, we're not.' The fact that he couldn't see how bad it was made it all the funnier.

'I think you're both heartless. It took me all day to make that.' Thomas looked at her like a wounded puppy, his soft brown eyes melting under his hair.

She regained control of herself. Thomas was right; he'd done the best job he could, and it was heartless to laugh at him. 'You've done a good job and with a little adjustment here and there, like you said, I'm sure it'll be fine.' She'd get Jarin to fix it when Thomas was out.

'I'll look at it again tomorrow, but now I need to check something in my charts. I've been wanting to look at them all day.' Thomas sat down, spreading the papers out and looking down at them with keen interest.

She ambled over to join him. She'd often wondered what was so important about those papers, and this seemed as good a time as any to ask. 'What are you looking at?'

'My almanac and chart. It gives dates and shows the movements of the planets and stars. If you know how to read them, they can predict things and tell you when it's right to make decisions. I use them all the time. Take a look, it's fascinating.'

Leaning over his shoulder, she peered down at the mass of dots, lines and letters that covered the parchment and held no meaning at all for her. Ma had taught her to read and write numbers in the mill, and she was proud of that, but she'd always wanted to learn to read. To think a few lines and squiggles could speak to you! It was like magic. Her Pa could read enough to deal with merchants but had refused to teach her. He'd always said reading wasn't for maids, even though she had never understood why. After all, if she'd been born a noble like Maria, she would have learned.

'Is this the night sky?' she said, leaning closer and pointing.

Thomas nodded. 'The stars change as they move around us. A few ancient philosophers, like Aristarchus of Samos, think that we move around the sun, but I'm not sure—'

'What're ye doing, Rose?' William stood poised on the threshold, his broad frame casting a long dark shadow across the floor.

There was that possessive tone again. She turned and lifted her chin in her best imitation of Maria. 'Thomas is showing me the stars.'

'Shut the door! The wax is going on my chart!' Thomas ordered as he pushed the pewter candle holder to one side and brushed the spots off of his parchment lovingly.

'Stars?' William snorted. 'That'll be a great help this winter!'

'The charts help Thomas make decisions,' said Rose as though she'd always known it. 'That seems helpful to me.'

'Oh, aye? And was it those charts of his told him that this'd be a good place to come?' William demanded, the derision in his voice stronger than ever. 'If so, he'd be better off—'

'Move yourself, boy!' Peter barked from behind William. 'God's bones, I've made so many nails there's enough to mend a village full of roofs.' He pushed his way in, sniffing the air appreciatively. 'That smells good. Ye make a fine potage, woman, I'll say that for ye.'

William followed Peter inside, letting the door slam shut behind him, and Thomas yelped.

'Mind the draught! I've a precious chart here.'

'I should give up if I was you,' said Rose.

Thomas sighed and started tidying his parchments onto his mattress. 'You're right. I'll show you another time, if you want.'

'I'd like that,' she said with a smile, and meant it.

William dragged a stool close to the hearth. 'Sit here, Rose,' he said, patting the top, fixing jealous eyes on Thomas.

She wanted to say that she was quite capable of choosing where to sit, but the others might think her surly, so she perched on the stool as far away from him as she could.

'What do ye want with stars?' William said, leaning so close that she could smell the embers and ash seeping from every part of him. 'I can show ye real stars in the sky if you've a liking. In the spring when we go home and are wed, we can look at them from our place in the yard behind Pa's forge.'

The corners of his eyes crinkled, showing her a glimpse of her old William. For the tiniest moment, she wanted to say yes, but one glance at the empty sleeve tucked into his belt and all that it meant soon changed her mind.

'There's no haste,' she said. 'I mean, getting wed isn't something we should rush into, is it?'

The crinkles changed to disappointment. 'But we're promised. Ye knows that.'

She sighed. Deep down, underneath her disgust, she felt sorry for him. It wasn't his fault he'd lost his arm, and it certainly wasn't his fault that she didn't want to be wed off like other maids. Sometimes, she wished that she did; it would make life much easier.

Letting him down was going to be harder than she thought, but if she didn't do it now, it might be too late.

'I don't think we are promised,' she said in a low voice, 'and I hope you're not going around telling folks—'

'I tell ye, m'young lord, my Will made nearly as many nails as I did, and him with only one arm too.' Peter announced. 'How's that for a boy?'

William turned around. 'Pa, I'm not a boy—'

'In the spring, boy, when we're back home, I'll get ye fixed up as me apprentice proper. I'll learn ye all I know and in a few years, I'll get ye to the guild for your seal, just like your grandpa wanted. He slaved like a cur for young lord's Pa, as they all did.' Peter nodded towards Thomas, who kept his head down. 'Night and day as the head stableman and he tilled the communal fields and cut the harvest. No thanks from the lord, mind. Worked his fingers to the bone, he did and saved his silver pennies so I could get a trade. When the good Lord takes me, the forge'll be yours and your son's after, safe from any lord, just like your grandpa wanted.' Peter sat down by the hearth, looking far more relaxed and at home in the house than she suspected Thomas ever would. 'The work killed him in the end,' he said in a more somber tone. 'Lord of the Manor threw me and me sister, Annie, out on the street.'

She shivered. Ma had often talked about that. It had been a dreadful business.

'I know, Pa, you've told me.' William shielded his mouth with his hand. 'I bet he doesn't pay me,' he whispered to her.

'I heard that, boy! I'll pay ye when you're worth paying and not before. Come on, woman, that pot's teasing me gut.'

'I am not a boy—' William tried again.

'Now, tell me, m'young lord, how comes that Gee and his son are staying?' Peter demanded.

She was beginning to see where William had got his stubbornness and unwillingness to listen.

'Ye promised no one would find us and I reckon if they did, what's stopping others?'

Thomas squirmed. 'I didn't think anyone would.'

'Thomas wasn't to know. Anyway, they haven't got the Pestilence.' She accepted a bowl from Janet and nestled it in her hands, breathing in the smell of herbs as her stomach growled in anticipation. She didn't know how Janet did it, but she could make a tasty dish out of nothing.

'The next lot might. I'm telling ye—'

'And they might not.' That Peter was like a cur gnawing a bone, and she hastened to change the subject. 'Thomas, have you found any bees for us yet?'

'Two days ago, and El has made a skep for them. She did such a good job that I've put her in charge of all basket and twine making from now on.'

'Can you get the nest?' said Simon.

'Oh yes, I used to help Brother Matthew with his bees all the time.'

'Finally, sommat he can do,' Peter muttered just loud enough for everyone to hear.

Eleanor and Maria giggled behind their hands. Rose shot them a hard look, turning it on William when he stifled a laugh. Why didn't Thomas stand up for himself more? She would do if she'd been the lord.

Thomas deliberately placed his bowl on the floor and slowly wiped his hands on his hose. 'You can laugh, but I'll get the bees. I'll show you,' he said.

'Not tomorrow, you won't,' said Simon. 'The reeds are dry

and the beams are ready. Tomorrow we start on the roof.'

No sooner had he said it than a drip landed on the hearth, followed quickly by another and another.

She looked up, the dread in her heart mirrored on the others' faces as they all stared at the roof, feeling the drips on their faces.

It was raining.

CHAPTER 8

'The food! Save the food!' Rose ran to the corner, Janet close behind, and started gathering everything she could reach, piling jars, baskets and bowls into her kirtle. 'Maria! Don't just stand there; help us!'

'Me embers! Boy, come on, save me embers!' Peter was out the door in two strides with William on his heels.

'El, pails! As many as you can find!' Simon shouted, running to the door and grabbing two pails of his own.

'The mattresses!' Rose shouted over her shoulder. 'They're getting soaked. Thomas, get them out and take them to the linhays.'

Rose's voice snapped Thomas out of his dread stupor, and he raised a hand to his cheek, feeling the raindrops there. It was real. The rain had come, and it would destroy everything; the mattresses, the food—his charts. He'd left them on his mattress!

He crossed the distance in two gigantic steps and seized his charts, clutching them to his body, hunching over to try and protect them while fumbling in his purse for the key to his chest. Something loud crashed behind him. Turning, he saw his shelves cascade sending jars and baskets rolling across the floor and spilling precious beans and grain into the mud. All thoughts of charts forgotten, he watched the last shelf groan and fall to the ground to join the rest of his hard work in an ignominious heap in the dirt.

'Quick!' Rose shouted to the room. 'Get the covers from the mattresses to shield the food and scrape the beans off the floor!' She dropped to her knees, scrabbling through the mud to try and save what precious stores she could.

'Thomas!' Simon yelled, lugging two overflowing pails to the door. 'Don't stand there gawking like a cow! Get the covers and take those mattresses to the linhays!'

'I'm putting my charts away.' Thomas said, now grappling with the key in the lock.

'Forget your damn charts. The food's more important.'

Not to him, it wasn't. His hands shaking, he thrust the key into the lock. He opened the chest, threw the charts inside, then slammed the lid and snatched the covers off the mattresses. 'Here they are.'

'Don't give them to me, you nuddlejade!' Simon said. 'Give them to Rose!'

Thomas held out the covers to Rose, who snatched them from him with a look of contempt to mirror Simon's.

'I'll do this! For God's sake, get those mattresses somewhere dry!' she ordered.

No sooner had the words left her mouth than a large wedge of thatch slid off the roof and landed with a splat on the floor between them, as the timbers above their heads began to creak ominously.

'The roof's going!' Simon shouted. 'Everyone get outside.'

'Wait; Pa's flour! Thomas, for the love of God, *help* us!' Rose began dragging a sack towards the door, but water was already seeping in from outside, turning the floor slippery and treacherous.

Skidding, fighting to keep his feet every step of the way,

he grabbed a corner of the sack, but it was sodden and refused to budge. Overhead, the creaking stopped for a split-second, as if the beam was unsure, then one of the roof timbers crashed to the ground, missing him by inches.

'Get out!' Simon shouted.

'But the flour—' said Janet.

'Leave the flour! It's no good to you if you're dead!' Simon yelled. 'Come *on*, before the whole lot caves in.'

'Janet, leave it!' Rose screamed from the threshold, as one end of the roof collapsed to the ground in a shower of splintering timber. She grabbed Janet by the arm and the two women struggled through the door to safety. Thomas seized his chest, half carrying, half dragging it and followed them as the rest of the roof gave way.

Outside, they huddled together in numb silence, as the world they'd been working so hard to build fell apart in front of them.

'Look!' Eleanor pointed across the yard.

In a final gesture of defiance, the river burst its banks and raced towards them. There was nothing any of them could do except watch the yard turn into a lake as the river came closer and closer.

A white flash split the sky, followed by a threatening rumble that built to a deafening crescendo of thunder that shook the very ground beneath them.

Eleanor screamed and covered her ears.

Maria clung to Janet, and the older woman crossed herself. 'God help us! It's the devil and his evil spirits in the air!'

'We've no bells to scare them away. Shout! Everybody shout!' Rose opened her mouth and screamed at the top of her lungs, shaking her fist at the sky.

'It's not the devil,' Thomas said. 'It's just the light

disturbing the air causing —'

Simon grabbed him and pulled him away from the others, shaking his head. 'God's balls, not now, Thomas.'

'But if they'd only stop shrieking and listen to me, they'd understand and then they wouldn't be frightened —'

His protest was drowned in another rolling roar. As it died away, everyone held their breaths to the sound of beating rain.

Slowly, Eleanor uncovered her ears. Maria stopped clutching Janet, who looked up from her prayers, and Rose lowered her fist as Peter and William came out of the forge with grave faces. Water dripped off their clothes as they looked at the carnage in stunned silence.

Weeks of work, all destroyed on a whim of God. Nothing remained of the roof, and only the four walls of the house were left standing naked to the sky like a shipwrecked boat lost at sea.

'Just when we were starting to make it work,' said Rose quietly.

'Me embers are out and me iron's wet. It'll rust now. There'll be no nails and nothing else 'til I can fix the forge,' said Peter to the ground.

'Why didn't God wait a few days?' said Eleanor, sobbing.

Janet put her arms around her. 'I don't know, El. Nobody knows.'

'I want to go home,' said Maria plaintively.

'We all want to go home, but we can't, and moaning about it won't help,' said Simon. 'If you'd cut the reeds right in the first place —' he glared at Rose — 'and if Peter had helped more with the building instead of wasting days on that forge, we might have had a roof, and then we wouldn't be standing here soaked to the skin with nowhere to sleep tonight.'

'Simon —' Thomas began.

'If you'd told us what you wanted at the start, we would have cut the reeds right. We're none of us thatchers, so don't blame us!' Rose flashed back. 'And it's not our fault it's raining.'

'Lass is right,' Peter agreed. 'Besides, no forge means no nails, and no nails means no roof of any sort, thatched or no.'

Simon sighed, running a hand through his sodden hair. 'I know. I'm sorry, it's just—*look* at it!'

'Me and Pa heard the noise.' Jarin ran into the yard. 'I come as fast as I could, but—' He saw the wreckage and stopped dead. 'God's blood, what a mess. What're we going to do now?'

The group turned to Thomas, the same question in their eyes, exactly as they had when they first arrived. Again, they expected him to have the answer. And again, he didn't have one.

He was only human. No different to them, except he'd been born with a title. How was he supposed to know what to do? In truth, he agreed with Maria; he wanted to go home, but they couldn't.

They were still looking at him. He had to think of something to say.

'There's only one thing we can do,' he said, his words sounding more confident than he felt. 'We'll have to start again.'

He heard their sighs and saw the doubt on their faces. Hope, that was what they needed. 'Tomorrow, we'll clear up and see how things are. I'm sure it's not that bad.' His words sounded as feeble as he felt, and there wasn't so much as a glimmer from any of them. He tried again. 'Things won't seem so bad in the morning. They never do,' he added lamely.

Nothing. He might as well have addressed his remarks

to the ruined house. Clawing for something to save himself, he spotted the wagons beside the house and pointed. 'We can sleep under the shelter of the wagons tonight. It looks a bit drier under there.'

Peter raised his eyebrows, his expression bordering on pure derision.

'Come on, woman,' he said to Janet. The two of them walked away, in the opposite direction to the wagons. One by one, the rest of the group followed him.

Behind him, the last beam surrendered with a groan and fell to the ground. Even the house was giving up on him.

Alone in the middle of the yard, water dripping down his neck, he lifted his eyes to what was left of his Great Plan. He was no good at this lord thing.

Soft footsteps stopped beside him, and a gentle hand rested on his arm.

'Don't mind them,' Rose said quietly. 'It must be hard to be the new lord and always know what to do.'

How right she was. He didn't answer, didn't even look at her. After a while, Rose took her hand away and walked after the others, leaving him alone in the ruins of everything he'd been trying to achieve.

CHAPTER 9

Early the next morning, Thomas crawled out from under one of the wagons, every part of him damp and cold. Muxy axle! No matter how much he'd shifted position, it was always there, digging into his back or his hip or some other part of his body. He'd had to curl up into a ball to get away from it, and now he was paying the price; his body was stiff and painful.

Wincing, he pulled himself to his feet, clinging to the cart for support. He rolled his shoulders, hearing his back crackle, and tried to stretch, only to find that his arms were too cramped to go much higher than his ears.

The morning was calm and bright, making a mockery of last night's storm. He hesitated, as though putting off the evil moment would somehow turn back the clock, then took a deep breath and turned to see what was left of the house.

It was a sorry sight. The stone walls were still standing, but the roof was gone, as if some giant hand had reached down and plucked it off, leaving only the two largest end beams.

How were they going to mend this? Where was he supposed to even start?

As he watched, the door opened. Rose and Janet emerged, carrying one of the mattresses between them, which they propped against the wall to dry. Rose rubbed her forehead with her sleeve and said something to Janet that made her smile weakly, then they went back inside and came out with another mattress.

He felt as though he should be helping, but after the stinging rejection of last night, he didn't know if they'd want him to. He'd had no idea Rose – *Rose*, the miller's daughter of all people – had seen through him, and now he felt even more vulnerable. If she'd recognised his act for what it was, then the men must all have realised it too.

If only he had someone to talk to, like the monks back in the monastery. Someone he could bounce his thoughts off, talk things over with. Someone who shared his passion for learning and debating. Simon would listen, but he wouldn't really hear him. He'd just stand there, waiting patiently until Thomas finished talking and it was his turn to speak, and then he'd slap him on the back and tell him he worried too much.

He wished Father Rulf had stayed. Priests were educated men; he could have had an equal conversation with him. He could imagine the two of them in a hot debate. Father Rulf had said he'd come back and see them again. Maybe he'd keep his word, or maybe another priest would come along. One who wouldn't leave.

More than any of that, though, he wished his brother Richard had never died and he could have stayed as just plain Thomas.

Heavy footsteps came from behind the house. Simon and William rounded the corner. Their shoulders were slumped, their arms heavy and tired-looking with the weight of their axes.

'I thought we'd finished with cutting trees,' said William.

Simon sighed, knuckling his eyes. 'So did I. There's

nothing else for it, though; we'll just have to get it done.'
He glanced up and saw Thomas watching them.

'Hail.' Thomas raised a hand.

Simon saw him, then walked off with William without troubling to return Thomas's quavering greeting.

Thomas let his hand fall to his side and watched them cross the field and head to the woods until they were out of sight. In the crisp air, he could hear Peter shovelling dead embers inside the forge with a grinding noise that made his teeth tingle: *scrape*, load, throw, *scrape*, load and throw.

Jarin appeared in the forge's doorway, pushing a loaded cart and whistling as he went.

'Stop that racket! I'm not in the mood!' Peter shouted from inside.

Thomas kicked a stone across the yard, meandering in Rose and Janet's general direction. He wasn't in much of a mood either.

Rose and Janet came out again, carrying another mattress, neither of them looking in his direction as they propped it up with the others. He didn't think he could face either of them just then, and so he ducked behind the wagon.

'That's the last one.' Janet eased her headdress up enough to wipe sweat from her forehead, then tugged it back into place. 'I suppose El and I will have to turn the reeds again?'

'Afraid so,' Rose answered. 'Simon's planning to have the extra trees cut for the roof by tomorrow, and Peter says he and Jarin will split them the day after. Simon wants to start building the roof as soon as he can even if the timbers are still wet, and he says we're all to help. As if I don't have enough to do clearing up this mess.' she added with a sigh.

'I can't believe it happened,' Janet said wearily. 'Dare I ask how much food we've got left?'

'I've still got to sort through it all, but I reckon we've lost over half, and the flour's all ruined,' Rose answered. 'You'd better start thinking about how we can make our stores last, because I doubt we've enough to keep us going to Christmas. Tell Peter to get out his traps and I'm going to ask Gee to start picking wild grains for flour.'

Janet froze, her face suddenly as pale and unmoving as a marble statue's. 'What makes you think Peter's got traps?'

Rose raised her eyebrows. 'Just ask him. It shouldn't be a problem. Thomas probably has more on his mind than catching poachers. Besides, if we're trapping food for the lord's table as well as our own, I'm not sure it is poaching.'

'I'll mention it.' Janet reached down and picked up a fragment of broken pot, turning it over in her fingers. 'We're not going to grind the grain by hand in the old way, are we?'

'How else are we going to do it? Have you seen Thomas?' Rose put her hands on her hips and gazed around the yard.

'Not since last night. I don't know where he slept.' Janet laughed a little. 'I can't think he'd be such a nuddlejade as to actually sleep under a wagon like he said, though, can you?'

Nuddlejade. His face burned. Peter's open contempt was bad enough, but hearing his people laugh at him behind his back was somehow far worse. And from Janet of all people, who wouldn't say boo to a goose.

Rose snorted. 'After last night, I'm beginning to think nothing would surprise me about him anymore.'

'I know what you mean. Did you see how furious Simon was?'

'I did.' Rose's voice grew more excited as she picked up the thread of gossip. 'You can't blame him, though. I mean, Thomas just stood there! It was plain as the nose on your face that he didn't have any idea what to do, even with Simon yelling orders. When he moved at all, it was only to try and save those muxy charts of his.'

Janet nodded. 'He's clear addled on those charts, and for what? We can't eat parchment, can we?'

Rose's laugh rang across the yard, stabbing him in the heart. 'Maybe he thinks we can spread them out and use them for roof tiles instead of clay!'

'Or fashion them into kirtles?'

Now Rose was giggling so hard she could barely stand upright. 'Yes! That way, he can talk to us and read his charts at the same time. Can you imagine it?' She pretended to examine Janet's shoulder and 'read' her arm, then deepened her voice a little and put on a refined accent. 'Oh, Janet, I'm ever so sorry to trouble you, but might you turn around so I can finish the chart?'

As Janet bobbed a curtsy, Thomas cringed and tried to make himself even smaller. 'Yes, m'lord.' She turned around, presenting her back to Rose. 'Is m'lord finished?'

Rose made a show of pretending to read Janet's back, then lifted her arm and craned her neck into an interesting variety of poses before clearing her throat. 'Hm, hm. Yes, it's quite clear. Tomorrow night, the stars will dance in circles, so we must all wear sheep hooves on our noses if we want a good harvest.'

Sheep hooves indeed! The redness in his face was as much indignation as shame now.

'Don't get me wrong,' Janet said, still chuckling a little. 'I do like him, but folks need to respect their lord and know he's in charge. Last night proved what we've all been thinking: he doesn't know what he's doing.'

Rose nodded, more serious now. 'I feel a bit sorry for him. It can't be easy.'

'I suppose not, but he is the lord' Janet answered. 'And take the Lady Joan; she ruled the estate well enough without charts telling her how to do it. Sir John wasn't much of a ruler, but he was a lord. When he spoke, folks jumped or he'd know the reason why.' She studied the broken piece of crockery in her hands. 'This was my favourite pot,' she added sadly. 'My Ma gave it to me when Peter and I wed.'

Rose cast around on the ground for a few seconds, then picked up a basket and held it out. 'You can put the broken bits in here. You never know; Jarin might be able to mend them. He seems able to do most things.'

'It won't be the same.' Janet tossed the pieces of pottery into the basket with a sigh.

Thomas's boot slipped in the mud and he put out a hand to stop himself from falling, biting back a curse. Rose and Janet looked in his direction, and he ducked down behind a wheel. He had to show himself sometime but if they saw him hiding, they'd think him the coward he was. Besides, he couldn't face them just then, not after hearing them make such a jest of him.

Janet wiped her hands on her apron, businesslike again. 'Well, those reeds won't dry themselves. I best find El and get started.'

Rose nodded. 'I'll come and help as soon as I'm finished here.'

Thomas waited until both women had disappeared – Janet across the yard and Rose back indoors – before squeezing out from his hiding place and wishing he'd never left the monastery. As if being the lord wasn't bad enough, Janet thought he was weak, Rose pitied him and both of them were laughing at him behind his back. The others were probably doing the same thing.

Quick footsteps brought him back to the present as Maria swept over to him, heading for the fowl house, an egg basket clutched tightly to her chest. 'Oh, there you are. Why didn't you sleep with us in the linhays last night?' Without waiting for an answer, she jabbed a thumb toward the house. 'You need to tell that maid in there to stop bossing me around. If she says the word *idle* to me again, I swear I won't be responsible for my actions.'

'It's just her way.' Thomas stared at his boots. 'Someone has to organise things.' And it wasn't going to be him by the looks of it.

'So you're not going to tell her?' Maria said.

He shook his head. After all, his sister was idle and the last thing he needed was a confrontation with Rose. 'No. She's only doing her job.'

Maria sniffed and clutched the basket tighter. 'Why am I not surprised? God's teeth, you're pathetic!' In a huff of skirts, she stalked off in the direction of the fowl house.

He sighed. Was he pathetic? Richard wouldn't have been pathetic. His older brother had been brave enough to be made a knight.

He kicked another stone across the yard and ran a hand across his chin. Still smooth. Damn it, how could he be expected to act like a man all the time his body refused to grow into one? Maybe it never would. He'd seen freaks like that in the stocks. Stop it. He might be a terrible lord, but he wasn't a freak. He just needed a way to redeem himself. He'd take a walk; he thought better when he walked.

Straightening his tunic, he began walking alongside

the river towards the mill, on a path he'd discovered not long after they'd arrived. It was narrow, a little overgrown and no more than a sheep track, but no one else used it, making it the perfect retreat for when he needed to be on his own. That was what he missed most about the monastery: the solace and peace to think. There were days in the house when he was reading his charts trying to calculate the best times to make decisions, and Janet would be chopping at the other end of the table and Rose would be bustling around and sniping back and forth with Maria until he thought his head would explode. That was when he'd pack up his charts and come to his refuge.

He pushed aside a branch of gorse. The yellow flowers smelt strong and sweet. The skylarks trilled high in the sky and swifts skimmed across the water like black arrows. It was a good place.

A furlong further on, and he was none the wiser despite his best effort to think of something. With a sigh, he sat down on his favourite perch; a flat stone overhanging the river. It was a quiet spot with thick velvety brown bulrushes bursting their seeds in creamy tufts along the banks. On the opposite side, a line of willows draped their long branches, their leaves stroking the water like green fingers. Thomas dangled his legs in the water, letting the tranquility lull him back to simpler times. He used to sit like this with William when they'd gone fishing together as boys.

He could try fishing now. Rose was worried about the state of their stores, so if he could tickle a few trout for a meal, everyone would be pleased. He couldn't do that here, though; this stretch of the river was running too fast. He needed to find quiet waters, where trout basked in the shallows. Then he could creep up behind them, being careful not to cast a shadow, lower his two hands in the water and slowly move in until he could touch their belly with his fingers, sending them into a trance. After that, it was a simple matter of cupping his hands underneath and flicking them onto the bank.

He'd often tickled trout when Mama took them on picnics by the river. It seemed like another life. Pray God she was still safe.

A fly landed on his hand, and he went to flick it off, only to stop when he saw the telltale yellow and black stripes on its body.

Slowly, a smile spread across his face. He knew what he was going to do.

Two days later, just after dawn, Thomas was ready. He had a pail full of smoking-dried dung over one shoulder, a basket over the other, his gauntlets tucked into his belt and a ladder under one arm.

He scanned the yard. No one was about. Good. He hadn't exactly lied when he said he knew about bees – he had helped Brother Matthew tend the hives – but those hadn't been wild bees, and he'd never retrieved a nest. If he was going to make a fool of himself, he'd rather do it on his own.

'What are ye doing with all that?' said William, leaning over the forge door.

He hadn't noticed William., 'Nothing much,' he mumbled.

'Doesn't look like nothing.'

'I'm collecting some bees, that's all.' He didn't break stride. With good fortune, William would have work to do in the forge, and that would be an end to it.

'Wait a moment, I'll get Pa.' William turned and shouted

into the forge. 'Pa! Thomas is fetching bees, want to come?'

Peter joined his son, leaning over the door and grinning at the sight of Thomas's burdens. 'Now this, I've got to see.'

'There's nothing to see,' Thomas protested. 'Really, there's no need for—'

'I must tell Rose,' William pushed open the door to the forge and came out at a run. 'Rose! Rose! Thomas is fetching bees!'

Thomas cringed. This hadn't been in his plans, but before he knew it, he had an audience standing expectantly before him.

'They won't buzz around, will they?' Rose said. 'Only I was stung once when I was little and I don't like them too close.'

What did she expect? Buzzing around was what angry bees usually did. The memory of Rose and Janet's previous mockery was still painful – if he failed at this, would they make fun of that too? He replied in a sharper tone than usual, 'They very well might if—'

'Wait for m-me!' Eleanor bustled out the door, her face pink with excitement. 'I've got the skep! M-Maria, make haste!'

Maria emerged onto the threshold. 'I'm coming, but why you want to see stupid bees, I don't know.' She fixed Thomas with a haughty stare. 'Are we going now? Only I've more firewood to collect. She—' Maria nodded towards Rose— 'says I've to fill the linhay. God knows why.'

'For the cold months and cooking, unless you want to shiver and starve,' said Rose.

'Look, if you *must* come, you'll have to be quiet,' Thomas said sharply. 'Bees don't like noise. Now let's go.' He walked off briskly, inwardly cursing the lot of them with words that would have brought a swift smack from his Mama, had she been able to hear him.

It was all going wrong. His plan had been to bring back the bees in triumph and win his people's esteem, but that clearly wasn't going to happen now. And if they saw him fail again, it would only make his position worse.

Word travelled fast in a community as tiny as theirs, and by the time he had reached the bottom of the old oak tree, Janet, Simon, Gee and Jarin had joined the party.

He looked up at the tree towering above him and swallowed. It was higher than he remembered, easily three or four times taller than he was. Heights made him dizzy and he'd never liked ladders, but he'd reckoned that he might be able to do it if he took his time, and if he failed, no one would have known.

Unfortunately, the presence of everyone in the whole muxy settlement had put an end to that idea, and he had no choice but to get it over with.

Carefully, he leaned the ladder against the trunk, making sure it was firm, then pulled his hood forward and put on his gauntlets. He looked up again and his stomach churned. What a nuddlejaded idea this was. What had possessed him to think he could do it?

His heart pounding, he took a deep breath and curled his fingers around the ladder. Keeping his eyes fixed firmly on the bark in front of him, not daring to look up or down, he put his foot on the first rung and slowly began to climb. As he stepped onto the fourth rung, the bees swarmed around him, darting in and out like evil needles wielded by some unseen hand. More than anything, he wanted to slither down the ladder and run, but the nest was still out of reach. He had to go higher.

From below, several pairs of eyes bored into his back

as he inched his way up rung by terrifying rung, his legs heavy and his chest heaving a little.

Please God, don't let me fall. He risked a quick look down.

Bad idea. His head began to swim, and his hands were sweating so much they slipped on the ladder. Everything inside him screamed to get down, but Peter was grinning up at him and he couldn't give in now.

He gritted his teeth and continued climbing until he was level with the hole in the trunk where the nest was hidden. The bees were coming thick and fast in an angry black cloud, charging at him like tiny black knights. The blood pulsed in his neck, and he clung to the ladder like a baby to its mother.

'Are ye doing it?' Peter's voice came from below, echoing strangely in his ears. 'Only them bees look right vexed from 'ere.'

'They're fine! I'll have them in a moment!' He shouted back, or tried to. He could barely hear his own voice, choked and hoarse with terror, but God's bones, he would not fail again.

The first thing he had to do was mollify the bees. With his heart in his mouth, he let go of the ladder and raised the pail of smoking dung until it was level with the hole. The smoke billowed and stung his eyes, turning everything into a watery blur.

If Brother Matthew was right, the bees formed a tight ball as the days shortened. He planned to scoop as much of the ball out in one go. Pulling his gauntlets as far up as he could, he dropped the smoking pail to the ground, turned his head away and put his hand into the hole.

Brother Matthew was right. He could feel the ball of bees, still sleepy in the grip of the smoke. He had to act fast. If they woke up and swarmed before he could get away, being laughed at would be the least of his worries.

It was now or never. Taking a deep breath, he swept the ball into the basket and slammed the lid in one swift move. He had no idea how many bees he had and didn't have time to breathe before the ladder swayed, knocked off balance by his sudden movement. It wobbled beneath his feet, tilting away from the tree.

Terrified, he clung on as the ladder rocked. Sweat trickled down his neck. The ladder swayed and teetered. He braced himself for the fall. The ladder poised then fell back against the tree. He was frozen. He dared not move. His fingers gripped the ladder so hard they hurt.

But he had to get down. He focused on the now-familiar tree bark inches from his face. Slowly, he felt for the rung below with his boot. When he was sure, he took a deep breath and inched his way down, rung by rung. He didn't know how far he'd gone until he felt the soft earth beneath him.

He stood there, his knees weak, his head bowed and his heart still pounding as he clung to the ladder and the sweat dripped off his forehead.

'Didn't think ye'd do it,' Peter said.

He turned to find a sea of smiling faces. As one, the group started to clap, and a smile spread across his face.

'Now we'll have honey, thanks to m'young lord,' said Peter.

His heart soared. It was the praise he had longed for. And even the appellation didn't sound nearly as obnoxious as it had before.

He had done it. He had finally won their respect, and he felt ten feet tall.

CHAPTER 10

Rose sat back on her heels with a groan. God, her arms ached. If only she was back in the mill. Her Pa would have ground all this grain to flour in the time it took her to do a mere handful. Despite working until her shoulders and arms hurt, she'd only finished half a basket and there were two more waiting to be done. How in God's name had people coped before mills were invented?

'God's teeth, I hate this!' she said, glaring at the grinding stone as though she'd like to kill it. It wasn't even a proper grinding stone; not like you'd get in a real mill. She and Jarin had found a flat stone and dragged it into the house two weeks ago, and she'd been grinding wild seeds and grain on it ever since. Now she was ready to scream.

'I thought you were jesting when you said you planned to grind in the old way.' Janet scooped a careful measure of beans into a small cup and added it to the stew pot.

'There's no mill, so how else can I do it?'

Looking at how much grain she still had to do, Rose wished with all her heart that she'd never started. Ma was always saying that one day, she'd open her big mouth so wide she'd fall right into it, and it looked like that day had finally come. What had possessed her to say she could grind with stones in the first place? And even after all her effort, the flour she had made was coarse, which meant the bread would bake hard and dry.

'Bread fills bellies, so we'll need as much grain as we can find.' Janet peered into the pot and wrinkled her nose. 'You did say only one cup of beans or peas and two carrots to a pot, didn't you? It doesn't look much, and the men are complaining they're hungry.'

'We're all hungry, but we have to make the food last,' she said. And by the new year, it would be down to half a cup and one carrot, but she kept the thought to herself.

Gee pushed his way through the door and dumped a basket on the floor, spilling a handful of seeds in the process. 'I've scoured the fields and that's the last I can find. No more oats or wild wheat but there's a little barley in there and the rest is grass seeds.'

She wasn't sorry to hear there would be no more grain to grind, but four baskets weren't going to make many loaves. Even the ones they made would have to be small loaves, to make supplies last.

Resting both hands on his stick, Gee glanced around. 'I see you've cleared the place up after the flood. Nice solid shelves in the corner and a table and benches.'

'It's been a lot of hard work these past weeks,' she said resuming the grinding.

'Well, not much left of it, was there? The new beams look good. I watched Simon and Peter haul those up with ropes. Fair cursing they were,' Gee added with a chuckle.

She paused in her work to look up. Over her head, thick strong beams spanned the width of the house supporting thinner beams that were spaced along the length in pairs, and depending on how the tree had grown, meeting at the top to form irregular arches.

'El and I made the ropes from bramble,' said Maria,

frowning with concentration as she slowly braided grass wicks for tapers. 'That's the strongest material, so it should last for a good while.'

'And my lad carved the pegs to join the beams,' said Gee proudly.

'Peter made the nails and said he had to make a spear to hammer holes through the ends for those pegs,' said Janet.

Didn't she know it! While Peter and Simon hammered and cursed above, she'd been below grinding grain, listening to it all day until her head was ringing like a bell and ready to burst. They had done a good job though, and soon she would be able to relax in the secure knowledge that there was a roof over her head keeping the precious stores safe and dry.

'Now, where's my bread?' Gee held out a grubby hand, his chewed nails black with dirt.

'I haven't made it yet,' she said. 'God's bones, I'm still grinding the flour.'

'That's what you said last time. One flat round for every sack, that was our agreement. That's four you owe me now.'

'What agreement?' Maria looked up, adding the finished wick to the pile. 'Peasants don't make agreements. They do as they're told.'

Gee thrust a finger at her. 'Don't you call me that! I'm no muxy peasant.'

Maria flinched. Despite the animosity between them, Rose could only admire how quickly and smoothly the noble girl recovered, tilting her chin and looking down her nose. 'What are you then? You're certainly no noble, and you live on Lord Thomas's estate at his discretion and do his work. That makes you a peasant.'

Only Maria could spit out the word *peasant* and make

it sound like something she'd trodden in.

Gee tapped his nose. 'I'm a traveller, belonging to no man.' He turned his dark face back to Rose. 'I'll be back for my dues.'

Not to be outdone, she sat up and lifted her chin. 'And what about the hares?'

'Rose—'

Taking no notice of Janet she pushed on. 'I know Jarin's set traps, but he's only brought me one hare in two weeks. The fields are full of them, so where are they?'

'Has he? Then I'll be seeing him later. Anything he catches stays with us.'

'That's poaching,' Maria chipped in. 'Lord Thomas could have you hanged for that.'

'Then tell *Lord Thomas* to come hang me himself,' Gee drawled, his mouth twisting into a sarcastic smile.

Rose wanted to say she'd do just that, but they both knew Thomas wouldn't. 'I told you to stone rooks and blackbirds, but I haven't seen any of those either. You have got a sling, haven't you?' She too could be sarcastic.

Gee nodded. 'Oh yes, but I've been picking seeds, haven't I? I can't do both. Now that's done, I'll see what I can hit. I'll keep the linnets and blackbirds, but you can have the rooks. They're too tough for me. The meat gets stuck in my teeth, see?' His grin broadened, showing a few black stumps of teeth.

Revolted, she turned her head, and Gee bowed majestically to Maria before walking out of the house, whistling with his stick clipping the ground as he went.

'Oh, that man! Who does he think he is?' Maria scowled at her. 'You're supposed to be in charge. You should have said something.'

Normally, she would have but Gee was intimidating

and didn't care what he said. Being in charge wasn't as easy as she had once thought. She'd come to learn very quickly that it meant more than giving orders; she had to make decisions while others relied on her.

She was also beginning to understand how Thomas must feel. Her tasks were nothing like being a lord, of course, but she was responsible for running the house and the food. The days were already getting shorter and the nights colder. Folks were always hungrier during the dark months, and she often lay awake at night wondering how she was supposed to manage everything.

There was also a lack of firewood, no fat to make tallow candles and no swine to kill on Martinmas Day, a few weeks before Christmas. If they wanted meat, they'd have to kill one of their precious sheep. There was no barley to make ale, and with only one barrel of cider left, they'd have to rely on what they could press from the orchards, but the hot, dry summer had meant the apples were small and hardly worth pressing at all.

Oh yes, she had a lot to think about.

Simon was the only one who understood how dire their situation was, but every time she tried to talk to him about it, he shrugged and said there was no point worrying, that they could only do the best they could, and with God's blessing, they'd survive. She hoped God was in a good humour because the future looked very bleak, and after the Pestilence who knew what He would do?

'I can't force him, can I?' she snapped at Maria. 'I don't know how many hares Jarin catches.'

'Someone talking about me?' Jarin stepped through the door, a bright smile on his face. 'Simon wants you outside. Says he's ready to start the thatching.'

'Your Pa's looking for you,' Maria said. 'He wasn't

happy about that hare you gave us.'

Jarin's face paled as he looked at Janet. 'I told you not to tell him!'

'I didn't, I—'

'I did,' Rose interrupted, 'and it's fine, Jarin. You were only doing as I asked.'

'Oh Lord, he'll be furious.' Jarin seemed to shrink before her eyes. She had seen that look on the faces of village lads and some wives too frightened to go home. She'd wager Gee used his belt.

'Please don't ask me again.'

'I won't, but if you happen to leave one behind, by mistake…' She let the sentence trail off suggestively.

'You're as weak as my brother,' Maria said to her. 'Since when did the peasants tell us what to do? Mama would never have tolerated such a thing. She'd have put *you*—' she looked at Jarin— 'and that Pa of yours in the stocks or worse.'

'I know.' Jarin squirmed from foot to foot. 'I know the rules but Pa doesn't see it that way.'

As far as she could tell, Gee didn't see anybody's way but his own.

'Are ye coming to help us?' Peter demanded, poking his head around the door. 'Or are ye going to sit there blathering all day?'

Grateful for the chance to escape, Rose went outside and waited beside a stack of bundled reeds, tied with twine.

'Rose! What d'ye think?' William shouted down from the roof where he was sitting astride and grinning from ear to ear. 'I thought I'd get a bit of practice for building our place!'

God's teeth, William shouldn't talk like that where anyone could hear him. Before she knew it, she'd have

Janet twittering on about wedding dates and Eleanor picking flowers for her hair.

'Will, you have to—' she began, then stopped. She couldn't put off the conversation any longer, but this was neither the time nor the place to have it. As soon as an opportunity presented itself, she'd grab it with both hands, tell him straight and pray God he listened.

'We've c-come to help!' Eleanor announced, skipping into the yard, while Thomas followed at a more sedate pace. 'We've p-picked loads of apples, haven't we, T-Thomas?'

He nodded. 'Nearly a cartload. But they're hard and small, and the wasps have got into a lot of them.'

'And T-Thomas and I saw some swine, didn't we T-Thomas?'

'You saw swine?' said Simon, turning sharply round, only just beating Rose's identical question.

'Briefly from a distance, yes,' Thomas answered. 'Unfortunately, they disappeared.'

'You mean you just let them wander off?' Simon ran a frantic hand through his hair. 'God give me strength! We could have had meat for weeks and fat for candles and hide for leather. Did you even try to catch them?'

Thomas coloured. 'It was only a small group, and we didn't let them wander off. We tried to catch them, but by the time we got close, they'd run into the woods and we couldn't find them.'

'You should have got help. They'll be long gone by now.' Simon raised his eyes to the heavens and sighed heavily.

'We did our best,' Thomas protested. 'I'm sorry.'

Simon turned away. 'So am I.'

'I'm sure Thomas would have sent for help if there had been time,' Rose put in. Much as she sympathized with Simon's frustration, a part of her couldn't help feeling he was being unfair. What did Thomas and Eleanor know about herding swine? They hadn't any of the tools or experience farmers possessed, and swine could turn vicious. Seeing Thomas's downcast face, she felt sorry for him.

'Me and the boy will see if we can find 'em,' Peter announced. 'Get down from there, boy, and bring that broken hurdle standing behind the door of the forge. Ye needs that to keep the hogs walking straight.'

'Exactly!' Thomas looked at Simon, a slow flush creeping up his cheeks. 'I've never herded swine in my life; I would never have thought of that.'

'Well, you should have!' Simon shot back.

'Why? Because I'm the lord? That doesn't make me omniscient. How many lords have you seen handling swine? I came back, I told you about them and now the job's going to get done by people who have probably forgotten more about herding than I'll ever have to know!'

Silently, Rose applauded him. He did have some grit about him after all. A shame he didn't show it more often.

'You'd better get up there and replace Will,' Simon said at last.

Thomas swallowed, the red of his face paling rapidly to white. 'M-me? Up there?'

'I'll go up, I'm not scared.' Jarin jumped onto the ladder and scrambled to the top as fast as a squirrel climbing a tree.

'I'm not scared. I think I'd be better down here organising the lasses, that's all,' said Thomas.

Organising the lasses! She hoped that didn't include her. She was trying to support him, but he was too dense to see it, and one look at his ashen face told her he was quaking in his boots.

'I'll go up, then,' she said, stepping forward.

'Fine. Sort it out between you. I need one of you at the top of ladder to pass the reeds to me or Jarin for fixing. I don't care who. The rest of you, make a line to pass the bundles along and for God's sake let's get started! It's already midday.' Simon put his foot on the ladder. 'Pray God, we can get this thatch to stay on,' he mumbled into his beard.

She wasn't meant to hear it, but she had and grabbed his sleeve. 'What do you mean?' she hissed. 'Don't you know how to do it?'

'Of course I do, but when have you seen thatchers working in autumn?'

'Well, now that you mention it, never,' she admitted.

'There's a reason for that. Thatchers cut reeds in the new year after they've flowered and when the stalks are thick and brown. They dry them until spring and do their work in the summer, using the thick stalks to make spars to fix the thatch.' Simon picked up a box of nails and the hooks and lowered his voice. 'We can't wait that long, so the reeds are thin and short. I've no idea if this will work.'

She didn't want to consider that possibility. Making the roof had brought them together, giving them a common purpose and had kept them going all this time.

'Apart from getting wet, what are we going to do if they don't work?' she whispered.

Simon looked her straight in the eye and said in a frighteningly calm voice, 'Die. If this doesn't work, none of us will survive until spring.'

CHAPTER 11

December 1348

Despite the strongest winter winds any of them could remember, the nails and hooks had worked and the thatch held fast, much to Thomas's relief. If it hadn't, he supposed that would have been his fault too.

He looked down at his chart, but the letters and figures all seemed to swim around on the parchment. He threw down his quill in frustration, pushed away the chart and slumped back in his chair. He hadn't the heart for it, and his mind had been wandering too much these days.

Pulling his surcoat tighter, he blew on his frozen hands to get some life back into his fingers. God's teeth, it was cold, but Rose insisted that they didn't have enough sticks to keep the fire blazing all day. That was only allowed in the evenings when everyone huddled close around the hearth with their hands held out, their skin tingling in the warmth.

Since the autumn, the baskets of beans and the sack of carrots had been steadily dwindling to a meagre pile. Nobody had commented as the potage became thinner and the bread ran out. Then last month Rose had wiped away a stray tear and announced that their two bowls a day would have to become one. Nobody had complained. They were all too tired and scared to do anything apart from pray and drag themselves from one day to the next.

He had heard of peasants starving in the dark months – it happened every year – but he'd never realised until now how it felt. He'd always had plenty to eat in Mama's house, and the food he'd eaten with the monks had been *plain but plentiful*, as Brother Luke had put it.

Now, there were times when hunger made his entire jaw throb and tingle, like he'd bitten on a sour apple. His stomach was the worst; it would go numb for a while before suddenly twisting and knotting into stabbing hunger cramps that were like no pain he'd never felt before in his life. Cramps that left him briefly doubled over like an old man.

Much like his people, he'd stopped caring what happened. Some days, he had no strength to move or do anything other than lie on his mattress waiting for dark and blissful sleep. On days when the hunger got too great, he would scour the hedgerows for a leaf or a hidden nut the squirrels might have missed, anything that he could chew. He'd even ripped bark off the trees and gnawed it, which had brought a small amount of relief, but that hadn't lasted long.

He had to keep busy, because if he didn't, his mind would drift away to thoughts of food, torturing him with images of dishes piled high with beef in saffron and lamb with roasted apples that were so real he half believed he could taste them.

Idly, he glanced around the room through the thick acrid smoke of tallow candles, where he could see Rose sitting in her usual place by the hearth staring into the grey embers with her chin cupped in her hands. William was sitting close to her, his sunken cheeks making his eyes appear too large for his face. Did he look as bad as they did? He ran a hand down his cheeks and was shocked to feel harsh cheekbones jutting through the skin.

In the shadows on the other side of the room, Maria lay on her mattress with her cover pulled tight to her chin, her hair lank and loose around her shoulders. When had she last combed it? Thomas couldn't remember and couldn't bring himself to care either. Hunger had shrunk her beautiful face making her look old beyond her years.

Eleanor was next to her, her once childish rosy cheeks now pale and pinched. Even she wasn't so cheerful these days. Simon was lying on his back on the floor staring at the roof with his hands behind his head. Close by, Peter perched on a stool by the hearth, scratching at the lice in his hair.

His people. The people he had promised to look after, the ones he had brought here nearly five months ago when they'd all been healthy and full of expectations. Rose had even called it an adventure.

Some adventure. They were cold, weak and starving with neither the will nor strength to do anything, and he had stopped caring about anything except his own belly. Maria had spotted a dropped nut a few days ago and grabbed it, and his first thought had been to beat her into the ground and take it from her. He hadn't, of course, but the sheer force of his instinct had shocked and terrified him.

He should never have brought them here. He'd only done what he thought was best, and he'd genuinely tried to be a good lord. It wasn't his fault that he wasn't a natural leader like his brother Richard, and felt more at home with a quill than a billhook. Rose at least understood, but there were moments when even she'd seemed to despair of him, like the day when he'd seen the wild swine in the orchards. Peter and William had managed to catch one of them, but the others were nowhere to be seen. If he'd only stopped to think, he could have sent Eleanor to fetch help; then they'd have caught all of them and would have had enough meat to last until the spring. Instead, they were starving, and it was his fault.

He had found the bees, though. The honey had been good while it lasted, and the beeswax had made a few candles, which cheered the place a little. And Rose's bread may have been coarse, but it had filled their bellies for a while and they'd managed to build a roof, so they were dry. Simon had been especially pleased about that.

The door opened and Janet stood on the threshold, holding a bowl and smiling from ear to ear.

'Surprise!' she said.

'What it is?' said Rose, not looking at her.

Janet placed the platter reverently on the table and removed the linen cover with a flourish.

'Dried hog meat and bread,' she announced.

One by one, they all turned to look at her.

'Did you say dried hog and bread?' Maria pushed away her cover and sat up.

Janet's smile spread into a grin, and she nodded. 'I did.'

Simon stirred from the floor, and William levered himself to his feet and peered into the bowl.

'Where did you get that, Ma?' He stared at the viands as though he'd never seen anything like them.

Thomas could already taste the meat that was sitting tantalisingly on the table, just inches from his nose.

'I saved it for today. It's Christmas, and I thought it would cheer us up.' Janet clasped her hands and bit her lip. 'You are pleased, aren't you?'

Peter stood up, rubbing his hands together. 'Ye may be a cloth head, woman, but sometimes ye do me proud!'

She beamed at him, basking in his rare praise. Everyone laughed, and even the house seemed to smile in approval.

'El, you get the bowls!' Rose said. 'Maria bring the cups. It's Christmas Day!'

Was it his imagination or did Rose take the chance to shift her stool away from William's? Yet William had been telling everyone that he and Rose were promised, so he wasn't sure what was going on. He didn't dwell on the thought, though; he only had eyes for the bowl on the table.

'I'll fetch the cider. I think we can treat ourselves.' Simon got to his feet.

Seven ravenous pairs of eyes watched Janet break the bread equally into the eight bowls. When Simon took the knife from his belt to cut the first slice, the entire room seemed to freeze as his blade disappeared into the meat and cut it. Almost reverently, he slid the blade under the piece and placed it into the first bowl.

There wasn't a lot to go around, but Thomas's mouth watered as he cupped his bowl as though it was made of gold. His mind screamed and his fingers itched to pick up the food and stuff it into his mouth, but he made himself wait, wallowing in delectable self-torture, breathing in the rich smell of meat, and anticipating the crunch of the bread.

At last, he couldn't wait a moment longer and picked up the piece of meat and put it into his mouth. Closing his eyes, he fought the urge to chew, letting it rest on his tongue to savour the taste for as long as he could, feeling the juices slowly melt. Never had anything tasted so good. And when he crunched the bread, it tasted not like the dry peasant bread it was, but like the softest and finest white bread his Mama had ever served on the high table.

Two mouthfuls and it was gone. His tongue demanded more, and his stomach growled in protest at being teased. She had no right to torture him like that. He'd got used to his meagre daily ration, and now he'd have to start accepting it all over again.

He glared across the room at her, his frustration building, the harsh words ready on his tongue. He must have been scowling, because Janet looked nonplussed at him.

What was happening to him? This wasn't her fault. It was like Maria and the nut all over again; his emotions were threatening to overrule his thinking. During these last weeks, his mood had swung from hating everything and everyone to staring into space in despair and – God forgive him – praying to his maker to either provide for him or take him.

He forced a smile. 'I've never tasted anything so good. God bless you, Janet.'

'We should t-toast the house to keep the evil spirits away,' said Eleanor.

'You're right.' Rose scrambled to her feet. 'Let's do it!'

'And I've a surprise of me own. I was saving it for the new year but now's as good as then.' Peter nudged Simon in the ribs. 'Can't be outdone by me woman, can I? 'Tis outside the forge hiding under a sack, m'lord. I'll show ye.' He stood abruptly and crossed to the door, then turned and grinned at their blank faces. 'Well? What ye all waiting for? Outside!'

In a flurry of tightening shawls against the cold, putting on hats and chattering excitedly, they bustled out of the house and gathered in the yard as they had five months ago.

'What's that smoke?' said Eleanor suddenly.

Thomas followed her pointing finger, seeing a thick, dark grey column rising from beyond the moors.

'Hope it's not a gorse fire,' said Rose.

'Not at this time of year. Whatever it is, it's too far away to affect us,' said Simon. 'Now come on, Peter, what's this surprise?'

Peter stood by the forge door, his legs straight and his thick arms crossed over his chest guarding the mysterious object beneath the sacking. He waited until Eleanor and Maria stopped talking and everyone was looking at him. Dramatically, he swept off the sacking and stood back proudly.

Thomas stared at what was underneath, hardly daring to believe his eyes. 'It's a bell!'

Peter nodded. 'Ye said ye wanted one. Go on, m'young lord. Try it.'

A bell. A real bell. Thomas's face split into a beaming smile. He gripped the rope, his stomach now quivering with excitement instead of hunger, and swung it. It didn't matter that it clanked instead of rang. It didn't matter that it was shaped like an upturned cheese instead of being delicately curved. To him, it was the best bell he had ever seen or heard because Peter had made it for him.

He swung the rope again and looking at Peter, they shared a grin.

As the tone faded, Thomas lifted his chin and gazed at his people, whose faces were full of respect. He allowed himself a moment to enjoy the feeling. Maybe he had been too hard on himself. After all, they were all still here.

He glanced at the house that nestled in the base of the tall wooded slopes as it had for centuries. Combe Hide was now a safe refuge and it had been his idea. The once dirty moss-covered stones were now washed light grey. The repaired shutters closed tight and the front door hung straight. In the low sunlight, the thatched roof tinted gold. There were a few thin patches and ragged ends but it kept them dry.

The gaps in yard walls were filled, and the spit was still there from the day Peter herded the hog down from the woods. Rose had said they should celebrate and Janet had made dough cakes as a special treat. As the hog had crisped brown and the fat dripped into pots below for Eleanor's tapers, Peter had brought out his pan flute and they had danced around the spit until the meat was cooked. How they had laughed as the juices dribbled down their chins.

Thomas's eye moved on to the smithy with its new roof. Peter was right about the sight and smell of burning embers, they did give the place a sense of home.

'Thomas, we're waiting,' Simon whispered in his ear.

He breathed deeply and stood tall. He wiped his palms on the back of his surcoat, cleared his throat and raised his voice. 'We came here to avoid the Pestilence and we have. We rebuilt this place from a ruin.' He swept his arm in an arc. 'I know we're hungry, but we've come this far and we will survive.' He paused to blink back the hot tears that were stinging his eyes. Lords didn't cry. He took a deep breath and continued, his voice quivering slightly. 'And in the spring, we shall go home.'

Home – how he longed for it. The high table laden with silver bowls full of fruit and nuts, fine French tapestries on the walls and his thick feather mattress. He and Mama sitting in front of a blazing hearth, talking and playing chess. He had taken his easy life for granted, but he never would again. It had been a hard lesson but well-learned.

He lifted his head and raised his cup to the sprig of rowan poking up at the far end of the roof, put there by William to ward off evil spirits.

'God bless this house!' he cried, as the house blurred with his tears. 'To going home in the spring!'

'A blessing on the house and home in the spring!' they cheered.

CHAPTER 12

April 1349

Thomas placed a hand to his forehead, shielding his eyes from the early sun, and stared up the valley. Nothing. He sighed and started pacing back and forth in the lane for what felt like the tenth time that morning. A light scent of blossom drifted from the orchards and early bees foraged the primroses, but he barely noticed.

At last, he saw what he'd been waiting for: Simon cantering down the track towards him. Thomas waved frantically and cupped his hands over his mouth.

'Yes or no?' he shouted.

Simon pulled up his horse a few paces away, his face unreadable. 'I rode a couple of miles along High Drovers Road.'

'And?'

'There was no sign of travellers, and the tracks are clear,' Simon answered with an air of satisfaction. 'It looks like you can go.'

'Praise God!' He punched the air triumphantly. 'We're going home!'

'I think so, but you've got to go first,' Simon said. 'Make sure it's safe before we pack up here.'

Even the reminder of their arrival to Combe Hide months ago wasn't enough to dampen Thomas's enthusiasm. 'It'll be safe; I checked my charts this morning. We're going home!' He hadn't been so excited since Brother Luke awarded him the accolade of top scholar last year. At last, he could get out of this place, get back to his studies and not have to worry about being the lord. Mama would take charge as she always had, and this whole nightmare would be behind him.

Feeling as though his heart would burst with pure joy, he raced down the lane and into the yard shouting at the top of his voice. 'The tracks are clear! We're going home!'

William poked his head over the forge door, yawned and ruffled his hair.

'Come on, Will! Make haste, we can go!' Thomas had imagined this moment so many times during the harsh cold months. Now that it was here, his mind was buzzing so fast that he didn't know what to do first.

Calm. Think. First thing: change into his boots, grab a few clothes and – remembering his ride from Tavistoke – Brother Luke's dagger, and he mustn't forget a token for Mama. Bursting through the door into the house, he shouted again. 'The tracks are clear! We're finally going home!'

At the trestle, Rose dropped her knife, the beans she'd been preparing forgotten. Maria threw aside her stitching and squealed. Eleanor grabbed Maria's hands and danced with her around the room.

'We're going home, we're going home!' she sang at the top of her voice. 'C-come on Rose, join us, we're going home!'

Rose wiped her hands on her apron. 'You are going to check if it's safe first, aren't you, Thomas? Only I'm not travelling if the Pestilence is out there.'

'Of course I am. And it'll be safe; the charts said so.' He rummaged around in his coffer and started pulling out various items of spare clothing, stuffing them into his bag. 'Where's my spare flagon? I know I put it here somewhere. And Rose, could you cut some apple blossoms for Mama? They're her favourite.'

'Don't you want t-to go home, Rose?' Eleanor asked, pausing in her dance to look at Rose with a worried frown. 'You don't look like you do.'

Maria giggled behind her hand. 'She doesn't want to be a miller's maid again.'

Rose flushed. 'I heard that, and of course I want to go home. I just don't want to get my hopes up, that's all.' She swiped her knife off the trestle and flounced to the door. 'And your flagon is right where you left it: on the shelf next to my basket of spinning wool,' she added over her shoulder, letting the door shut behind her.

Janet bustled in. 'Will's told me! Isn't it exciting? You'll be needing something for the journey. I've only got a few apples, and they're a bit wrinkled. Sorry, but they're the end of the barrel.'

Sitting on the floor, grappling with his boots, Thomas didn't care if the apples were wrinkled or not. Tonight, he'd sit with Mama in front of the big stone hearth, which would be ablaze with logs, and have a proper meal with meat before going to sleep on a feather mattress.

Throwing his woollen mantle over his shoulders, he fastened his gold brooch at the shoulder. A simple gold ring with a centre bar, it was one that Mama had given him for being the top scholar in Greek for three years in a row, and one of his most treasured possessions.

In the stable, his fingers refused to work, fumbling as he attempted to buckle the girth and bridle his horse. Finally, his bag strapped behind the saddle, he checked the dagger on his belt and led his horse outside where he mounted, his stomach churning with excitement.

'Will, make haste!' he called. 'We've miles to cover before nightfall!'

William sauntered out of the smithy at a leisurely pace pulling his surcoat over his tunic. His belt was twisted and by the look of his red sunken eyes, he was suffering from too much cider.

'You look dreadful,' said Thomas.

William grinned sheepishly and casting a furtive look over his shoulder mimed a tankard going to his lips.

Thomas's jaw fell open. 'Since when have you started drinking like a sot?'

'Shh, keep your voice down!' Pa'll take his belt to me if he knew. Since I can't sleep for thinking of Rose.' He winked.

Thomas shifted in his saddle. He'd never had a sleepless night over a maid, but then he only really knew his sister, and she certainly didn't count as a prospective conquest.

'Alright.' He gathered his reins impatiently. 'Fetch your mount and let's get going.'

'Wait!' Eleanor called, hurrying across the yard. 'T-tell your M-Mama I'll be home soon, and give her this.' She held up a posy of primroses.

He had nowhere to put it, so he stuffed it inside his surcoat. 'Yes, I'll tell her, now—'

'And this kerchief's from me. Tell her I stitched it myself.' Maria thrust a square of azure satin at him.

He sighed again and put it next to the flowers. Forget the evening meal with Mama; at this rate, he'd be lucky to arrive in time for breakfast tomorrow.

Rose hurried over and tucked some sprigs of apple blossoms into the top of his bag. 'God's speed, and give Ma and Pa my love,' she said.

William gingerly settled himself on his grey pony, his long legs nearly touching the ground.

'Can we go now?' Thomas demanded, as he picked up his reins again.

William winced. 'Not so loud.'

Thomas turned his horse's head and moved forward, closely followed by William. They'd gone all of two yards when Janet ran out of the smithy waving a goatskin. 'Take this in case the ground's damp!'

God's teeth, the woman was an old fussbudget. He sighed audibly as William reached down to take the goatskin.

Peter leaned over the forge door. 'And don't ye forget, boy: say *Hail* to Malcolm and tell him he owes me an ale. And pick up me long rasp from the smithy. The old horse will need seeing to if he's to get back on all four feet.'

God's bones, would these people never let them leave? He kicked his horse into a trot and rode out of the yard, the last messages ringing in his ears. As soon as he and William splashed through the ford and was out of sight, he let out a whoop, put his heels to his horse and charged for home.

By the time they pulled up at midday, Thomas could see the grey stone tower of Ashetyne church in the distance. They'd ridden hard; his horse had steaks of white sweat on his neck and the pony was blowing from trying to keep up.

'We'd best give the horses a rest before tackling Six Mile Hill,' Thomas said, dismounting and wincing as he landed on stiff legs. Leaving his horse to crop grass, he looked up to where Six Mile Hill rose ahead in shades of purples and greens, greeting him like an old friend. The sun struggled behind high clouds, too weak to give much warmth, but he didn't pay it any mind. He was nearly home; it could have been pouring rain or hailstones for all he cared.

Ignoring William's jeers of behaving like a lass, he spread the goatskin on the grass, silently blessing Janet for thinking of it. Without it, sitting on the ground would have been a miserable experience as the damp seeped through his woollen hose to make his legs itch interminably.

William took a bite of an apple, swallowed and took another bite. They sat there for a long while in silence before William spoke.

'Rose is everything to me,' he said abruptly. 'We've been friends since the time ye went to that monastery of yours.' He tossed his apple core into the heather. 'And her and me, we've got an understanding.'

'I know.'

William gave Thomas a hard look. 'Just so's ye do. I mean us to wed as soon as we're home.'

Wed? He had seen how Rose acted around William, the little twitches of revulsion whenever her gaze fell on his missing arm, the way she always tried to shuffle away from him at the hearth without being too obvious about it.

'I'd heard you talking, but do you actually mean that?'

'Don't look so shocked. I'm fifteen, nearly sixteen summers. 'Tis time and many a lad will have his eye on a lass like Rose.' He held his stern gaze.

Good Lord, did William think he had sleepless nights over Rose? 'Will, Rose helps me out and I've been very grateful for her support over the months, but that's all it'll ever be.'

Slowly, William nodded. 'So long as it is. I know she's different to other lasses, and Pa says I'll have me hands full 'cos she says what she thinks, but I like that. Wouldn't want her messed with if you get my meaning.'

Thomas shivered. There was no chance of that. The thought of messing with any lass terrified him.

William took a swig of cider and wiped his mouth with the back of his hand. 'Every time I see her with her buds pressed tight against her tunic, I get such a longing. Ye know what I mean?' His eyes glinted like those of the lads Thomas had seen teasing maids at the harvest festival.

He didn't know what that felt like, but he nodded anyway. He wished William wouldn't talk like that; it made him feel so young. There was nothing wrong with him, he was sure of that. William was growing into a man faster than he was, nothing more. Soon, he would have hairs on his chin and be thinking of maids too. Pray God, it would be soon; it was difficult being a boy and a lord at the same time.

'It's like old times, isn't it?' he said, moving to safer ground. He didn't like being at odds with William or anyone for that matter. He only had two friends – William and Simon – and he valued them both. 'We used to sit on the bank of the river, dangling our feet over the edge. We were always fishing but never caught anything.' He leaned back on his elbows. 'They were good times.'

'Aye, they were. We was just boys then, but how come your Pa let you mix with the likes of me?' said William, handing him an apple.

'Oh, he never knew. Mama was careful to make sure of that,' he said biting hungrily into the apple.

'And now you're Lord of the Manor and I'm still the smithy's son. Only now, thanks to your Pa, I've only got one arm.' William snorted. 'Ever tried shoeing a horse with one arm? Can't be done, though Pa thinks it can. So, what kind of smithy does that make me?'

What could he say? Apologies were meaningless, and it hadn't been his fault.

The clouds had cleared and the sun was coming to the third quarter. They'd already stayed longer than he intended.

'We'd better get going,' he said, getting to his feet. 'I'm glad we spoke about Rose, though.'

'Don't do to fall out over a lass.' William wiped his mouth with his sleeve and stood up. 'Not far now. How're ye feeling? Me stomach feels like a twist of rope.'

'Mine too. I've been counting the weeks until I can see Mama and have a decent meal again. I can already smell Cook's bread, soft and white with a crisp golden crust, dipped into a large bowl of proper meat stew with carrots and beans.' He closed his eyes and breathed in slowly. He could taste it now; the bread crackly on the outside and velvet-soft inside, the rich, warm gravy of the stew...

'Wouldn't mind some of that meself. You always liked your food, and you're thin as a starved crow,' said William.

'We all are, but we made it through. 'Thomas dusted himself down, clipped his leather flagon to his belt and swung himself onto his horse. 'Race you!' he said, grinning and set off at a gallop before William had a chance to mount his pony.

Leaving William behind in a thunder of hooves and clouds of dust, he reached the top of Six Mile Hill and pushed his horse on for the last few miles until reaching the open moor where he stopped and drank in the barren landscape laid out in front of him.

It was wild and forbidding, especially in the dark months when the cold winds drove the rain in horizontal sheets that cut your face like daggers, but he loved every inch of it. Today, it looked exceptionally welcoming with dots of yellow gorse spiking throughout the heather and cushions of cream woolly sheep and brown wild ponies grazing amongst the stones at the foot of the high granite tors.

He dropped his gaze to a wooded valley nestling below, looking for a sight of his home, Court Barton.

Nothing. He frowned and checked his surroundings. Yes, this was the right spot. He should be able to see Court Barton from here.

He screwed up his eyes, squinting into the sun, and what he saw made a chill crawl up his spine.

William pulled up beside him. 'You cheated! I wasn't ready! Thomas?' William persisted. 'What's wrong? You look like you've seen a ghost.'

He couldn't speak, he couldn't think, it wasn't real. He raised a trembling finger and pointed to the valley.

'God's blood, what happened?' William said beside him.

Thomas shook his head. 'I don't know,' he said as he looked at the remains of the manor house standing naked and charred with a few blackened roof timbers jabbing into the sky like accusing fingers. Others lay scattered on the ground, fallen and broken like the bones of a skeleton and black as the Pestilence.

'I don't know,' he said again in a hoarse, cracking voice that didn't sound like his own. 'I'm going down.'

He was grateful for William's company. His heart numb with dread, he reached the bottom of the hill and stopped. The place was eerily still, as though even the wind and the birds wanted no part of what had happened there.

There was little left of the house, and most of the other buildings – the Great Barn, the dairy, the stables and the cart linhay – were piles of rubble and burnt timbers. Even Mama's favourite rowan tree was nothing but a black stump.

'Mama!' he shouted, his voice echoing in the ruins. He leapt down and threw his reins at William. 'Hold my horse!'

'Thomas, no—'

'I said, hold him! Mama is here, I know she is.' She had to be. She just had to.

Taking the bunch of apple blossoms from his pack, he picked his way over the remains of a wall and climbed through a gap where a shuttered opening had once looked out onto the yard. Standing in the remains of the grand hall, he turned around slowly, gazing at the devastation. No beautiful tapestries lined the walls, no silver candlesticks and platters gleamed on the table and no chairs, benches or stools stood by the hearth. All that remained was the stink of death.

He looked to the far end of the room. The high table had once held pride of place there, where Mama and Papa had sat looking down on their people. He could see Mama wearing her favourite yellow kirtle, a dazzling jewel at her throat and her hair braided with matching ribbons and pinned in coils behind her ears.

He saw the flaming torches in their wall sconces along the walls and heard the clink of silver goblets that sparkled in the light of wax candles that were placed in neat lines along the trestles. He could hear the pipes of visiting players, the laughter of guests, and he smelt the dishes of roasted meats in herbs and spices. But mostly, he heard his mother's laughter ringing in his ears.

'Mama?' he whispered.

Behind him, he heard the familiar light trip of her slippers. He spun around, his pulse racing with new hope, but there was no one there.

He glanced up. All that remained of her bedchamber were two blackened floorboards jutting out against the grey sky like spears. At the other end of the hall and above the charred remains of the grand door was a gaping hole so large that he could see clear across the passageway to the orchards.

How many times had he stood outside those doors, plucking up the courage to go in? It felt like only yesterday but he'd been six summers when he and Annie-healer had stood in that passageway listening to his Mama and Papa having one of their rows on the other side of the doors. What he'd heard that day had changed his life. It had been the day when Papa had denounced him as weak and useless, thanking God for his capable son Richard. His Papa, whom he had idolised and whose approval he had desperately sought, didn't want or even like him.

He hung his head at the memory.

Ashamed of his cowardly tears, he had run away. He remembered racing across the orchards until his chest burned, then falling to the ground and sobbing as his heart broke. He had tried so hard to be as good as Richard, but he could never compete. And when he had tried to show Papa how clever he was at script and reading, the one thing Richard hadn't shown much aptitude for, Papa hadn't even looked, saying he was too busy.

He had always been too busy.

That day, Thomas had thought about running away for good, but he hadn't known where to go. Instead, he'd asked Mama if he could go to school a year early. To his delight, she'd agreed; he had been glad to leave a few months later.

He wiped his eyes. The only happy part of his childhood had been with Mama. Now this was all that was left of it.

'Thomas?' William whispered. 'I don't like this. We should go.'

He shook his head. 'I need to find Mama. She must be here somewhere.'

He felt William's hand on his arm. 'Thomas, there's no one. Maybe we'll find out more in the village. Come, there's no point staying.'

William was right but he felt sure…

As he turned to leave, something in the ashes caught his eye. He took a hesitant step towards it. His heart stopped and he crossed himself.

From the ground, two dark empty eye sockets stared up at him. The jaw gaped open showing teeth in a hideous smile. The remains of the skeleton lay strewn across the ground, the rib cage broken and scattered haphazardly. He'd seen dead sheep on the moor like that after the foxes and crows had finished with them.

He didn't know why but he was drawn. He knelt. Three bone fingers poked through the ash, beckoning, calling him. He reached out.

'Don't!' William clutched his arm. 'Ye mustn't disturb the dead.'

He shook him off. His hand trembling, he touched the cold, hard bones.

And he knew.

In the ashes something glinted. It was a small gold cross and chain. Cradling it in the palm of his hands, he knelt back and gently turned the cross over. In the centre was a small red jewel.

His chest tightened as death's hand closed around him, squeezing out every drop of hope and love to lie in the ashes beside her. Clutching the cross, he crumpled and wept.

He didn't know how long he stayed like that but he felt William's hand on his back. He lifted his head and looked at his friend. 'It was Mama's,' he said. 'She always wore it. Her mother gave it to her on her wedding day.'

It was all he had left of her. The bones were no more than a mockery of the woman she was. A testament to God's cruelty.

'God rest your soul,' he said, kissing the cross before carefully putting it in his purse.

William tugged on his arm. 'Come away, there's nothing ye can do.'

'She must have been trapped by the fire. There's a pile of fallen timbers across the doorway. She must have been banging on the doors, frantic to undo the bolts in her effort to escape the flames.' He squeezed his eyes tight shut to obliterate her cries against the cracking of burning timbers. 'I should have stayed. Maybe if I had…'

'Thomas, don't do this to yourself,' William pleaded. 'Come away.'

'She wouldn't have had the last rites. God won't let her burn in hell, will he?' He looked deeply into William's eyes. 'I can't leave her like this. We must bury her and say a few prayers.'

'We can't. She may have had the Pestilence. She's at home and she'd understand. Come, best we leave her in peace.'

He didn't want to go but William was right: she may have had the Pestilence and she had told him to stay safe. He could do that for her, at least.

Gently, he laid the apple blossom close to her, then took the kerchief and crushed posy of primroses out of his surcoat and put them alongside.

He got off his knees and crossed himself.

'God take care of your soul,' he whispered. 'I vow to make you proud and be the lord I promised you I would be.'

There was nothing more he could do. The pain and grief were too raw to deal with, but one thing he did know, he would do his damnedest to keep his promise.

He and William remounted and rode in silence to the village. The first cottage they reached was boarded up, and the next stood empty, its door open in a sinister grin. There was no smell of woodsmoke or the familiar blue haze misting the lane, only a veil of death cloying the air as they passed cottage after cottage in eerie silence.

'The place is deserted,' said William in hushed tones. 'Not even fowl scratching the dirt.'

Tightly, Thomas nodded. It didn't feel right to break the silence.

Across the lane, the scattered remains of two skeletons lay in the dirt. Another was on the grass beside the pillory. Thomas crossed himself and looked away.

'Dear God, the Pestilence must have come,' William whispered. 'Do you think they all died here or did some get out?'

'I don't know. Pray God some of them escaped. I should have taken more people with me,' he added, more to himself, forgetting that they'd struggled to feed the few mouths they already had.

A crow cawed and took wing, reminding him of the corpse he'd seen in Tavistoke with the eyes pecked out. He shivered and pushed his horse to walk a little faster.

They continued through the village in cold silence, the only sound the gentle thud of their horses' hooves. As they passed the deserted inn, echoes of men's rough voices drifted through the closed door, and ghosts of women stood gossiping in groups along the lane, their willow baskets resting on their hips.

He could feel their spirits turning to watch him as they passed. Pulling his mantle close, he glanced over his shoulder, but the lane was empty.

When they reached the smithy, they stopped and exchanged nervous glances.

'Do you want me to come in with you?' Thomas asked.

'No. I'll call if I need ye.' William turned the heavy iron ring and pushed open the door, which scraped across the cobbles as it always had.

Before long, he emerged again, shaking his head. 'No one's been in, it's as we left it, like we were never there. We'd better check the mill and see if Geoffrey and Mary are there. I promised Rose.'

William's dour expression looked about as hopeful as Thomas felt. He wasn't sorry to leave and they headed out of the village to the ford. The air seemed fresher there, or maybe it was the sound of the clear water rippling over the stones.

As they drew nearer, William slowed to a halt. 'Ye stay with the horses. I'll go.'

Thomas let the horses drop their heads and drink and watched him walk along the towpath to the mill. He had stopped here so many times as a boy. With his back to the ghost village and the constant chuckling of water, everything he'd seen so far seemed surreal, as though he and William were intruders in someone else's nightmare.

It wasn't long before William returned, and his ashen face told him all he needed to know.

'They're not there, are they?' he said.

William shook his head. 'Oh, they're there alright. Bones lying on their mattresses with their arms holding each other. The rats have taken over and the mill's a mess. Sacks gnawed through, pots everywhere, and the stench made me guts heave. The cottage is the same.' He sighed. 'What am I going to tell Rose?'

Thomas didn't know. What did you say to someone whose family were nothing but bones? He would live with the image of his Mama lying in the ashes until the Lord took him. At least Rose had been spared that.

Death and evil emanated from everywhere he looked: only the river kept happily gurgling on its way over the stones, *forever-and-ever-amen*.

'Let's get out of here,' he said. 'Did you get the rasp your Pa wanted? He'll need it for our journey back here.'

'Damn, I forgot.' William looked him straight in the eye. 'But they've had the Pestilence and the fire's destroyed the manor. We can't come back.'

He felt sick, the hard truth of his friend's words hitting him like a punch in the stomach. William was right: they would never come back. His world and the life he'd dreamed of returning to were as dead as the ashes of his old home.

He was the last de Chiddleigh. He was the Lord of Combe Hide. He was on his own, and he was terrified.

CHAPTER 13

Thomas rode away from the village. Outside, he was calm. Inside, he was dying. An unseen thread was pulling him back to his home and the life he was promised. The force of it threatened to break his heart but there was no going back.

He no longer noticed the green hedges or the spring sun on his face or the nutty scent of the may trees crowding the sides of the track. He was a puppet doll, torn and discarded with a burning resentment smouldering within as he rode forward into an unwanted future.

'We can still come back,' he said. They'd rebuilt Combe Hide; they could rebuild Court Barton.

William shook his head, kicking his pony into a trot to keep up with the long strides of Thomas's horse. 'We can't.'

'So you're giving in?' He stared at William. 'I never took you for a coward.'

'Don't ye get vexed with me. It's not my fault.'

'I know it's not, but we *can* come back. We could rebuild.' He knew it was unrealistic, but he had to have something to cling to.

'Are ye willing to risk the Pestilence? Who's going to do the work? There's nothing but burnt timbers and ash left.'

'The Pestilence won't be there forever, and we can start again. We did it at Combe Hide. Mama would want—' He broke off. It no longer mattered what Mama wanted.

William sighed. 'Don't be a nuddlejade. There are only eight of us and four are women. It's not possible.'

'Will, I can't—'

'Shh!' William pulled his pony to a stop.

'What?'

Barely whispering, William said, 'Up there, on the left. I'm sure I saw someone duck behind that boulder.' He pointed at a dark grey rock twice the height of a man and just as wide.

Thomas squinted, but the only movement he could see was a linnet darting and trilling amongst the bushes.

'Are you sure?' he whispered back.

William nodded and walked his pony forward, Thomas alongside. Cautiously, they approached the rock, the blood beating harder and harder through Thomas's neck with every step they took. An attack was the last thing they needed. He clutched the bone handle of his dagger, and the harder he clutched, the harder he stared at the rock until his eyes blurred and he had to wipe them on his sleeve.

Suddenly, William stopped short and drew his knife. 'I know you're there! Show yourself!' he ordered.

Thomas focused on the boulder, slid his feet from the stirrups and slipped the dagger from his belt.

'Show yourself or we'll come in and get ye!' William shouted.

Thomas swallowed he wasn't sure about that; he'd rather make a run for it.

The bush twitched again and a small worn boot with a hole in the toe inched into view. A pale face peered around the stone and then a small woman dressed in a ragged grey kirtle and dirty linen apron emerged.

William leaned forward and frowned. '*Aunt Annie*? Is it ye? God's teeth, ye gave us a fright.' He laughed and sheathed his knife. 'Put your dagger away, Thomas. It's Annie-healer.' He jumped from his pony and opened his arm to her.

The woman visibly sagged and ran to William. 'Praise God! I thought you were travellers. I've been so afraid!'

Thomas knew Annie-healer. She was – had been – a friend of Mama's, but he hardly recognised her. Her cheeks were sunken, the skin tight and drawn over the bones. Her hair, usually neatly tied at the neck, hung lank around her face in a dark curtain.

William put his arm clumsily around her and let her cry on his shoulder, patting her back with a sheepish grin at Thomas.

Thomas slid off his horse. 'We thought everyone had gone.'

Annie drew away from William and held out her hands with a smile. 'It's good to see you, Thomas. I've been praying for you. God spared me but I'm the only one left.'

Her eyes misted. Thomas hoped she wouldn't want to cry on his shoulder next. He stepped aside just in case. 'The village is deserted. Why didn't you leave with the others?'

'I wanted to but Ellyn was old and frail. The demons were in her head. Some days she didn't know me. She couldn't travel and I couldn't leave her. It was a mercy when God took her in the darkest months but by then everyone had left...or died.'

'I'm sorry,' said Thomas, which was a inadequate response, but he didn't know what else to say. At least Ellyn had lived her full time, he thought bitterly. That was more than Mama did.

'She was nearly fifty summers, I reckon,' said William.

'I suppose she must have been,' said Annie, dabbing the corners of her eyes with the hem of her apron. 'And the others who went with you? Are they well?'

'Well, but thin. Ye know how it is during the dark months. We've been on one bowl of potage a day since before Christmas. Ye look a bit thin yourself,' said William.

'I lived on gorse flowers. They're always around, but they're bitter and the thorns are vicious. Good for staving off hunger pains though. They saw me through many a day. Things are beginning to grow again and I was foraging when I heard you coming.' Annie held out the pocket of her apron. 'I've found some primroses, wood anemones and early nettles. I was going to boil them with an egg tonight. I've only one fowl left. I was so hungry I ate the others. It's been the worst time I've ever known.'

They stood together in a sorrowful trio for a while before Thomas summoned up the courage to ask the question that was burning his mind in its demand to be answered.

'We went to the manor. Do you know what happened?'

Annie shook her head. 'Not really. The fire started on Christmas Day, I know that. I was feeling particularly miserable, Christmas can do that to you, can't it? I remember thinking about you all having a merry time and how I wished I was with you. Ellyn was asleep so I wandered outside to look for sticks. That's when I saw the smoke.

'I ran to the manor but when I got there, the flames were already raging through the roof. The smoke was so thick it was covering the lane and I couldn't see across the yard. I shouted and shouted but I couldn't hear my voice over the noise of splitting timbers and crashing beams.' She looked down, her face dark with grief. 'I tried to get to the house but the smoke and heat were too bad. I covered my face with my shawl but it didn't help. I couldn't even get to the well. Then folks started arriving from the village but when they saw how fierce the fire was they panicked, saying it was another sign of God's wrath. Most of them fled, packed up and left the village that night. By New Year's Day, everyone had gone.'

'Did no one survive the fire?' Thomas asked.

Annie shook her head again. 'I'm sorry, but no.'

'Do you know what caused it?'

'I don't, but the week before, I met your mother in the orchard to give her periwinkle lotion to keep the buboes away, and she was worried about talk of purifying the house. Whether the folks she was sheltering started the fire to do that, I don't know. I don't think we ever will. It doesn't matter, does it?'

Yes, it did. If he discovered that his people, the very folks his mother had taken into her home for safety, had caused the fire which killed her, he would never forgive them. 'I found Mama…' he started.

Annie nodded. 'Thomas, I'm so sorry. I wanted to bury her but I had Ellyn to think of. What if the Pestilence was still there and I got sick? What would happen to her? I couldn't risk it. After God took Ellyn, I went back to the manor, but it was the dark months, and the ground was too frozen to dig a grave. I said some prayers though. I did try, forgive me.'

He nodded but didn't look up. He was fighting his tears, as she was. 'When Mama sent me away, she asked for my forgiveness. She said that *it wasn't her fault* and that *we did what we thought was best*. I've been trying to work out what she meant. Do you know?'

Was he imagining things, or did Annie hesitate a little?

'No, I can't think,' she said. But her voice was a little too casual, and he couldn't help noticing that she didn't quite meet his eyes when she said it.

'By *her*, I wondered if Mama meant you,' he persisted. 'You were her friend, and you were always with us. If you know anything, please tell me. I need to know or I'll never be able to rest.'

Now Annie looked at him defiantly. 'I told you, Thomas, I have no idea.'

That was a lie. He knew that as well as he knew his own name, but he couldn't think what to do about it.

'That's the last of the jars. I've got the mortar and pestle, the last of the dried herbs, my sacking for straining, beans, peas and seeds for planting, and Will's just putting the fowl in the basket.' Annie checked her belongings that were piled high on the hand cart outside Ellyn's cottage.

Thomas dragged a thick straw mattress and fur coverings out of the narrow cottage door. 'I don't know how we're going to get these on. Do you have to bring them?'

'Yes, I do. Joan gave them to me when Ellyn took me in after Pa died and I had nothing.'

He couldn't argue with that, but the cart was already piled high. Lord knew how they were going to push it through the ruts and stony tracks.

'Got the fowl. God's bones, how are we going to take those?' William blew out a whistle through his teeth as he caught sight of the furs and mattress.

Thomas nodded. 'That's what I said, but she won't leave them behind.'

'No, I won't,' Annie said firmly. 'There's some nettle and willow twine inside. We'll tie them on the cart, and if we can't do that, I'll strap them to my back and carry them.'

William ran his fingers through his hair and muttered something under his breath but managed to secure the mattress and covers onto the cart. 'Are ye ready now?'

Annie cast a last gaze at the small cruck house clinging to the hillside with its stick and mud walls with a thick mop of bracken thatch.

'Ready as I'll ever be,' she said, gripping the rough wooden handles and heaving the cart forward. 'Not going far, I hope?'

'Combe Hide, my great-uncle Boren's old place on the east of the estate,' Thomas said. 'He lived there with his two sons, Gilbert and Aldred. I don't suppose you've heard of them.'

Annie stopped, something dark flashing through her eyes. 'Oh, I've heard of them.'

There was a grim note in her voice that he had never heard there before. Puzzled, he watched her put all her weight into getting the cart moving.

Annie was a strange one. A kitchen maid turned healer wouldn't cross paths with exiled nobles like Aldred or Boren. What could she mean?

He sighed. He'd thought that coming back to Court Barton would have solved all his problems. Instead, he was left with far more questions than he'd started with, and with Mama gone, there didn't seem to be anyone who could give him the answers.

CHAPTER 14

The cart lurched to the left and dropped into a rut for what felt like the thousandth time since they'd left.

'Damned thing! I've got another splinter and we've covered less than a mile.' Thomas dropped the handles and sucked his finger. 'Why did you have to bring all this stuff?'

'That *stuff* is all I've got to my name. You'll be pleased to have my healing herbs one day,' said Annie. 'Here, let me take a turn.'

He caught sight of William's smirk and sucked harder, trying to get the stubborn splinter out of his finger. 'We can take it in turns, but I'll pull more. It's not fair asking a woman to do it.'

Annie gave him a withering look. 'Being a woman's never bothered me before, and it'll not stop me now. You men haven't a clue how hard we work. And if you don't stop picking at that finger, the bad humours will come to the top, turn it green and make it drop off. I've got yarrow lotion on the cart – didn't I just say you'd be grateful for my herbs?'

He winced and didn't answer. Annie sounded exactly like his mother had when he was a little boy.

They went on, taking it in turns to push the cart, and had travelled halfway back to Combe Hide before dusk fell and it became too dark to continue. They found shelter behind some large boulders off the track and ate the plants Annie still had in her apron. Grateful now for Annie's mattress and fur covers, they settled down to sleep.

After a night of tossing and turning, Thomas woke to a heavy sky covered in iron-grey clouds. He lay on his back and stared up, wondering if his Mama was up there looking down on him. She'd been a good woman. God shouldn't have taken her. He didn't need her as much as Thomas did.

The dark, sullen-looking clouds matched his mood. He was glad to see them; he couldn't have borne a bright sunny day after yesterday. Maybe he'd never be able to bear the sun again.

Worst of all, he knew that the moment he and William arrived back at Combe Hide, everyone would swarm around them, clamouring for news. How was he going to tell them what had happened? How could he make them believe it when he was still struggling to believe it himself?

'Looks like rain,' said William, stretching out of his cover. 'We best make haste.'

William was right. They still had a good six miles or so to cover, and the cart would be even harder to push over rain-soaked ground. With a heavy heart, he rose and helped Annie reload the furs and mattress back onto the cart and reluctantly took the first turn to push.

Just after midday, as they left High Drovers Road and entered the wide valley leading to home, the heavens opened and rain exploded out of the sky. Water ran off Thomas's hair and down his neck, and in moments, his surcoat hung in sodden folds around his knees.

'God could have waited,' said William pulling the hood further over his face.

He could have, but Thomas wasn't surprised. God had it in for him.

A furlong or two ahead, he could see the bend in the track leading to Combe Hide. Maybe they'd been seen. Maybe his people were already waiting to greet him with excited, expectant faces, eyes full of hope that would die the instant he began to speak.

Pushing the cart into a deserted yard, he dropped the handles and flexed his aching hands as the door to the house banged open and Rose ran out, clutching a shawl over her head, closely followed by Maria and Eleanor.

'You're back!'

Thomas sighed. He'd hoped for a *little* more time before having to break the news to his people.

'Annie!' Maria squealed, throwing her arms around her.

Eleanor grabbed Rose's hands and danced her around the yard, splashing in the puddles. 'They're back. They're back and we're going home! Going home!' she sang.

Janet peered out from the forge and rushed out. 'Peter! Peter, come quick! They're back, and they've got Annie with them! Praise God, Annie, it's good to see you!'

'Lass! Ye look right worn out, but what are ye doing 'ere?' Peter strode out of his forge, wiping his hands on his leather apron and pulled Annie into a rough hug before turning his attention to William. 'Tell me, boy, how's old Malcolm? Did he buy ye an ale and give ye any message for me?'

William took Peter's manly slap on his back with a tight grimace. 'I'll tell ye later, Pa. Let's get out of this rain.'

'Annie?' Rose stood by the cart fingering Annie's belongings, a look of faint suspicion on her face. 'Why have you brought your things?'

Eleanor giggled. 'Yes, that was s-silly of you! When we go home you'll have to take them back. We've already started p-packing, haven't we, Rose?'

'Yes.' Rose looked hard at Thomas. 'We have. Thomas?'

He couldn't tell them now. Not here in the pouring rain.

'Plenty of time later for all the news. Let's get in before we're all drowned!' said Annie, bustling the girls towards the door. 'Come on, El, get that wet shawl off and sit down by the hearth. I want to hear all about what you've been doing!'

He shot her a grateful look, but she was already at the house and didn't see it.

'Ye can bed down with us, lass,' Peter called after Annie and, picking up the handles, wheeled the cart across to the forge as though it was nothing.

Thomas watched him go. If only he could be that strong.

He went inside and sat down by the warm hearth, feeling a tingle spreading from his toes to the tips of his fingers. Annie was doing a good job holding off questions by insisting they get dry and have something to eat first.

Peter and Janet joined him but he avoided looking at them, letting the conversation drift. Rose gave him a bowl of potage, her eyes looking straight through him, hard, suspicious. Hungry as he was, the smell of the potage made him feel sick and he put it on the floor.

Peter finished his bowl and wiped his mouth with the back of his hand. He was looking at him questions written all over his face. Peter wasn't stupid either; had he realised something was wrong too?

Maria put her bowl on the floor and five expectant faces turned towards him. Seeing them, he bit his lip.

What could he say to ease the crushing blow that he was about to inflict?

Nothing. At least, nothing that he could think of.

'Well, m'young lord, and how was Malcolm?' said Peter, his face challenging, as though he already knew the answer.

Thomas had never been in front of a sheriff, but he'd attended many of his father's manorial courts as a boy, and Peter's question made him feel like he'd already been accused and found guilty. His courage melted, and he glanced to Annie for help, but she was looking into her lap. He shifted his gaze to William, who was staring fixedly at the roof. No help there either.

He took a deep breath. 'We went to the village and —'

The door banged open. Simon stamped his boots on the threshold. 'God's teeth, it's pissing spears out there!' He shook his mantle before tossing it onto the bench. 'It's good to have you back. And Annie! Praise God, He spared you. I was on the top fields when I saw you arrive and got here as quick as I could.' Simon went to the fire and held out his hands to the warmth, water dripping off his sodden clothes to form a puddle at his feet.

'Have some potage; that'll warm you up,' said Janet handing him a bowl.

'Have I missed anything?' Simon shoved his mantle to one end and settled himself on the bench.

'Young lord 'ere was just telling us how Malcolm was.' Peter said. He stared hard at Thomas. 'Weren't you, m'lord?'

God's bones, Peter wasn't making this easy. Best to come straight out with it. He took a deep breath.

'Malcolm wasn't in the village,' he said. 'Nobody was.'

'They'd be tilling the fields for sowing,' said Simon. 'Did you go to the fields?'

There was a hint of contempt in his voice that Thomas didn't much like, as though Simon considered him too foolish to have thought of that himself.

'They weren't in the fields either,' he said. 'They weren't anywhere. The whole village was deserted. Some folks had died, and judging by the boarded up cottages, it looked like the others had fled.'

There, he'd said it. He stared around at them, waiting for his words to sink in and the barrage of questions that was sure to follow.

There was a shocked silence, which Peter broke first. 'I knew summat was up as soon as I saw lass with her cart. I said the Pestilence would come to the village. A good job I came with ye. Did Malcolm flee, do ye know?'

Peter had a short memory, Thomas thought savagely. He'd been against coming from the start and had ridiculed him ever since. He kept that thought to himself though; arguing wouldn't change anything.

'His cottage was boarded up, so I think he must have,' said William.

Peter nodded. 'Well, that's summat then. Happen he might make his way here too.'

'What about Ma and Pa?' Rose lifted her head, her eyes full of hope. 'Did you go to the mill?'

Thomas exchanged a glance with William and then studied his hands. This one was down to William, and he didn't envy him one bit.

'Aye, I went to the mill as I promised,' said William.

'And?'

'And I found their bones.'

Thomas winced at his choice of words.

'Their — no!' Rose stood up and backed away, her eyes large and desperate. 'You're wrong. You're wrong, it couldn't have been them.'

'I'm telling ye, it *was*!'

'Thomas?' Rose turned the terrified look on Thomas. 'Thomas, tell him he's wrong!'

He couldn't answer and Rose's face crumpled.

'It's true, Rose.' Annie's voice was very quiet. 'I went myself at the start of the dark months to look for supplies. They were lying peacefully together. *Weren't they, Will?*' She glared across the hearth.

'Oh aye, very peaceful like.' William stood up and walked over to Rose, putting his arm around her and pulling her clumsily toward him. 'Come here, lass, ye have a good cry on me shoulder. I'll take care of ye now.'

'*Get off me!*' Rose threw off his arm so violently, she sent him stumbling to the side. 'I don't want to cry on your shoulder, and I don't want you taking care of me! You're always sidling around me, pawing at me and trying to touch me. Just leave me alone!' With her face in her hands, she ran from the room.

'Rose!' William was on his feet before the door stopped rattling. 'Rose, come back!'

'Leave her be,' Annie said, so firmly William stopped in surprise. 'She didn't mean any of that. She's just upset.'

William ran a hand through his hair. 'She's my lass. I was only trying to help. I thought she'd want me help, being as how we're promised and all.'

'After the way you blurted it out about her parents?' said Thomas, who would have gladly followed Rose through the door for a few pins.

'Ye *were* a bit blunt, boy,' said Peter.

William snorted. 'That's a good jest, coming from ye!'

'There's no sense getting heated,' Simon interjected. 'Rose has had a terrible shock. Right now, she doesn't know what she wants. Sit down, Will, and do as Annie said: give the poor girl a few moments to herself.'

'I suppose...' Subdued, William took his seat.

'When did the Pestilence come to the village?' Janet asked.

'Don't matter when it came, ye cloth head woman!' Peter burst out. 'The question is, are we going back or not? Me, I don't see how we can, not with no folks living there.' He crossed his arms with macabre satisfaction.

'Don't say that! The thought of going home to see Mama is all that's kept me going.' Maria flared up. 'We are going home, aren't we, Thomas?'

There it was. The question he'd been dreading. Seeing his younger sister's large, innocent eyes made him feel like a traitor. The urge to follow Rose and run out of the house was almost irresistible.

'Well, m'young lord?' Peter demanded. 'Are we or aren't we?'

Thomas cleared his throat. 'The thing is...I mean, when we arrived...' Desperately, he looked at Annie.

'You said there was no one in the village, but what about the manor?' said Simon. 'Lady Joan was taking in families when I left. We could start from there, and folks may come back.'

Annie darted Thomas an anxious look, but he pretended not to notice.

'How *is* Mama, Thomas?' Maria asked, the question piercing him deeper than any sword. 'You still haven't said.'

He couldn't tell her. He just couldn't.

'There was a fire,' Annie said quietly. She looked pointedly at Thomas, clearly willing him to pick up the thread of the story, but he averted his eyes.

'Not me forge! God's teeth, lass, tell me the old place is still standing,' said Peter.

Annie managed a thin smile. 'Your forge is safe and just as you left it. No, the fire was at the manor house.'

'A fire?' Maria echoed. 'What happened? Is Mama alright? Where is she? Will one of you please tell me.'

Annie looked up. 'The fire started on Christmas Day.

'C-Christmas Day? We saw smoke over the moors on Christmas Day,' said Eleanor.

Simon let out a long, slow breath of comprehension. 'And I said it was too far away to affect us. If only we'd known.'

'Couldn't 'ave done aught, even if we had,' Peter pointed out.

'Annie?' Janet's voice was very quiet. 'What happened?'

'I ran down the hill...' As Annie retold her story, Thomas pictured his Mama inside the burning hall. He heard her screams against the roar of the flames, heard her fists pounding on the giant doors and heard her coughing as the smoke overwhelmed her.

A tear trickled down his cheek and he wiped it quickly with his sleeve. Why was God so cruel?

'...I did try, really I did, but there was nothing I could do but stand and watch the place burn until it was charred timbers and ash.' Annie finished her tale in a low, quiet voice.

'Mama died in the fire, didn't she?' Maria said. '*Didn't she*, Thomas?'

She made it sound like it was his fault. He wanted to be strong and tell her everything would be alright, but the words wouldn't come.

Annie nodded. 'I'm sorry, Maria. Lady Joan was inside the house when it burned, and yes, God saw fit to take her.'

Maria burst into tears and stumbled forward into Annie's opened arms, sobbing onto her chest.

'God will t-take c-care of her, Maria.' Eleanor patted Maria's shoulder, fighting her tears. 'She's in Heaven now. She's listening to His angels s-sing.'

Annie took her kerchief, no more than a scrap of linen, from her purse and wiped Maria's eyes as though she were a young child. 'Folks packed up and fled after that, saying it was God's wrath. God took Ellyn not long after and I was left alone on the hill.'

'It was God's will,' said Janet and crossed herself.

Simon cast a serious look around the group. 'God's will or not, this is now our home and there's no going back.'

They sat in sombre silence, their faces shadowed in the dimming light.

'I'll miss me forge,' said Peter staring at the embers.

'I'll miss my cottage,' added Annie, holding Maria and Eleanor.

'Who am I going to chat with as I card the wool?' Janet pulled a loose thread from her apron.

'Mama won't see me married.' Maria twisted an imaginary ring around her third finger.

'I miss Lady Joan,' Eleanor sniffed.

'Who will wed me and Rose? We've no priest.' William asked the room.

Thomas watched the last drip of fat run down the candle and congeal in a pool on the table, his own thoughts too painful to put into words.

CHAPTER 15

Rose had an itch in that infuriating place: in the middle of her back and just below her shoulders. It didn't matter how much she tried, she couldn't reach it. The mattress had never been the same since the flood. She should have restuffed it months ago; well, today she would.

Letting her arms flop down, she stared at the sky through the smoke hole. Judging by the pale yellow, it was nearly dawn. Three days since they heard The News. Three days for faces to morph from resentment to resignation. And for every one of those three days, she had woken to the same heavy feeling of remorse.

Unlike the others, she was happy to stay. She liked her new life with responsibilities and freedom. It was the guilt she couldn't come to terms with. As soon as she'd heard of Thomas's plan to leave Court Barton last August, she'd been hopping up and down with excitement. It had been even more thrilling when her Pa refused to abandon his mill and said she was to go on her own.

On the day of departure, she'd hardly given a thought to her parents in the mounting excitement of the adventure. Oh, she'd cried when the time had come to go, but her tears had dried before she'd reached the top of the hill out of Ashetyne.

And while she'd been thanking God for her independence, her Ma and Pa had been dying of the Pestilence.

Rose glanced around the room, which already held fond memories: the shelves in the corner that Thomas had tried to make and Jarin had had to repair; the grey walls that she and Janet had scrubbed clean, and the wattle fencing at the far end. Once, it had separated the area where the livestock used to live. Now, it held their stores. Above her head were the new beams and thatched roof that everyone was so proud of.

It was home, but she had to admit that it was a far cry from Court Barton. No wonder Thomas looked so miserable.

Five straw mattresses lay in a row along the opposite side of the room, next to the wall. Only two were occupied, and as she watched, Maria emerged from under her covers, yawned and stretched her arms lazily above her head.

Rose rubbed the sleep out of her eyes, threw back her own woollen cover and reached for the untidy pile of clothes next to her.

'It's nearly dawn,' she announced. 'Time we were up.'

'It's too early. How do you sleep in that smock? I sleep with nothing on,' said Maria running a hand down her silky white arms.

Rose smoothed down her crumpled under-smock self-consciously. Even after waking, Maria looked elegant. She'd wager no straws poked her back during the night. 'You've got a fur to lie on.'

'So I have.' Maria snuggled back down with an impish smile.

Rose shook out her brown kirtle furiously and wrestled it over her head. 'You're not at the manor now, Maria. You've fowl to clean out and feed and eggs to collect, so get up and start working. There's no maid here. Although you use Eleanor like one,' she couldn't resist adding.

'El likes doing things for me. Besides, now Mama's gone—' Maria crossed herself— 'I'm the Lady of the Manor.'

She was right about that, and Rose would have given anything to swap places with Maria for just a day. She'd parade across the yard in her silk kirtle, jewellery sparkling at her neck and on her fingers, and she'd nod down her nose as others curtsied in her path. It would never happen, of course – she was a commoner, a nobody in the eyes of nobles like Maria – but she could dream.

'You're not the only one to have lost their Ma, but things still need doing. You don't see me moping around, do you?' Rose tightened her belt with a hard tug. She could do it up two holes tighter than last year, but she'd never be as willowy as Maria, no matter how much weight she lost.

With a sigh, she thrust her feet into her wood and cloth shoes and threw a handful of sticks on the hearth, then picked up the two pails by the door.

'I'll fetch the water, then, shall I?'

Maria gave a lazy wave of dismissal that made Rose want to slap her hand hard, just like her Ma once had when she'd caught her sticking grubby fingers into the flour.

She stalked out and slammed the door hard behind her. She didn't think she was a horrible person by nature, but Maria's endless superiority and habit of talking down to her got her prickled, as Ma would have said.

Annie came out from the forge, and Rose hastily smoothed her face into an over-bright smile.

'Hail,' she said. 'A bright morning today.'

'Yes, it is.' Annie scrutinised Rose's face with a concerned healer's look. 'How are you?'

'I'm fine,' she lied.

'Hm.' Annie peered closer. 'You've dark circles under your eyes. Are you sleeping? Come round the back and I'll give you some poppy tincture to take at night.'

'I'm really very busy,' she said. Annie meant well, but she didn't want poppy tincture or any of Annie's other cures. The only tincture she wanted was one to wipe out guilt, and she doubted that even a healer as skilled as Annie could give her that.

'It won't take a moment. This way.'

With a sigh, she put down her pails and dutifully followed Annie through the forge to a small open-fronted linhay at the back.

'Isn't this new?' Rose said, staring around at it.

Annie nodded. 'Peter built it for me. He said my baskets and dried flowers were cluttering up his forge and would cause a fire.'

Ducking between bunches of dried flowers hanging from the low roof, she couldn't help thinking Peter was right. Annie had pots arranged in sizes from small to large. On the shelves, neat rows of clay jars jostled for space, while piles of nettles, primroses, blackthorn blossom and grasses littered a trestle below.

'You're well organised,' she said.

Annie shoved the plants to the end of the trestle. 'When you're troubled, it's best to keep busy. It helps you forget and heals the hurt.' She picked up a small clay jar, removed the reed stopper, sniffed the contents and nodded in satisfaction. Wedging the stopper back into place, she added, 'We're all upset, but we need to be kind to each other.'

There was that guilt again, creeping up Rose's spine. Did Annie know she'd been nasty to Maria? Maybe she had the healer's extra eye. Ma said she had.

Annie held out the jar. 'Poppy tincture. Take a spoonful every night.'

Eleanor ran in, clutching a wilted-looking bunch of primroses and violets, beaming. 'Annie! I've p-picked you some flowers.' She held out the small posy. 'I like your healing p-place. It smells pretty, like a flower m-meadow.'

Annie took her present and sniffed the flowers. 'Thank you, Eleanor. That was very kind of you.'

Eleanor's beam widened. 'There're *m-masses* of flowers up the valley. Shall I pick you some more?'

'I think these will be enough for now.' As Eleanor's smile faded, Annie added, 'Besides, if you pick all the flowers today, tomorrow they'll be all gone. When I need more flowers, you'll be the first person I ask.'

Eleanor clapped her hands in glee. 'I can be your helper!'

Annie smiled. 'You certainly can. My helper in charge of flower-picking, how does that sound?'

Eleanor nodded hard, the beam back. 'I'm glad you're here. We're all together again like we used to be, aren't we, Rose?' Her bright eyes dulled for a moment. 'Well, not quite. Poor J-Jay, dying in the fire like that. I wish she was here.'

'So, do I,' said Annie. 'But Joan wouldn't have suffered, Eleanor. The smoke would have made her feel very tired and she would have just gone quietly to sleep.'

Eleanor frowned, biting a forefinger. 'Like Thomas's bees? The smoke m-made them sleep too.' 'Yes, just like that. It was a much better end for her than dying from the buboes.'

Rose doubted that was true, but that was Annie all over. Always the healer, always finding a way to make folks feel better.

'El?' Maria's voice came from somewhere across the yard. 'El, where are you?'

'Maria's calling me! I have to g-go. I'll see you later.' Eleanor skipped away, humming a tune.

'She's going to cope better than any of us,' Annie said, putting the posy in a blue jar next to half a dozen similar posies. 'I'm hoping she'll help Maria in her innocent way.'

'She misses Lady Joan,' said Rose.

'Yes, but she'll bounce back quicker than the rest of us. Children always do, and that's really all Eleanor is, for all she has the body of a maid.'

She could do with a bit of Eleanor's childish bouncing, but she had the hogs to feed and water to fetch for cooking and washing bowls. 'I've got to go too.'

Annie nodded. 'Don't forget to take the tincture. I'll see you at the morning meal. Simon says we've got to make plans; I can't wait to hear what he has in mind.'

Neither could she.

By the first quarter, she'd finished her jobs and, holding the door open with her back, struggled in with two pails of water. It was a long way from the river to the house with iron handles digging into her hands. She must remind Simon about getting the well at the back of the house cleared out.

She put the pails by the shelves, taking care not to spill any of their precious contents, and rubbed the life back into her hands. 'Where is everyone?'

Maria was sitting on her mattress while Annie replaited her hair. 'Thomas is out somewhere. Staring at the sky, I shouldn't wonder. He hasn't said a word since he got back. Simon is Lord knows where, and El will be checking the sheep in the orchard. But you should know that since you gave her the task.' Half-turning to Annie, Maria added. 'We have our orders from Rose. My tasks are to see to the fowl and collect sticks for the fire, and she's always saying I don't do it right.'

'I'm only doing as Simon told me,' said Rose.

'But I'm the lady, and you've mud on your face.' Maria delicately raised her hand and held out a finely carved bone comb in Annie's direction.

Savagely, Rose wiped her hand across her grubby cheeks, snatched the bowls from a shelf and slammed them down on the table without answering.

'You are the lady, but life is different now,' said Annie, running the comb through Maria's long tresses. 'We all have to help, and that includes you.'

Maria turned sharply. 'I do help! Rose knows I do my tasks, even though she's always moaning at me about them.'

'They're all you do,' Rose retorted from the corner of the room. 'As soon as you finish your tasks, you think you're at liberty to lie idle for the rest of the day. At least Thomas is always doing things.'

'Oh, Thomas is hopeless,' Maria said. 'He's trying to run this place like a monastery — ouch!'

'Sorry, hit a knot.' Annie continued combing, and Rose wondered just how much of an accident that particular knot had been. 'That's the only life he knows.'

'And it's about as much use here as a horse with three legs,' Rose muttered.

'I'm sure he's doing his best,' Annie said. 'He needs our help —'

'Who needs our help?' Peter demanded, his stocky frame filling the doorway. He glanced over his shoulder. 'Stop ye fussing, woman, and get inside.'

Janet squeezed past and poked the fire into life as Peter sat down by the hearth.

'Meal won't be long,' she said, heaving a heavy iron pot onto the hook above the spit. 'Potage again. I'm sorry, it's all we have left in the stores.'

'It's all folks ever have this time of the year,' Annie said, as Simon ducked through the door, closely followed by Thomas. 'But things are growing again, the hens are laying and I'll go foraging later.'

'Talking of which, Thomas and I wanted you all here because we need to plan for the future.' Simon reached out to the waking embers, warming his hands.

Rose looked at Thomas, who had sat down on the floor with his knees tucked up to his chin. He looked hurt and sad, much like a puppy she once had.

'And what plans do ye have for us this time, m'young lord?' said Peter, dipping a finger into the pot.

'I never said I had any plans,' Thomas muttered to the floor.

'Let's wait for the others and then we'll talk,' said Simon.

'They'd best make haste then,' Peter grumbled. 'I've timbers to cut and me belly's empty. Leave off stirring that pot, woman, before ye stirs a hole in the bottom.'

William brought in a pail of water with Eleanor close behind, carrying a bowl of eggs.

'I d-did the fowl like you asked, Maria,' she said.

Rose spun round. 'You lazy sow! You lie there, having Annie do your hair, which you could do yourself, send Eleanor to do your work and still call yourself a lady? Us common folk have better manners than that.'

'Maria's sad and I d-don't mind.' Eleanor set the eggs very carefully on the side.

'See? El doesn't mind.' Maria lifted her chin. 'And what would you know about manners?'

'More than you, and we're all sad. El, let Maria do her work from now on.' She grabbed a stool.

'You two should stop quarrelling,' said Simon, taking a seat.

'I'll do your braids later, best join the others,' said Annie, handing back the comb.

Rose ignored the scowl as Maria took her seat and spread her kirtle daintily over her knees. William put his stool firmly next to her, his leg resting against hers. God's teeth, if he sat any closer she'd be in his lap. She shuffled her stool towards Eleanor.

'I'm sorry there's no bread,' said Janet.

'There's been no bread for weeks and me belly doesn't need reminding.' Peter tipped the bowl to his mouth, wiped up the last of the contents with his fingers and licked them. 'Now, m'young lord, I can't wait to hear this plan of yours. There's just us here and we can't go home, so how are we going to manage? That's what I want to know.'

Thomas continued to stare at his boots. 'I don't have a plan.'

'There's a surprise.' Peter tutted to the roof.

'Give him a chance. Honestly, sometimes I think you've fewer brains than the iron you work with,' said Rose. 'He's just lost his Ma and his home.'

'He's the lord, it's up to him to sort things. Who's going to work the acres? Can he tell us that? There's eleven of us and only five of us are men. Well, six if you count Gee but he can't do much—'

'I can do the work of any lad,' she said.

Peter snorted through his nose. 'You're a lass.'

'You didn't say that when I was hauling sheaves of reeds up the ladder for the roof.' She threw back at him, even as she knew it was useless. Women were only considered capable when it suited men.

'Stop bickering.' Simon silenced them. 'Peter's right, we can't manage on our own. We need help. It's lambing season, we've ditches and banks to repair, hedges to lay, stones need taking off the fields, there's ploughing, tilling, sowing, walls that need building, more wattle fencing for pens, we'll need more sheep and—'

'C-cows and goats too,' Eleanor added. 'I like goats.'

'And the well at the back needs fixing,' Rose put in. 'I'm sick of going to the river for water.' 'Where ye going to find this help?' said Peter, rubbing his chin.

'I saw a lot of travellers passing through. Most of them were just roaming. We could try and get some to settle here,' said Annie. 'Of course, we don't know if the Pestilence is over.'

'Well, I'm building a place behind the forge, and I'm not taking to the roads looking for no folks.' Peter crossed his arms emphatically.

'I don't want to stay here,' Maria protested. 'It's boring and miserable. I don't see why we can't go back to the village. Thomas said it was empty.'

'There's no m-manor house in the village,' Eleanor said. 'Where would we live?'

'The men would build me one.' Maria stroked the folds of her kirtle and smiled sweetly at Simon. 'Wouldn't you?'

Simon shook his head. 'No, I wouldn't. The village has had the Pestilence; it's not safe anymore. This is our home now, so you'd better get used to it.'

'What do you think we should do, then?' Annie asked.

'I think Thomas and I should go to the Chiddleigh lands to the north of the estate and see if there're any folks still there. If there are, we'll bring them here. You'd be best staying here, Peter. We need more tools and another plough.'

'I'm a smithy, not a carpenter,' Peter said. 'I can't do it all.'

'I know that, but with God's blessing, we'll find more men and you can get back to your forge.' Simon ran his fingers through his hair. 'We're all disappointed, but we've got to make the best of it.'

'We'll need more fruit and nut trees planted and more swine to give us meat, fat for candles and hides for leather,' said Rose.

'I can m-make c-candles, said Eleanor.

'What about a dovecote?' Maria said suddenly, twisting a strand of hair around her fingers. 'Then we'd have meat, eggs and feathers.'

Peter snorted. 'Talk sense! Where're ye going to get fancy doves?'

'The markets, I suppose. How should I know? I was only trying to help.'

'There won't be any markets if the Pestilence is still coming, you nuddlejade!' said Rose.

'Don't you call me a nuddlejade!'

'This isn't helping!' Simon's voice silenced them. 'There's no point getting sour with each other. We have to work together, like before. This place—' he swept his arm around the room— 'was a ruin when we came here, but we rebuilt it. Think of what else we've achieved. We can make this a proper estate, can't we, Thomas?'

Thomas shrugged. 'I haven't got a choice.'

Rose gritted her teeth. God, she wanted to shake him! Couldn't Thomas see Simon was giving him a chance to assert himself? That was what lords did and what folks expected. God help them all if he didn't learn soon.

'We can catch fish from the river and there's loose stock roaming. We could round up some of those,' Annie interjected. 'And I know you'll think me a cloth head for saying this, but we should plant madder roots.'

'Ye can't eat madder,' said Peter.

'Lady Joan found a way to make a bright scarlet dye for cloth. I know how to do that. But we'll need madder roots, lots of them.'

So that was why she was busy spinning, Rose realised. Whenever she wasn't concocting tinctures and gathering herbs, she was working with her drop spindle, like she was now.

'It's *food* we need,' said Peter. 'Making dyes and selling cloth; ye're talking muxy, woman.'

'No, she's not.' Simon regarded Annie thoughtfully and nodded. 'She's absolutely right. This is the new manorial home, so we have to think ahead and plan for the future as well as now. The land is poor for farming, we know that, but if we can spin and weave enough wool, that scarlet cloth could be the saving of us. The Flemish merchants can't get enough of it, and it fetches huge prices.'

Rose listened intently. If that were true, the estate could have huge potential. 'I think it's a good idea.'

'Now I know the devil's in your 'ead,' said Peter.

'I c-can find m-madder for you, Annie,' Eleanor piped up. 'M-Maria will help me. Won't you, M-Maria?'

'It'll be better than looking after fowl,' said Maria with a shrug.

'You'll still have to do that,' said Rose.

'Mama would like that,' Thomas said to the ground. 'The cloth, I mean.'

'Yes, she would,' Annie said softly. 'We'd be finishing what she started.'

Simon nodded. 'Good. Find a spot for planting and we'll get digging.'

Peter snorted. 'Thinking like that, we'll need all the help God gives us. It's now we've got to think of.'

'Oh, you're like an ox with a thick head sometimes!' Rose wiped her hands on her apron and handed her empty bowl to Janet. 'Just get on and make another plough.'

'If we could rebuild the mill, we could grind grain for flour. Maybe even sell it.' Simon looked at Rose. 'You know all about that, don't you?'

God's bones, that was the last thing she wanted, to be dragged back into life as a miller. Still, it wouldn't be forever; only until they found an actual miller to take over. 'I don't know how to build a mill, but I know how to work one,' she said.

'She's bright for a lass.' William beamed at her, shifting his stool a little closer.

She moved away. She didn't need compliments from him. If only he would leave her alone for just one day. A few days would be better. No; a few weeks. She was sick of having to check every corner to see if he was waiting for her. What would it take to stop him?

She glanced at Thomas and a thought struck her. William could hardly refuse a direct order from his lord, could he? If she could find a way to win Thomas to her side, she might yet be safe.

'We c-could scratch messages on the beams to keep the bad spirits away,' said Eleanor.

Rose blinked. She'd been so caught up in trying to rid herself of her unwelcome suitor that she'd all but forgotten their current discussion.

'That's a good idea!' Maria's eyes sparkled. 'What shall we write?'

'I'm not g-good with letters. You do it.'

'God's teeth, I've more to do than listen to a couple of wenches blathering on about scratching letters.' Peter rose to his feet. 'Boy, come with me! I'm going build us a place to live. I'll need stones, so you, woman—' he pointed at Janet— 'get us some from the ancients' places up the valley.'

One by one they drifted outside, leaving her alone with Thomas. She thought he was crying, but he was staring at the ground scratching lines in the dirt with his boot. Thank the Lord for that. She wouldn't know what to say to a lad who cried, let alone a lord.

She moved closer and peered down at the lines in the dirt. 'What are you drawing?'

'An isosceles triangle.'

'Oh...yes.' She was none the wiser, but pretended to admire it anyway, squatting down in front of him. 'It's hard, isn't it?'

He didn't look at her. 'What is?'

'Losing our mothers. I mean, we're on our own now.'

No response. She might as well have appealed to the dirt or his icy-lees triangle for sympathy.

'Do you know the worst of it?' she continued. 'The guilt.'

Thomas stopped drawing triangles and looked at her. 'What have you got to feel guilty about? I was the one who brought us here.'

'You were only doing what you thought was right. And where would we be if you hadn't?' He looked so vulnerable, she had an overwhelming desire to hug him, but held back. Lasses didn't do that to lads, especially not when one was a peasant and the other a lord. 'I doubt any of us would be alive if we hadn't come here. You should feel proud, not guilty.'

He tilted his head, showing the enchanting lines of a frown under his hair. 'I never thought of it like that. But what have you got to feel guilty about?'

'I couldn't wait to leave the mill and hardly gave Ma and Pa a thought.' Speaking the words aloud made her feel cleaner, somehow, as if she'd confessed to a priest.

'They wanted you to go. *Give our daughter a chance*, your mother said. They'd be pleased you survived.'

'She did say that, didn't she? I'd forgotten.' She looked into his eyes. She'd never noticed before what a pretty shade of light brown they were, like the seeds on a soft-rush. 'We're a right pair, aren't we? Both feeling guilty when all we did was exactly what our mothers wanted. We'll make this place work, you'll see.'

For a brief moment, she felt the possibility of a friendship, or at least an alliance. She could help him if he'd let her; she understood her people in a way that he didn't and never would. She waited hoping for some sign or response to show that he felt the same way, but he just shrugged and returned to his triangle.

'I suppose,' was all he said.

Feeling ridiculously disappointed, she stood up, adjusted her coif and retied her apron. He was right. The whole idea was impossible, him being a lord and she a miller's lass.

'I've got work to do,' she said, picking up a basket. 'I'll see you later.'

Stopping at the door, she cast a glance back over her shoulder. Thomas wasn't looking. He hadn't even moved. Frustrated, she stalked outside and let the door bang shut behind her. It didn't seem like there would be any hope from that quarter.

CHAPTER 16

Carefully,. Rose carried the earthenware pot to the trestle.

'The first ewe has lambed! I've just milked her. Remember milk?' She dipped a finger into the bowl, sucked off the milk and savoured the taste of the creamy liquid sliding down her throat, closing her eyes in pleasure.

Eleanor looked over. 'M-milk? That m-means cheese!'

'It certainly does, and what are you doing up there?' Rose threw her coif on the trestle and rubbed her greasy hands through her hair. Eleanor was balancing precariously on the same stool that Maria was sitting on and reaching up to the beam.

'We're cheering ourselves up by scratching stick p-people on the beam to bring us good fortune. Aren't we, M-Maria?'

'Lord knows we need it,' Maria said. 'Poor Mama, I can't bring myself to do much at the moment.' She dabbed the corner of one eye with a fine lace kerchief.

'No change there, then,' Rose muttered to herself.

'You—' Maria started to rise.

'Maria, don't m-move!' Eleanor cried. 'This stool's only got three legs and one of them wobbles.'

Rose sighed. Maybe she was being harsh. Maria was younger than she was, and she had lost her Ma.

'I'm sorry, Maria.' She forced the words out through a tight smile. 'I know how you feel. I lost my Ma and Pa too.'

'How could you possibly understand how a noble feels? For your information, a lady is taught not to show her emotions, so I keep smiling despite all the hardships I've had to endure since leaving home.' Maria sniffed delicately.

If Maria was a real lady, she'd hide her moans and groans. Rose took a deep breath and tried again. 'It must be difficult for you.'

'Hm. Well, at least you won't have to worry about it soon,' said Maria examining her hands in her lap.

'What are you talking about?'

'I'm talking about what Simon was saying last week, about making this place like the old home with peasants and a dairy and a mill and men to work the land.' Maria held up one hand, admiring it. 'I hope it happens soon. Then I can have a maid again.'

'I braid your hair and p-pin it in loops how you like it,' said Eleanor.

'Yes, but you're more of a helper and companion, El. One day, I'll marry an earl or a duke and have a proper maid. I'll live in a castle and wear silk kirtles every day with jewels and velvet slippers, and I'll be invited to banquets, like Mama and Papa.' Maria held a long-fingered hand up to her eyes and smiled, as though she could already see the rings that would adorn them.

'It will take years to rebuild this place, and I still don't know what you meant,' Rose said, taking one last taste of the milk. 'Why won't I have to worry about it?'

'Don't you know?' Maria tilted her head, her eyes dancing. 'Simon's going to rebuild the mill, just as soon as he gets more men. Think, you'll be all snug and cosy in your little cruck house and you can have your old job back as a miller's maid.'

She hated to ask, but she had to. 'What cruck house?'

'We heard Will talking to T-Thomas. He said you and he are p-promised, and he's building a c-cottage so you can get married and—oh!' Eleanor covered her mouth with her hand. 'I forgot! It's a surprise; I wasn't s-supposed to say anything.'

It was a surprise alright. William had no right telling folks they were promised, let alone building a muxy cruck house for her. A *cruck* house! Those who lived in them were considered poor even by peasant standards, so what did that tell her?

'Oh, I'm such a cloth head.' Maria smiled sweetly. 'I do hope we haven't spoilt it for you, but Will's been going around telling everyone. Still, it won't be long before you're wed and living with your husband in your little home of sticks and mud.'

Rose gritted her teeth. God's bones, she'd like to wipe that smile off the little vixen's face, sitting there looking so innocent, but she wouldn't give her the satisfaction.

'Oh, you haven't spoilt anything,' she said with an airy wave of her hand. 'Will and I have often talked about it.'

She turned away and furiously started rearranging the pots on the shelf, her mind racing. Maria and Eleanor had done her a service, albeit accidentally. If the pair of them hadn't let it slip about the cottage, she wouldn't have known and it would have been too late until he gave her a muxy ring. It was no good putting it off any longer. She had to stop him.

'Your t-turn, M-Maria. Are you going to do one, Rose?' Eleanor scrambled off the stool and handed the nail to Maria.

'Later.' She shoved the last pot back on the shelf and grabbed her shawl. 'I've got to go out.'

Her skirts swished savagely through the grass, scattering early brimstone butterflies in a cloud of yellow as she marched along. Cruck house indeed! She'd soon get to the bottom of this. First, she had to talk to William and find out just how much of Maria's words were true. She wouldn't put it past that one to spin lies just to vex her.

There was no way she was going to marry William, let alone live in some makeshift house of sticks and mud as a peasant wife owned by her husband.

If the estate succeeded, Maria would be the Lady of the Manor until Thomas married. That was a terrifying thought. She could see her now with her nose in the air, sitting on a chair covered in furs and velvet, wearing fine clothes like Queen Philippa and ordering everyone to do her bidding.

A cold shiver ran down her spine as a new, worse thought struck her: *what if Maria made Rose her maid*? She'd make her curtsy and have her working from dawn till dusk and there would be nothing anyone could do about it. God's teeth, she'd be a slave to both Maria and William!

Never. Never, never, never. She'd rather die. Gritting her teeth, she increased her pace, looking neither right nor left until halfway along the valley, where she found a plot marked out with hazel poles.

It was larger than Gee's, about fifteen yards wide and going back to the field some fifty yards behind. The ground had been cleared in readiness, and there was no mistaking the first row of stones marking out a small rectangle of a cottage.

Damn it! William *was* building a cottage. There was nobody else it could be. The quicker she dealt with this the better, and there was only one way to do it. Rose turned on her heel and stormed back down the valley, back to the house.

'Rose!' William hurried after her with a pail in his hand, slopping water with each heavy stride of his boots.

She stopped and waited, her hands already on her hips.

'What ye been doing?' William's pail swung in his hand, splashing water over her shoes.

'Watch what you're doing!'

He grinned sheepishly. 'Sorry.'

'I've been walking up the cleave,' she said, feeling the water seeping through the toes of her woollen stockings. Any minute now, her feet would start to itch. 'And you?'

'I've nearly finished mending the plough.' He puffed his chest out with pride.

He had to be jesting. He couldn't use a saw or hammer a nail with only one arm; she'd seen him try.

'William, this has got to stop.' She spoke slowly and loudly, as though he were deaf.

'What has?'

She'd never noticed before, but when he frowned, his brow furrowed in deep ugly tracts making him look like a soured apple. 'You telling people we're getting wed, that's what! And now you're building us a cruck house.'

William's face fell. 'I put a lot of work into that and it's not a cruck house. It's a proper stone cottage with shutters and that. It was supposed to be a surprise for after we're wed. What with losing your folks, I thought it would cheer ye up.'

A stone cottage? Many a lass would come running at the promise of a stone cottage, but she wasn't one of them. 'Will, listen to me. We're not getting wed, and I don't want a cottage.'

'But we're promised. Ye can't go back on that. What's changed your mind?'

Seeing his confused eyes made her feel dreadful. She didn't want to hurt him, but he wasn't leaving her much choice. 'Oh, Will. Nothing's changed my mind because there is no arrangement. You've got to believe that.'

'But we've always been together since we were children—' he began, his gaze imploring now.

'As children, yes, but we're grown up now.'

'Aye, I know.' He smiled at her, set down the pail and took her hand. 'My woman.'

She wrenched herself free, backing off a step. 'Will, please. You've got to stop telling folks we have an arrangement or they'll start believing it, and it isn't true.'

He chuckled. Not a laugh of disbelief, but a knowing, patronising, manly chuckle. 'I know your problem. It's the wedding jitters.' He shook his head, grinning. 'Ye lasses are all the same, but ye'll be fine on the day.'

God give her strength. 'There won't be a day! I. Am. Not. Marrying. You.' She didn't see how she could say it any plainer.

'But Rose, don't ye see? I'm a man. I want my own place with a wife. I'm sick of being Pa's boy.'

So, it wasn't just her he wanted and that gave her an idea.

'Well, if you're trying to prove yourself a man to your Pa, don't do it by telling folks we're promised. Why don't you ask Simon if you can go with him instead of Thomas? You managed the sheep coming here, and if you brought down more livestock, it would show your Pa you're not tied to the forge and can do other things, like a man.'

She waited, trying to gauge his reaction. Would he go for her idea?

William frowned. 'I do like the sheep.'

'There you are then! You could round up hundreds of them.' She didn't know if there were hundreds but if he thought there were, that was all that mattered. 'We'll be needing as many as possible for milk and wool.'

William hesitated, then shook his head. 'No. It wouldn't be fair to leave Pa on his own.'

'But that's the point. You'd show him that you're independent, that you're a man. Do you want to be a smithy? It can't be easy, not with…' Her eyes flicked to his empty sleeve. 'And anyway, your Pa won't be on his own. He's got Jarin.'

'Will! Will, where are ye, boy? Stop blathering and get in 'ere with the pail.' Peter's voice came from the smithy doorway.

William glanced at the forge and then back at her. A slow smile spread across his face. 'I'll do it. Thanks, Rose, ye're a fine lass. I'll ask Simon today. And when I get back, I'll finish the cottage and we can wed.'

'*William!*'

'Stop worrying. I told ye, it's just maid's nerves. Coming, Pa!' he yelled over his shoulder. Grabbing the half-empty pail, he ran to the smithy.

Dear God, what was she going to do now?

CHAPTER 17

Soft grey shadows extended like fingers across the yard, and the early morning warmth brought colour to Thomas's cheeks. Praise God William had taken his place with Simon; he wasn't in the mood for travelling. Some days, he felt quite optimistic about the future. On others he'd be checking the hedges for gaps or doing some other menial task and his mind would drift to Oxford and the gloom and frustration would descend on him as he thought of everything he'd lost.

He stretched his arms wide and breathed in deep lungfuls of air. Listening to the skylarks high above him, he smiled. It was going to be a good day.

The smithy door crashed back against the wall.

'This is all your doing!' William roared, marching towards him, his face black as thunder and his fist clenched at his side.

Thomas backed off rapidly. William's temper was no jesting matter. 'What's wrong? What have I done?'

He felt the cold stones of the wall behind him and cursed his stupidity. William was coming straight for him and now he was trapped against the building.

'God's blood, I ought to knock that pretty face off your shoulders!' William stopped so close that he could smell his sour breath. 'I know your game!'

He stared into William's blazing eyes, racking his brain furiously to think of what he might have done. 'What game?' he protested in a voice that was little more than a squeak.

'Don't give me that! Ye knows what I'm talking about.' William inched closer.

'I don't, really I don't.' He shrank against the stones as William towered over him.

'Last night, I got to thinking and it came to me. No lass could have thought of it on her own. Ye put the idea into her head, didn't ye? Oh, I'm not blaming her. She's just a lass and thought she was helping me. She had no idea ye—' William prodded Thomas hard in the chest— 'were plotting to get me away so ye can take my place with her.'

'*What?* No, I didn't, I swear. I don't want Rose. She's your lass.' Frantically, he looked around for someone to help him, but the yard was empty. He opened his mouth and tried to shout for aid, but his mouth and throat were so dry he could only croak.

'Don't ye lie to me! I've seen ye showing my Rose those parchments of yours. What does a lass need with parchments?' William leaned in, the smell of the smoky forge on his breath making Thomas gag. 'I was going to see to ye last night, but Pa said I was to cool me 'ead, and just as well for I'd have killed ye.'

He looked like he was going to kill him now. Thomas swallowed and glanced at William's clenched fist. If he was going to hit him, he wished he'd get it over with.

He screwed his eyes shut and turned his face aside, bracing himself for the blow, trying to back even further into the cold, unyielding stone wall. When nothing happened, he risked opening one eye in the hopes that

William had backed off, but he hadn't. William's face was now less than three inches away from his own.

Slowly, William pressed hard knuckles into Thomas's cheek, his voice low and venomous. 'Rose's my lass. Ye stay away from her. Do ye hear me?' He pressed harder.

Thomas tried to nod, but the pressure from William's fist was too strong. Something of his intention must have been visible, though, because William nodded in satisfaction.

'Good.' Grabbing Thomas's tunic, he pulled him off the wall. 'Because if I come back and hear ye've been anywhere near Rose or so much as looked at her, I'll not waste time with words,' he growled, releasing Thomas with a hard shove that sent him staggering back into the wall. 'Filling the lass's head about me proving myself to Pa!'

From somewhere, Thomas found his voice. 'Will, I swear to God that I didn't fill her head with anything. You said yourself that Peter calls you a boy and that you struggle with the work. I think you going with Simon is a good idea; it'll show your Pa you're not a child anymore.'

William snorted. 'Ye know your trouble? Ye think too much. If anyone around 'ere needs to prove himself a man, it's ye. Take a look at yourself in the river with your scholar boy's hands and a chin as smooth as a fowl's egg.'

Thomas forced his hand not to stray to his chin. 'It isn't smooth. It doesn't show because I'm fair, that's all.'

They stared at each other in a long silence. Just as Thomas was beginning to hope it was all over, William spat at his feet. 'Pa was right all along. You nobles think ye can do what ye like with us. And I'll tell ye summat else: you're weak and not fit to be lord, ye and your fancy ideas. You're not capable of running this place, everyone says so. Ye'd be lost without Simon or my Rose. Well, we don't need ye. Why don't you go back to that monastery where ye belong?'

Thomas felt a sharp pang of guilt. He'd barely spared a thought for the monks recently; he'd been too busy trying to work out how to be a lord.

He fixed his eyes once again on William's fist. 'If you want, you can stay here and I'll go with Simon.' Getting away suddenly seemed like a very good idea.

'And have folks think I'm scared?'

God's teeth, he couldn't win. 'Will, I'm your friend. I told you before: I'd never try to steal Rose from you.'

'Ye're no friend of mine!' William snarled. 'Leave her alone, or I swear to God I'll swing for ye!'

William turned and marched back across the yard. When he was safely inside the forge, Thomas peeled himself off the wall and breathed a long sigh of relief, rubbing his cheek. He'd have a good bruise on his face by tomorrow.

Whatever Rose had said to William, she had given him completely the wrong idea, and once William made up his mind to something, there was no shifting him. He was right about one thing, though: he was incapable, and everyone knew it. He saw it in Maria's disdainful looks, heard it from Peter and felt humiliated every time Simon took charge.

But he wasn't interested in Rose in that way. She was a good worker and he relied on her; nothing more. He'd never thought much about lasses, although he would never tell William that. Did not thinking about them make him a boy, as William had said?

He stroked his chin. Still no sign of hair. William was growing a beard, and he was broad and muscular. He felt his arms: thin and weak like a maid's. Maybe there was something wrong with him.

The skylarks had vanished. Two crows were mobbing a buzzard, driving it away.

He knew exactly how it felt.

The next day, Thomas stayed in the shadows at the side of the house and watched as Simon led his horse from the stable, threw a hide bag onto the back of the saddle and tied it tight. A leather flagon swung from his belt as he pulled a large sleeveless surcoat over his tunic and gathered the folds with a wide leather belt that concealed his knife and purse.

William brought his pony alongside. Thomas had thought about offering his horse but then thought better of it. William would only say it wasn't for the likes of him.

Janet bustled out of the smithy and Peter leaned over the door. Annie, Maria and Eleanor stood on the threshold of the house. Rose, he noticed, stayed behind the half-opened door. She'd been very quiet since he'd told her what William had said. It looked like she was hiding. They had that much in common, at any rate.

'Thomas!' Simon shouted across the yard. 'We're leaving!'

He cringed. The last thing he wanted to do was to see them off, but it would look odd if he didn't. Jogging to join them, he pretended to be out of breath and bent his head between his knees.

'Sorry, I was checking the ewes in the top field. Praise God, I didn't miss you.' He wiped his dry brow.

'While we're gone, there are the fields to plough, harrow and seed,' Simon said, settling himself in the saddle. 'If you've time, there are drainage leates to dig through the reed marshes – Rose knows – and keep an eye on the ewes. Some still need lambing.'

'Yes, I know. When do you expect to be back?'

'There's no knowing. Haymaking time, maybe, but it all depends on what we find.'

'And when we get back, I'll finish the cottage and Rose and I can get wed.' William looked directly at him. 'Remember what I said. I meant every word.'

He didn't doubt that for a moment.

'Don't forget to go to Holdesworthe to see if the market's trading again,' Simon added. 'We need grain and seed.'

He nodded. Going to the market was something he thought he could handle. 'I'll do that.'

Simon nodded back and rode out of the yard, a stony-faced William following. One by one, the others drifted away until he was alone.

He looked up at the sky. The sun was nearing the first quarter. By the time Eleanor rang the bell, Simon and William would be on High Drovers Road heading north.

He glanced around. Everyone was busy with their work. Good. He had a plan of his own and not much time to do it.

CHAPTER 18

A log slipped into the glowing embers of the hearth, sending a small puff of grey ash onto the floor.

Thomas picked up his bag, took a last look around the room and closed the door behind him.

He'd tried his best to be a lord, and he'd failed. He was tired of trying to be someone he wasn't. The only thing he seemed to have got right were the bees, and that had been forgotten during the dark months. He couldn't look after his people. It was time to look after himself.

There were no doubts, no *what ifs*; just a growing excitement that came from knowing his troubles were finally over. He hadn't felt this happy since Brother Luke had praised him for his Greek pronunciation. That had been exactly a week before the same Brother had sent him home and bolted the garden door on him.

It would be good to see them all again. Brother Luke with his straight, no-nonsense approach. Brother Mark, with his dry wit that had always seemed at odds with his sacred calling and Brother Leviticus, with his keen, inquiring mind that seemed to penetrate so much more of the world than Thomas thought he would ever understand if he lived a hundred years.

He hurried across the yard to the stables, then slowed to a stop as a cold sensation crept up the back of his neck.

Someone was watching him. He was certain of it. Slowly, he turned and glimpsed a fleeting shadow darting behind the back wall. He waited, but the figure didn't reappear.

Had he imagined it? He could have sworn there was someone there. If there was, the only place they could hide was in Annie's linhay. It couldn't be one of his people; they wouldn't hide from him. Investigating was out of the question; whoever it was might be desperate, or they may have lost their wits or be bigger than him. Worst of all, they may have the Pestilence.

He was torn. He needed to get on his way but if they did have the Pestilence, he should do something.

With a wistful glance at the stables, he drew his knife and crept over to where he'd seen the shadow. When he reached the corner where the wall abutted the linhay, he flattened himself against the stones and listened, his heart pounding in his chest and throat.

He could hear nothing but his own breathing. Gripping his knife, he inched forward and peered around.

'God, you made me jump! What are you doing skulking around corners and scaring folks out of their wits?'

He leapt back, his heart jumping into his throat. 'Annie!'

'Yes, of course. Who did you expect? And put that knife away.'

'I thought I saw someone back here.'

'Me, who else would be here?'

He felt rather foolish but the dark figure he'd seen had looked more like a man than a maid.

'I'm sorry, Annie. I thought…' What? That a mysterious dark figure was sneaking around and watching him from the shadows? The idea seemed ridiculous now.

'Well, no harm done,' she conceded. 'And I've been wanting to speak to you.'

'Can it wait? I'm going to saddle Henry.'

'We can talk as you do that.'

Damn. He wanted to get on his way without anyone knowing.

'What do you want to talk about?' He sauntered into the tack room and picked up Henry's saddle. 'It's not like you to be in here. You don't like horses,' he said walking to Henry's stable.

Putting the saddle on Henry's back he reached underneath for the leather girth. He might still be able to get away, if Annie didn't take too long.

'Horses make me sneeze, but I want a word with you about the dye shed. I need poles to make drying rails and barrels for soaking and mixing, and I've a list of other items that's as long as my arm. I know I won't be making dye for a while, since the madder has to grow first, but as Ellyn always said, no harm in being prepared.'

'Poles are easy enough. There's a stack of coppiced hazel in the barn that you can use. I don't know about the barrels, ask Simon.' Thomas checked his stirrup leathers. The one on the left had some loose stitching, but it didn't look too bad. Pray God it would hold until he reached the monastery.

Annie nodded. 'I'll speak to him when he gets back. Where are you going?'

'Oh, um, just checking the ewes.'

'At this time?'

'Yes, I need to look for any newborn lambs. Don't want the fox getting them. I thought I'd ride. Henry's been getting fat on the spring grass; he could do with the exercise.' He kept his back turned and began tying the large leather bag to the back of his saddle.

'That's a big pack for a ride to check ewes.'

Annie never missed a thing. He should have waited until she'd gone. 'I thought I'd make a day of it.'

She sighed. 'Thomas, I've known you since you were a baby. You couldn't fool me as a child, so don't start thinking you can do it now. What are you really up to?'

She wouldn't leave until she got the truth. He gritted his teeth, summoning his courage, and turned to face her. 'If you must know, I'm going back to the monastery where I belong.'

'And what about us?' she said, her eyes boring into him.

'You don't need me. Will was right. I am an incapable and useless lord.'

'No, you're not and I'm sure he didn't mean it. I know you've got a lot on your young shoulders, but there's no need to leave. You'll find a way.'

How many times had he heard that? 'No, I won't. I'm not a lord, Annie; I'm a scholar. That's the life I know and it's what I'm good at. I want to go to the University of Oxford and learn to be a physician.'

She considered that for a moment, her gaze holding him in such a way that he couldn't have looked away if he'd tried. 'We can't always do what we want. If your brother Richard—' something seemed to flicker in her grey eyes— 'had lived, he'd be the lord instead of you. If the Pestilence hadn't come, your Mama would be running the estate and none of us would be here. But that wasn't God's plan. It's hard for all of us, but we must make the best of it. You included.'

Thomas stared at his feet. He felt like he was back in the passageway of Court Barton, waiting with Annie in front of the imposing oak doors that led to the hall, listening to one of his parents' furious arguments. He was standing just as he had been then, his head down, his hair flopping over his face and scratching his boot in the dirt as his father denounced him as useless and a weakling.

Annie had tried to persuade him to stay then, but he'd turned and run away. Now he was grown and was running again.

'I miss her too, you know,' she said, stepping closer.

'I know.'

'Your Mama wouldn't want you to go. She'd want you to stay and be strong—'

He glared at her. 'You don't know what she'd want!'

Annie's grey eyes darkened to iron. 'Oh yes I do, Thomas de Chiddleigh! I knew your Mama better than you'll ever know. She wanted you to be a good and better lord than your—' She broke off abruptly.

'Than Papa,' he finished lamely. 'I told you: I've tried and I'm no good.'

'Running away isn't the answer. You have to face what God wants you to do.'

'Brother Leviticus says that life is more about science and the stars than God.'

'Does he?' Annie raised her eyebrows. 'I'm surprised at that, him being a monk and all.'

Thomas tried and failed to smile. 'They're not all prayers and chants, you know.'

'Well, I'm not learned, and I don't know about what your Brother Lavi-Lavit—'

'Leviticus,' he corrected her.

'—what your Brother Leviticus says, but if there's one thing I do know, it's that your Mama wouldn't have run away.'

God's teeth, why did she have to come and start meddling? He wasn't as strong as Mama, and he'd felt so certain of his path until she interfered. 'She was never in my position.'

Annie snorted. 'Oh yes she was. When your Papa became a drunken sot – and yes, we all knew it – your Mama could have run home to her family, but she didn't. As the Lady of the Manor, she had obligations to her people. She faced her problems squarely, and you must do the same.'

'How did you know her so well?'

Annie sighed, leaning against the stable wall. 'We were both fifteen summers when we met. Your Mama was very much the new Lady of the Manor; innocent, lonely and unsure of her position. A bit like you are now.' She smiled. He didn't return it and she continued. 'I was a kitchen maid, and we secretly became friends.'

'If you were friends for so long, you must know what she meant when she asked for my forgiveness.'

'I told you I don't.'

Was it the harsh voice or the defiance in those eyes? Either way, he was certain that Annie was lying.

'Why won't you tell me?' He reached for the bridle hanging on the iron hook by the door.

'Because I truly don't know.' Emphasising each word, Annie sounded as she did when he was little and scolded him for some misdemeanour. 'But if there's one thing I do know, it's that your Mama was very proud of you, and she'd want you to stay and be the lord. It'll work out, you'll see.'

Her voice was overly bright, as though she was kissing his grazed knee better and telling him that everything would be alright. Well, he didn't have a grazed knee and nothing was alright anymore. It hadn't been since the day he'd brought them all here.

'I've told you, Annie; I keep getting it wrong. I'm no good with people, and I don't like being in charge. If Mama was here, then maybe I could have coped, but she isn't and I can't do this on my own.' He turned away to hide the tears filling his eyes and threw the reins over Henry's neck.

Annie gripped his arm and pulled him around. 'You're not on your own. You've got me and Simon and the others. Think how we all worked together to make this place fit to live in. That was your idea, and now you've got to keep everyone together to make it last.'

'No.' He shrugged her off. 'I know you mean well, but my mind's made up. Isn't it better for me to be an absent lord and leave building the estate to those who are capable of it? Better to be a successful scholar than a failed lord.' He bit his cheek to stop the tears from falling.

Annie grabbed his shoulders and shook him. 'Now you listen to me, Thomas de Chiddleigh. Your people are relying on you. Do you think you're the only one to have hard times in life? God knows, I've a had a few. Don't stand there with your head bowed feeling sorry for yourself. Lift that Chiddleigh chin and show them what you're made of.'

He could feel her nails digging into his skin through his good linen clothes and feel her hot breath on his face. He didn't want to be a coward but he wasn't sure he could be a hero either.

'I'm sorry.' He untied his horse and turned to lead him out.

Annie grabbed the reins. 'Wait! Think how you'll feel when you come back, and you will have to come back for taxes and money and things. What will your people think of you? How will you feel having to face them knowing you ran out and left them on their own?'

'They'll probably be glad.' He snatched the reins out of her hand.

'Do you want them to think you weak?'

That was a cruel blow. She knew how much shame he felt over Papa's brutal dismissal of him. He wouldn't be weak in this, his nails dug into the palms of his hands. He needed to leave. He would leave. Mama would understand.

'Come on, Henry.' He started to lead his horse outside, but Annie blocked his way.

'Thomas, the good Lord saw fit to take your Mama. We can't change that. And there will be times when you hurt, and times when you'll be angry – as I am – but running away won't help.'

'I'm not running away!' As he said it, a tiny part of him whispered that yes, that was exactly what he was doing.

Annie didn't move. 'At least wait until Simon returns. He's your bailiff, and he was good to you when you were a boy. You owe him that.'

Simon had been like a brother to him. He didn't know what he would have done if he hadn't been there letting him ride the estate with him and talking to him when his Papa never did. He lowered his eyes and swallowed. God help him, he could feel his determination slipping away.

Annie put a gentle hand on his arm. 'You say you want to study? Well, think; if you stay here long enough to get this place up and running as a proper estate, the coins will flood into your coffer chest. Then you can go to Oxford and pay reeves to help Simon. There's many a lord who lives away from his manor, you were right about that.'

'I know, but—'

'And that dream is what will keep you going, so that when the day comes, you can leave with your head held high as a lord having done his duty, and not as a coward running away.'

He raised his eyes to meet hers. She relaxed her grip and stepped aside. 'Yes, well, I've said my piece. It's up to you now.' She tightened her brown woollen shawl and hitched her basket onto her hip. 'I've herbs to pick before it gets too light. They lose their potency in the sunlight. I'll see you later.'

He watched her go in a shimmering mist of held tears. He didn't want to be a coward, but he wasn't sure if he could be a hero either. If he stayed, his plan hadn't failed, it had just been delayed.

A small delay. That's all it was. He lifted his chin. He was a Chiddleigh and he'd damned well show it.

CHAPTER 19

It was light and the room was silent. He must have slept the entire night. Gingerly, Thomas turned his head and regretted it at once. His neck was stiff, and his skull felt like it had been stuffed full of wool. He lay there, lacking both the power and inclination to move.

It had been two days since his conversation with Annie. Two never ending days of ploughing, which had been his not-so-bright idea.

He had cursed under his breath and gritted his teeth when the plough lurched sideways, he'd ignored every jar in his bones when the wooden blade hit a stone, and he'd hidden his blisters when he handed over the mitts to Rose for her turn. He'd even kept pace with the goaders leading the ox, even though his calf muscles had cramped into an iron ball and were screaming at him to stop.

But he hadn't stopped. He'd kept going. He'd shown them.

Somehow, he summoned up the strength to look around the room. The mattresses were empty. Upturned bowls on the shelf dripped water onto the floor, and fresh sticks smouldered on the fire. They'd gone without him.

Part of him wished they'd woken him, or that he'd woken up himself – sleeping in hardly fitted the image of a strong leader – but another, much larger part was secretly glad they hadn't. He yawned. He could sleep for a hundred days. He tried moving his legs, but they were as stiff as boards and the attempt was enough to make him groan. The thought of another day's ploughing was enough to make him want to snuggle back down and let them get on with it, but he could imagine Peter's jibes if he did.

He was a Chiddleigh, he reminded himself and took a long, deep breath and forced himself to rise and dress. What he needed was a wash to wake himself up. He went to the pail and splashed his face with cold water. The water hit his hands like a thousand needles and he yelped and squeezed his hands tight under his armpits. When the pain had settled to a steady throb, he risked opening his fingers to look.

Bloody red blisters covered his palms, making them look like slabs of raw meat. There was no way he'd be able to hold the plough with those.

He couldn't honestly say he was sorry, but he wasn't going to admit he wasn't fit to work either. They would think him soft – Peter would probably say so to his face – and he would lose the respect he was working so hard for. What he needed was a plausible reason to get out of ploughing, one that wouldn't reveal his feebleness.

Simon had told him to go to Holdesworthe for grain, and today was market day. He didn't relish the thought of the six-mile journey, but it was better than looking a fool in front of the others.

Forcing his hands to work, he harnessed the old carthorse, Ted, to the wagon and turned onto the track.

The early morning light shone low over the dew-drenched field, covering the grass with thousands of sparkling jewels. On either side of him, curtains of spiders' webs glittered with dewdrops on the hedges. On any other day, he would have stopped for a while to admire God's work, but today, he wasn't feeling his best.

Looking over the hedge, he saw that the others were already busy ploughing. Rose was leading the ox with one goad line, and Annie was keeping pace with the other. Rose wasn't what anyone would call comely with her tangle of curls and freckles, and she was as strong as any lad and knew her own mind. Maybe that was why William was so besotted. Certainly she was unlike any maid Thomas had ever known, although his experience in such matters was somewhat limited.

Peter deftly turned the plough close to the hedge to begin the next row. He made it look easy. Thomas wagered he didn't have blisters.

'Where are you going?' Rose called over her shoulder.

'To Holdesworthe for seed grain,' he called back.

'Wait! I'll come with you.' Rose dropped the line and hurried towards him.

William's warning echoed in Thomas's head, and he swallowed. 'There's no need. It would be better for you to stay here and plough.'

Rose stood with one foot on the step of the cart, her hands already gripping the side as she looked at him with a clear challenge in her eyes. 'Do you know good grain from bad? Wheat from oats? Which seeds are for sowing and which are for grinding?' she challenged.

He shrugged. He'd assumed grain was just grain.

'I thought not,' she said pushing her coif back off her eyes. 'Well, I'm a miller's daughter and I do. I also know the trickster merchants who weight the sacks with stones or fill them with rotten grain with just a sprinkling of fresh on top to fool you. Make room.'

'It might be a good idea to have Rose with you,' Annie interjected.

There she went, interfering again. It was all her fault that he was here and not in the monastery where he belonged. He stared daggers at her.

'I can decide for myself.'

'Yes, of course.' Annie lowered her head submissively and drew back a step or two.

Before he could stop her, Rose had climbed the steps of the cart and was settled on the bench beside him. 'Good, that's decided then.' She took hold of the reins. 'I'll drive. If we meet trouble, you've got the better knife.'

He would have preferred to go on his own, but she knew about grain, and he couldn't afford to get it wrong. He looked at Peter. 'Will you manage on your own?'

'Happen we'll 'ave to,' said Peter. 'El, take the line with Annie and let's keep moving or we'll be 'ere 'til Michaelmas.'

Rose slapped the reins and the cart lurched forward. The regular click of the solid cartwheels and the steady clomp of Ted's hooves soon had Thomas feeling drowsy. Before they reached the end of the valley, his chin fell to his chest.

The wagon swayed, jolting him awake. They were on High Drovers Road. All signs of the valley were far behind them, and the square grey tower of Holdesworthe church was visible through the trees a few miles ahead.

He sat up and wiped the sleep from his eyes. There was something he had to say to Rose. 'Will mustn't get to hear of us going to the market on our own,' he said. 'He wouldn't like it.'

Rose gave him a sideways glance. 'Even Will could see the sense, me being a miller's lass and you knowing nothing about grain.'

'I'm not so sure. You didn't see the way he pinned me against the wall. I thought he was going to hit me.'

'He's got a temper on him, I'll give you that. Never used to have. It was the war that changed him. He won't speak about it; I've tried. Get up, Ted!' She slapped the reins. 'Poor old horse should be out to grass.'

Maybe if he pleaded William's case, it wouldn't matter that he and Rose had gone off together. 'Will's worked hard on the cottage,' he said. 'He's serious. When he returns, he means for the two of you to wed.'

'I know, but I won't do it.'

'Why not? He's a good lad and there's no one else, unless Jarin wants you. I mean, all lasses get married, look after their man and have children. It's the way of things.'

Rose shot him a reproachful look. 'I want to be me, not William's wife or John's mother. And as I said, Will's changed and—oh, you're a lad, you wouldn't understand.'

That was true. Everyone knew that lasses had less sense than lads due to their smaller heads, and as Simon had once said, there was no understanding them. He certainly didn't.

'When Will's back, I'm keeping my distance,' he said. 'You'll have to sort it out between you; I'm not getting involved.'

'Don't worry, I'll tell him again. If that doesn't work, I'll find another way.'

They had reached the outskirts of Holdesworthe and were passing a straggle of cruck houses, their thin reed thatch showing the ravages of winter storms. A door or two gaped open, but there was no sign of women and no children playing outside or fowl pecking the dirt.

It reminded him of Ashetyne, sending a chill down his back. 'Do you think the whole town is deserted?' he whispered, as if respecting unknown souls.

Rose shrugged. 'We'll soon find out.'

That was a hard response for a lass. Did she have no soul at all?

They turned right, passing a row of narrow merchants' houses squeezed tightly together with their upper stories jutting out and casting dark shadows over the lane. There was little sewage or rubbish in the street, which was odd. He shivered as an eerie silence enveloped them.

The sound of the wheels seemed to grow louder with every turn, echoing off the buildings. He could feel hidden eyes watching them from behind barred shutters, and put a hand on his knife. Pray God he wouldn't need it.

The larger houses gave way to poorer single-storey cob cottages as they neared the heart of town, passing the empty pillory on their left. A woman stood in a doorway, watching them pass with a grim stare. Ahead of them, an old man bent over a handcart and next to him, a stout woman dragged a reluctant goat behind her. There were still some folks then.

'Looks like there is a market,' he said.

'I hope so, but the place is dead. Where're all the folks and rotting shit in the middens? I can't smell a thing.' Rose steered Ted past a couple of lads rolling a barrel down the middle of the lane. 'Shift yourselves, you lubbers! Ted's got big feet, and he's not fussy where he puts them!'

Thomas smiled weakly, she even cursed like a lad. Rose kept the horse moving, forcing the lads into a ditch at the side, clutching their barrel. He pretended not to hear their reply.

'Can't be doing with it,' she muttered.

The lane ended in the town square where a few sellers had their goods laid out on cloths or displayed on the back of a cart. Leather goods, ironware, last season's wrinkled fruit; nothing of much interest that he could see.

'I'll stop us in the corner,' said Rose turning the wagon.

His legs were stiffer than ever, and he struggled off his seat, hoping Rose wouldn't notice. 'I've never seen a market so quiet. Even the shops around the square are shuttered. Where are the jugglers? The dice tables and the dogfighting pit? Usually, you can't move for folks pushing and shoving.'

'All in the pits themselves, I shouldn't wonder.'

He winced and wondered if Rose would be so coarse if she'd heard Simon's tale of Exeter where men swathed in cloths dug pits for hundreds of bodies, all ravaged by rats and flies.

Rose tied Ted to a rail. 'I'm off to look for grain merchants. Coming?'

He had no intention of showing his ignorance to the merchants. Haggling with them was her business, not his. 'I'll catch you up.'

Instead, he decided, he'd take his time and wander around. Drifting past the sellers, he saw people – many barefoot – slouched with sagging shoulders, their faces grey, their clothes threadbare. The stink from them made him step back and put an arm across his nose. Judging by their language, a lot of them weren't local. Probably wanderers having fled their homes from the Pestilence and looking for somewhere to settle.

The place didn't feel right. He liked markets with music and street entertainers, and pedlars' voices shouting their wares amidst the hustle and bustle of livestock and crowds. Market day was a merry time when folks gathered, caught up on gossip, got drunk and enjoyed themselves. This was too quiet, and people shrank away, wary of others.

His stomach growled. He hadn't seen any food sellers with trays strung around their necks or heard the cry of *Hot peascods!*, his favourite. There wasn't even a pie-man, although he was never sure what went into the pies. A fellow scholar once told him it was rats. He may have been jesting, but Thomas had never bought another pie after that.

Disappointed, he returned to the wagon. Only too glad to sit down, he reached for his flagon. Rose would be a long time yet, and he was still exhausted from the ploughing he'd done yesterday and the day before. How peasants toiled in the fields from dawn to dusk, day after day, was beyond him. He leaned back, enjoying the warm sun bathing his face, and closed his eyes.

Someone kicked his foot. 'Take this.'

He woke with a start, seeing Rose's outstretched hand looming over him. 'What?'

'I found us a nice cock-hen and some geese. God's teeth, I had to haggle hard, but I got a good price in the end. Get your purse out.'

He blinked at the mean-looking cockerel that was eyeing him through the bars of a willow cage. 'Why a cock-hen?'

Rose raised her eyebrows. 'You remember what Janet said: we'll be needing more fowl. We're not getting enough eggs.'

'Alright, but why geese as well?' He thought of the few meagre coins in his purse. They wouldn't last long at this rate.

Rose looked at him as though he was a numbskull. 'Why do you think? Eggs, meat, fat and feathers, and if a fox comes sniffing around, the gander will soon let us know.'

'Oh, I see. Good idea. Did you remember the grain as well?'

'Of course I did. Wheat, oats and barley; the lad's bringing the sacks over. Bargaining for that was easy; folks are desperate to sell.'

The lad arrived, loaded the sacks onto the wagon and walked away, clinking the silver pennies from Thomas in his hand.

Thomas looked at the few coins left in the bottom of his leather purse. They wouldn't get him very far to Oxford. He sighed, drew the string of the purse and tied it back onto his belt.

'Let's go home,' he said with a yawn. 'You drive.'

He slept for most of the journey and awoke to low rays from the sun blinding him as Rose turned the wagon into the valley. They were nearly home.

'Have a nice rest, did you?' said Rose with a superior smile. The cart jolted and she winced. 'Muxy ruts! I'm surprised the left wheel's still attached.'

Thomas cursed himself and rubbed his eyes. 'I'm sorry.'

'No need to be. Ploughing's hard work. I was impressed by the way you kept going, but I'll wager those blisters hurt.' She grinned sideways at him.

He slid his hands under his tunic.

'Oh, you thought I didn't notice? We all get blisters the first time. I still remember mine; my hands were bleeding and felt like fire. They took a week to heal,' she added proudly.

A week? He couldn't wait that long to pick up a quill! He had work to do on his charts.

'I've enjoyed our day out together,' she added, smiling at him.

He didn't see it as a *day out together*. That sounded far too cosy. 'We only went to the market. You make it sound like we're friends or something.'

'Don't look so horrified; I didn't mean it like that. But we have got a lot in common; losing our mothers and all. Anyway, you're a lord and I'm a miller's lass.' She laughed, but there was something behind her laughter that made him feel uncomfortable. Next time, no matter what, he would go on his own.

The wagon rattled down the slope to the open valley. The last time he'd been here was when they'd arrived nine months ago. So much had happened since then that it felt more like a lifetime.

As they approached Gee's cottage, he saw the old man sitting on the wayside, whittling a piece of chestnut wood.

'I see the ploughing's started,' Gee said, not looking up. 'Jarin can steer a plough.'

Jarin! Thomas could have kicked himself. He should have thought of Jarin. 'Rose, stop the wagon.'

'The going rate is four pennies a day.' Gee continued his whittling.

'How much?' Rose demanded. 'A master craftsman only gets six pennies.'

For once, he was glad she'd butted in. He had no idea how much peasants earned, and added that to his list of things to find out. He hadn't given so much as a thought to wages.

Gee stopped his knife mid-stroke and raised his head. 'Times are changing. Craftsmen are asking a shilling and getting it.' He tapped the side of his nose with a finger. 'No workers, see? They're all travelling or dead. The nobles can't get men to work their lands. Desperate, they are. Some have sold acres or left. The peasants have the say now.' He smiled the smile of an avenged victim. 'You wait 'til harvest, you'll see. Be no fields to reap and no corn to buy, and that means those who have it will get top money. You could be one of them, my lord, but seems to me that you need all the help you can get.' He returned to his whittling.

Thomas knew he needed help, but peasants setting the rates? Whoever heard of such a thing? He couldn't pay half what Gee was asking. God's bones, he couldn't pay anything at all at the moment.

But if Gee was right, and if Simon found peasants to join them, he'd have men to plough, sow and reap a good harvest. He'd be one of the few getting top money.

'I can't pay you until after harvest on Michaelmas Day.'

Gee's voice turned hard. 'Agreed. But mark my words, ways are changing. I've seen peasants take over places like this. You lords won't be having it your own way for much longer. And don't expect no dues come Michaelmas Day, not unless you pay us first.'

'That's for Lord Thomas to decide,' said Rose.

'Everything will depend on the harvest,' said Thomas.

'And we'll be needing a few acres for grazings and the plough, my lord,' Gee added.

For an old man, he was sharp. They'd be demanding the freedom to own their homes and the right to leave their lord's lands next. 'I'll decide that later, when my bailiff returns.'

Gee rubbed his chin and drew a long breath through his teeth. 'That'll do for now. Jarin will be ready to plough at dawn, my lord.'

Thomas thought he'd handled it rather well, but as they drove away, uncertainty began to slither into his mind. Times were changing, and it was hard enough to be a lord when the nobles ruled. What if Gee was right and the peasants demanded more freedom? What would he do then?

He shook his head. He was worrying over nothing. Peasants telling their betters how to rule them; the very notion made him smile. Oh, certainly things were different now, but society would go back to the way it should be as soon as the Pestilence was over. Gee's ridiculous prophecy could never come true.

Could it?

CHAPTER 20

June 1349

Rose stopped the drop spindle. She'd been spinning all morning and her wool basket was almost empty. They were running low on the fleece they'd brought with them, but they'd be shearing again come July. She must remind Peter to sharpen the shears, and they'd need looms for the women to weave cloth during the dark months while the men worked on the hedges and ditches.

It was nearly midsummer and time for haymaking, and the dark months would be upon them again before they knew. Worse; William had said he'd be back at around this time. Pray God he'd changed his mind about marrying her. Folks believed him when he said there was an arrangement, and she'd need a very good reason to get out of that. Saying that he had no future because he was a cripple and not good enough for her would destroy him, and much as she'd come to dread being in his presence, she didn't want to do that. But if she couldn't think of another way, then her dream of being free would be nothing more than that: just a dream.

Shoving the wool back into the basket, she turned her thoughts to the travellers. Gee was a nasty old man, but she liked Jarin. He was different to his Pa with his constant smile and cheerful ways. He was a good worker too and could turn his hand to anything. Peter had been wary of him at first, but only the other day he'd told her that having Jarin in the forge was the best idea he'd ever had.

She wasn't entirely sure if it had been his idea, but that was Peter for you. When Jarin wasn't helping in the forge, he was building a wattle and stone cottage for him and Gee to live in. She'd seen him taking the best stones from the ancients' circles to do it as well. William wouldn't be happy about that. He'd have to search further afield for stones for his cottage. And it would be his cottage, since she had no intention of living in it.

Rose put the basket of fleece on the shelf, she'd card it later. At the table, Thomas was bent over his charts and in a world of his own, and she sighed. She'd dared to hope that they were becoming friends, but he'd killed that thought on the way back from the market.

She hadn't given up on the idea, though. After all, being the lord must be lonely, much like she was. Thomas could use a friend, and he was fair to look at...if a bit boyish.

She ambled over to the table. 'I'm glad the fields are finally finished and the grains scattered. What're you doing?'

'Trying to work out how I got it wrong. When we arrived last August, I checked the movements of the stars on the charts. I was sure we would be going home in the spring, but we didn't, and I can't see where I missed it. The charts also guide me to make decisions and haymaking is coming soon.' Thomas ran a frustrated hand through his hair and pushed the chart away.

'Maybe the chart was wrong,' Rose ventured.

'The charts are never wrong. If only Brother Leviticus was here to show me.'

What strange names those monks had. She supposed it came of being learned. 'Have you ever thought of going back to see him?'

Thomas flushed and rolled the chart up quickly. 'Of course not! Why do you say that?'

'Seems to me you're happier staring at them charts than pushing a plough.'

'I won't always be pushing a plough. Simon's bringing more men and they'll do the work.' He tied the green ribbon around the charts with meticulous care and tucked them in the corner of the oak chest that he kept beside his mattress.

'If we can make that scarlet cloth, you'll be wealthy and the lord of a grand estate. You'll need reeves to manage things for you and you'll be looking for a high-born wife. Or are you promised?'

'Not that Mama ever said.'

'I don't suppose you want a wife now. I mean, wives cost money and there's so much to do here. What help would a noble lady be? She'd have nothing to do but sit around and look pretty.' She glanced around. 'And it's not as if you could entertain guests, since you haven't got a hall.'

'I don't know anyone to invite. Even if I did, I haven't the money for banquets. Why the sudden interest?'

'Oh, nothing; just curious. What's in there?' Rose peered over his shoulder at a box about a foot square made of dark wood and intricately carved with oak leaves and acorns with a gold clasp on the front. She reached out, intending to run a hand over the polished wood.

'Don't touch that! It's precious.' Thomas caressed the lid. 'It's a chess set Mama gave me for my tenth birth date.' He hesitated. 'Would you like to see it?'

'I'd love to.' She had heard of the nobles' game of chess but had never seen it. She pulled up a stool and watched him lovingly take out each carved piece and place them on a square wooden board. 'They look like people. That one's got a crown, like Edward III, and she must be Queen Philippa. Can I hold her?'

'If you're careful. The dark ones are carved from oak and the light ones from beech wood. And you're right; that's the king, and the one you're holding is the queen.'

Rose turned the delicate-looking piece over in her hand. Whoever made it had taken a lot of trouble to cut small stars into the folds of the dress and put tiny red jewels in the crown. 'It's beautiful. She's even got a face.'

'This one's the bishop. The knight stands next to him here and —'

'Don't tell me; the castle! It's the royal court living in their castle!' She laughed delightedly. 'What do you do with it?'

'It's a game for two, but I've no one to play with, so I play on my own.'

Was that a hint? 'I could play if you teach me.'

'Are you sure? It's quite complicated, each piece can only move in a certain way and you have to think ahead.'

Rose nodded. 'How do the pieces move?'

'Take the bishop – he can go diagonally but only two squares at a time, like this. The pawns that guard the front can only move one square forward at a time. If I move a piece and it lands on your piece, I take it off the board.'

'So how do I know when I've won?'

'Like in a real royal court, each piece is guarding the king. You win when the king can't move without being taken. That's called checkmate. The other way to win is if you capture all the pieces except for the king, but that rarely happens. If you want to surrender, you tip the king over.'

Rose blinked, her head spinning a little from Thomas's enthusiastic explanation. This chess sounded a bit dull compared to her favourite games of marbles and knucklebones. But maybe learning to play would help her get closer to him, and it would also be one in the eye for that insufferable vixen, Maria.

She shifted her stool closer and smiled. 'It sounds wonderful. Please teach me.'

'Really?' Thomas's eyes lit with excitement. 'Alright. Well, the king…'

He described each piece and its moves in intricate detail, and by the time they started the game, she could hardly remember what went where or why.

'It's a wonderful game, and the more you play, the better you'll be, and that's when it gets really exciting.' He rubbed his hands together.

Rose stifled a yawn, picked up a pawn and noticed Thomas's frown of disapproval but moved it anyway. She hadn't a clue what she was doing, and when was it going to end?

'This is where you're skulking. Shut the door, El.' Maria put a bowl of milk on the trestle. 'What are you doing, Rose? Chess is a noble's game, not for the likes of you.'

'Who are you to say who can and can't play?' She picked up a piece at random, hoping it was the bishop; she could remember how that one moved.

'Rose wanted to learn, and I've no one to play with.' Thomas frowned again. 'I wouldn't put the bishop there if I were you. If you do, I'll take it with my knight. See?'

She didn't see at all, but replaced the bishop and picked up a castle instead.

'You'd do better teaching me—' said Maria.

'You, such a fine lady and don't know how to play? I am surprised.' Rose put the castle firmly on the board as though she knew what she was doing.

'That's a good move. I didn't see that coming.' Thomas rubbed his chin. 'You're learning quickly.'

She could have kissed Thomas for that, although she had no idea what was so good about her move. 'It's not that difficult.' Rose looked smugly at Maria. 'I wager even you could learn.'

'I could have. I just wasn't interested, that's all. While you've been idling in here, El and I have milked the ewes. Though I only got a few drops from the one with twins, and she's usually got plenty to spare.'

'The lambs will have been tugging at her all day and sucked her dry, that's why. And we're not idling. Thomas is learning me to play chess, and I was up and doing long before you were awake.'

'Aren't you the good one? And it's teaching, not *learning*. Annie's planted her madder and is now planting the beans on her own,' said Maria.

'I've finished m-making the skeps you wanted, T-Thomas. Why do you want them?' Eleanor put down her bowl, a worried frown creasing her forehead. 'Aren't the bees happy in the ones I m-made?'

'I'm sure they're very happy, but when there are too many bees, they make another queen and some of them leave with her to find a new home,' Thomas explained. 'That's called swarming, and they'll be doing it soon. I'm going to put the new queen and her bees in the new skep before they fly off and we lose them.'

'So we'll have m-more bees making m-more honey.' Eleanor's face lit up at the prospect. 'I like honey!'

'So do I.' Thomas stood up. 'I'd better go and check them. I could do with some help,' he added.

Rose shook her head. When it came to bees, Thomas was on his own. She remembered the first time she'd been stung. She'd been no more than four summers, playing indoors at being lady in her castle. Ma's best earthenware jug had been on the shelf, and she had thought it just the thing for her high table. Ma was out, and she'd had to stand on tiptoe to reach it. As soon as she'd grabbed the handle, she felt a pain like a thousand knives and dropped the jug, which smashed into tiny fragments at her feet.

She'd tried to scream but it came out as a choke. She couldn't breathe and remembered being scared about what Ma would say when she saw the jug. Her Ma had come running in, taken one look at her and gone white, screaming for Rose's father.

There had been a lot of commotion after that. Her Ma had clutched her and was crying, Pa had shouted for a lad to fetch Ellyn-healer, and all the time she had been swelling like a stuffed sow and struggling to breathe.

Ellyn had arrived and given her some sour tonic, which she could hardly drink because her throat was so swollen. Whatever it was, it had worked, because she had been able to breathe again shortly after taking it. Ellyn had said it was probably a bee sting and she was to keep away from bees in future. She'd been scared of them ever since.

'I'd better help Annie,' She glared at Maria and reached for a flagon of cider. 'I can't have folks saying I'm idle, can I?'

'We'll have another game later,' said Thomas, packing his pieces back into their box.

She smiled sweetly at him, pleasantly conscious of Maria fuming in the background. 'Yes, I'd like that.'

'Thomas, come here.' Maria beckoned him over and lowered her voice. 'I overheard something that you might like to know.'

Rose busied herself readjusting her coif, straining to hear.

'As I was crossing the yard to the field, I saw Annie talking to Peter. I couldn't hear Annie but Peter said *Say nothing and keep your lips sealed, I'm telling ye. The last thing we want is for anyone to know about that.*'

'And?' said Thomas.

'That's it, they saw me and El, and went inside the forge.'

Thomas sighed. 'God's teeth, Maria, they could have been talking about anything. Why should I be interested?'

Maria lowered her voice until Rose could barely hear her. 'Because, my dear brother, you are the lord, and lords should know what's going on. There might be a plot to overthrow you.'

'Oh, don't be ridiculous. Lords can't be overthrown. Annie was probably talking about William and his marrying Rose or something.' Thomas took his gauntlets and turned to walk away.

Maria shrugged. 'Well, it sounded odd to me. I won't bother to tell you next time.'

Rose inched up the door latch, hoping to leave unnoticed, but the latch gave her away with a loud clunk. Maria jumped and stared at her.

'I thought you'd gone. What are you still doing here, listening to your betters' conversations?'

'I wasn't,' Rose picked up the flagon and opened the door. Stepping outside, her mind was racing. It didn't sound like Annie had been talking about William; there were no dark secrets there that she was aware of. Lady

Joan, perhaps? But then, what would Peter know about her? As far as she could tell, he and Lady Joan had never interacted much.

Any thoughts she might have had about learning more flew out of her head when she turned the corner of the house to the vegetable area. Gee was leaning on the fence, talking to Annie on the other side and by the looks on their faces, they weren't having an idle chat.

'I know what's best for my boy—' Gee was wagging his finger at Annie as Rose drew nearer.

'I saw the bruises! Jarin's a good lad and far too loyal to you. He refused to say where he got them, but I know a beating when I see it.'

Rose stepped forward. 'Gee, what are you doing here? You're supposed to be scaring crows off the fields.'

'I have been.' He held up a makeshift slingshot. 'But it's not easy with one hand on my stick.'

'Then wave it at them or shout or something. Whatever you do, you'd better get back to it or we'll have no wheat to harvest.' Rose thrust open the gate and stepped through, avoiding meeting Gee's rheumy eye.

'I was just going. But you—' he pointed his stick at Annie— 'you keep your meddling healer's nose out of my affairs.'

Rose waited until he was out of earshot before turning to Annie. 'What was that about?'

'He beats Jarin. I know he does, and the poor lad doesn't deserve it.' Rose had never seen Annie look so vexed. 'I'd like to take that precious stick of his and beat him, see how he likes it.'

'Gee's a horrible old man. Jarin had a bruise on his face when they first arrived, do you remember? I thought it was a buboe. If Gee gives you any trouble, you will say, won't you?'

'I don't know what good that'll do. I'll keep an eye on him, though. Jarin's a nice lad; I feel sorry for him.' Wearily, Annie picked up her basket of beans and walked to a patch of freshly dug soil at the back of the garden. Dropping to her knees, she began putting beans into the holes she'd made with a wooden dibber.

'Need a hand?' Rose asked.

Annie patted the ground flat and wiped a thin, muddy hand across her face. 'Please. There're more beans to plant, and I've still to scratch out the ground over there for carrots and peas. The ground's so dry and stony it's hard to work.' She stretched and eased her back.

The ground was thick with buttercups and dock weeds, and Rose groaned. She preferred hedging to gardening, but her conscience wouldn't let her walk away. Annie was a good woman – if something of a busybody – and she looked exhausted. Her hair was streaked with grey and her face and brow deeply lined.

How old was she? Rose wasn't sure, but she guessed that Annie must be at least thirty or forty summers, and few lived longer than that.

Besides, if she helped Annie, she might learn more about her and Lady Joan. Annie was also close to Thomas, *and* she was William's aunt. Maybe she'd be able to convince him not to wed.

Rolling up her sleeves, she made a start. When she'd finished digging one row, she had a pile of stones on the side and a heap of weeds on the other. The job was endless, there was yards still left to dig. She ran a hand around her damp neck and took a swig of cider, then offered the flagon to Annie.

'Want some?'

'You're an angel. I'm dry as chaff.' Annie drank deeply. 'What have you been doing today?'

'Thomas has been learn—teaching me to play chess.' Rose waited, and when Annie didn't answer, asked, 'Did you play chess with Lady Joan?'

'Whatever gave you that idea?' Annie dried her mouth with her apron.

'Everyone knew that you were close friends.'

Annie fumbled the wooden stopper, almost dropping it before pushing it back into the flagon. 'Yes, well, folks would do best keeping their noses out. We weren't that close.'

That wasn't true. She had heard Ma and Ellyn talking in whispers many a day about the Lady of the Manor being seen walking the fields and sitting by the river with a common lass like Annie. When she'd asked why, they'd told her it was adult talk and best she didn't know. She'd reckoned Annie knew something terrible about Lady Joan, otherwise why did she and Ellyn get all those presents from her: mattresses, goatskins, furs and the like? That had been before her time, but the gossips were still talking about it years later.

'It must be nice to have a special friend and share secrets,' she tried.

'It is, but Lady Joan wasn't a special friend. I helped her, that's all.' Annie handed back the flagon. 'God's bones, the sun's moving fast today. Best get on.'

Annie was hard to work out; secretive yet motherly and caring. She reminded Rose of her Ma in some ways.

Ma. Rose welled up and bit her cheek to stop her chin from trembling. She'd have given anything to have her here. Ma would have known what to do about William.

'Oh, Rose,' Annie drew her close and hugged her tightly. 'You have a good cry, lass.'

For a moment, she wanted to sink into Annie's arms and be a little girl again but if she wanted respect, folks couldn't see her weeping like a weak maid. But there was no one around, it wouldn't hurt to talk. She inched out of Annie's hold. 'When I think of Ma and Pa, I miss them. I miss them so much. And Will keeps on about us getting wed. I've told him I don't want to and that we don't have an arrangement, but he won't listen.'

'You poor lass. Of course you miss your Ma. It's only natural. I don't know what we'd do without you, and all the time you've been carrying your grief and worrying about getting married. But don't you fret about William. All lasses get wedding nerves.'

'I haven't got lasses nerves. It's not just William. I don't want to marry anyone. You're not wed, I thought you'd understand.'

Annie's eyes clouded over. 'I might have been, once, but God had other ideas. Anyway,' her voice took a brighter note. 'I became a healer, and healers don't have time for a husband. But you listen to me,' she said, taking Rose's face in her hands. 'Will's a fine lad and you'll feel differently on the day. From now on, we'll look after the vegetable garden together and you can help me with my lotions and tinctures. That way, you can talk to me anytime. I'll show you how to make the red dye. It'll be fun for both of us.'

Rose wasn't sure about the fun part, but Annie wasn't getting any younger and one day, someone would have to take her place. The red dye was a new idea. The future of the estate could depend upon it, and if she knew how to make it, that would put her in a very good position. Equally, healers were respected; they lived independent lives and most of them never married and were never expected to. The thought of spending her days picking herbs to be crushed and mixed made her want to scream but if that was what it took to retain her independence, she'd do it.

'You're very kind. I'd love to learn.'

Annie beamed. 'Wonderful! We can make a start right now. I've had enough of this planting, and I need some willow leaves and clover for fever tonics. I make a lot of those; they're one of the easier mixes. It'll be your first lesson. Let's take a walk and pick some.'

There had to be easier ways to avoid getting wed. She forced a smile. 'That sounds lovely,' she said, picking up a basket.

What she really wanted, she now realised, was to be was a reeve. Reeves oversaw men's work and were at the heart of running the estate. They earned good money – enough for her to live on without the need for a man – but as a woman, it was unheard of. She'd have to work hard on Thomas to get him to even consider it.

She bit back a sigh. It looked like there would be a lot more of those interminable chess sessions in the future...

CHAPTER 21

Thomas looked down the length of the open field at the tall dry grass rippling in the breeze. Above it, a flock of goldfinches was swirling in chittering circles of golden streaks. He ran his hand through the stalks and bent to listen. Simon had said that the time to make hay was when the seed heads rustled and before the grass turned yellow. And, Thomas thought dourly, before the birds ate all the seeds.

It sounded like it was rustling, the grass had a tinge of green and his charts indicated it was a good time to take action. He tilted his head back and checked the sky, seeing nothing but high wispy clouds. If only he could be sure it wouldn't rain.

He could wait for Simon to bring more men, but there was no telling when he'd be back or how many men he'd bring with him. If the grass turned before then, they'd lose the hay, but if he timed it right, they'd have a good yield.

He turned to survey the long stretch of field again. His heart told him to cut, but his head wagged an admonitory finger and said it was more sensible to wait. Frowning, he bit his lip.

Right now, he'd rather be galloping towards Tavistoke. He could be in the monastery by nightfall and sitting in his old place in the quiet of the refectory, listening to one of the Brothers reading from the Bible. After his meal, he would take a candle by the door and walk through the aged cloisters to his cell, as the Brothers called the bedchambers. In the security of the wise stones, he'd kneel in silent prayer before settling on his wooden bed with a straw mattress and woollen cover. And a little after sunset, he'd hear the comforting tone of the bell ringing for Compline.

It was tempting.

Show them. Annie had said. She had a lot to answer for. If it hadn't been for her, he would be in the monastery now.

He looked back to the house. His people were down there. What would they think if he deserted them like a coward on a battlefield? He laughed to himself at the comparison. That was exactly how he felt: like a knight surrounded by constant blows and confusion, having to stand fast when he all he wanted to do was run away to find peace and calm.

His brother Richard, the brave hero knight, wouldn't have run.

Thomas clenched his fists. He had made a promise to himself. He was here to prove himself, and God's teeth, he would do it.

Early the next morning, he stood in the same spot at the end of the field and yawned. He'd not slept last night for worrying. Looking at the field afresh, it seemed a hopeless task. The scythe felt heavy and clumsy in his inexpert hands as he practised a few swipes.

He looked over his shoulder to where the others were dawdling behind him. 'Make haste!' he shouted. 'We need to get started!'

They gathered in a reluctant group in front of him, and he looked from one to the other. Peter, his face lined with the years, dressed in a torn tunic stained ash grey from the forge; Jarin, his smooth youthful face with creases yet to come, yawning next to him; Rose, alert and wearing her herringbone apron with her coif askew as always. Next to her, Annie stood neat and tidy, her hair now showing grey under her pinned headdress. Maria; her shoulders down and her face telling the world that she didn't want to be there, but still managing to look highborn in her working kirtle. And Eleanor, bright as always, and finally Gee, his face sour and his hands clutching his stick.

'We'll spread out in a line across the strip and cut as we move forward.' Thomas's voice sounded small in the vastness of the field. 'We'll work until midday, have a rest and work on until it's too dark to see. Tomorrow, the men will cut and the women will follow and turn the hay to dry.'

Peter eyed him from under his hood. 'I'm thinking tis too soon for the hay. Happen we wait and see what Simon says before we start.'

Thomas eyed him straight back. 'As I said last night, if we wait, we could lose the crop. It's my decision, and I say we cut now.'

Peter drew himself up to his full height. 'And I'm saying 'tis the bailiff's job to decide and Simon knows what he's about.'

'Meaning I don't?'

Peter didn't flinch. 'Meaning we should wait. There're acres of it! There's only me and Jarin who's ever swung a scythe, and the two of us can't cut all that. We need more men…m'lord.'

God's bones, Peter was stubborn as an ox. They'd argued this last night and hearing it again only increased his own doubts. He squared his shoulders. 'We don't know when Simon will be back.'

'Don't know what I'm doing here,' Gee muttered. 'What am I supposed to do with one hand on my stick?'

'You can pick stones or something.' Thomas ran a hand through his hair. He'd wager they wouldn't argue with Simon like this.

Rose put her hands on her hips. 'You should do as your lord says. I can use a scythe and I bet Annie can too, so that's four of us.'

Annie didn't look too sure about that. 'Well, I have used one but—'

'Ye are only women. Scything is men's work,' Peter cut in. 'Scythes are heavy and unwieldy, no lass can swing one.'

'We'll help, won't we M-Maria? It'll be fun,' said Eleanor.

'God help us.' Peter folded his arms and turned away.

'How dare you! El can help, and I'm as good as any lad. Give me that scythe and I'll prove it to you.' Rose thrust out her hands, but Peter held on to his scythe, giving her a contemptuous look.

'Well, I'm not using a scythe.' Maria folded her arms. 'I say we wait for Simon to bring more men.'

'Anything to get out of work,' Rose muttered just loud enough for everyone to hear.

Thomas stood there awkwardly, his hands clutching his own scythe. He knew he should put a stop to the bickering, but he wasn't sure how.

'You're being very quiet, Annie. What do you think?' he asked. Annie would support him. After all, it was her fault he was here.

Annie glanced between Thomas and Peter. 'More help would be nice—'

'There ye are, m'lord,' Peter said triumphantly. 'Another one agrees with me.'

'Actually, I was going to say that there's no harm in starting, and we should do as our lord bids us.' Annie nodded in Thomas's direction.

He threw her a grateful smile.

'Then ye and ye—' Peter glowered from Annie to Rose— 'can get on with it, for I'll not be helping. And I'd like to see the mess ye make of it.'

'What do you think, Jarin?' said Annie, ignoring Peter's offer of his scythe.

'The boy'll do as I tells 'im,' said Gee.

'Jarin?' she asked again, turning her back to Gee.

Jarin shifted his feet and glanced through his hair at Gee. 'Like he says, I do as I'm told.'

Rose raised her eyebrows. 'You should think for yourself. You're not tied to him.' She turned her attention to Peter. 'Thomas could make you cut the hay, you know. Go on, Thomas, tell him.'

Dear God, Rose was making things worse. Peter was the last person he wanted to cross, and now all eyes were on him: Peter's hard and contemptuous, Rose's expecting him to be strong, Maria's expecting him to be weak, Annie's pleading with him to get it right, Gee's challenging and Eleanor's simply smiling. Only Jarin was still staring at his feet.

Peter was openly defying him. As lord, he should call him to his manorial court for trial and punishment, but Peter was the only smithy they had and, if he was honest, still scared him.

He cleared his throat, striving for a tone of lordly magnanimity. 'I could, but I won't —'

Peter stifled a laugh, and Thomas wanted to crawl away.

'Don't laugh!' Rose's hands were back on her hips. 'He's your lord. Show some respect.'

'I'll give 'im respect when I've cause to. Now hold your tongue; you're nothing but a maid. And you nobles are all the same, hiding behind your lands and fine clothes.' Peter's face darkened. 'When I think of what your Pa did to me —'

'Peter! Not again, not now,' Annie put a hand on his arm, but Peter's look froze her to silence.

'What did Sir John do?' Gee asked. 'Go on, speak your mind, smithy; I'm sure we'd all love to hear.' He glanced around the group for support.

Annie gave him a furious look. 'You keep your nose out of what doesn't concern you!'

'But what d-did he do?' asked Eleanor.

'Nothing,' Annie said firmly. 'It's just Peter getting worked up. You know how he is.'

Thomas felt it was time he stepped in. 'I'm not my father,' he said. He glanced at Maria, who didn't look like she understood Peter's words any more than he did. 'But if there's something I should know, now is the time to say it.'

Peter slowly shook his head. 'Happen Annie's right. No good raking up the past. But at least Sir John had guts.'

'Peter! Don't mind him, Thomas, he's got a touch of toothache that's addled his temper.' Annie glowered at Peter as she pulled him away. 'Come on, you! I'll give you some cloves.'

'What are ye blatherin about? I've not got toothache; and get off me woman, I can walk on me own...' Peter's grumbling voice faded into the morning air as Annie pulled him away.

Thomas twirled his scythe. He'd only wanted to make hay. Why did everything always have to be so difficult? For a moment there, he'd thought he was in control, but then it had all gone wrong and he didn't know how to put it right. He sighed.

'P-pipes!' Eleanor said suddenly. 'I can hear pipes!'

'Oh El, that's just the birds,' said Maria.

'No, wait.' Rose frowned. 'I hear them too. Listen, they're coming from over there.' She pointed up the cleave.

Thomas strained his ears, and the faint sound of trilling pipes drifted towards him.

'Do you think it's t-troubadours or jesters? I love jesters with their brightly c-coloured clothes and asses' ears on their caps. They have bells on their legs too!' Eleanor was jumping up and down with excitement. 'Oh, I hope they want to stay. Say they c-can, Thomas!'

'There's a drum and a fiddle—' said Maria.

'I can see them!' Eleanor pointed. 'They're coming down the c-cleave! Look!'

'Let's go and see!' Maria gathered her skirts and started running for the lane.

'There're c-cows and goats too! M-Maria, wait for m-me!' Eleanor ran off, clutching her hat to her head.

'Troubadours don't travel with livestock,' said Rose, shielding her eyes against the rising sun. 'I can see five – no, six – carts, and folks walking alongside. And there must be hundreds of sheep with them.' She looked meaningfully at Thomas. 'It looks like Will's back.'

It did indeed, and he wasn't looking forward to seeing him.

CHAPTER 22

A colourful line of people and livestock were making their way down the cleave. Thomas stared. William and Simon's figures were unmistakable even at that distance; Simon on his chestnut horse, and William bringing up the rear on the shaggy grey pony.

'I'm going to see,' said Rose. 'Are you coming?'

Thomas saw William's fierce face in his mind and heard his warning. He didn't want to be on the end of William's fist. 'You go on. I'll follow.'

When she was a hundred or so yards ahead, he put down his scythe and headed for the lane. He wasn't looking forward to his reunion with William.

Simon stopped the first of the wagons halfway down the valley. 'First wagon in here! We'll mark out plots tomorrow. Next wagon, pull in by the hawthorn tree and watch out for the boulders. Thomas, hail; how fare you? You won't believe who we've got with us.'

'Who?' he said, trying to summon some enthusiasm. Simon's easy mastery of the situation only served to heighten his despondency.

Simon laughed. 'What's wrong? You've a face on you like a sow's backside.'

'Nothing. I'm fine. Just didn't sleep much last night, that's all. Who have you got with you?'

'Only a miller and his son. What do you think of that for a piece of good fortune? We came across them just outside Torrington on our way home. Josef had his own mill on the River Torridge. His wife's at the back of the wagon with their two young boys, and he's got a grown son, Lief.'

'Did you tell him our mill's a ruin?' Thomas muttered.

'Is that all you can say? Thomas, we've a miller who can get the mill running again. What's wrong with you? I thought you'd be thrilled.'

He could hardly say that he'd just experienced his greatest failure yet, was terrified of meeting William again and found Simon's success irritating. 'I told you, I'm fine.'

'You don't look fine.' Simon cupped his hands around his mouth. 'Not *there*! Move down to make room for the cart next to you! God's bones, some folks haven't got the sense of an ass. What have you been doing whilst I've been away? Did you go to the market as I said?'

'Yes, and we've ploughed and sown two strips of wheat, two of oats and one of barley, although I don't know whether there are enough weeks for them to grow. I was going to start cutting the hay this morning, only…' his voice trailed away.

'You weren't seriously intending to cut the hay with only seven of you, were you? Last cart in there by the boundary ditch! You should have waited for us. I said we'd be back for haymaking.' Simon rubbed his forehead and blew out his breath with a whistle. 'God's teeth, but I've had a trial of it organising this lot. I'm glad to be home. Will and I found six families on the estate and about a dozen travelling men who joined us on the road. One's a sawyer. Not a Guild carpenter, but he reckons he can work wood well enough. The others are general peasants but a strong looking lot, and Will's discovered a talent for working sheep. He's a natural.'

As if to prove Simon's words, William chose that moment to herd the sheep expertly into the end of the large open field. Nervously, Thomas glanced around, searching for Rose.

She was with Annie, talking to some women unloading the first wagon, and he breathed a little easier. Even William couldn't say anything about that.

'We've brought over a hundred sheep, a few cattle and some wandering goats came with us, so that'll please El.' Simon turned to survey the field. 'The hay looks ready. Is it rustling?'

'Yes, I checked. You and Will have done well.' He forced the words out, when what he really wanted to do was bury his head under his bedcover and beat his pillow to death.

'Good. We can get started on that, then.' Simon stood in his stirrups and raised his voice. 'You men without carts, make what you can for yourselves along the cleave. Everyone get settled, then go to the field behind you. We're cutting hay. Those with tools, bring them. Tomorrow we'll carry on cutting and mark out your plots and sort acreage for freemen.'

'They won't like that,' Thomas said, his blood already curdling at the thought of another confrontation. 'They've been travelling and must be worn out.'

'They'll do as they're told. Most of them were starving when we found them, and the others were wandering with nowhere to go, so they're grateful to be here. You can meet them tomorrow and introduce yourself.' Simon jumped off his horse with an energy Thomas could only envy. 'You look like you need your bed. Go home and take your boots off.' He clapped him on the shoulder. 'Don't look so worried. With these extra men, I'll soon have the hay cut and gathered for you.'

Bed was a wonderfully tempting thought, but how would that make him look in front of his people, both new and old? 'I don't need my bed. I'm coming with you.'

Simon shrugged. 'As you please, but we can cope fine.'

That was the problem as far as he was concerned. He was supposed to be the lord, a strong symbol of knowledge and authority, and yet his people had no interest in one of those attributes and no respect for the other. Simon was right; they could cope without him.

He stayed until the men stopped for a rest at midday, but there was nothing for him to do except watch them work, and so he went back home and flopped down onto his mattress, where he dreamt he was on his own, cutting fields of hay as storm clouds gathered around him. Peter stood by laughing and others joined in. He cut faster and faster until his hands bled, but every time he reached the end of the strip, the field stretched out again and he had to keep cutting.

Peter's laughter grew louder, echoing until he could stand it no longer and screamed, covering his ears in a vain attempt to shut it out. The skies darkened, the thunder rolled and the rain came down in torrents. He was alone in the middle of the field watching his hay turn black.

'Thomas! Wake up!'

He blinked his eyes open to see Simon's face looming large in front of him.

'It's well past the third quarter. Have some ale. Rose told me about your trouble earlier with Peter. I spoke to him and put him back in his place. He's now cutting hay with the other men. I doubt you'll have any bother from him for a while.'

'She'd no right to do that. I could have dealt with him,' he muttered, although he doubted his own words.

'It was best sorted quickly before he started bragging to the new men. It's good news about the extra workers. They're good peasants who'll stay and serve their lord.'

'How am I supposed to pay them?' Thomas sat up slowly, rubbing the back of his skull where he could feel a thumping headache developing. 'Gee demanded four pennies a day for Jarin. He said that's what peasants are getting now.'

Simon sat on the mattress next to him and grinned. 'Not anymore they're not. King Edward's changed all that, and about time too. We stopped at an inn three days from here and while we were enjoying a bowl of rabbit stew, an argument over wages blew up between some roaming peasants and the bailiff from the nearby estate. Got a bit heated and wagers were being placed on who would throw the first punch, but the landlord stepped in before it got to that.' He poured out two cups of ale and handed one to Thomas. 'Turns out that the peasants did have the upper hand for a while and were demanding four pennies a day and moving to the next estate if they didn't get it. The nobles paid because they had no choice, but it was never going to last. According to the innkeeper, the nobles pressed the king for action and he passed a new law called the Ordinance of Labourers.'

'What does that mean?'

'Apart from merchants and craftsmen, everyone under sixty has to work and cannot be paid more than they were earning before the Pestilence. They also have to stay on the estates they're bound to and if they don't, they're imprisoned,' said Simon. He refilled their ale cups and took a long drink.

Thomas's bones went soft with relief. 'Thank God. I've been having sleepless nights over how I'm going to pay everybody. Though I've still nothing in the coffers unless we sell the surplus hay and reap a good harvest.'

'That's months away. You worry too much. I saw the planting by the way. You did a good job there.' Simon tipped the dregs onto the floor and got up. 'Well, I must get back and see to the hay. You still look pale. Do you want Annie to take a look at you?'

No, he didn't. His problems weren't physical. The cowardly part of him was saying that Simon was back and now was his chance to gallop out of there as fast as he could. His conscience, on the other hand, said it was his duty to stay. Damn it! Why couldn't he make up his mind to do what he wanted instead of always having to think of his people?

He watched Simon walk out and sighed. How much longer would his dream have to take second place to his duty?

CHAPTER 23

Rose opened the door and looked out. William was in the yard. Maybe if she was quick, she could slip around the back without being seen. She crept out, turned and closed the door behind her as softly as she could.

Not softly enough. William looked up as the latch fell into place, and a huge grin appeared on his face. Before she had time to move, he was striding towards her.

'I can't stop; I'm on my way to milking,' she said before he was more than halfway across the yard. She held up her bowl and kept walking.

William blocked her path, his silhouette gigantic and dark against the sun. 'The ewes can wait; I've summat to say. Sit ye down.'

The lines in his jaw told her that he wouldn't take no for an answer. She'd done well to avoid him for this long. Warily, she perching on the edge of the chopping log.

William threw the axe to one side and sat beside her, his arm resting on his knees. His shoulders were broad, his skin tanned and leathered from travelling and his beard had grown thick and dark. She couldn't deny it; he was a handsome young man.

'I've said nothing to no one, as I wanted to tell ye first. I was angry having to go with Simon, and I think ye knows that. But while I was away, I got to thinking, and I been a fool.'

Hope blossomed in her. Did he mean what she thought? Had he finally given up all thoughts of forcing her into marriage?

'Thomas is the lord,' he went on. 'What interest would he have in a miller's lass like ye?'

She raised her eyebrows. 'You know how to make a lass feel good.'

'Oh Rose, I'm not good with words. Ye knows what I mean. Thomas is highborn, and ye're one of us. But ye're still the best lass, and ye're mine, not his.'

She wasn't anybody's lass, but nobody would care about that. Men controlled, and lasses did as they were bid. 'Will, I'm not yours. I've told you and told you—'

'Listen and ye'll think differently,' he interrupted. 'As I said, I got to thinking, and Thomas was right. I'll never be a man if I stay with Pa. I'll always be his boy, and I'll never be any sort of smithy with my one arm. I was a fool to think otherwise. Thing is, though, I like working with the sheep. 'Tis something I can do, and I'm good at it.'

'You want to be a shepherd, is that what you're saying?'

'Not just a shepherd, a head shepherd. The lands up there go on for miles of open grazing, and it all belongs to the Chiddleighs. There's sheep roaming – hundreds of 'em – and no one to tend them. I reckon we'll need more wool for that red cloth Annie's so excited about.'

The cloth had potential, she knew that. If William was as good a shepherd as he said, they could be making ells and ells of scarlet cloth for the Flemish buyers. Thomas would need someone to manage that. Annie would never give up her healing, and she couldn't do both.

She smiled. It was an important role. If she was successful, she might even persuade Thomas to promote her to reeve. Wouldn't that be something?

'Rose, are ye listening?'

She jolted back, scrambling through her mind for what William had been saying. 'You want to be the head shepherd to give us more wool for cloth. I think that's a very good idea.'

'Ye do?' His face lit up. 'Then wait until ye hears the rest of it. On our way home, we passed a stone house. Simon said it was the old bailiff's place, and do ye know what I thought?'

She had a horrible feeling she did.

William leaned in close and squeezed her knee. 'That's just the place for my Rose, that's what I thought.' He sat back, triumphant, but didn't remove his hand. 'It could be our home, and ye'd be a head shepherd's wife. The place hasn't been lived in for years, but I'd do it up. It's a grand place too; a longhouse with a cross passage and everything.'

She pushed his hand away and fought the urge to rub the feel of his touch off her leg. 'It doesn't make any difference, Will. I don't —'

'I'll make it nice for ye. I'll weave hazel wattles to go around the front, and there's a good square patch at the back for your vegetables. Needs digging but ye'll soon have that done. Ye can have fowl and a few swine, and I'll plant us a small orchard and there's a stream nearby for fetching the water and washing the pots so ye won't have to go far. I've got it all worked out.' His words tumbled eagerly over each other.

Like he'd worked out the stone cottage. And she'd thought the trip might have made him see sense.

'Ye'll love it; I know ye will. Think, me as a head shepherd and ye as my wife. What do you say, Rose?'

She didn't want to say anything; she wanted to scream. Living in the middle of nowhere growing vegetables and playing the obedient wife? It was her worst nightmare.

'I don't know what to say. Is there a village?'

'About four miles away, I reckon, though folks have gone. But they'll be back, or others will move in.'

On her own with William? She'd end up madder than a fly-ridden donkey. 'I'd have no one to talk to.'

'Ye'll have me. Though I'll be out most days tending the sheep, and happen I'll have to stay away some nights, especially at lambing. Like I said, the land goes for miles, right north to the sea. I'll wager ye've never seen the sea. I'll take you one day. Ye'll like that.'

No, she wouldn't. She had never wanted to see the sea, and she'd hate all of it. Did he really believe a trip to the sea would sway her? It was clear to her now what she should have seen months ago: he saw her as a wife and nothing else. He didn't know her at all.

'Course, we'll get wed before we leave—' William went on.

'There's no priest!' she blurted out.

'We can handfast at the manor in front of the others. I know Thomas'll agree. I'll make ye an iron ring in the forge, and we'll state that we accept each other as man and wife.'

'I know what handfasting is, but I don't want to.'

William waved his hand. 'Oh, I know it's not as holy as a proper church wedding, but it's all legal and proper. There'd be nothing sinful in it.'

God give her strength. 'Will, listen to me. I don't want to handfast. I don't want to have a church wedding. I don't want to marry you.'

His face fell. 'Why not? It would be a grand life, and I thought ye liked me.'

She looked at his crestfallen expression and felt dreadful. Most lasses would jump at what he was offering, but not her. 'I do like you but not to get wed. It's not your fault, but please believe me and find another lass. What about that good-looking maid with the fair hair living in the first plot? Alviva, she seems nice.'

'I don't want no other maid. You're my lass, and we've an arrangement.'

He didn't understand. He never would. 'I don't remember any arrangement, and besides, Thomas may not want a head shepherd.'

'Oh yes he will, and he's in the lane. I'll ask him. Thomas!' William was up and gone before she could draw breath.

She squeezed her eyes shut, praying to God and the Blessed Virgin for strength. William wasn't making this easy, and Thomas was so desperate to be liked he'd agree to anything. Picking up her skirts, she hurried after him.

William turned a beaming face on her. 'See, I told ye! Thomas likes my idea, so there's nothing stopping us.'

Her blood turned to ice. She would have to persuade Thomas otherwise. 'What about the work I do here? You've no one else to do it. Maria's hardly capable of it.'

'True, but we'll need more wool for the red cloth and someone upcountry to tend the sheep,' Thomas said. 'You know I rely on you, Rose, but if this is what you want, then I'll not stand in your way.'

'It's not what I want. I don't want to get wed. Why won't anyone believe me?'

William looked at her, and his voice softened. 'I don't blame ye, Rose. Ye're just a lass with wedding nerves.

But don't worry your little head about it; I'll sort it. Pa'll say there's an arrangement and when ye hears that, ye'll be fine.' He turned toward the forge. 'Pa!'

Rose grabbed Thomas's sleeve. 'Do something. I don't want to wed him!' She hissed shaking his sleeve.

He looked at her, his face soft and bewildered. 'What can I do? I don't want to get on the wrong side of Will again. I told you: you'll have to sort it out between you.'

Peter was bound to side with his son, and if she refused to honour an arrangement, folks would shun her. Her life here would be as good as over. She could either be the obedient wife, all alone with William, or an outcast here. She didn't like the sound of either of them.

Peter strolled over, wiping his hands on his leather apron, with Janet scurrying behind. 'What's doing, boy?'

'I've been telling Thomas my plans to wed Rose and go upcountry to be head shepherd. Ye don't mind, do ye, Pa? Ye've got Jarin now. Thing is, Rose's got the lass's jitters. She's saying as how she don't remember us being promised. Tell her we are, Pa.'

Peter stroked his beard and drew in a long breath through his teeth. 'I knew summat was up. Ye've bin right quiet since ye got back.' He nodded slowly. 'Head shepherd, eh? That's a step up, and happen ye'll be a better shepherd than ye are a smithy.' Turning to Thomas, he said, 'What do ye say to all this, m'lord?'

Thomas shrugged. 'I do need someone, and if it's what Will wants, then I've no objection.'

'What about what I want?' she said.

'Keep out of this, Rose. I'm sorting it.' William turned his back, shutting her out.

'Alone up there, ye'll need a wife to look after ye,' Peter said. 'And ye've a liking to Rose; I've known that a while.'

'Don't I have any say in this? You can't make me get wed,' she said, but the men didn't reply or even turn around to acknowledge the fact that she'd spoken. Her whole life depended on what Peter said now, yet she wasn't even consulted.

'It's true Geoffrey and I talked,' said Peter, scratching his jaw. 'I didn't hold much with him. Too above himself. But as to an arrangement, I never agreed. Not proper like.'

She waited for the *but*. It never came. Slowly, her gaze travelled from Peter to Thomas before finally resting on William.

William frowned and shook his head a little. 'Ye...never agreed? But ye let me tell folks and go on thinking. Why didn't ye say?'

'Made no odds if the lass wanted ye.' Peter raised his eyebrows at her. 'Is it the jitters, or don't ye want my boy?'

Finally, the men were listening to her. 'It's not the jitters and it's not William's fault; I don't want any lad right now.' She looked sadly at William. This wasn't how she'd wanted it at all. 'I'm sorry, Will.'

William glared at the pair of them, a slow crimson staining his cheeks. 'Ye knew how I felt, the pair of ye. Ye've made a fool of me!'

'Will, I told you over and over again how I felt, but you wouldn't listen.'

'Don't ye speak to me! Ye're no better than a teasing mare!' The veins on William's neck stood out, his fist clenched at his side. She could feel the rage and humiliation emanating from him like heat from a fire.

'Now, boy—' Peter began.

'I am not your boy!' William yelled, the fury burning in his eyes. 'God's blood—' He drew back his fist.

'Will, don't!' She grabbed his sleeve. 'I'm sorry, truly I am. You'll find another lass.'

His arm relaxed. For a moment, she thought he'd seen reason, but then he shrugged her off.

'Ye're not sorry. None of ye are. What do ye say, Ma?'

Janet wrung her hands. 'I can't go against your Pa, son. I'm sorry.'

'I should have known. Ye're against me too.' William turned to her, his eyes pleading. 'Ye'd be a head shepherd's wife, and I'd look after ye. We'd be happy in our house with just the two of us. Say yes, Rose, please.'

It tore her apart to see the pain and hurt in his eyes, but she couldn't, not after she'd come so far. 'I wouldn't be happy with no friends around.' Unable to look at him a moment longer, she glanced at the tree as if seeking inspiration, but saw nothing except a sparrow.

'What if I was to stay here and go north now and then to tend the sheep? We'd still have the stone cottage, and ye'd have your friends.'

She shook her head slowly. 'No, Will,' she whispered. 'I can't.'

'Ye're like him,' he snarled, thrusting an accusing finger at Peter. 'I'll wager ye were laughing behind my back and all. There *was* an arrangement, and ye all knows it. Well, I'm not finished yet. Rose's Pa's not here and when there's a dispute amongst folks, it's for the lord to decide. Thomas, tell them I'm right. Rose is to wed me, isn't she?' He fixed his eyes on Thomas, who visibly paled.

That was it then. All her dreams were shattered, for now another man held her future in his hands. Not just any man, but a weak one who looked as though he wanted to crawl into a hole and die. There was nothing left but to hang her head and pray.

When Thomas said nothing, she dared to raise her head. He was frowning and rubbing his hand around the inside of his collar.

'It's not fair to make Rose do what she doesn't want,' he said, glancing at her beneath his hair.

Her jaw fell open. Had she heard him correctly?

There was a long, hot silence.

'So that's it then, is it?' William demanded. 'Ye're siding with her. I always knew ye wanted her. Ye're the same as all nobles.' He spat the words with disdain. 'Pa warned me ye were; I should have listened.'

'Will, I don't want her. I'm just trying to do what's right.' Thomas reached out a hand.

Will looked at the hand, scowled, raised his fist and punched Thomas in the face.

'Will!' Rose screamed.

William rained blows on Thomas who cowered away with his arms up to protect his face.

'Don't! Will stop!' Janet cried.

Rose started forward, but before she could take more than a few steps, Peter charged like a bull, tackling his son around the waist and bringing him to the ground.

'Don't be such a damn fool! He's not worth it!' he yelled.

William thrashed his legs and flailed his arms, but Peter was stronger and held him until William was spent. Breathless and on their knees, they eyed each other. Peter wiped his mouth with his sleeve and got to his feet. Looking down at his son, he offered his hand.

'Get up. I spent months chained in Lyndeford Gaol. I won't see ye in there for the likes of him.'

William knocked his father's offered hand aside and staggered to his feet.

'Tis all your fault, ye vixen!' He thrust a finger at Rose.

She didn't answer. She'd never meant for things to go so wrong. All she'd wanted was the right to choose. She forced herself to look at him and saw the pain and humiliation behind his anger and her conscience gave her a painful jab. He wasn't a bad lad.

William turned to face Thomas with visible loathing. 'Am I still your head shepherd, or are ye taking that from me as well?'

'If that's what you want, you can have it.' Thomas croaked, his face drawn and pale.

'I do, and I'll be the best head shepherd ye've ever seen. I'll show ye.' William swept his arm wide. 'I'll show all of ye! Even with only one arm, I'll rebuild that house so as any lass would be proud to live in it. I'll look after the sheep, do the shearing, and be back come harvest time with stock and wool for sale and spinning. Ye'll see. Pack me things, Ma; I'm leaving!' He spun on his heel and strode off.

'Ye don't have to go right now, boy.' Peter called after him.

William stopped and turned around, his face red, his jaw tight. 'I said I'm leaving, and don't call me *boy*. I'm a man and a head shepherd. That makes me your equal, Pa, so don't tell me what I can or can't do. I'll be taking a wagon, with my lord's permission.' Mockingly, he bowed low to Thomas.

Thomas took a step forward. 'Take what you want, but don't go like this—'

'I'll go how I likes, *m'lord*,' William said, and strode off.

Rose looked at Thomas, whose face was already swelling slightly on one side. He looked so pitiful that she felt a pang of guilt about him too.

'Will!' She ran after him. 'Will, you don't have to go. I never wanted you to leave.'

William stopped, turned and looked down at her. 'I don't care anymore what ye want. One day, when ye're still working here as a lowly maid, I'll be living in my big house, wearing my fine clothes and with silver groats chinking in my purse. Ye'll look at me then and wish ye'd wed me as ye should have. Only don't ask, 'cos I wouldn't have ye if ye begged on your knees.' With a look that made her feel like she belonged in the gutter, he stormed off towards the stables.

'Will...'

'I'll give him a hand with the wagon.' Peter pointed a finger at her. 'And ye best stay out of his way 'til he's gone!'

He strode off, Janet following close behind.

She watched them go, her conscience coming more and more alive with every step they took. As Thomas walked past her, his face white and tense, she reached out and caught his sleeve.

'Thank you. I'll never forget how you helped me. I'm sorry it turned out like it did,' she added.

'*You're* sorry?' He rounded on her, his face so uncharacteristically furious that she fell back a few paces. 'How do you think I feel?' He cast her a derisory look and marched away.

She felt his contempt as deeply as if he'd thrust a dagger into her heart. She'd won her freedom, but it was a hollow victory.

CHAPTER 24

Shaking, Thomas crossed the yard. He couldn't believe how quickly everything had gone wrong. Damn women; they were nothing but trouble, and Rose in particular! And damn his duty and his conscience. He could have been out of here by now.

He rubbed his cheek, wincing, and ran a tongue around the inside of his mouth. At least William's punch hadn't knocked any teeth loose. That was a blessing.

What he needed was a walk to unscramble his mind. The men were taking care of things under Simon's leadership, so he could go off without worrying. Pulling his cap firmly down, he strode up the hill behind the house.

Halfway to the top, he paused to kick a stone across the path and watched it bounce down the slope. William was as bad as Rose. He should never have got him involved, especially when Rose had made her feelings so clear.

He resumed his pace, his boots pounding the path with every furious step.

He'd tried to be a fair lord and look where it had got him. His best friend had left and would probably never speak to him again, and everyone believed he was chasing after Rose. Well, they were wrong; he didn't want her or any lass, and if this was the kind of trouble women caused, pray God he never would.

He stroked his chin. Why couldn't he grow a beard and be broad like William? If he looked more like a man, maybe he'd be treated more like one. He stopped and kicked another stone. And where was God in all this, with His Pestilence?

Thomas marched on until he reached the top, where he stopped, swiped off his hat and wiped the sweat from his forehead. Combe Hide sat innocently below him with plumes of blue woodsmoke drifting up between the trees and covering the land like a shroud. Looking down, he saw William cross the yard and disappear into the forge. He'd be leaving soon.

Good.

Up the valley, folks were setting up their plots. Some had already laid the first stones for a dwelling; others were claiming their territory with makeshift hurdles. Two women carrying bowls walked across the orchards, their heads bent in conversation, probably looking for windfall fruit to stew.

Life was going on as normal, but it didn't feel very normal to him. All of this – the land, the crops, the people – was his, and he couldn't think of a good word to say about any of it.

He turned away and kept walking. A few yards further on, the path forked. If he went left, the way he usually went, he would be in the woods. Feeling contrary, he turned right for the first time.

After a furlong or so, huge boulders towered on one side. On the other, smaller rocks that were cloaked green with moss scattered their way down the hillside where a few hardy rowans and gorse fought for soil to cling into. The path narrowed, and the only way through in places was to squeeze sideways with his back against the boulders. It was peaceful; he could hear nothing but a few birds darting amongst the bushes. Breathing in, he felt calmer.

Perching on a stone, he gazed into nothing. He hadn't felt this calm since the monastery. What were Brother Luke and the others doing now? Pray God the mob hadn't got to them, and they were safe. He should have gone back to them when he'd had the chance, but Annie had pricked his conscience.

'Muxy on the gorse; another thorn in my hand!'

He leapt to his feet, his knife already in his hand and his chest pounding in his ears. Judging from the heavy tread, the speaker was coming his way. A shadow grew around the boulder.

He gripped his knife and tensed.

'Who goes there?' His voice wavered as he held the knife out in front of him, staring at the anonymous dark outline.

The shadow grew and then shrank again as a man in a priest's cassock rounded the boulder. He raised his eyebrows at Thomas and the knife and spread his arms wide.

Thomas swallowed, the knife already limp in his hand. 'Father, forgive me! I…'

The priest smiled. Above his mouth, two piercing blue eyes held Thomas in their thrall.

'Hail, and there's nothing to forgive. These are uncertain times.' The voice was soft and entrancing, and there was something familiar about it and the face, which seemed young for a priest. He looked to be no more than fifteen or so summers older than he was. Where had he seen him before?

'May I move?' the priest asked, 'or do you intend to hold me at knifepoint all day?'

'I...er, no.' Thomas sheathed the knife so hurriedly that he almost nicked a finger. 'Sorry, Father.'

'Then come take some wine with me. I haven't spoken to anyone in months.'

'Wine? Do you live nearby? I've never seen you.'

The priest chuckled. 'It's not real wine. I make it from what I can forage. And yes, I suppose you could say I live nearby. Come, I'll show you. What about Gee and Jarin? Are they still on the estate?'

'Yes, and you're Father Rulf, I remember now. I was sorry to see you go, I was looking forward to some educated conversation.' That sounded ungenerous, and he floundered. 'I mean, the others are good people but—'

'But of limited topics?' Father Rulf threw back his head and laughed. 'I understand. I enjoy a good debate myself. I intended to spend the dark months in a monastery further north, safe from the Pestilence, but the doors were closed and they weren't going to open them.'

'Not even for a priest? That's dreadful! The monks are men of God; their doors should be open to all men in need.' Thomas thought back to his own monastery and added, 'Abbot Bartholomew would have welcomed you.'

An enigmatic smile played around Father Rulf's lips. 'I would like to think so, but these are changing times. We can't depend on anyone now.'

Thomas frowned. The abbot would never change. He had closed his doors to the townsfolk, that was true, but only because there had been so many of them.

'But come,' Father Rulf added briskly, 'let's have that wine and indulge in some good conversation.'

He stepped past, gathering the thick folds of his cassock around him, and led Thomas along the path, his strides easy and sure. Thomas hesitated before following him, but not for long. The man was a priest, so he wasn't dangerous, and there was something compelling about him; a tantalising hint of secrets yet to be told.

A few yards on, Father Rulf stopped before an opening between two solid square rocks, which Thomas hadn't noticed earlier. 'My humble abode. I bid you welcome,' he said, sweeping his arm low into an exaggerated bow.

The entrance was dark, and Thomas had to duck his head to pass through. Two steps inside, he found himself inside a cave that rose to twice his height and opened to about fifteen paces across. In the centre of the floor was a ring of flat stones with the remains of a fire.

Father Rulf picked up a stick, poked the ash and added a few more twigs.

'Be seated.' He indicated a tree trunk placed on two rocks at the side of the cave. 'Not luxury, but it suffices.'

Thomas took his seat, glancing around at the priest's home. At the back of the cave was a line of various clay pots and a few flagons. Along the wall, an untidy pile of clothes had been thrown on the floor and a leather bag put next to them. Opposite, a rough hollow had been scooped out of the earth floor; presumably where Father Rulf slept. It was basic but as homely as such a place could be.

'Did you spend the cold months here? It must have been freezing.' It wasn't that much warmer now; Thomas rubbed his hands together in an effort to generate some heat.

Rulf smiled. 'I've been in worse places, but no. The may trees were flowering when I arrived, and I watched your comings and goings below but kept my distance. The Pestilence, you understand.'

'So it was you who was watching me! I thought the demons had got to me.'

Rulf chuckled. 'Oh yes! It kept me amused on many a dull day. Although I did have one or two scary moments. The day I ventured to the healer's linhay was nearly my undoing. Such is the price of curiosity.' His eyes twinkled. 'Try my nettle and primrose wine.' He offered Thomas a cup and squatted on a boulder, a cup nestled in his hands.

Thomas eyed the drink. It was a muddy dark green colour and smelt of damp wood. He smiled politely and took a sip. The acrid taste hit the back of his throat like fire, and he coughed as he forced it down.

Father Rulf laughed. 'Awful, isn't it? It gets better the more you drink.'

'It's fine, really, Father.'

The priest laughed again. 'No, it isn't and I lied, it doesn't get any better. Call me Rulf. And you are?'

Rulf's cheeks were smooth with just a hint of colour. His dark eyebrows arched over those intense blue eyes, and his full mouth turned a little at the corners as though ready to smile. He was regarding him in a way that made it impossible for Thomas to look away.

'Thomas. Lord Thomas de Chiddleigh, for my sins,' he said, cursing the heat rising from his neck and across his face.

'Ah, a reluctant lord. Then we have a lot in common, for I am a reluctant priest.' The lines around Rulf's eyes creased as he smiled.

'A reluctant priest?' He tried not to stare at him. 'But how can that be? You have the word of God!'

Rulf took a long drink, grimaced, and tipped the remains of the green liquid onto the ground. 'Can I trust you?' he said, tilting his head a little to one side, his gaze suddenly focused on Thomas as though drinking in his very soul.

Thomas squirmed a little under the intense scrutiny, but nodded. 'Yes, of course.'

'Yes, I do believe I can. You have the angelic face of one who is trustworthy.' Rulf smiled. 'You ask how I can be a reluctant priest when I have the word of God? I don't believe I do have the word of God.' He spoke the last words slowly, although no emphasis was needed. 'I often wonder if any priest truly does.'

He had never heard such blasphemy. '*All* priests have the word of God—' he began.

'Do they?' Rulf interrupted. 'You're from noble stock. You know as well as I do that sons are sent into the church by the wishes and ambitions of their families.' He steepled his fingers together. 'As a lowly third son, such was my fate.' He smiled again. 'And you? What makes you so uncomfortable in your role?'

Such an enthralling voice and such radical words. He was both shocked and captivated. 'I was the second son. If my father had had his way, I would have been a scribe in a monastery. It's a long story. What are you doing here; have you no parish to tend?'

'Like you, mine is a long story, and no. I'm a priest without a church. And—' Rulf held up his hand as if in explanation— 'happy to be so. Does that shock you?'

He wasn't so much shocked as astonished. He'd never met anyone like Rulf. For some inexplicable reason, he was drawn to this stranger. If the priest had asked for his deepest secrets, he would willingly have told him.

'You remind me of Brother Leviticus in the monastery where I was a scholar,' said Thomas abruptly. 'He was a man of science and studied the stars. He gave me some charts and an almanac before I had to leave.'

'You study the stars? Then you're a man after my own heart. I'd love to see your charts, and I have something that will interest you.' Rulf went over to the leather travelling bag and delved inside, tossing a blue tunic, a pair of green hose and a cap onto the floor. 'Here it is! Safe and sound.' He returned to his seat and held out a solid brass disc about eight inches across.

'An astrolabe!' Thomas had only seen one in his life and he had always longed to have one. Most priests condemned the science of astronomy as being against the word of God. This Father Rulf was certainly full of surprises. 'Brother Leviticus had one but not as fine as this; his was made of iron. May I hold it?'

'Of course.' Rulf had the long slender fingers of a lute player. 'Note how the rete rotates over the face, its pointers showing the positions of the stars marked in images and in Arabic. Look at this symbol. Do you know which star it is?'

Thomas peered at the outline of a bird. 'No, I don't.'

'The bird represents the beak of the constellation, Corvus, the crow.'

Thomas ran his hand gently over the face of the astrolabe in wonder. 'It's a fine instrument. I envy you. Brother Leviticus used his for calculating the altitude and positions of the stars, but I can't remember how he did it. On the back —' he turned it over — 'yes, here we are; the circles relating to the calendar to keep track of saints' days.'

Rulf chuckled, 'Indeed, but I mislaid my charts somewhere on my travels. Or maybe they were stolen; I don't know. But you say you have charts, so between us, we have everything we need.'

'Tell me, do you believe in the idea that the earth goes round the sun?' said Thomas, reluctantly handing back the astrolabe.

'Now that is a subject I look forward to discussing. As a priest, I should say you speak blasphemy and give you penance, but I have studied the theory and discussed it with others of a like mind. And yes, I believe it is a possibility.' Rulf stood up. 'Regrettably, though, that's for another day, I must check my traps if I'm to eat tonight.'

Thomas glanced towards the entrance of the cave. The light was mellow as the day slipped towards evening. He didn't want to leave. No, that wasn't right; he didn't want to leave Rulf.

'Why don't you come and eat with us? You could stay there. There's room in the house, it's warm and there must be a spare mattress somewhere and —'

Rulf's laugh cut him off. 'Apart from my clothes, do I look like a priest? My hair hangs to my shoulders and I've a thick beard that drives me as mad as flies around a horse. What would your people make of a priest with a beard?'

'They'll understand and welcome you with open arms. The house isn't a manor, but it's warmer than this cave.'

'They may not like the idea of a priest staying with them. This outfit makes people uncomfortable. No; I've made this cave my home. I can stay a little longer.' Rulf handed Thomas his hat. 'But you must come back and bring your charts, and if you have a pair of scissors so I can do something about this hair...?'

'I'll come tomorrow.' Another wonderful thought struck him. 'Do you play chess?'

'My dear young friend, don't tell me you have such a thing as a chess set?'

'A rather fine one. I'll bring it.' He couldn't wait to show it off and pit his mind against his new friend.

'I look forward to it. I'll wager you're a mean player, but I warn you, I have a trick or two up these sleeves myself.' Rulf smiled, walking with Thomas to the cave exit. 'Until tomorrow then. God's speed.'

Thomas almost skipped along the path but stopped himself. Rulf might be watching. All thoughts of William had vanished in the sheer joy of this new acquaintance. He couldn't wait for tomorrow.

CHAPTER 25

Thomas hitched his satchel over his shoulder, his charts poking out of the top. The chess set weighed heavily in his bag, but he didn't mind. He was on his way to see his new friend. A man who could give him a decent game of chess and who was as interested in the stars as he was.

Arriving at the cave, he straightened his tunic, ran a hand over his face and combed his hair with his fingers before ducking through the narrow entrance. Inside, the fire burned with a steady flame, sending purple shadows across the walls and flickering on the mute paintings of large bison and stick men with spears, the artwork of ancient dwellers.

The cave was empty, and he swallowed his disappointment. Not for the first time, he wondered what sort of man Rulf was. He was a strange priest, certainly, but beneath that cassock was an air of mystique that he found irresistible.

The leather bag still sat in the shadows of the cave, a pot or two stood close to the bench and a pile of sticks was thrown haphazardly near the hearth. There was no sign of a rabbit. Perhaps Rulf wasn't a good trapper.

Close to the bench stood an upturned tree trunk which hadn't been there yesterday. It would make a fine table, and Thomas began setting out his chess set.

Putting the last pawn in place, he stood back proudly to admire his work.

'Thomas! Hail, I see you're ready for a game.'

He spun around and his mouth fell open. 'You're wearing clothes!'

Rulf laughed. 'I don't look very pretty without them!'

Colour flamed in Thomas's cheeks. 'No, I mean you're not wearing your priest's cassock. You look different in a tunic and hose.'

'I've been scrabbling amongst the briars, cutting strands for rope. The long folds of the cassock get snagged on the thorns.' Rulf leaned over the table, closely examining the pieces. Glancing at Thomas for permission, he picked up the black king. 'This is a fine set. Where did you get it?'

'Mama gave it to me for my tenth birth date. Apart from her gold cross, it's all I have left of her.'

'It must mean a lot to you. Your Mama; was it the Pestilence?' The firelight danced across Rulf's face, creating soft shadows on his cheeks.

'I don't know. I was with the monks as a scholar in Tavistoke when the Pestilence swept through the town. They sent me home, but the Pestilence had already reached the manor before I got there.'

'Is that why you came here?' Rulf returned the king to its rightful place, positioning it precisely on the square.

Thomas nodded. 'I begged and pleaded with Mama to leave but she wouldn't. She said she belonged with her people. I brought a small group to this remote farmstead, thinking we would be safe and could go home in the spring. A few months ago, I went back to the manor, but it was burnt to the ground. I found her bones in the ashes, along with her cross.'

It was the first time he'd spoken of it to anyone, and he didn't know why he was speaking of it now. Maybe it was because Rulf was a priest and listening to people was part of a priest's duty. He bit his cheek, cursing the tears he could feel building behind his eyes. 'I had no choice but to return here, and now I'm trying to make it my manorial seat.'

Rulf put a hand on Thomas's shoulder. 'You mustn't blame yourself for what happened. Your mother did what her conscience told her to. God has His reasons for our journey in life, and I'm sure you'll succeed and be worthy of your title.'

Rulf sounded like the priest he was, but he preferred the other Rulf; the one who cursed at gorse bushes. Thomas stared at his feet. 'Mama made me promise to be a good and fair lord and to look after my people, something my father wasn't very good at. I wish she hadn't.'

Embarrassed, he scratched the dirt with his boot. He wanted to say more, tell Rulf about the secrets that Lady Joan had hinted at, but if he said another word, he'd probably burst into tears. Better to keep quiet and not make a complete fool of himself.

'You're young and a lot has happened to you. Give it time and I'm sure you'll be a very good lord.' Rulf's voice still had the patronising tone of a priest.

'I don't want time!' He burst out. 'Don't you see? I loathe all this. I don't want to be a lord; I want to go to the University of Oxford and study the stars and learn to be a physician. That's all I've ever wanted.'

Rulf raised his eyebrows and stroked his beard thoughtfully. 'Is it indeed?'

Maybe he was wrong, and Rulf was like all the other priests. Thomas didn't want Rulf to be his priest, he wanted—what did he want? His friendship? To be his equal?

'Some wine as we play?' said Rulf, reaching for the jug.

'I've brought some cider,' Thomas said, untying the leather flagon from his belt.

'Not willing to risk my wine again? I don't blame you. The wild parsley is a little better, though not much.' Rulf's eyes glinted playfully as he grabbed a stool, settling himself behind the black pieces. 'You start.'

They played in amiable concentration, and Thomas noticed that Rulf didn't drink the wine either. They were evenly matched but eventually, Rulf tipped over his king with a sigh and declared himself beaten.

'You play a devious game, Thomas. Though, in my defence, I've not played since Oxford,' he said.

'You were at Oxford?' Thomas's eyes lit up. 'You never said.'

'Didn't I?' Rulf's eyes glinted mischievously. 'My family sent me there nine odd summers ago when I was sixteen.'

'I thought you were much older than—' He broke off and wished he could bite out his tongue as heat spread across his face. 'Prithee, I didn't mean...'

Rulf chuckled. 'Travelling on the road ages a man. Having to constantly keep your wits about you for thieves, never knowing when the next meal is coming from and sleeping in ditches takes its toll. Wearing the cassock helps, for not many would dare assault a holy man, but it's still hard.'

'I can't believe you were actually at Oxford. I've never met anyone who has been there. What's it like? Were you a scholar?' Thomas sat forward, eager to devour every detail.

Rulf put his hands behind his head and let out a long sigh. 'Not a very good one. As I said, I was the third son. What else was there for me to do but become a priest?'

'You don't sound local. Where are you from?'

'If you want my story, you'll have to fill my cup with cider. I'll stir the fire and we can sit by the warmth. That's the trouble with living in a cave, it's always cold.'

Leaning back against the stones, they stretched their legs in front of them, watching the flames spring into life. Rulf finished his drink, put his empty cup on the floor and wiped his mouth with his sleeve. Folding his hands behind his head once again, he said, 'For what it's worth, my name is Rulf de Beauchamp. The Beauchamps were French nobles with lands in Normandy. When William, Duke of Normandy, invaded England a few centuries ago, my ancestors supported him. It's said they fought in the famous battle at Hastings. As a reward, they received lands in the shire of Sussex; a place called Ditchling. Have you been there?'

'No, I've only been to Tavistoke.'

'You must go. The inn serves the best bowl of mutton I've ever tasted, and Sussex is covered in dense hunting forests. For the king's use only, of course.'

From Rulf's knowing smile, Thomas wondered if he had risked his life to hunt the king's deer. He'd wager he had. There was something bold and daring about Rulf that he couldn't help but admire. It made his own life seem so dull.

'Towards the south, there are acres of pasture on high downland with miles of dazzling white cliffs along the coast. It has an air of civilisation but then it's closer to London and the ports. When I came west, I couldn't believe so isolated a place could exist in modern England. I thought I was amongst heathens.'

'We're not heathens,' Thomas protested. 'We have towns and a high sheriff.'

'Ah, but your towns are small and primitive. I saw no midden ditch for the waste outside any town wall.' Rulf's mouth turned into a teasing smile.

'Exeter has a midden and a new cathedral. I bet your Sussex hasn't got one of those.'

Rulf chuckled. 'Actually, it does. There's one at Chichester. I admire your loyalty, but trust me, if you travel east, you'll notice the difference. Better roads, better buildings and the weights and measures comply with the king's standards. Early on, I was constantly tricked by the Devonshire traders who insisted on giving me only fourteen ounces to the pound when everyone else gives sixteen. Your narrow deep twisting lanes make miles longer and your acres are smaller. Look at your Devonshire hills and valleys littered with rocks. Here, the area tilled by one man with an ox in one day is only half what he could do in Sussexshire.'

'I'm surprised you stayed here.' Thomas picked up a stick from the pile and idly scratched an isosceles triangle in the dirt.

'I stayed because I didn't want to go home. I still don't, and I'll admit there's a certain something about this place.' Rulf's eyes twinkled as he smiled directly at Thomas who tried not to notice. He wasn't sure if Rulf was serious or not.

'Whatever you make of it, I'm proud to be a Devon man,' he said, 'but I want to hear about Oxford. I imagine large libraries with shelves stacked high with books and heated debates taking place between learned men sitting in corners.'

'Merton Tower has a library, but it's small and I didn't spend much time there. Whilst other scholars sat crammed together on hard pews in small sweaty rooms, craning their necks to hear words of wisdom from the tutor peering down from his dais, I spent my time in the inns. I wasn't the only one and by evening we were usually drunk and made merry on the streets. On a good night, there'd be a fight between the two factions of students: us Southerners against the Northerners from Queen's College.' He smiled. 'The town people hated us, but they were fun times.'

Students drunk and fighting in the streets, upsetting the locals? That didn't sound like the studious place he had imagined. It was hard to believe that scholars fortunate enough to be there would behave in such a manner. He certainly wouldn't waste his time in the inns.

Rulf regarded him, his head tilted a little to one side. 'I think you would be one of the serious scholars who made good use of his time, unlike me.' He spread his hands on his lap as a way of apology.

'I'd spend time in the inns too.' He didn't want Rulf to think him a sop. 'I'm surprised you had fights. I thought Oxford was a quiet and serious place. Didn't you want to learn? I mean, it's not cheap being a scholar, and how did you get your degree if you didn't study?'

'I wasn't paying and was quite happy to spend my parents' coins on ale. But you're right; most of the masters charged two shillings and sixpence for their lectures.'

'Two and six!' Thomas thought of his empty purse and his dream seemed ever further away.

'Some charged more, and we had to buy books, ink, parchments and pay for our food and lodging. I never wanted to be a scholar, let alone go into the priesthood. Just because you're at Oxford, you don't have to take the exam and get a degree. The place is full of sons from rich families who either don't know what to do with them or who are sent there to further their parents' ambitions, and few are interested in studying. The alehouses are far more entertaining than the lecture rooms, believe me.'

'Did you get your degree?' Thomas asked.

'I never intended to bother but surprisingly, yes. When I returned to start my fifth year, the corridors were buzzing with talk about a radical master called John Wycliffe who gave his lectures and preached in English, and he was challenging the church. Well, anyone with the nerve to do that had to be worth listening to, so I went along to one of his lectures.' Rulf paused and, looking straight at Thomas, said, 'John Wycliffe changed my life.' He refilled his cup and downed it in a single gulp. 'He spoke with passion. He believed in what he said, and I started to believe it too.'

This was more like the Oxford he'd imagined. 'What did he say?'

'He criticised the church, saying the bishops and abbots thought themselves high nobles and lived like princes when they should be helping and leading the people to Christ. He dared to accuse the church of corruption and self-indulgence. I'd never heard anyone speak like it, and the more I heard, the more I wanted to hear.'

'That's blasphemy! He can't say things like that. What did the clergymen at Oxford think?'

'They weren't happy, but they had to be circumspect. King Edward is an advocate of the English language and they feared his reprisals. And John was careful, although he did go so far as to suggest that no pope, abbot or council was infallible. Some were corrupt and there were times when they were wrong.'

Thomas stared in wide-eyed disbelief. 'He didn't! You didn't agree with him, did you?'

'Yes, and I still do.' Rulf stated. 'You were at a monastery. Think about it. I wager your abbot lived like a lord.'

Thomas had been inside the abbot's house once. A roaring fire warmed the vast hall in stark contrast to scholars' cells which were cold and damp. Rich tapestries adorned the walls, and he remembered a fine oak table under the windows laden with expensive gold candlesticks and silver dishes full of nuts and fruit. It had reminded him of home.

'Abbot Bartholomew had a large house befitting his status but, on his orders, the brothers gave leftover food to the poor queues every morning, and he'd never be corrupt. He was a good God-fearing man.'

'I'll wager he was, but did you really – I mean really – believe everything he said?' Rulf leaned forward, his eyes challenging him.

'Of course! He was the Abbot speaking with God's voice, as He speaks through all priests. You should know that. You're one too.'

Rulf burst out laughing. 'My dear young friend, it's because I am priest that I know God does not speak through me or other priests. They're just men like me and it's all an act—'

Thomas was beginning to question his liking for this priest who was laughing at him. 'That's not true! If all priests are false, as you say, they would receive the wrath of God, and they don't.'

Rulf shook his head. 'Maybe we will in time, but I assure you, I speak with my own voice and not with God's.'

The whole idea was outrageous, and he didn't know what to say, so he said nothing. He'd think about it later, but he was certain of one thing: Rulf was wrong about Abbot Bartholomew. He would never be false.

Rulf reached for the flagon and topped up their cups. 'After I first heard John Wycliffe, I was spellbound and attended every one of his lectures. He predicted that one day the Bible would be translated from Latin into English so the common people could understand it.'

'The authorities would never agree to it. It wouldn't be the same.'

'But what of those who don't understand Latin? Shouldn't they know what's written in the Bible and what's being said during Mass? Or is the church afraid that if the general populace understood, they might start asking questions?' Rulf's face hardened as he spoke in earnest. 'If that happened, the church could lose not just its control but its wealth, most of which it gets from the common people. The authorities wouldn't want that.'

'But the church has control through God. That's the point.'

Rulf got to his feet, ran a hand through his hair and paced around the cave, then turned suddenly. 'Yes, that is *precisely* the point, and people – even educated people like you – go on blindly believing in them. Haven't you ever stopped to think?' He looked down at Thomas and shook his head. 'No, I don't suppose you have.'

Thomas wasn't sure what to make of any of this. He didn't like the mocking side of Rulf that made him feel naive, and his first thought was to get up and walk out.

Rulf sighed. 'I can see I've upset you. I meant no offence. Let's not quarrel so early in our friendship.' His voice and eyes softened. 'Shall I continue my story?'

Thomas nodded, keeping his eyes fixed on the ground as Rulf sat back on the floor next to him. After taking a good draft of cider, he continued. 'There was a buzz around Oxford. It was exciting, and I wanted to be part of that. For the first time, I wasn't just the third son. I had a purpose in life. I went back to Oxford for my final year and took my degree. A few of us wanted to start work on translating the Bible, but John said no, the authorities weren't ready. So—' Rulf paused, his eyes shining with mischief— 'three of us decided to make a start in secret.'

'Isn't it dangerous? With the authorities, I mean?'

A wry smile played around Rulf's lips. 'Only if they find out.'

Radical and brave, Thomas thought. He drank the remaining dregs of cider and fastened the flagon onto his belt. Next time, he'd bring two. 'It must be satisfying to be part of something that will change the realm.'

'I admit, the secrecy is part of the thrill, but yes, it is worth doing. After I got my degree, I managed to stay on for a few months working on the translation until my allowance ran out and I had to go home. I never said anything about John Wycliffe, though. My uncle's a bishop and I needed his patronage.'

'How could you take your vows if you don't believe in God?'

'I never said I didn't believe in God. It's the arrogance and authority of the church that's wrong, but as John Wycliffe said, change can only come from within. So, I made my vows like hundreds of others who do the same and have done for centuries.' Rulf smiled a little at Thomas's expression. 'Don't look so shocked. It's an easy living, especially if you're given a parish on your family's estate like me and know you'll be the bishop one day.'

Thomas rearranged his face into what he hoped was a more accepting expression and waited to hear the rest of Rulf's story.

'I was soon working as an acolyte to a priest there, tending the candles. I suppose you'd call it an apprenticeship. I saw first-hand the evidence of what John believed, particularly regarding my uncle who lived lavishly, entertained often, and did little to warrant his lifestyle beyond paying the odd visit to his priests to collect money and prove that he existed. Thanks to him, I was made a deacon within a year and ordained in the spring of '48.' Rulf shrugged. 'Hypocritical, I know, but I needed an income if I was to save enough to get back to Oxford and continue my work with John.'

There had to be some genuine priests out there, but Thomas didn't much fancy getting into another argument with Rulf. 'So what happened?'

'The Pestilence happened. My family fled to the north, giving me the perfect excuse to go my own way. I packed a few things and headed west, simply because my family went north and the Pestilence was coming from the south and east.' Rulf idly poked the fire and watched as the embers sparked into life. 'One day, when the Pestilence is over, I shall return to Oxford and continue my work.' He wiped his hands on his tunic and turned to

Thomas. 'Forgive me, I've talked too much. Tell me your story. I'm sure it's far more interesting than mine.'

He doubted it. He was still wrestling with the blasphemy of John Wycliffe, the idea that priests weren't all they seemed and that maybe Abbot Bartholomew shouldn't have lived like a lord. 'You've already heard most of it.'

'Tell me what happened when you came here. Don't mind if I close my eyes, I am listening.' Rulf put his hands behind his head, stretched out his legs and settled back as Thomas began his tale.

He spoke of how he could never match up to his brother, Richard, and his father's disappointment in him. He spoke with enthusiasm of finding salvation in his studies with the monks, and of his brother's death and then his father's, making him lord, and when the Pestilence struck, how his mother had sent him away and he'd come to Combe Hide.

'That's it.' He leaned back against the wall, wishing they hadn't finished the cider and wondering if he dared risk another go at Rulf's wine. 'New people have joined us, but I need more to make the place a profitable working manor. I'm planning to make red cloth, like Mama. *Chiddleigh Scarlet* she called it, and the Flemish merchants paid well for it. Annie-healer knows the dye and has already planted madder but we'll need lime, a dying shed, looms and people to weave. And a lot of the land needs draining, there are more acres to till, hedges to lay, haymaking, harvesting, my bees—the list is endless.' He ran his hand through his hair. 'I'm a bit like you, I suppose. You have your purpose in life and I have mine.'

'It seems we tread similar paths. Neither of us wants to be where we are and both of us have barriers blocking the way to where we want to be. What a pair we are.' Rulf stretched up, reaching behind him until he could touch the cave wall. 'But we'll succeed; you'll see.'

'I wish I had your faith.' He caught Rulf's eye and their smiles matched the irony of his words. 'I'm not a very good lord. I nearly ran back to the monastery.'

'What stopped you?'

'Annie found me and said I would be a coward to run, that I should prove myself and leave when the estate was profitable and I could employ reeves. Well, I've tried to prove myself but so far, I don't seem to have managed it.' He dropped his gaze to the ground. Did Rulf think he was feeble? Maybe he shouldn't have said anything.

'It shows great strength to put your duty ahead of yourself. I admire that.'

Thomas looked up swiftly. 'You do?'

'Yes; you've done well and against your own desires. Look at what you've achieved in such a short time. I think you're a better lord than you realise, and one day you'll achieve your aims.'

Here was someone who not only admired but believed in him. For a moment, his spirit soared, and then he thought of William and Peter's defiance and the long list of other failures. He and Rose hadn't exactly parted on good terms, and what did Peter think of him? Did he believe he was trying to steal Rose and had ruined everything for his son?

He wouldn't mention any of that to Rulf, though. For some reason, even the implication that he wanted Rose felt disloyal.

'I hope you're planning to stay longer this time,' he said instead. The thought of Rulf leaving was an alarming one.

Rulf shrugged. 'Where else can I go? I don't want to go north to my family and until the Pestilence is over, I can't return to Oxford.'

'So you'll stay? The place would feel more like a proper estate if you did. We could have Mass on Sundays again.'

Rulf reached for his jug of wine. 'God's teeth, I haven't given Mass for years.'

'But you must know how.' Thomas held out his cup. Bad as the wine was, he needed a drink.

'I haven't got a Bible.'

Thomas choked again on the wine and put down the cup. Maybe he wasn't all that thirsty after all. 'I've been to enough Mass services to quote it from memory, so I'm sure you can.'

'Then you do it.' Rulf finished his cup in one swig and poured another.

'I'm not the ordained priest here, you are. The people will look up to you, give you their confessions—'

'No.' Rulf looked at him sharply. 'I'm not doing that.'

'Why not? None of us has confessed since the Pestilence. Our souls are in danger if the Lord saw fit to take us. It wouldn't hurt to hear us.'

Rulf's eyes darkened and his voice had an edge. 'Do you have any idea what it's like to take on the sins and secrets of others? A few prayers, a bit of penitence and they walk away happy with a cleansed soul, safe in the knowledge they've avoided the flames of hell. What about the priest? He's now burdened with secrets he'd often prefer not to know. How does he unburden himself? He can't. He can tell no one. He has to carry it in his mind and on his shoulders. He sees that same person knowing he's an adulterer or worse. He greets the innocent wife, or husband, as though everything is right. Inside, it makes me want to scream but I can't. So no, I'm not keen on confessions.' He drained his cup again and shook out the dregs.

Thomas didn't know what to say. 'I'd never thought about it like that.'

'Folks never do.' Rulf got up, found another jar of wine, poured a cup, downed it in one, poured another and kept his back turned. 'It's not like I can unburden myself to a priest, since that would violate the seal of the confessional and result in a *latae sententiae* excommunication.'

Thomas stood up. 'I'm sure our confessions wouldn't keep you awake at night. We're none of us adulterers,' he added in a jesting tone. 'The peasants would build you a cottage; you can't live in this cave forever, and there's plenty of space along the valley —'

Rulf turned. 'Your peasants would be better employed working on that list of yours. I don't need a cottage, and I'm not living amongst others. I've been on my own for too long and enjoy my own company. If I am expected to be their priest, I might have to leave before the spring.'

Thomas swallowed. Rulf – the only person he'd met since the monastery who understood him – was slipping through his fingers. It hadn't been until he met Rulf that he realised just how lonely he'd been. 'If I can find you somewhere else to live, will you stay? You can choose wherever you want.'

Rulf shook his head. 'I told you. I'm not the voice of God, and your people will believe that I am. I'm not comfortable with that.'

Thomas ventured a step forward. 'You said many priests feel like you, but it doesn't stop them. Even if it's true, you're still looking after their souls and surely that's what matters?'

Rulf smiled wryly. 'And who is looking after my soul as I play out this deception?'

Thomas shifted his weight, racking his brains for things to say. He had to make Rulf stay. He needed him to stay. 'Don't decide yet. Janet makes a tasty bean pot, we'll have more cider and this year we'll have enough honey to make mead and grain to make ale. And you said you wanted to look at my charts.'

'I'll think about it. But if I do decide to stay, it will only be until I can return to Oxford in the spring.' Rulf's mouth hinted at a smile, creasing the corners of his eyes. 'I will join you tonight though, for I've not eaten a bean pot since I can't remember. But it had better be as good as you say.'

Thomas thanked God as he lost the fight to keep the grin from his face. 'You won't be sorry. Now, let's take a look at my charts.'

CHAPTER 26

Later that afternoon, Thomas sat on his favourite rock near the mill and pulled his knees tightly towards him, his thoughts tumbling like the waters at his feet. Could Rulf be right when he said some priests preached without the voice of God? How would the congregation know? Brother Luke would never do that, and Brother Leviticus was a man of science; he would never lie.

Rulf had said he admired him. Maybe he hadn't done so badly and even though Simon was back, he didn't want to leave now that he'd met Rulf. He'd wait and maybe they could go to Oxford together. Thomas hugged his knees in celebration of the idea.

He'd never been drawn to anyone so strongly before, not even Brother Leviticus. Rulf was worldly-wise when the furthest he had been was Tavistoke. Rulf probably thought him naïve, and with good reason. All the more proof that his decision to leave one day was the right one.

The way Rulf threw his head back and laughed and those eyes that —

'There you are! I've been tramping the fields since midday looking for you.' Simon's accusing voice jarred his thoughts.

Thomas stared at an emerald-green dragonfly zigzagging over the water and suppressed a groan. It had been such a good day, and now Simon was going to spoil it.

'What in God's teeth has been going on? The place is buzzing with the news that William tried to kill you and fled when he failed.' Simon stood with his fists on his hips, the heavy folds of his over-tunic catching the breeze. 'Some people are saying he punched you, others say he had you by the neck and tried to slit your throat, one man insists William hurled you off the roof of the house, and I can't get any sense out of anyone!'

Thomas sat up straighter. 'Will didn't flee; he went north to be my head shepherd. And how could he hold me by the neck and try to slit my throat when he only has one arm? Who told you that story?'

'Gee said—'

'Gee wasn't even there. What would he know about it?'

'I know, it's absurd, but I was still worried sick when I heard. So, Will didn't attack you?' said Simon.

'No. He was angry with Peter who said there was no marriage arrangement between Will and Rose. Will lost his temper — you know how he is — and accused me of wanting Rose. He did hit me, but Peter made him see sense,' Thomas said in a light voice, trying to breeze over what had shaken him to the core at the time.

Simon visibly relaxed and sat down next to him. 'Well, I'm pleased to hear it, but Will shouldn't have done that. Was making him head shepherd your idea? Get him out of the way?' Simon nudged him knowingly. 'I'd have thought you had enough on your mind without lusting after Rose.'

Thomas sighed. He was beginning to sympathise with Rose and her endlessly futile attempts to convince people she wasn't getting wed. 'I'm not lusting after Rose or any lass. Why won't anyone believe me? It was all William's idea; he wanted to wed Rose, become the head shepherd and take her north with him. The trouble was, Rose didn't want to marry him at all, let alone live up there. That's how it all started.' He took a deep breath. 'We need someone up there for the sheep, and I don't have to discuss everything with you. I can make decisions on my own.'

'I know you can.' Simon opened his hands by way of an apology. 'Look, I've had a tiring journey, and then to hear all that and you not around. I was worried out of my mind. Tell me exactly what happened.'

Thomas knew that Simon wouldn't be going anywhere until he'd heard every thing, so he related the events of that day in as much detail as he could remember.

'What could I do?' he finished. 'I knew Rose didn't want to marry Will. She'd made that clear before you both left, and I wasn't going to be the one to make her. Can you imagine if I had? She'd have given me hell.'

Simon chuckled in a way that reminded Thomas of Rulf. 'She would that. I wouldn't want to be on the wrong side of her. I assume you don't want me to fetch Will back for a manorial trial? I mean, he did hit his lord.'

'Of course I don't. He was just Will being Will. And maybe it all worked out for the best. I mean, he's good with sheep and we'd have missed Rose. I can't think who would replace her.'

'Neither can I, but I hope Will's coming back for the harvest. I'll need every pair of hands I can get,' said Simon.

'He said he would, and he'll be bringing wool and lambs for the sales. I hope he's calmed down by then and we can beg pardon. I don't like being at odds with him.'

Thomas sighed and switched the conversation to a more comfortable topic. 'How did you get on at Okewolde market?'

'Place was almost empty. Remember the high prices when you and Rose went to Holdesworthe? Now they're lower than I've ever seen. Not enough people to buy. Makes me wonder how many died in the Pestilence, but that's something we'll never know.'

'I suppose that's good if you're buying, but not if you're selling, and I have to sell to get coins in the coffer. Otherwise, how am I going to pay the men come Michaelmas? They're already waiting for their money as it is. There'll be a riot if I can't pay, and I've no rents coming in until next year.' And I need to start my Oxford fund, Thomas added to himself.

Simon raised his eyebrows. 'Difficult times. There's no grain to be had, so we could do well if we reap a good harvest. Folks always need grain. What are you doing up here, anyway? If you're thinking about repairing the mill, forget it. I can't spare men until after harvest. We can store surplus grain in the barn, but we'll have to grind it by hand.'

'The women will love that.' Thomas plucked a long thin piece of grass and chewed the end. If Maria was right and Peter and Annie's earlier conversation did concern him, maybe Simon could enlighten him. 'Can I ask you something? Was there anything in my past that I should know about?'

Simon blinked at the rapid change of topic. 'What sort of thing?'

'I don't know. A scandal when I was away at school? Or something else that Annie and Mama wouldn't want anyone finding out?'

'Not that I know of. What's brought this on?'

Thomas shrugged. 'Something Maria overheard Annie and Peter saying. It's probably nothing, but Mama begged my forgiveness before I left, and I can't help wondering what for. How can I forgive her without knowing what she did?'

Simon wiped his face, leaving brown streaks down his cheeks. 'Your guess is as good as mine. Lady Joan was living with the Pestilence, fearing her end. Folks say all sorts of things when they think God is about to take them. If you want my advice, forget it. And I should be getting on.' Simon stood up, stretching.

'Before you go, do you think there's enough room for a cottage over there?' Thomas turned and indicated a small flat area of grass on the other side of the path.

Simon studied it, frowning. 'A small one, perhaps, but who'd want to live up here on their own?'

'A priest I just happened to meet,' he said in a casual tone, enjoying Simon's look of surprise.

'A priest? Where did you run into him?'

Thomas hesitated. Something wanted him to keep quiet and not share Rulf's friendship, although he didn't understand why. 'His name is Father Rulf. He's coming to eat with us tonight and he wants to stay.' That wasn't quite the whole truth, but once Rulf had met everyone and settled into his role, he was sure to stay.

'It would be good to have a priest around the place. Lord knows I've not been to confession in a while, and I've got a few sins weighing on my soul.' Simon wiped his hands on the back of his surcoat. 'Well, now I know you're not dying somewhere, I've got a wagon that needs mending. I look forward to meeting this priest of yours.'

Thomas sat there for a little while longer, enjoying the return of his solitude, then went back down to the house to tell the others about Father Rulf.

He very soon regretted it. Anyone would think it was May Day or Christmas, the way they reacted to the news. All buzzing and fluttering and chattering excitement until his head spun and he wanted to go back to his quiet rock by the river.

Janet put her hands to her face saying the beans wouldn't cook in time and she'd already got a pot on the hearth. She followed this with a lot of muttering and a burst of frenzied activity that included delving into jars and sacks of beans and, it seemed to him, anything else she could throw into the pot.

Maria agonised to the point of panic over which of her two satin kirtles she should wear and finally decided on pale blue, since that colour represented purity. He doubted if Rulf knew or cared about the meaning of colours.

Eleanor changed into a yellow kirtle he'd never seen before and entwined yellow marguerite daisies around her head like a coronet. Even Annie rearranged her hair in a twist at the back, and he found it in himself to smile at her. He could forgive her for interfering now. If she hadn't stopped him from leaving that day, he would never have met Rulf.

As the sun dropped below the hills, the bean pot was bubbling, and Janet was wearing a clean linen apron with green herringbone stitches gathering the pleats at her waist. Peter arrived in shining boots and wearing a green tunic in place of the usual ash-stained brown. Thomas wagered that was Janet's doing.

Rose hadn't bothered to change except to remove her apron saying just loud enough for Maria to hear that it was a priest coming and not King Edward. Thomas prayed they wouldn't start sniping at each other, but Maria was too absorbed in having Eleanor braid her hair.

Looking at the small group, he wondered what Rulf would make of them and what they would make of him.

When he opened the door and saw Rulf standing on the threshold, he wished he had followed his people's example and changed into something more appropriate. Rulf seemed much taller and broader than in the cave. He'd shaved, and his dark hair no longer fell to his shoulders in tangles. With his full-length priest's cassock gathered at the waist with a fine leather belt, Rulf looked every inch the man of authority.

'Father, be welcome.' Thomas ushered Rulf forward, feeling strangely shy.

'And God keep you,' Rulf replied, lowering his hood.

As Rulf stepped into the room, all eyes turned to him.

'Father, sit ye down here. I'm Peter the smithy, and I praise God to see ye.' Peter crossed himself and wiped his cap along a bench closest to the hearth.

To Thomas's dismay, Eleanor and Maria burst into a fit of giggles behind their hands, making Annie tut and Rose scowl.

'You must be Eleanor. I've heard all about your weaving skills,' said Rulf, taking his allotted seat. 'And...Lord Thomas's sister, Maria, if I'm not mistaken?'

'Yes, Father.' For once, Maria was lost for words and dropped her eyes coyly.

Rose raised her eyes to the heavens, but Thomas frowned at her. 'This is Rose and Janet, and Annie-healer. Simon'll be here soon,' he said, avoiding the space next to Rose and choosing instead to sit next to Rulf.

'Janet who makes the best bean pot in the shire, so I've been told.' Rulf flashed her one of his smiles across the bubbling pot hanging over the hearth.

'It's not much, Father. I hope you like it. I'm afraid the bread's a little hard, we're nearly out of grain. Sorry.' Janet blushed, scrunched the top of her apron between her hands, then fled to the safety of stirring her pot.

Thomas waited for Peter's usual tart remark and breathed more easily when it didn't come. Like everyone, Peter was on his best behaviour.

'Don't mind me asking, Father, but how come ye found us tucked away down the cleave here?' said Peter.

'By God's will. Last summer, I left the southern shires to escape the Pestilence, letting Him guide me. I sheltered in the king's hunting forests for the dark months, and when the tracks cleared I headed west. Once in Devonshire, I followed the stone crosses marking the monks' route from abbey to abbey across the moor. I was hoping to find sanctuary, but the abbeys were either abandoned or the monks refusing entry to a stranger, even one of their own. I met Gee and Jarin on High Drovers Road and arrived here with them but only stayed for one night.'

'So ye did! I remember ye now.'

By God's will? Letting Him guide me? That wasn't what Rulf had told him, and his voice had changed. He spoke smoothly with the pious monotone typical of all priests. Was this the same man who cursed and stretched bare feet to the fire?

'When I left here, I headed north but couldn't find anywhere to stay and by the time I arrived back here, the May trees were in flower. I remember the day clearly. It was pouring. I was soaked cold and tired. My feet ached and I'd hurt my leg when one of my boots broke and I fell on the moor a few days earlier. I needed somewhere to rest and as the rain came down, God took pity on me, for as I sheltered against some rocks near the woods above here, I noticed a cave. I only intended to stay until I was fit to move on.'

'A secret c-cave? In our woods?' Eleanor's face lit up at the thought.

Rulf chuckled. 'Not so secret but yes. It's above where the new settlements are now.'

Thomas bit his lip. Rulf was a good story-teller but he wished he hadn't mentioned the cave. It was their place. Now everyone would be going up there to find the priest for a quiet word.

'Father? What did you eat?' Eleanor piped up.

'Stop asking so many questions, El. Sorry, Father.' Rose wiped her hands on her tunic. Even Rose was on edge.

'Eleanor can ask whatever she wishes.' Rulf rubbed his chin. Maybe he was missing his beard, Thomas thought. He ran a hand over his own jaw, which still annoyingly smooth.

'I made traps and caught the odd rabbit, but I have a confession to make.'

Thomas could hear the gasp of shock rippling around the room. The girls looked at one another, Rose's jaw dropped and Annie's eyes were as large as the pot hanging over the hearth.

Thomas held his breath. Surely Rulf wasn't going to say he didn't want to be a priest and had no intention of hearing their confessions?

'I'm not a good trapper,' Rulf went on, 'and there were times when I was hungry and came down here at night to raid the hen house and take milk. Which isn't easy from a reluctant ewe in the dark.' Rulf caught Thomas's eye and smiled. 'And Peter, I borrowed your hammer and a few nails to mend my boots and make a bench but I returned it. I trust you found it on the wall?'

Peter's eyes went as round as the bowl in his hand. 'It was ye, Father, skulking around in the dark! Praise God.' He crossed himself and began to laugh. 'For a while, I thought 'twas the little people from the moor playing tricks.'

'Why didn't you make yourself known to us, Father? We'd have been pleased to have you here,' said Annie.

Because he doesn't want to be your priest. 'Rulf was making his way to Exeter—' Thomas began.

'The truth of it was I could see by your empty barns and few livestock that you had little enough for yourselves, and I didn't want to impose. God will provide.' Rulf smiled benevolently and made the sign of the cross, a signal for everyone to do the same. 'I managed quite well with a little of your help – even if you didn't know it.' His eyes twinkled in the firelight.

The door opened and Simon, his hair awry and his hands covered in grime, stamped the dirt off his boots on the threshold. 'Forgive me for being late, one of the goats had her horns stuck in the wattle fencing. God's arse – sorry, Father – she put up a fight. Father, be welcome, I'm Simon de Perceaux, Lord Thomas's bailiff. It's good to have a priest join us and take care of our souls.'

Rulf flicked a more serious glance in Thomas's direction, the question written all over his face. Thomas shrugged and stared at his feet.

'We'll build ye a church and a dwelling, Father,' Peter said. 'Can't have our priest living in a cave, can we, m'lord?'

'If that's what Father Rulf wants.' Thomas avoided Rulf's eyes.

'And Father, I'm wondering when ye'll start the Mass again and take my confession?' Peter added eagerly. "Tis a long time since I spoke to a priest, and my soul's in sore need.'

Rulf went to run his hand through his hair but stopped himself. He looked at Thomas as if to say *I told you so*. 'I'd prefer the sanctity of a church to hear a confession,' he said.

'Then the sooner we build ye one, the better. Can ye give the Mass outside until it's finished?'

Rulf inclined his head. He had easily slipped into his role of the priest sitting with his hands clasped loosely in his lap, a gracious smile playing around his mouth and not a hint of disdain for the church authorities or that he was not the voice of God, but Thomas wondered what he was really thinking.

Rulf talked to Simon about work on the estate. He praised Janet's meal, showed sympathy when Maria took pains to tell him how she'd worked alongside the others even though she was of noble birth, and he made Rose laugh. Thomas was speechless. Rulf should have been a mummer in a travelling play.

When the last taper sputtered, Rulf stood to take his leave. Amid thanks from Rulf and agreement that they were glad he was staying, Thomas accompanied him to the door. No sooner had the latch dropped into its bar than Rulf grabbed his elbow and steered him around the corner out of earshot.

'What was all that about me staying and them building a church and a dwelling for me?' he demanded. The change in him was as instant as the sun going behind a cloud.

'I told you they wouldn't have their priest living in a cave.'

'I'm not their priest,' Rulf hissed.

He shook off Rulf's grip and faced him. 'What did you expect? You are a priest. They were in awe of you, and having you here gives them a sense of security.'

Rulf sighed. 'I know.' He ran a hand over his short-cropped hair. 'My office does carry obligations, and I suppose I should earn my keep as your priest. But only until I can return to Oxford or my conscience gets the better of me.' He leaned close and searched Thomas's eyes. 'But hear this: when I wear this cassock I am the priest your people need me to be. Only you, my friend, are privy to the real Rulf de Beauchamp.' Rulf's eyes were dark and serious, then he blinked and they twinkled once more. 'Come by tomorrow and I'll beat you at chess.'

With a wave, Thomas watched Rulf walk up the field until he was lost in the darkness of the woods. He was an intriguing, fascinating man. He liked Rulf the man, but he still wasn't certain how he felt about Rulf the priest.

Smiling, he returned indoors.

CHAPTER 27

'Did you see him? When he stood in the doorway last night, I had goosebumps all over. And those eyes! Have you ever seen such blue eyes? And the way he looked at me.' Maria stood in the centre of the room with her hands clasped to her bosom and her eyes closed.

Eleanor giggled. 'You shouldn't speak like that. He's a p-priest.'

'She's right. You should be ashamed, talking like that about Father Rulf,' said Annie, her fingers flying on her drop spindle.

'I know, but one day I'll marry a handsome earl who looks just like him. He'll buy me silk kirtles embroidered with the finest gold and silver thread and stitched with hundreds of pearls, and gold necklaces and exquisite cremesin velvet slippers with jewels on the toes. We'll be invited to all the best houses, wining and dancing and everyone will admire me.' She wrapped her arms around herself and danced across the floor.

Annie stopped spinning and fastened her drop spindle back onto her belt. 'You'd do better helping Eleanor comb that fleece than wasting your time with such idle thoughts.'

'Yes, we're tired of hearing about your earl,' Rose added, from where she was busy with her mending. 'You're never going to meet one. Thomas hasn't a penny to his name, so he'll not be visiting the best houses any time soon.' She broke the thread with her teeth, admired the darned patch on her skirt and waited for the response she knew would come.

'He will one day, because Thomas isn't promised. He's the last Chiddleigh and will need a wife to give him an heir. Until he finds one, I'm the only noble here so he'll take me as his escort.'

Rose could just see the two of them dressed in their noble's finery. Maria would be even more insufferable than she already was. 'I can't see Thomas enjoying that. He'd rather look at his charts than be wining and dining.'

'He may not enjoy it but he'll have to do it,' said Maria, slumping back on her stool.

The green asp of jealousy slithered around Rose's neck and settled on her shoulder as she thought of high born young ladies in their silks and jewels catching Thomas's eye. She saw him gazing into their upturned faces while they danced, hands touching. He'd never admire her in that way.

'You'll have to confess your sinful thoughts about Father Rulf to Father Rulf,' she remarked to Maria. 'I'd love to hear you do that.'

'M-Maria, you c-can't! It would be too embarrassing,' said Eleanor.

'Be quiet, El. You're just jealous, Rose-miller, because I shall meet my earl and be a countess and you'll be stuck here as an old maid. Even William left you.'

Rose bit back a smile at Maria's attempted insult. Inside, she was dancing on clouds. William was out of her life, and now she'd got over her initial guilt, she felt light-headed with joy and relief. She was free and wanted to shout it from the hilltops. No more skulking across the yard in case he saw her, no more squeezing onto the end of the bench to avoid his too-friendly arm and no more breathing the stifling smell of ash oozing from his clothes.

She straightened her face. It wouldn't do to look too happy; folks would think her heartless. 'William didn't leave me. It was a misunderstanding, that's all, and I can't wait for you to marry some miserable old earl. And he will be old and miserable, because you're not pretty enough for a handsome young noble to want you, and then you'll be gone and I won't have to listen to you—'

'Stop it you two! Or I'll need a dose of my yarrow tonic to clear my head. Maria, you help El, and Rose, you come with me and see what I've been doing in my dyeing shed.' Annie threw the last of her wool into a bag, went to the door and held it open, an impatient grimace on her face.

Rose had little choice but to pack away her threads. 'You might have your dreams, but I have mine,' she muttered under her breath, thrusting her feet into her shoes.

Annie marched to the linhay, the folds of her skirts slapping against her boots. 'You and Maria should beg pardon,' she said as Rose scuttled alongside to keep up. 'We're all sick of your bickering.'

She'd never do that. Provoking Maria brightened her day. 'She started it, so she's got to say first.'

'I don't care who started it or who begs pardon first; just stop squeaking and squabbling with each other like a pair of babies. Now, let's go in.'

In a line down the middle of the linhay stood a row of three large open-topped tun barrels, and two rows of hazel-drying poles hung from the beams along the back wall, suspended by willow twine. On one side, crude wooden trestles bowed under the weight of bowls, pots and baskets of all sizes.

'I wanted somewhere close to the river for water. I must be getting old; the pails seem heavier every day. We can't start making the dye yet because we won't harvest the madder roots until the autumn,' said Annie.

'I thought we'd use the leaves,' said Rose.

'Not for this, but I do use them to help women get with child. I make a tonic drink, something else I'll show you.'

She wasn't interested in making tonic drinks for barren old women, but the potential for the madder and Chiddleigh Scarlet did interest her. 'Tell me about the dye.'

'We'll have to replant new madder every year,' said Annie. 'In time we'll have them growing at all stages. I want to try harvesting two-year plants; they'll have bigger roots. That's something Lady Joan never tried. I must ask Thomas if we can have a corner of the field behind the orchards.'

More gardening?

'I'll show you how to make the dyes,' said Annie, warming to her subject. 'It's fun; I know you'll enjoy it!'

Rose doubted that, but if she were to take over the dyeing and cloth-making, she needed to know all she could. Besides, Annie was alright as a friend. A bit fussy, but she would be a good ally. After all, she was respected by folks and close to Thomas, who'd seemed preoccupied since William had left. And she might learn something more of Annie's friendship with Lady Joan. It mightn't be so bad after all.

'I expect I shall,' she said with a smile.

'The madder roots are boiled in water until they turn to a pulp, then strained through wooden sieves into the first barrel.' Annie talked quickly, her cheeks flushed with enthusiasm. 'Then we add alum if we can get it, but if we can't, there's a moss that works well.'

'Did you and Lady Joan use that?'

'Yes. In the beginning, we used too much and the cloth went sticky, but we got it right in the end. After adding the moss, we mix it with long poles, something else we'll need. Then we boil it all together in limewater.'

Rose edged a little closer. 'How did you get involved with Lady Joan's dyes? Were you helping her as a friend?'

'I suppose so, but I'm interested in anything to do with plants.' Annie walked over to the last barrel and stood by it, resting a proprietary hand on the top. 'In here, we do the exciting bit. This is where—'

'Only when I was little, I used to watch you and Lady Joan having picnics on the other side of the river with her three children and with Eleanor,' Rose interrupted. 'You played bears, chasing each other around the trees. It looked like fun and I wanted to play bears too, but Ma said a miller's lass wouldn't be welcome. Why were you with them?'

Annie pursed her lips and thrust her hands deep into her apron pocket. 'I wasn't always with them. I went on some of the picnics for the children, that's all. Thomas was a frail little boy and Lady Joan wanted me there.'

Thomas was still frail; that was what she found most attractive about him. Annie's story sounded plausible, but according to the gossips, she and Lady Joan had been friends since long before Thomas was born. What made them friends in the first place?

'Now, are you interested in the dye or not?' said Annie.

'Yes, of course,' Rose said. 'What happens next?'

'We can add other ingredients, like brazilwood, to get different shades of red, but it grows in the hot eastern lands where the spices come from and is expensive and difficult to get. But it's the bright scarlet that everyone wants, and I know the recipe. I'll tell you the secret ingredient, but you must swear on your soul not to tell anyone. I'm only telling you because if God should take me, you'll have to take over the dyes.'

She didn't intend to wait that long, but nodded seriously. 'Of course I promise.'

Annie leaned close and whispered, 'It's feather moss.'

'Feather moss!' She choked back a laugh. Based on Annie's secrecy, she'd been expecting a story of a secret flower that only bloomed under the full moon, or some such tale. 'Is that all?'

'Shh! Keep your voice down. It grows on the peat bogs on the high moors. We'll have to gather it. I thought of using that because Ellyn and I used it to make a soothing lotion and when you pulp it, the juice is red. It took Joan and I months to learn how much to use. When it finally worked, we were so excited, we danced around the shed together.' Annie stared into the barrel and cleared her throat, rubbing a hand across her face. 'My, the dust in here is terrible!' Flustered, she moved to the last barrel. 'The last thing we do is add urine to fix the dye. It stinks and stings your eyes but you get used to it. That's it really.'

Dancing around a shed with Lady Joan? Crying at the memory? Rose was bursting to know more, but her Ma always said she had a nose the length of a snuffling sow after acorns. Better not to push Annie too far. Maybe Thomas knew something, but she'd hardly seen him since that priest arrived. After the way William left, she needed a way to make friends with him again, and Annie had just handed her the perfect excuse.

'I'm looking forward to making the dye; I've not done it before,' she said. 'I think I'll speak to Thomas about that extra ground. Any idea where he is?'

Annie shrugged. 'Last time I saw him, he was heading for the woods with his chess set tucked under his arm.'

She would wager the few silver pennies in her purse that Thomas was going to Father Rulf's cave. He could have asked her if he wanted a game. They hadn't played chess for weeks.

Stepping back into the yard, she leaned thoughtfully against the water trough. If Father Rulf took her place at the chessboard, she'd lose her best opportunity to be with Thomas, and she liked being with him. He was clever and gentle, quite the opposite of William.

She lingered over images of the way he smiled and the flop of hair falling over his brow making him appear vulnerable then shook herself and straightened her skirts. What was she thinking? She'd just got her freedom from one man, and here she was daydreaming about another! Anyway, it was impossible, Thomas was highborn and she was common folk. He'd never be interested in her in that way.

Eleanor started ringing the bell for the third quarter with her usual gusto. Where had the day gone? She had meant to meet the new women and start allocating tasks. There were a couple who looked young and strong; she'd put them to digging Annie's extra madder plants. It would save her the job. The children could work with Gee scaring crows off the crops and picking stones from the fields.

Jarin came out of the smithy carrying heavy lengths of iron.

'Are the scythes ready for the harvest?' she called across to him.

Jarin dropped his load by the door and wiped his brow. He looked up and his round face turned into a smile. 'They are that, honed and sharp as an old wife's tongue.'

'Did Gee do that?' She pointed to his left eye which was black and swollen.

Jarin hung his head. 'He don't mean nothing by it. He just gets the drink in him some nights.'

'God's teeth, Jarin; you should hit him back. You're strong enough.'

'Couldn't do that. He's my Pa and he's old.'

'I would, and you should see Annie, she's bound to have something for the swelling.'

'I will.' He cocked his head to one side. 'Can you keep a secret?'

Two secrets in one morning? This was turning out to be quite a day. 'Of course.' She stepped closer.

'I've started watering his drink, so he doesn't get so violent.' Jarin grinned sheepishly.

'Good for you. How are you settling in?'

'I like it here. It's good to have my feet in one place. I've spent my whole life travelling with Pa, picking up work where we could and making and selling a few bits here and there. I learnt a lot and can turn my hand to most things, but I like the forge. I'm thinking to be a proper smithy one day.' Jarin's face grew wistful. 'Do you think Peter would take me on as an apprentice?'

'He might but it would cost. Can Gee afford it?'

'Doubt he'd pay even if he could. He's tight as a sow's arse. Best get back, have to keep the embers hot or Peter'll be after me.' His cheeks dimpled as he grinned before dashing back into the darkness of the forge.

He was a good lad, and according to Peter, a hard worker who never complained. She hoped Peter would take him on. Jarin deserved a break.

Whistling coming from the lane made her look up. It was Thomas. He'd been doing that a lot recently, and he walked tall with his head high and he laughed more. Why, she had no idea. Hastily shoving stray curls under her coif, she hurried to meet him..

'I've been looking for you,' she said.

'Oh? Well, now you've found me.'

He was heading for the house. The women would have to wait. She turned and walked with him.

'We are still friends, aren't we?' she said. 'After William, I mean.'

'I don't hold a grudge, if that's what you're asking,' he said throwing open the door with a grand gesture.

It wasn't, exactly, but it was better than nothing. She watched as Thomas went to his chest and put away his chess set.

'Was that what you wanted to see me about?' he said, closing and locking the lid.

'That and Annie needs more ground for planting madder. Can we use the corner of the orchard?'

'Of course, but the field might be better. Take both if you want. Our future rests with the dye.'

'I'll tell her.' She bit her lip. 'And…I was hoping we could have a game of chess, but it's too late now. The others will be back for their meal. Maybe tomorrow?'

'T-Thomas can't tomorrow. We're taking the first honey and c-combs from the bees, and he's chosen me to help him, haven't you T-Thomas? And Annie and I are going to m-make candles with the wax. I'm m-making wicks, see?' Eleanor held up a length of braided reeds.

'You deserve the honour of taking the first honey, and you're doing a fine job,' said Thomas.

She doubted he'd know a good wick from a bad one, and a week ago, he wouldn't have cared.

'And Janet and I are making the mead. It's all arranged,' said Maria, smiling sweetly.

'C-can I help? How do you m-make mead?' said Eleanor.

Rose bristled. She was in charge of the house, and in her book that included things like honey, candles and mead. 'You can help me, El. I'll show you.'

She glanced at Thomas to see if he would respond, but he seemed lost in his own little world, still humming that interminable little ditty. She would give a good deal to know what was making him so cheerful.

The following morning, Rose waited by the trough in the yard for Thomas and Eleanor to get back with the honey. She had no idea how long they would be, but there was no way she would let Maria take over the making of the mead, so she had got there early. And she wanted to see Thomas about a game of chess before he sidled off somewhere.

Idly, she ran her foot through the dust. Things were different since the new people came. Everywhere she went, folks were busy in the fields, and she couldn't remember the last time she walked the valley without having to dodge someone.

Cruck homes and cottages of various designs were springing up beside the path, and the sawyer, the tall thin one with a finger missing, was building a saw pit halfway along the cleave. Men were digging drainage ditches for more grazings and earthlings were ploughing strips ready for sowing wheat and oats for the next year. The wash pool, once a quiet place, was now over run by groups of women gossiping as they cleaned their pots or under garments with stones. Simon was organising work as he used to and the place had the buzz of a real manor. They even had a priest.

She should be pleased, but in many ways, she'd preferred the way it was when they'd first arrived. The eight of them had been like a group of friends, and Thomas hadn't seemed like a lord. Now, folks were bowing to him and doffing their caps as he passed and he seemed to like it. If this carried on, she'd be bobbing a curtsy to him herself.

She glanced up at the sun. It was nearing midday and it felt like she'd been sitting there forever. Last night, Simon and Thomas had been talking about getting the mill working over the coming dark months. Simon even suggested he return north to find more folks. Annie had poked her nose in and said with the extra sheep, they needed a proper dairy to make and store cheese and what about using the old cart sheds? If Annie had any thoughts about her working in the dairy, she had another think coming.

And how long before Simon appointed a reeve? When he did, where would that leave her? She hated to admit it, but Maria was right: she could easily end up as a maid in the mill and then she'd be back where she started.

She needed Thomas's friendship more than ever.

Janet came into the yard with pails and an assortment of bowls. 'Rose, hail. They should be here any moment.'

And as soon as she'd said it, Thomas and Eleanor walked into the yard with baskets laden with honeycomb.

Peter must have been waiting for them too because he hurried across from the forge. 'M'lord,' he said, lowering his hood. 'I've found a spot for Father's Rulf's church. 'Tis a fine site. Can I ask ye to take a look?'

'I hoped we'd have a game of chess.' said Rose.

'You said we'd m-make m-mead,' said Eleanor, her face dropping. 'You *promised*.'

'We will,' she answered, 'but we've got to let the honey drip first.'

'I can't now, anyway,' Thomas said, and she wasn't sure if he was talking to her or Peter. 'I'm seeing Father Rulf.'

''Tis only up the hill, m'lord,' Peter persisted. 'I've got something to see to in the forge – it won't take long – and then can ye take a look at the site?'

'Quickly then, but your work here comes before any church building. There's no need for haste. I'll walk on, you can catch me up.'

That was that, then. So much for a cozy game of chess.

'We can m-make the m-mead now, can't we Rose?' said Eleanor, smiling at her.

She was in no mood for Eleanor's constant questions. 'I said we had to let the honey drip first! Don't you ever listen?'

Eleanor's chin wobbled and her eyes began to water.

'She was only asking, Rose. No need to snap like a cur with a bone,' said Janet, collecting the baskets. 'Don't worry, El, I'll make the mead with you. Fetch some water and pour five jugs into another pail. When the honey has dripped from the comb, add one jug of honey to your water. Can you remember that?'

Eleanor nodded. 'Then can we drink the mead?'

'No, we have to leave it in the sun for six weeks and when it's got bubbles, we'll do the next bit,' said Janet.

Eleanor left for the river, a pail swinging from her hand. Janet spun back to face Rose, her mouth stretched in a tight white line.

'Can't stop; I have to help Annie,' Rose said hastily, turning on her heels. She hadn't intended to be mean to Eleanor, but God's bones, that girl was just so frustrating. With no hope of spending time with Thomas, it wouldn't hurt to help Annie with whatever she was doing.

Passing the forge, she heard Peter's voice, low and hushed. Curious, she crept to the side of the open door and listened.

'As I was saying, keep your lips sealed,' Peter said. 'Ye didn't say nothing to m'young lord, did ye?' said Peter.

She shuffled closer just in time to hear Annie reply, 'No, but—'

'But nothing!' Peter interrupted. 'I don't care what Lady Joan said. Best if Thomas never finds out. Do ye hear me?'

'Oh, I hear you, Peter.' Annie chuckled, but there was no humour in it and the sound froze Rose's blood. 'You and I both know that there's a lot Thomas should never find out.'

CHAPTER 28

Two weeks later, Thomas arrived at Rulf's cave. It wasn't only playing chess with an equal opponent that he looked forward to, although he relished the challenge; it was simply being with Rulf. He could be himself when he was with him and not worry about behaving like a lord. It was as if they understood each other without having to speak.

Ducking through the entrance, he saw Rulf rummaging through his bag.

'Rulf, hail.'

'Are you here again?' Rulf asked, tossing clothing across the floor. 'That's every afternoon this week. I could have sworn I put my belt in here.'

Thomas hesitated, suddenly unsure. 'I thought you liked me coming.'

'Here it is! I do, but not if you're neglecting work elsewhere.' Rulf looked thoughtfully at him. 'I have things to do too, you know, but they can wait. Let's have a game of chess; I'm keen to seek my revenge. Some wine?'

Thomas shook his head. After drinking it yesterday, he'd had a stomach pain that twisted inside like a hot knife for most of the night, and it had still been there when he woke up.

'I've brought cider.' He took his usual seat on Rulf's bench and began setting out the chessboard.

'I was in the woods yesterday.' Rulf sipped his wine and grimaced at the taste. 'Why are the men cutting trees and dragging them up the hill?'

'Peter's got men helping him build your church. Didn't I say?' he said, placing the knight on its square.

'You said you'd seen the site, but you never said it was on top of the hill. Is he trying to kill me? By the time I've walked up there, I'll have no breath to give the Mass. You're the lord. Tell him to build it in the valley.'

'He says you're God's gift to his soul, and your church has to be closest to Him. Never knew he was so pious. Anyway, he's already laid the stones and there's nowhere in the valley to put a church. We need more peasants and they've got to live somewhere. Simon already has the sawyer building a sawmill close to the river, Annie wants to grow more madder for the scarlet dye and Rose thinks we should use the wet reed beds for carp ponds.'

'With all that going on, no wonder you escape up here.' Rulf smiled. 'I'm pleased that you do.'

He felt ridiculously elated. 'We're both escaping,' he said.

'Hiding more like. Peter cornered me again yesterday, begging me to hear his confession. Do you know, every time I step outside this cave, I find myself looking over my shoulder expecting him to pop up behind a bush? He says I'm his saviour and pesters me to cleanse his soul. I suppose I should get it over with, but I'm beginning to dread what I'm going to hear,' said Rulf, positioning the last two pieces on the board.

Thomas knew there were a lot of people waiting to confess, himself included, but he'd be too embarrassed to tell Rulf his innermost sins. He'd have to see the priest at

Holscombe next market day. 'I thought you took the Mass very well the other day. You sounded like a real priest.'

Rulf laughed. 'I am a real priest. My time as an acolyte wasn't completely wasted, no matter what my bishop uncle said at the time.'

'Yes, but I mean with the voice of God.'

Rulf raised his eyebrows. 'If God speaks through me, I've yet to hear it but I'll let you know if it happens. Now, before you open play there's something I'm rather excited about. Take a look at this.' Rulf spread Thomas's charts on the floor. 'At first, I didn't believe it, so I used the astrolabe and drew the charts further ahead. My drawings aren't fine, but I think they're accurate.'

Kneeling beside Rulf, Thomas was aware of the other man's closeness and felt heat rise to his face. In an effort to cover his confusion, he pulled the charts closer and spoke quickly. 'I didn't know you have parchments and ink. I've only four pieces left. We'll start making our own from goat and sheep hides soon, but I'm nearly out of ink. It's expensive and I'm trying to save.'

'For the great day of escape.' Rulf chuckled. 'Why buy ink when you can make it? It's simple enough.'

Thomas focused entirely on the chart, but could still feel Rulf looking at him and wished with all his heart that his cheeks weren't still hot and flushed. 'I don't know how. At home and in the monastery, the ink pots were always full.'

'Then I'll show you but not until after we've harvested the grain. That's the time to do it. Now, forget that and tell me what you think of this.' Rulf ran a finger along a black line on the chart.

Thomas followed the line, paused and then traced another line back across the parchment. He turned the charts around and then back again. Frowning, he bit the inside of his cheek in concentration and retraced the lines a second time.

'I'm right, aren't I?' said Rulf leaning forward. 'See here and here, how the lines converge.'

Slowly, Thomas sat back on his heels. 'Yes, you are. Dear God, you know what this means?'

Rulf nodded sagely, 'I do.'

'I can hardly believe it. There's going to be an eclipse.'

'Not just any eclipse, my friend, a full eclipse.'

They stared at each other, then simultaneously, their faces stretched into broad grins. Rulf clasped his hands on Thomas's arms, pulled him close and slapped him on the back as they burst out laughing.

'If you were a maid, I'd dance you around the floor,' Rulf declared. 'What a discovery! Assuming my calculations are correct, it will happen in two years, just after harvest time.'

'Not a bad omen, I hope,' said Thomas.

Rulf laughed. 'You don't believe in that nonsense, do you? Drink up, we're celebrating.' Throwing the remains of his wine on the ground, he poured two full cups of Thomas's cider. 'To the eclipse!'

'The eclipse,' he echoed, clinking his cup against Rulf's. 'It's every astronomer's dream. The last one was over a hundred years ago. People thought a dragon was eating the sun and it was the end of the world!'

Rulf topped up their cups and resumed his seat, dismissing the comment with a flick of his hand. 'Foolish folks' tales. Accounts of it say that day becomes night quicker than the sun rising. The air turns cold, birds roost and the land falls silent. For those who dare to look, it appears as though the sun is being eaten, bite by bite until it's nothing but a black disc with a ring of flames.'

'The Devil's Ring of Fire. I've heard of that. It's said you can go blind looking at it.' Thomas sipped his cider.

'I'll take the risk. You know as well as I do that it's not the devil's work, just the moon coming in line with the sun and the Earth. You'll have to prepare your people nearer the time, though, or they'll panic.' Rulf chuckled. 'How you're going to do that, I've no idea.'

Neither did he, but God willing, he'd be in Oxford by then, and his people would be someone else's problem.

CHAPTER 29

September 1349

In the flickering light of a taper, Thomas sat with his charts spread out before him, lost in a world of lines and predictions. The signs boded well for a good harvest, but it was the eclipse that was exciting him.

Since the day he and Rulf had celebrated the discovery, he had checked and rechecked their calculations and was confident that in two years they would witness the greatest of all astronomical events. Hopefully, he'd be with Rulf in Oxford on that day, but only if things went well here and Rulf agreed not to leave in the spring.

If Rulf left, he didn't know what he'd do. His life would become a lot duller, but it went deeper than that. He felt a sense of rightness when he was with Rulf, as though they belonged together. Part of him enjoyed such closeness, but the other part didn't like how vulnerable it made him feel.

He pushed his charts away. He should be checking the fields for reaping. It was the most important time of the year. This was the time that would decide whether they would have enough to eat or struggle through another winter on meagre rations. It was also a time when he'd know whether he could pay the men. He had no idea what he'd do if he couldn't.

Stepping outside, he glanced skywards for signs of rain. Praise God, there were no clouds. Rose was in the yard, chivvying folks to finish their tasks in readiness for the coming harvest. Women were stacking baskets of twine in piles around the yard, and Jarin's newly honed scythes stood in neat lines against the wall like soldiers lined up for duty. Rose was good at her job; he couldn't deny that.

Reaching the fields, Thomas shielded his eyes against the sun. Strips of golden oats and wheat stretched before him, standing alongside bands of pale green barley and covering the ground like a patchwork blanket. It seemed impossible that five of them had ploughed and planted all that. Rulf had said he should be proud, and he was.

He snapped an ear of wheat and rubbed it between his hands as he'd seen Simon do. The grains came away from the husks easily. They were ready.

Above him, swallows swooped in graceful arcs, and Thomas paused to watch them. They had always fascinated him. Every year, they gathered in large chittering groups as the leaves began to fall, and by morning they would be gone until the spring. He'd never seen them leave, and as far as he knew, neither had anybody else. Maybe it was true that they wintered at the bottom of rivers, but if they did, why didn't they drown? More of life's questions to be answered.

The rumble of cartwheels and a cacophony of bleating sheep disturbed his reverie, and he turned to see a huge flock coming along the trail.

William was back.

His shoulders tensed as he watched the tide of sheep coming towards him. Whatever happened, there was little he could do. Pray God, he and William could beg pardon, laugh at their foolishness and be friends again. William had certainly done well; there were two, maybe three hundred sheep. That was a lot of cloth. Figures clicked rapidly in his mind and came to a tidy sum.

A couple of men with crooks walked among the flock, calling and keeping the sheep together. Following them were three wagons, and bringing up the rear was a rider mounted on a fine chestnut horse.

There was no sign of William astride his shaggy grey pony with his long legs dangling, his feet nearly touching the ground. Thomas's gut twisted. Was William still so angry that he'd stayed behind, or had something happened to him?

'Will's back,' Rose said in his ear, making him jump. Wherever he was, she popped up. Whatever he was doing, there she was again, offering to help or butting in or pestering him for a game of chess. He was getting tired of it.

'You'd best go back to the house,' he said, deliberately not looking at her.

'Why? They'll be ages yet, and Will won't see us from here.'

There was no us. He moved away. 'Go and help Janet get food and drink ready. They'll need it after their journey. And go to Simon up at the mill. Tell him Will's back and he's to come down.'

That was assuming William was back. Keeping his back turned, Thomas half-smiled at the exaggerated sigh and furious ruffling of skirts, followed by the thumping of boots as Rose stomped away.

He could be firm when he tried. It was easier these days, and he had Rulf to thank for that. When Rulf was present, he had to act more like a lord, he didn't want Rulf to think him weak.

The new folks helped too. They took his title for granted and paid him due respect. Even Peter had dropped the *m'young lord* to just *m'lord* and removed his cap or lowered his hood. True, he only did it in front of Father Rulf, but it was something he thought he'd never see. Yes, he had a lot to thank Rulf for.

The drovers whistled and waved their crooks as they herded the flock through the first gateway into the valley field. Simon had organised hazel fencing from the top hedge to the bottom to create a separate field from the crops for precisely this purpose. It had been a huge task; cutting and pointing the poles, weaving thinner branches to make panels and securing them with strong bramble twine, all of which had taken a dozen men over a week to finish.

The drovers closed the gate and secured it with twine as the oxen ambled passed with the wagons, accompanied by the sound of a sickening crack when a wheel dropped into a rut.

Thomas hurried across the fields and was waiting in the yard as the first wagon turned through the narrow opening, piled high with wool. He watched the man on the fine chestnut dismount, and without a word, a young lad scrambled off the first wagon and hurried over to take the horse. The man turned, and Thomas couldn't believe his eyes.

It was William, looking very different from the angry young man who had left a few months ago. His face was well-tanned, his old straggly beard was neatly trimmed, and his hair was cut straight to the shoulder. He wore a cream linen over-tunic of fine cloth, drawn in at the waist by a well-crafted leather belt with a large shining buckle, and his knee-high boots, though dusty from travelling, were of quality leather. How had he been able to afford such things?

William removed his blue felt feathered hat and bowed low with a sweeping flourish. 'Sheep as I promised, my lord,' he said, rising. 'And two wagons of fleece, separated into long outer layers and shorter, inner layers, washed in water and lime to remove the grease, dried and beaten to separate the fibres and now ready for combing and dyeing for you to spin or sell as you desire.' He stood before him with an air of satisfaction.

Thomas was lost for words and before he could think of something to say, William swept his arm wide towards the first wagon. 'Also, my lord, I have brought Mark and his family to settle here. They were travelling your lands and hail from the port of Portsmouth. They were driven out by the Pestilence and have been on the road looking for a place to settle.'

Mark pulled down his hood revealing a shiny bald dome, reminding Thomas of an egg, and dropped his chin to his chest. 'My lord.'

'This is Mark's son, Dain.' William indicated the thin young lad holding his horse. Dain was nearing Thomas's age with enough red hair for him and his Pa. 'You'll find he's a way with horses. Mark's wife and his two younger sons are in the wagon; they're strong and healthy. I thought they might be of use to you.'

William not only dressed like an equal; he spoke and acted like one. Even the way he stood, looking him straight in the eye, was disturbing. Where was the hot-tempered smithy's son? The more he regarded William, the more bewildered he felt.

'Be welcome, Mark,' said Thomas. 'You can take a plot along the valley next to the sawyer. Will—'

'Do my eyes deceive me?' Simon's voice carried across the yard as he walked briskly towards them, his arms outstretched in greeting. 'Will! Hail and God keep you.'

'And you, Simon.' Beaming, William clasped Simon hand to elbow as friends.

'What's all this? Fine cloth, high leather boots and a feathered cap? Found yourself a wealthy nobleman's daughter already?' Simon stepped back and laughed.

Thomas thought he should laugh too although he didn't find it very funny. William was dressed better than he was.

'Not exactly. I had a few coins put by and with a good run at the dice tables at the port...' William turned Simon away and lowered his voice, 'There's a certain wine merchant's daughter on the north coast near Bristol that I've my eye on, but I must raise my game to get her, you understand. You should have seen Thomas's face when he saw me!'

The two men laughed, and Thomas strained to hear more as they bent their heads close and moved away.

Mark turned his wagon and left the yard with the rest of the men, leaving Dain and Thomas staring at each other.

'You can put the horse in the stables behind the barn,' said Thomas. Turning, he saw Simon slap William manfully on the shoulder and felt like an outsider in his own yard.

William sauntered back and stood, jangling the bulging purse that hung from his belt. Thomas eyed it enviously. Damn it, William had more wealth than he did.

'My lord, I owe you for the horse. When I left, you said I could take what I needed, so I took one of your Ma's — I mean, Lady Joan's young mares. I had to put her to the saddle, and now I should like to keep her, with your permission, of course.' He half-bowed, rising with a mocking smile.

'Will, we said a lot of things we shouldn't have and I beg pardon for it. You may keep the horse and welcome.'

'My lord is most generous, but I couldn't presume. I have means and I will pay her worth. I could give you the coins now if my lord prefers—'

Thomas bit his lip. William was deliberately making him feel small, saying that he had wealth and Thomas didn't. He ought to charge the full price and take the coins, but that would only prove William's point.

'—although, it would suit me better if you deducted my dues from the wool sales,' William finished. 'I paid the workers and drovers from my own purse, and I'd be obliged if you could recompense my outlay.'

Thomas wanted to wipe the smug grin off William's face, but he wouldn't give him the satisfaction. Anyway, he'd only lose a fight between them. And since when did William speak in such a manner, talking about *recompense* and *outlays*?

'As you wish,' was all he said.

'Thank you, my lord.' William bowed, took a step back and replaced his hat. 'Come, Simon! We'll take an ale cup or two, and I'll tell you my news.'

William, once his best friend and Simon, who had been like a brother to him, sauntered away together like fellows in arms. Savagely, Thomas kicked a stone across the ground. William was a successful man, wealthy and comfortable in his own skin, whereas he was still an impoverished lord clinging to a hopeless dream.

He swung his foot, sending another pebble flying. Who did William think he was? He was nothing but a smithy's son, but was strutting around as if he owned the place, ordering folks around, showing off his money and speaking like a highborn. Well, he, Thomas de Chiddleigh was lord here and could be just as assured, and he'd go and see those new people to prove it.

Holding his hands behind his back, he lifted his chin and strode across the yard in long, deliberate steps. Turning left and beyond the orchards, he passed a string of dwellings put up by his new people. Most were poor cruck houses, some with crude hazel fencing around their boundaries.

The sawyer had built a more solid cottage with beams and wattle and daub walls but then he had the skills. Gee's place was a stone and cob cottage looking a little incongruous against the stinking slop pails left unattended and the untilled vegetable patch overgrown with weeds.

As Thomas approached, Jarin ducked out of the door his hands clutching his hood and his head down.

'You're an idle lubber! Get back to that smithy and earn coins!' Gee shook his stick from the doorway.

Jarin didn't reply and walked onto the track with his shoulders hunched and turned for the forge. He nodded respect to Thomas as he passed but didn't look up. Jarin reminded him of himself when he was a boy. He'd wager the lad yearned for a word of praise from his Pa, just as he had.

Gee returned indoors and slammed the door, and Thomas walked on to where Mark and his family were unloading their wagon. He'd show them who was in charge.

Mark and Dain removed their caps. Mark's wife bobbed a curtsy, her arms heavy with clay bowls. Two young boys played hide and chase around the wagon.

'Stop playing and show some respect!' Mark ordered them. 'My lord,' he said with a nod, waiting.

Thomas cleared his throat' This is your plot from the stones here—' he indicated a point on his left— 'to the hawthorn over there.'

'We're grateful to you, my lord. The head shepherd said you'd give us a place and that you'd see us right. *A fair lord* was how he put it.'

William had said that? Suddenly, he didn't feel quite so resentful. 'Yes, well, I try to look after my people.'

'He said you did, and me and the boys are strong and the woman's a fair hand with the spindle. We won't let you down.'

'See that you don't.' That was the sort of remark a lord would make, but coming from him, it sounded rather petty. 'Finish here, then find Simon. He'll give you your work,' he added with as much authority as he could muster.

Annoyed with himself for having misjudged William, he strolled away. As he passed the orchards he saw Simon climbing over the fence. Despite a voice telling him he didn't care, he had to ask.

'How's Will?' he called out.

Simon fell in step alongside him. 'Will's doing well for himself. Being a man of respect suits him. He's almost finished rebuilding the old bailiff's house, did he tell you?'

'No, he didn't want to talk to me. I'd like to be friends again, but I don't think he's forgiven me,' Thomas said, stepping past a peasant laden with hazel poles. 'I was about to beg pardon when you butted in.'

'I had to. I didn't know how Will would react upon seeing you again, and I didn't want a row in front of the new men. It would demean both your positions.' Simon stopped and looked Thomas firmly in the eye. 'You're no longer boys, Thomas. You're the lord, and Will's your head shepherd. That's how he sees it. The eight of us have worked hard to make this your manorial seat. You've got peasants to do your bidding, wool to weave cloth, land tilled, ditches drained, hay gathered and soon, a mill to grind your grain. You're free to do as you wish, as a lord should be. It's now your job to trust us and be the Lord of the Manor. Ride your lands and smile at your people as you pass. Peasants are simple, superstitious folk. They need a noble to look up to; it gives them security.'

Simon was right. He did have a job to do; he just didn't want to do it. 'I'll be there for the harvest—'

'No, you won't. At least, not until it's gathered and we're ready for you to present the corn doll. Will and I will oversee the reaping. It's time for all of us to move on, you included. And talking of that, I've decided to leave the house. I'm a bailiff and should have a place of my own.' Simon strolled on, Thomas alongside. 'There's a flat piece of land with enough acreage for my status. It's across the river, but the men can build a pack bridge. We could do with one of those anyway for when the river rises. Nothing too grand, just wide enough for a man and a horse, the wagons can use the ford. I was thinking of a dwelling similar to Pa's with a herb garden, small orchard, few outbuildings. You remember?'

Of course he remembered. The place had been like a second home to him. 'You can't move out. It leaves me alone in the house with Rose, El and Maria.'

'I must. And Rose can't stay, particularly after what Will said. It wouldn't be right. There's still some folks who think you've a fancy to her. Tell her she'll have to find a place of her own,' Simon said, as though it was the easiest thing in the world.

'You tell her.'

'God's bones, it's your job! Just say that I'm building my own place and it wouldn't be proper for her to remain with the lord. She'll understand.' Simon shook a piece of wattle fencing as he passed. 'That's loose; I'll have to get that fixed.'

Thomas raised his eyebrows. 'She won't like it. I'll speak to Annie. Maybe it'll be better coming from her.'

Simon stopped and faced him. 'Don't hide behind Annie's skirts, Thomas. You do it. Rose can still run the house and the women; she's good at that. And speaking of women, Maria is highborn and your sister. The peasants need to see her as such; she can't be knee-deep in muck tending the fowl.'

That was all he needed; Maria playing the lady with Rose at her command. He could see his sister flouncing her way around the house, lifting her chin and giving orders in her haughty voice. That would really make the sparks fly, and he'd be caught right in the middle of it. 'I'll be left with only Maria and El for company,' he protested, even as he heard how weak he sounded.

'Then marry a wealthy wife who'll give you an heir and find a rich husband for Maria while you're at it.' Simon nodded at the trees laden with small green and red apples. 'The fruit's swelling nicely. That spell of rain did them good.'

'How am I going to find a suitable match for either of us? I'm not wealthy enough to get invited anywhere or to put up a dowry for any decent arrangement for Maria. Meanwhile, I'm left with the three of them.'

'Not forever.' Simon reached for an overhanging branch and twisted one of the apples, which remained firmly on its stem. 'Not ready yet, but it should be a good yield. Did I tell you I managed to mend the apple press?

It doesn't stick now so it'll be easier to turn. We could do with another one, though; it would halve the work. You should think about it.' He released the branch and Thomas watched it spring back into place, the green fruit bobbing on the stems.

Another apple press. Yet more drains on his coffers.

'I will,' he said, knowing full well that he wouldn't.

They were almost at the end of the orchard. 'Will's got his eye on a wine merchant's daughter, and I'm thinking of getting a woman too. It's time I had a wench to keep me warm at night.' Simon grinned at him. 'And on that happy thought, I'd better have a word with Mark and make sure he doesn't take more than his due space, else there'll be trouble from the others.'

Thomas didn't bother to say that he'd already checked. He was still reeling from the day's events. When he'd woken up that morning, the sun was shining and all was right with the world. Now Simon was moving out, and he was being told to parade around his lands, find a wife, marry off his sister, and his two oldest friends were thick as thieves and taking over. They were welcome to the place but as for the rest — God's teeth, why couldn't he be left in peace?

And to add to his troubles, tomorrow he would have to tell Rose she needed to move out.

CHAPTER 30

Thomas sat at the table, staring at the smoke stains on the walls. If he gazed at them long enough, he could make out the shapes of animals. In the far corner was something that looked like an angel with outstretched wings. When he was a young boy, he used to play the same game with clouds.

He had to tell Rose to leave.

He'd consulted his charts for help but could find nothing useful. Rose was busy rummaging amongst the sacks at the end of the room. It would be easier if she stood still, but she'd been muttering and sorting all morning. There was never going to be a good time, so he had better get on with it.

'Rose? Are you busy?'

'What do you think?' Rose turned to face him, one hand on her hip, waiting. 'What is it?'

One look at her stern face, her challenging grey eyes and the severe way her apron was tied around her waist and all his conviction disappeared. Some lads might find such assertiveness attractive, but it scared him.

'Do you think this place is, well, a bit small for all of us?' It was a weak opening, he knew, but he had to begin somewhere.

'What are you talking about? Of course I don't; we've managed until now, haven't we? You do come out with the strangest things!' When he didn't answer, she shrugged. 'If that's all you wanted to say, I've got to get on. All these pots and things need cleaning before the fresh harvest comes in, which won't be long now. Annie was saying that the last beans are ready and the berries are ripe to pick.'

He watched her resume her task, wishing he knew how best to broach the subject. Maybe it would be easier to talk to her over a game of chess and slide it into the conversation that way.

'How about a game of chess?' he asked.

Rose turned around again, her hand back on her hip. 'Why? Is Father Rulf busy?'

He winced. She knew how to aim the arrow when it suited her. 'W-what do you mean?'

'You know very well what I mean. You were only too pleased to play chess with me until he came along. I've been asking you to play for weeks, but you're always going off to that cave with your box tucked under your arm. I'm not at your beck and call just when it suits you,' she said, throwing baskets into piles. 'Anyway, I can't now. I've all this to do, and if you've nothing better to do than think of playing chess, you can take these betony leaves to Annie and tell her they're the last.' She thrust a pile of green leaves into his hands. 'Chess indeed! And don't slam the door on your way out!'

Resisting the urge to do just that, he closed the latch quietly behind him and made his way over to Annie's place, cursing his weakness with every step he took.

In her linhay, Annie was busy making candles. Her eyes lit up when she saw what he had brought. 'Betony!

I'll be needing that to make poultices for folks' head pains. Put it on the bench, I'll sort it later.'

'Rose says it's the last.'

'She's done well to find it at all. It grows amongst the grass; did you know?'

He didn't. 'Are you and Rose good friends?'

Annie wiped her hands on her apron and leaned back against the bench. 'I suppose so. I'm teaching her my dyes and lotions. After all, I won't be here forever!' She laughed, but there was a seriousness behind her eyes. 'Why do you ask?'

Thomas shrugged. 'Simon is moving out. It wouldn't be right for Rose to stay, but I can't think of how to tell her.' He didn't add that he'd already tried and failed.

'Pass me those wicks, will you? I've got a lot to do today, so we'll have to talk as I go, thanks.' She scraped a pile of beeswax into an iron pot. 'You're certainly right; it wouldn't be proper for Rose to live with you like that. Maria's your sister and Eleanor, God bless her, has no more wits than a child, but tongues would definitely start wagging about Rose.'

'In a way, I'll be pleased for Rose to move out. She never gives me a moment's peace, always wanting my attention and asking to play chess.'

Annie smiled. 'She could be sweet on you, have you thought of that?'

'On me?' The idea appalled him. 'She's a miller's maid and I'm a lord! She can't seriously believe — I mean, we'd never — if that's how she's thinking, then the quicker she's out of my house, the better.' Rose wasn't even his idea of an attractive maid. He wasn't entirely sure what was – he'd never given the subject any serious thought – but he knew it wasn't Rose.

'Then you'd better make haste and tell her. Pass me those twigs and moulds.'

It wasn't the answer he wanted. He passed the twigs and three iron cylinders about six inches tall by three inches wide, one end closed with a small hole in the centre and the other end open.

'Has Peter ever said anything about my decision between Will and Rose?' he asked.

Annie licked one end of a braided wick and threaded it through the hole in the top of the mould, leaving an inch poking out. She tied the other end around the middle of a twig and balanced it across the bottom.

'Peter's pleased as a swine in muck. He never liked the miller, and I know he wasn't keen on Rose for Will. Said she was too above herself and would give Will a hard time. You did him a favour, though he'll never admit it. Of course, if we were at Ashetyne, Rose would be married by now. Maybe that's what she needs, and it would solve your problem.' She looked up thoughtfully. 'Lief, the miller's lad, looks nice. And Rose is a miller's lass; what could be better? Or there's Jarin, although I wouldn't envy any lass having Gee as a father-in-law, let alone living under the same roof.' She paused with the wick in one hand and a stick in the other. 'Gee beats Jarin, did you know? I feel sorry for the lad. Help me carry these to the hearth, will you?' She thrust the moulds into his hands.

Thomas followed her obediently into the forge. Annie put the moulds on a wooden rack and the pot of beeswax on the edge of the embers to melt.

'The bees have done us proud,' she said. 'El's scraping the last of the honeycombs, and I should have enough for another three or four candles. I'll keep them by for special occasions.'

Mama always had the finest beeswax candles especially when she was giving a banquet. As the estate prospered, he'd have to mix with the local landowners to trade and that would mean entertaining them. It was the only way to find a husband for Maria, but he'd have to build a great hall and kitchens and pay a cook. The very thought had the coins draining from his coffer.

'Did Mama have an arrangement for Maria?' he asked.

Annie frowned. 'Now you mention it, she did say something about Lord Halifax's son. Your Papa and Lord Halifax were both farming rabbits at the time. But the last I heard, the son died of the sweating sickness and Joan never said about anyone else. Why?' She poked the embers into life and stood back, waiting for the flames to burst into life.

'It was just something Simon said.' Thomas watched the embers begin to glow.

'Well, it's something you should be thinking about. Maria's fourteen summers. She'll soon be past marriageable age, and you can't expect her to stay here. A wealthy connection wouldn't do you any harm either. You'll need a wife.'

'Don't you start. You know what I want and it isn't a wife.'

'I know, and I'm glad you stayed. You were vexed with me at the time, but staying was the right thing to do, wasn't it?'

He saw his chance and seized it. 'Talking of the right thing to do, there's something I've been meaning to say. I'm sure you know what Mama meant when she asked for my forgiveness. I want to know.'

Annie paled a little, then looked him full in the eyes. She was going to tell him about Mama. He was sure of it.

Then she sagged as though all the air had gone out of her and shook her head, turning away. 'No. Peter's right, I can't. It doesn't matter, anyway.'

'Annie, if it's to do with Mama, it does matter and you should tell me.' Frustration at being so close to the truth and confirmation of his initial suspicions both prodded him on. 'What was she talking about?'

'Nothing. Leave it, please.' Annie began fiddling with the candle moulds.

She knew. One day, he would get to the truth, but that day wouldn't be today. Annie could be as stubborn as an ox when she wanted to be.

'One thing I will say,' she added, 'is that it's your duty to produce an heir and you'd best do it before you go off to that fancy Oxham place of yours.'

'Oxford, not Oxham, and everything is my duty. I sometimes wish I'd been born a lass, then I wouldn't have all this.' He watched the melted wax spitting in the pot.

'No, you don't, believe me. And I can't stand here talking to you all day. I promised El she could help me pour the wax into the moulds.' Annie pinned her headdress in place. 'Then, for my sins, I must go and check on Gee's eye, though I doubt he's used the cabbage balm I gave him. Take that pot off the hearth for me, will you? Be careful, the wax is vicious when it's hot.'

He had to say something now or he'd miss his chance. 'I'd hoped you might speak to Rose for me about moving out. It would be better coming from you, woman to woman.'

'Oh no. You're the lord, it's your job. But you can tell her that she's welcome to live with me until she sorts herself out. Now, I must find El before that wax hardens.' Annie brushed past him in a bustle of skirts.

Thomas felt like hurling something across the forge. He was out of options. He'd have to tell Rose himself, and he'd have to do it now while he was in the mood.

Everyone kept reminding him he was the lord. Well, God's feet, he'd act like one.

CHAPTER 31

The walk back to the house wasn't far, but it was far enough for Thomas to work out what he was going to say: *Rose, sit down and listen. We're an estate now and things are changing, Simon wants a place of his own, and it's not proper for you and me to live here, even with my sister and Eleanor. You'll have to find somewhere else to stay. Annie said you're welcome to go in with her.*

Yes, that was the way to do it. Be positive, be firm, be a lord.

Pausing with his hand on the latch, he took a deep breath. He was ready. Good; Rose was on her own, chopping chard at the trestle. He took a few determined paces into the middle of the room, squared his shoulders and put his thumbs into the top of his belt. His Papa used to do that.

'Rose, I've something to say—'

'And so have I,' Rose interrupted. She turned to face him, the knife still in one hand. 'When are we going to play chess again? And don't tell me you are too busy, because you're always going off to play chess with Father Rulf.'

That wasn't how it was supposed to go. He swallowed. 'I asked you earlier and you said you were too busy.'

'Just because I didn't have time earlier doesn't mean I don't want to play at all. I do.'

God's bones, he couldn't win. 'For your information, Father Rulf and I don't always play chess. He has discovered something exciting in the charts and we're studying them.' He pushed his thumbs further into his belt. 'As I was saying—'

'Every day? Don't tell me; he's found a way to predict the weather and we'll never have to worry about the crops again.' Rose resumed her chopping with such force, the trestle shook beneath the blade. 'I don't know what's the matter with you recently. You're living in some sort of dream.' Chop, chop, chop.

That was true, and it wasn't a particularly nice one. Events were crashing over him like a wave pulling him under. William and Simon were enjoying a friendship he used to share; Simon was telling him to find a wealthy wife and a husband for Maria; and Annie kept reminding him of his duty to get an heir.

And then there was Rulf. There was always Rulf. Wherever Thomas was, whatever he was doing, Rulf was in his mind. The way he glanced at him with creases dancing around the edges of his eyes. The way his voice lowered when he made one of his dry comments. His easy manner as they sat on the floor of the cave together, their legs outstretched, hands folded behind their heads as they talked away the afternoon. Sometimes, Thomas resented the intrusion, but mostly he welcomed it like a warm cloak. Rulf was the one bright spot in his life.

'Did you hear what I said?' Rose's voice sliced through the air like her knife.

'Of course I did,' Thomas lied, his mind jerked rudely back to the present. 'Rose, listen: Simon is building a dwelling, and I'm sorry but that means you won't be able to stay here.' He watched her reaction, waiting for the outburst that he was sure would follow.

It never came. Rose just regarded him with a calculating expression until the silence became unbearable. In an effort to fill it, Thomas added, 'I mean, what would folks say?'

'If Simon's moving out, of course I can't stay, but where am I supposed to go?' Her eyes fixed on him, making him shift uncomfortably. 'I'm a lot more than a maid around here, and you know it. I organise the women, manage the stores, make sure the fowls and swine are fed, that the eggs are collected and sticks are gathered for the hearth, not to mention helping Simon with planning the wattling, ploughing and harvesting and I don't know what else. If I was a lad, I'd have been a reeve by now.' Her mouth tight, she began a savage assault on the carrots.

Thomas didn't see what any of that had to do with it, but then, he never understood how a lass's mind worked. Women's smaller heads meant smaller brains, so expecting logic from them was out of the question. 'I know you are, and we're grateful. None of that has to change. Annie said you could move in with her until you find a place of your own. It would be nice; you'd be company for each other.'

'So you told Annie before speaking to me?' Rose slammed down the knife and swept the carrots and chard into the pot with one practiced move.

She hadn't seen this coming, at least, not so soon. Thomas was right; she couldn't stay when Simon moved out, but maybe she could use this to her advantage. Maybe this was the opportunity she'd been waiting for.

She poked the embers into life and hung the pot on the hook. 'Well, no good getting vexed with each other.' She pulled two stools close to the hearth. 'Let's sit down and talk about this.'

When Thomas was seated, she softened her voice. 'You need me to move out and to take care of things for you, and I'm happy to do that, but how about we come to some sort of agreement?'

Thomas inched his stool away in much the same way she had often retreated from William. 'What sort of agreement?' he said.

'I want respect for what I do. Make me a reeve.' That was number one on her list of goals.

Thomas laughed. 'I can't do that! You're a lass.'

She'd been expecting that. 'I'm a lass who does everything a reeve does, and I do it better than most men. You're the lord. You can do what you want.'

Thomas hesitated. 'The men wouldn't stand for it. I'd be the only lord in Devonshire and probably the entire kingdom to have a woman reeve. People would laugh at me.'

Her heart rose a little. If he was raising smaller, individual objections, then he was weakening. 'So be the first. I'm as good as any man. One day, women will be given credit for what they do, though I doubt I'll live to see it.'

When he didn't answer, she moved to number two on her list. 'I'm learning about dyes, so give me the running of the red dye and the cloth sales.' Annie wouldn't like that, but she'd get over it and it would be worth the dirty looks and silent treatment for a few days. If the red cloth was as valuable as everyone said, then one day the estate would rely on the money it made. That meant whoever was overseeing the red cloth would be a powerful person.

'I'll put a loom in every cottage,' she added. 'You'll have the peasants weaving so much cloth that you'll need another coffer chest for all the coins you'll get.' All nobles wanted coins in their coffers, everyone knew that. She tilted her head and waited for Thomas to see the possibilities.

He shook his head. 'I can't give you the dye shed. That's Annie's responsibility. You could run the cloth sales though, if she doesn't mind.'

Rose nodded. One out of two wasn't bad, and she'd be in an ideal position to take control of the dye shed when the Lord called Annie home. She made a mental note to chase the sawyer about the looms he was supposed to be making. 'Annie won't mind. Leave her to me. And there's one last thing.'

'Something else?'

'Teach me to read and write.' Number three on her list.

'Whatever for?' Thomas blinked in surprise. Well, she'd expected that. Peasants didn't need to be literate to work for their lord; just obedient.

'Ma taught me my numbers, but if I can read and write, I can handle the merchants better. They'll respect me and I can get better deals for you, keep the records and write messages to save you the trouble.' She leaned close and added the final sweetener to the deal. 'You'd have more time for your charts.'

Would it work? His face was giving nothing away. Thomas may not realise it, but he was never going to be any sort of lord. Look at the way he'd come in. He should have been firm and positive; she'd have respected that. What he needed was someone capable and practical with their feet on the ground. Someone to make decisions and run things for him. Someone happy to let him gaze at the stars and live in his dream world.

Someone like her.

'But I'll need the title of reeve if I'm to write on your behalf,' she said.

Thomas ran a finger inside his collar, visibly wavering. Excited now, she pressed harder.

'It's only a name and the men'll get used to it. They'll have to if you tell them to. After all, you are the lord.'

Thomas nodded. 'Yes, I am, and I do need more time to study the stars because there's an important event coming. Are you sure you can cope with the extra responsibility? It's a lot for a lass.'

Of course she'd cope; it was barely more than she'd already been doing all this time. 'I'll manage.'

Thomas hesitated. 'I don't know, though. A woman reeve and a peasant who can read and write? You're asking a lot. I'll have to see what Simon thinks.'

If he did that, she was lost. Simon would never agree. 'You're the lord, not him. And when I move out, I'll be an independent woman. That will add respect to my being a reeve. The men will accept me more easily, just as they accept Annie. Stop hiding behind Simon and make your own decisions for once!'

Thomas sat up and squared his shoulders. 'I don't hide behind him. I just—I need time to think, that's all.'

God's feet, why couldn't he make a decision? 'What's to think about? You need a reeve, and I can do the job. As for the rest, I'll move out and take over the cloth sales. Who will care if I can read and write? And you can get back to your charts.'

Thomas glanced towards his charts and frowned. 'I do need more time—'

'Then you agree?' She held her breath, waiting for his answer. She'd never get another chance, and she was so close. In the silence that seemed to stretch forever, she could almost see his mind swaying one way and then another. If he said no, it would be the end of her ambitions. She'd face life as an unpaid reeve or a miller's maid, and she didn't want either.

Thomas nodded and slapped his thighs. 'You're right. I am the lord and why not? It suits both of us.'

Her heart soared. She'd done it! She'd done what no other woman had ever managed. She was going to be a reeve and an equal—no, better than that, she was going to be *above* most men. She could live where she liked, do what she wanted and choose whether to marry or not.

She had found her freedom. *Freedom.* She let the word roll in her mind. How good it sounded. She wanted to throw her arms around him, but he would hate that, and the last thing she wanted was to make him change his mind. Instead, she forced the excitement that threatened to burst out in great clouds of euphoria to the back of her mind to enjoy later.

Smoothing her apron, she stood up.

'That's settled then,' she said, resuming her place at the trestle and picking up her knife.

She was independent and a reeve! The very stones of the house seemed to glow with admiration. Now she'd show them what a mere miller's lass could do.

CHAPTER 32

Thomas hummed a tune as he strolled along with a spring in his step, his bag swinging on his shoulder. It was liberating to be rebellious. He'd made a daring pact with Rose and he'd done it on his own. Let Simon scoff if he wanted; it was a good agreement that suited them both. He got the house to himself and time for his charts, and Rose got what she wanted. It was better than trying to wed her off, as Annie had suggested. After the William fiasco, he didn't dare think what Rose would have said about that.

He turned onto the gorse path that led to Rulf's cave. Rose would soon get fed up after a few reading lessons, and what was in a name after all? If she wanted to call herself a reeve, let her. He wouldn't go out of his way to make it known. And if she could make and sell the red cloth as she said, he'd only need one more reeve and he'd be on his way to Oxford in a year or two.

Thomas waited until he and Rulf had finished their game of chess before telling him what had happened. When he did, Rulf leaned against the wall of his cave, threw back his head and laughed until tears rolled down his cheeks.

'It's not that funny,' said Thomas, packing away the chess set.

'Oh yes it is! A maid as reeve and a lord teaching her to read and write? It's the funniest thing I've heard in years!'

'It won't hurt anyone, and it solves my problem.'

'What did Simon say?'

'I don't have to discuss everything with Simon. I can make my own decisions.

'Can you really see the men taking orders from her?'

Deep down, he couldn't. Maybe he should have thought it through a little more, but Rose had made it sound like a good idea. It's done now, the men will have to accept it.' He closed the box and stuffed it into his bag.

'My dear friend, I always knew you were a rebel underneath that innocent façade. You're a man after my own heart and I admire your bravery.' Rulf threw an arm around Thomas's shoulder.

He didn't feel very brave, but he basked in Rulf's praise and quashed the uncomfortable knowledge of how much the priest's good opinion mattered to him.

'It's a beautiful day,' said Rulf. 'What do you say to a stroll over the high fields?'

'I say it sounds like a good idea.'

They walked together in amiable silence, the sun on their faces and the sound of the long dry grass swishing against their boots. Thomas could think of no nicer way to spend an afternoon. He'd never met anyone like Rulf, who shared his love of science and was brave enough to voice his radical views, the very danger of which was tantalising. Rulf made him feel alive, and his days were consumed with thoughts of him.

Did Rulf think of him when he was alone in his cave, or was Thomas just someone to while away his spare time with? The thought stabbed him uncomfortably. Surely, he meant more to him than that. Snapping off a piece of grass, he chewed the end. Knowing Rulf was a little disturbing but that added to the excitement.

'Father! Father, will ye wait?' Peter's voice called from behind, breaking his thoughts.

Rulf sighed, changed his face to that of an understanding priest and turned around. 'Peter, God be with you,' he said, his hands already folded neatly across his chest.

'M'lord.' Peter gasped with the effort of running up the hill. 'Father, are ye going to see the church? I'd be proud to show it ye.'

Rulf flicked a discrete look to Thomas, who gave a slight shrug. 'I'd like that very much. I'm sure Lord Thomas would too.'

The lines of a half-smile gave away Rulf's true thoughts. The church was the last place either of them wanted to visit, but in their different ways, they both had a duty to this sincere man. Thomas bit back a sigh. No matter how much he tried to escape, it was always back to duty.

'M'lord, I think ye'll both be surprised. Father…' Peter walked in step beside Rulf who, in full priest mode, bent his head to listen as though every word was the most interesting thing he had heard.

Thomas smiled to himself as he followed them along a new wide path going straight through the woods.

'We cut this to get the horse through with the logs.' Peter strode ahead, eager to show his work, his voice trailing after him. 'I know 'tis a climb, but it's the closest to God I could get for ye, and the church will be seen for miles around. Folks will come flocking to hear ye. 'Tis a church to be proud of, Father.'

They stopped at the bottom of a long steep flight of wooden steps, Peter's ruddy face alight with childlike pride. 'Tis no Exeter Cathedral, Father, but I'm hoping ye like it.' He didn't wait for a reply but began climbing.

Looking up at the flight of steps, Thomas exchanged a resigned shrug with Rulf before following in Peter's wake.

As they reached the last step, a crude rectangular building came into view. Perched on the very top of the hill, it sat precariously as though trying to decide whether to cling on or give up the fight and topple over the edge. Thomas reckoned it was only twenty paces by ten, but to be fair, it wasn't finished.

Peter puffed out his chest as he led them around the outside, pointing out the wattle walls balanced on a stone base and the upright poles that held them. Horizontal poles kept them in place with nails, he explained, and naked roof timbers pointing to the sky in rough triangles were waiting to be clothed in thatch just as soon as harvesting was finished.

It reminded Thomas of the peasant cruck houses that dotted the shire, their shape dictated by the curves of the poles that supported them, but that was all the men knew how to build.

'What do ye think, Father?' said Peter, standing back proudly.

Rulf tipped his head, looking at the small building from all sides. 'I can honestly say that I've never seen a church quite like it.'

Peter's chest visibly swelled. 'I knew ye'd like it! I told them so. We couldn't fetch enough stones up this far, but I reckoned God wouldn't mind a wooden house. We've more roof poles to cut and with m'lord's permission, we'll thatch with corn stalks and bracken. See here, Father–'

Thomas thought Peter was going to grab Rulf's sleeve, but he stopped himself in time and led them to a gap in the walls.

'This here'll be the doorway. The sawyer says as how he'll make us a fine door, and I'm thinking to cut a few openings in the walls. Sawyer says he can make us some shutters as well. Do ye want shutters, Father?'

Rulf stroked his chin. 'I think God will bless it with or without shutters. You've worked hard on this, Peter, so you should decide.'

'Then shutters it'll be.' Peter hesitated. 'Father, I was wondering...can ye hear me confession soon?'

'Ah, the confessional. Of course, but let's not hasten. I believe God has called you to this fine work. He and I can wait a little longer.'

Thomas bit his cheeks to stop himself from laughing. Rulf was doing his best to put off the dreaded day but if he knew Peter, nothing would stop him from finishing the church and they'd be trudging up this hill every Sunday for Mass and to confess their sins. Peter wasn't the only one who needed to cleanse his soul. He hadn't been to confession since the Pestilence and would feel easier if he did, although confessing to Rulf would be a step too far. He didn't know which of them would be the more embarrassed.

'It's been interesting, but the sun moves on and I mustn't keep you from your work,' said Rulf, inching towards the steps.

'As ye say, Father. I've left Jarin trying his hand at making nails and—'

Thomas followed on Rulf's heels, not waiting to hear what else Jarin had been left to do, but Peter wasn't finished and stayed close behind. 'Father, when the church is built, I'll start on your cottage. I'm thinking of cob, what do ye say?'

They had reached the steps. As they side-stepped their way down, Rulf turned to Thomas and whispered, 'What's cob?'

'Low round houses with steep thatch roofs. You've seen them on the estate. The cob part is the walls; they're made of mud, dung and straw and anything else the men can find. They tread it down with their feet or by walking an ass on it.'

'You Devonshire folks are more heathen than I thought. I'd rather stay in my cave.' Rulf straightened up a little and raised his voice. 'Peter, you do too much for me. I can't presume.'

''Tis no trouble. Don't ye worry, Father! I'll have ye out of that cold cave and snug in a cob before the year's out,' Peter called after them.

'God's bones, spare me from men seeking favour from their priest,' Rulf muttered. 'You're a good man, Peter. God bless you.'

'He means well, and we need a church,' said Thomas.

'Not if he's thinking to make me the priest, you don't.'

There wasn't much he could say to that. Did it mean Rulf was still intent on leaving in the spring? He hoped not.

At the bottom of the hill, he and Rulf took the left path as Peter turned right. In the valley field, Red Admiral butterflies flitted black, red and white amongst the blues, purples and reds of autumn flowers. The oats and barley were at that autumnal stage somewhere between green and dry yellow. Thomas ran his hand through the stalks. If it stayed dry, they would soon be ready to reap.

He glanced across to Rulf. He couldn't imagine life without him. Surely he wouldn't go?

'This takes me back,' Rulf said unexpectedly. 'I did a lot of walking on my own when I was a boy. I used to sit for hours watching and thinking and puzzling over things.'

'What kind of things?'

Rulf laughed. 'Trivial things that only a child would think of, like why are leaves green and not blue? I puzzled over that one for a whole summer.'

Thomas looked at the leaves. He'd never wondered about that before. 'And why are they?'

'I don't know. I'm still trying to work it out. Sometimes, I took to walking late and would stare at the twinkling stars wondering if God was lighting his candles. I tried counting them once but there were too many. I suppose that's how I became fascinated in the skies. What got you interested?'

'One of my tutors, Brother Leviticus, talked about astronomy. He was a physician and introduced me to reading charts and an almanac. *If you want to cure people you have read their chart first,* he'd say. I wanted to be like him. I still do. Why were you on your own?'

'I was the third son. My brothers were ten and eight summers older, and I was a nuisance. No one was interested in me. There were two others, a boy and a girl in between us but they both died of the Devil's rash before they were two,' said Rulf.

'I don't believe it's the Devil's rash,' Thomas said. 'That's why I want to study. If I can discover what causes the ailments, maybe I can find a cure.'

'A worthy cause, and I wish you well, because in God's truth, looking at the colour of urine and patterns in sheep's entrails doesn't seem to help any of us.'

Rulf was right, but it was all they had and most physicians believed in it. If only he could get to Oxford and learn, then one day he'd find the answers and could cure hundreds of people.

They'd walked over the far fields and began following the river valley below High Drovers Road. Almost hidden by overhanging willows and alder, the water cascaded over rocks as it left the high moor.

There was an air to the place that demanded whispers and a soft tread, like entering a church. Whenever Thomas came here, he felt he was intruding. If there were little people on the moor (which of course there weren't) this was where they would live. He planted a discrete kiss on a boulder to appease them, just in case.

'I was a lonely second son,' he said. 'I was never good enough for my Pa.'

'You told me he called you a weakling.'

Thomas nodded. The memory hurt even now. 'I decided then that I would never try to impress him again, and I never did. Instead, I told Mama I wanted to go to school. I don't know how she managed it, but she did; I went to study with the monks at Tavistoke and loved every moment. When I was home, I rode with Simon on his work around the estate and that's how I met Will.'

They'd reached the ancients' stepping stone bridge, a platform of large flat boulders balanced on piles of rocks that spanned the river from bank to bank. Some said the ancients' spirits hid underneath waiting to pull down unwary travellers to a watery death. It was all fadoodle, but Thomas still crossed himself and hurried across as quietly as he could for fear of disturbing them.

Following the river, they turned towards home, much to his disappointment. He wanted to walk and talk with Rulf forever and slowed his steps to make the walk last longer.

'I was never close to my mother,' said Rulf. 'You were though, weren't you?'

'Yes, although I never met any of her family apart from Eleanor, who lived with us. Papa's parents died when he was young and Combe Hide was his Uncle Boren's place but we never spoke of him. An old family feud or something. And there are other secrets; Mama asked me to forgive her for something, but she wouldn't tell me what and it's been worrying me ever since. I'm sure Annie knows but she won't say.' He paused and looked deep into Rulf's eyes. 'I've never told anyone that before.'

'Some family secrets are best left unrevealed.' Rulf threw an arm around Thomas's shoulder. 'Come, the day is too bright for such serious thoughts, and we're dawdling.'

Thomas had never felt happier, and it was some while before Rulf removed his arm.

CHAPTER 33

Two days later, it was the start of the autumn harvest, the most important time of the year. A time when everyone worked, sang, rested and ate together. A time of camaraderie when old quarrels were put to one side, for it was a time that could decide the difference between life and death.

Before dawn, families gathered in the yard as Thomas looked on from the open door of the house. Outside the forge, men dressed in ragged tunics and woollen hose picked over the pile of sickles and scythes, checking the blades for sharpness.

Several tight circles of women stood gossiping, their hair tucked under their coifs, leather mitts stuffed into their aprons and their woollen shawls pulled tight across their chests as children played chase amidst the organised chaos.

Above it, Thomas heard Simon's quiet, experienced authority directing the oxen and wagons out of the yard. William followed behind with a column of peasants, the sound of their voices drifting behind them. Thomas strained to hear as they splashed through the ford and followed the track round the bend to the fields and out of sight.

This was what he'd worked for. To have others take over so he could be free to do as he wished. Now the time had finally come, he didn't feel free; only left out.

The place echoed with silence. Violently, he kicked a stone, sending it hurtling across the ground. It was fine for Simon to say lords didn't reap the harvest, but what was he supposed to do? Apart from Maria and Eleanor in the house, he was the only one not working. Janet and a few women would return at midday to fetch the flagons of cider and the bread and cheese to take back to the fields, but after that, everyone would be toiling until the moon was high.

He sat down on the cutting log by the door, picked up a stick and idly scratched an isosceles triangle in the dirt. It was always an isosceles. Why did he do that? Deliberately, he scratched an equilateral and then an acute triangle, just to be different. Irritated, he scrubbed them out, tossed the stick aside and watched it bounce across the ground. Letting out a loud sigh, he rubbed his hands on his thighs and stared around.

Rulf had said he was picking berries to make more of his disgusting wine. Thomas would enjoy spending a day wandering the hedgerows with him. He had no idea which way Rulf would go, but the other day, he'd seen masses of whortle berries and thick blackberry brambles while they'd been walking below High Drovers Road. That would be a good place to start.

He collected some baskets from the house and took the shortcut below Peter's half-built church, dropping down to the valley and heading for the sound of the river and the ancients' bridge. It was still early, but the heat was already rising, sending ribbons of heat shimmering from the path. There was no shade, just mounds of purple heather and spiked bushes of yellow gorse filling the air with a pungent nutty smell that announced the arrival of autumn.

When he reached the bridge, he stopped to splash his face in the cool water.

'Rulf!' he yelled. There was no response, only the caws of startled crows taking flight from a nearby copse of ash trees.

He'd carried the baskets all this way; he might as well pick something. Janet could bottle the berries in sweet mead or dry them for the winter. With good fortune, Rulf might show up later.

When he'd filled the baskets, Thomas stretched and wiped his red-stained hands on the back of his tunic. The sun was at its highest and beat down ferociously. He'd finished the last dregs of cider, but his throat was still parched and now his stomach was growling as well. The tinkling of the river was tempting, but fresh river water made you sick. No one knew why; only that it did. He wasn't going to meet Rulf now, and disappointed, he picked up his baskets and turned for home.

By the time he reached the high fields above Rulf's cave, his arms felt as though they were being pulled from his shoulders and the handles slipped through his sweating hands. Loud chittering gave him the excuse to stop and look up. A flock of swallows twisted and turned high on the wing, so fast he couldn't keep up. It was a good omen. What was the old saying? *When swallows fly high, the days shall be hot and dry.*

Pray God the swallows would stay high, for the barn was empty.

Thomas's feet throbbed, his tunic stuck to his back and his neck itched with dried sweat. Finding a boulder to rest, he dropped the baskets at his feet and flexed his fingers.

Tiny figures toiled in the shimmering cornfields below. God's bones, it must be sweltering down there. Working from dawn to moonrise, with so few peasants and reaping two acres a day at most...his cast his eyes along the valley and did the maths. It was going to take them weeks to finish.

In the still air, he heard the odd notes of men singing in rhythm to the swinging of their scythes. Right to left, right to left, inching forward, row after row. Women followed, their backs bent double, gathering the corn into sheaves and binding them with nettle or hazel twine. One woman gathered half a dozen sheaves and stood them on their ends in a tidy stook for the wagon to take them to the barn later.

When all the harvest was in, the women would thresh it. He had loved that when he was a boy. Two women would hold a large winnow basket full of stalks and toss them high into the air. The heavy grain would fall out or be left in the basket while the chaff and husks blew away on the breeze or fell like yellow petals to the ground. He would run through it trying to catch the pieces as they drifted and feel the husks tickle his upturned face. Then one of the maids would ruffle his hair and he'd watch more pieces fall around him in a shower. Everyone would laugh before refilling the winnow basket and the game would start over.

He was grown up now, and it wasn't a game. Everyone, lord and peasant alike, needed the corn to survive the winter. Every precious grain was needed for milling into flour or stored for winter cooking, saved to feed livestock or to sow in the following spring. With God's blessing, he'd have enough surplus to sell.

'Why so serious on such a glorious day?'

'Rulf!' Thomas jumped violently. 'You startled me! Where've you been? I've been picking berries and looking for you all day.'

'Wandering along the riverside. You've done better than me.' Rulf put his half-full basket on the ground and sat beside him. 'I see the harvest has started,' he said, helping himself to a blackberry. 'At this time, more than any other, I praise God I'm not a peasant.'

'I need a good harvest this year. If I don't have a surplus to sell, I won't be able to pay the men their dues come Michaelmas Day.'

Rulf threw back his head and laughed. '*You* are paying *them*? You never cease to amaze me. Most lords do it the other way round.'

Thomas started to scratch an isosceles triangle in the ground, stopped and changed it to an equilateral. 'It's just for this year. They're not serfs, so they do earn a few coins, but when they came here I'd no money, so I owe them. Next year, they'll pay rent and dues to me as usual.'

'No wonder you look serious. What you need is something to take your mind off it. What do you say we journey to Okewolde and take a look at the market?'

'I told you, I've no money.'

'Come, you must have an odd groat or two in that purse of yours. We'll have a few ales, play some dice and watch the troubadours. It'll do you the world of good.' Rulf looked up at the boiling sun. 'How far is it to Okewolde; twenty miles? If we make haste, we'll be there by nightfall.'

He did have a few groats, but they were the start of his Oxford fund, and it was too hot for a journey on the dry dusty tracks.

'Come on, stir yourself and stop looking like a sow's arse!' Rulf kicked the end of Thomas's boots and grabbed a handful of berries. 'I'll meet you at the monk's cross at the third quarter,' he added, tossing a berry into his mouth. 'And don't be late!'

Thomas stirred himself. The thought of a whole day at the market with Rulf was irresistible.

Late that evening, their horses cast deep night shadows as Thomas and Rulf rode down the main street into Okewolde. The town was eerily silent; its shops shuttered and the pillory empty.

A few yards along on the right, a large stone building hugged the street, its second floor jutting out over their heads. In the middle of the building was a wide arch, where a large board depicting the image of a white hart squeaked back and forth on its rusty chain.

'This is what we're looking for,' said Rulf. 'I'd prefer to stay in a private house, they're more comfortable, but it's too late to go knocking on doors. An inn will have to do. At least it's got heavy doors that close off the street, so it should be a better quality establishment.'

He didn't know about that; he'd never been inside an inn. Rulf slipped his boots out of the stirrups and flexed his ankles before slipping to the ground and leading his horse under the arch into a dark courtyard. Thomas followed, wearily dismounted and landed in a puddle of stinking horse muck.

'Take yer horses, sires?' A young boy came running from the shadows. Rulf flipped him a silver farthing and handed him the reins. Thomas wondered if a servant in the inn would clean his boots.

On one side was a two-storey timber-framed building with a steep thatch roof. A wooden stairway led to a first-floor gallery and a line of doors. There was a similar row of doors on the ground floor that reminded Thomas of the cloisters at the monastery.

What would Brother Luke say if he could see him now? He wouldn't be impressed, that was for sure. Brother Luke had always been more austere than some of his fellow monks and often held forth on the vices of visiting an inn.

'Let's make ourselves known to the landlord. I could eat an ox, tail and all!' Rulf slapped Thomas on the back and strode towards the entrance.

Thomas squared his shoulders, trying to look as though he was completely at ease, while his insides were twisting were nerves and excitement. He was about to cross the invisible threshold into a man's world. Once crossed, there was no going back. He wiped his sweaty palms on his surcoat, took a deep breath and followed Rulf inside.

The smell of stale sweat and acrid smoke hit the back of his throat. In the dim light, he could make out a long low beamed room, lit only by a few rushlights and tallow candles in wall niches. As his eyes adjusted to the semi-darkness, he saw men seated shoulder to shoulder on either side of a long trestle. It was nothing like the grand hall he'd imagined all inns to be.

The men stopped talking and turned to assess the new arrivals. Seeing nothing at odds, one by one they returned to their meal and conversations.

'Be welcome, sires!' A short, stout woman wearing a tight leather apron over a greasy skirt approached with wooden bowls of half-eaten mutton in her hands. 'Sit ye down. A jug of ale and mutton stew for the pair of ye?'

Thomas eyed the congealed yellow fat in the bowls. Oats and a few beans in a gruel might be better. 'Do you have potage?' he asked.

The woman bristled to her full height. 'If it's peasant food ye're after, ye'll not find it 'ere. It's the inn by the river ye'll be wantin'.' She leaned so close that the sight of her blackened teeth and the smell of her rank breath made him flinch. 'But old Jack there waters the ale.' She tapped the side of her nose and let out a raucous laugh.

The men on the benches exploded into laughter. Thomas's cheeks burned and he stared at his boots. He'd keep quiet in future.

'Prithee, my good dame. A jug of wine and a bowl each of your finest mutton, if you please, and lodgings for the night, if we may,' said Rulf, graciously removing his hat.

As soon as she'd disappeared to the back, Rulf gripped Thomas's elbow and steered him firmly to the benches.

'Why did you insult her?' he hissed in Thomas's ear. 'We need to keep her in good humour if we're to have a bed to ourselves tonight.'

He hadn't meant to insult her; he just hadn't liked the look of the mutton. The man sitting on the end of the bench reluctantly shifted up, leaving just enough room for him to perch. His neighbour eyed him up and down and flashed a toothless grin. He stank, his tunic was poor and filthy and his hair was crawling with lice. Thomas returned his smile weakly and sat as far away as he could.

'The pair of ye here for the market?' The man took a swig of ale, smacked his lips and wiped his beard with the back of his hand.

'We are,' said Rulf, sitting down opposite him. 'And your good self?'

'Aye. That and travellin' through. Tradin' in pots. No soft metal, mind; all iron. If you've a likin', I'll do ye a fair price.'

'Thank you, no—' said Rulf.

'Two mutton and the wine's just comin'. The innkeeper's wife squeezed her voluptuous bosoms between Thomas and his neighbour's shoulders, then slapped two bowls and spoons in front of him and Rulf.

Thomas regarded the stew with suspicion. It looked better now that it was hot, but it was still an unsavoury grey colour with a few lumps of what he took to be mutton and bits of carrot. If he hadn't been so hungry, he would have refused it. He watched Rulf take a mouthful and reluctantly, picked up his spoon. The stew was greasy and tasteless, but washed down with frequent swigs of wine, it was better than nothing.

'Tell me, any news of the Pestilence?' said Rulf to no one in particular.

Thomas's neighbour rested his elbows on the trestle. 'I've come through Winchester in the southern shires and heard from a traveller off the boats as how the Pestilence's still in London. Further out seems safe, though folks are still wary and some are desperate. If you're travelling, you'd do well to go with others. There's safety in numbers.'

'Any news of Oxford?' said Rulf, his face intent.

Alarmed at the word *Oxford*, Thomas rested his spoon.

'Some. I was within three leagues around haymaking. Seemed normal, though traders were saying it had the Pestilence earlier in the year.'

'So it's safe to go there?' Rulf persisted, a hint of excitement in his voice that Thomas didn't like at all.

'As safe as anywhere, I reckon. Now I wish ye God's will, I've some business to tend.' The traveller rose, belched and melted into the gloom to join a man seated at the other end of the bench.

Thomas breathed easier and shuffled up. Picking up his spoon, he stared at the remains his meal. The fat was already congealing into a yellow gloop. He dropped his spoon and pushed the bowl away with a shudder.

The men were telling bawdy stories, the ale flowed and as the evening wore on, their laughter grew louder as their stories grew ruder. Two of the men at the far end leaned close over the trestle, their voices raised. A bear of a man appeared inside the room, eyeing them, his thick arms crossed over his broad chest.

'The landlord,' Rulf said. 'I think it's time we left before a fight breaks out.' He caught the landlady's eye and raised his voice. 'My good dame, a moment, if you please! Our thanks for an excellent mutton stew. About our lodgings, do you have a bed for just the two of us? Preferably in a room of our own?'

The landlady put her hands on her hips and sucked through her teeth. 'Ye should have sent your servant ahead to save it for ye. I'm packed out with market folk.' Her eyes lingered on Rulf's purse, hanging from his belt.

Rulf smiled. 'Perhaps three pennies for the two of us would help?'

'Make it two pennies per night each for the bed, three pennies each for your meals and two pennies for each horse. One night is it?'

'Two,' Rulf said.

'Then that makes—' She stared at the roof and counted on her fingers. 'Thirty pennies, or two shillings and six.'

'No, it comes to—' Thomas felt a sharp kick on his ankle.

'—a very fair price, if I may say so,' Rulf interjected smoothly. 'Now, if you'll show us our room?'

The landlady held out her hand. 'Coins first. Two and six.'

'But it's only—' Thomas began, before Rulf glared him into silence and counted out the coins into the landlady's hand.

Scuffing her shoes in the mud, the landlady led them across the yard to a door on the ground floor at the far end of the row. She shoved open the door with her shoulder and stood to one side to allow Thomas and Rulf into the tiny room beyond.

As soon as Thomas stepped inside, the stench hit him. He swallowed a retch and covered his nose and mouth with his sleeve.

'Ye'll find a tallow on the side and the piss holes are outside next door,' the landlady said. 'Handy if ye need to go in the night. I'll leave ye to it.' She shut the door and Thomas heard her make her shuffling way back across the yard.

The room was barely large enough for him and Rulf, with the only furniture a wooden frame strung with rope and a thin, stained straw mattress. The thought of sleeping on it – of even touching it – made his skin crawl.

'We can't stay here; it's a dreadful place! I'll wager that mattress is crawling with fleas and lice, and why did you let her cheat us over our bill?' he said.

'My dear friend, as inns go, I've stayed in a lot worse. We're fortunate to have found a bed at all. As for the bill, an innkeeper can make your stay hell if she's a mind. We needed to keep her sweet or we'd be sharing a bed with three or four others right now.'

'But the smell—'

'If you're even half as tired as I am, you'll soon be asleep and oblivious to it. That's assuming that poisonous mutton doesn't get you up in the night. If it does, you might be glad of the piss holes so close at hand. Now, pull off my boots and let's get to bed.'

Thomas obliged and stretched out his legs for Rulf to return the favour. Rulf stripped off his clothes, leaving them in a heap on the floor, flopped onto his mattress and was soon sleeping like a baby.

Thomas couldn't sleep. The acrid smell from the piss holes filled his nose, he could still taste the mutton, and he was prepared to swear the mattress was alive beneath him. Next to him, Rulf's soft, regular breaths were quietly reassuring. He gazed at him. Was Rulf thinking of leaving? He was certainly interested in the news from Oxford.

Thomas couldn't bear the thought after everything Rulf had come to mean to him. He was more than a friend; he was a twin soul. Someone to share ideas with. Someone with the same passion for knowledge. Someone who gave him belief in himself when he had none. Someone who made him laugh. Someone whose very presence made him happy and someone he would miss if he wasn't there.

Rulf was sleeping on his side with a hand tucked under his head. A thin streak of light from a slit in the wall threw a trail of pale yellow across his cheek. He had extraordinarily long lashes that curled at the ends and his ears were small, neat and rather pink. Thomas had never noticed them before.

Slowly, he reached out and gently ran the back of his finger down Rulf's cheek. It was so soft...

What was he doing? He snatched his hand away and leapt up. His guts heaved. Grabbing his surcoat, he fumbled for the door and rushed outside. Reaching the piss hole, he emptied the entire contents of his stomach.

He stood over the hole, heaving with a sour taste making his mouth feel like the inside of a barrel. Had he really touched Rulf? What if the priest had woken up?

Thomas wiped his mouth on his sleeve. He was disgusting and weak, just like Papa had said. God's bones, he needed an ale, but that would mean going back inside the inn on his own, and he wasn't brave enough for that. He wasn't even sure about returning to the room, but there was nowhere else to go. He could hardly spend the night on the street at the mercy of cutpurses and thieves. And if Rulf woke up and noticed he'd gone, what would he think?

Thomas did what he always did when he was in a quandary. He stood and stared at the stars. All he'd done was touch Rulf's cheek. He didn't even know why. Was that so bad? Friends touched each other all the time; it didn't mean anything. Rulf was always slapping him on the back and putting an arm around his shoulders.

He was being foolish. He'd go back to bed and go to sleep. Things always seemed different in the morning.

Quietly, he pushed open the door and crept inside. Rulf hadn't stirred. He lay down next to him and stared up into the blackness, listening to the heavy steps of fellow guests hauling themselves up the stairs to the rooms above.

Why had he done it? It was a sin. He prayed for forgiveness, and he prayed that Rulf wouldn't leave. Rulf mumbled and turned over, his head inches from Thomas. He smelled faintly of herbs: he must use herbal water. It was pleasant; maybe he would start using it too.

He imagined Rulf opening his eyes, smiling. He'd reach out and Thomas would feel the comfort of his arms.

No! What was wrong with him? He flung back the woollen cover and ran his hands down his face. Rulf was a man. Worse, he was a priest; holy, chaste and untouchable. Such thoughts were unnatural and forbidden. He'd drunk too much. It was the wine making him feel like this. It had to be.

If it wasn't, then God help him.

CHAPTER 34

'Rouse yourself, you idler! Prime bell has rung and the traders are setting up their stalls.'

Thomas opened his eyes and groaned. So the inn hadn't been a bad dream. He pulled up the cover and hid his face.

'Wake up! There's a fresh pail in the yard to splash your face.' Rulf grabbed the cover and threw it back, leaving Thomas exposed. 'I slept like a log; how about you?' He ran his fingers through his hair and grimaced. 'God's teeth, I need a barber! Look at this mess.'

Thomas stretched and reached for his hose. Rulf's normal tones made him relax just a fraction. 'Oh yes, like a log.'

He had to act normally, pretend it didn't happen. Pretend he hadn't caressed Rulf's cheek in the way he had. Fumbling, he fastened the hose to his waist belt, pulled his tunic over his head and put on his belt.

Had he gone mad? He tried conjugating a few Latin verbs in his head. No, he could still do that, so his problem wasn't madness.

'You're not wearing your cassock,' he said, reaching for his boots.

'When did you last see a priest having fun? Did you manage to keep down the mutton? You were a bit pale last night; I thought you were going to be as sick as a cur.' Rulf slipped his surcoat through his arms and checked his purse was secure on his belt and well hidden.

'Oh, that was the wine. I'm fine.' Did he want to touch Rulf again? Yes…no…maybe. God, he didn't know. As he pulled his laces tight, a taunting whisper ran through his head: *sinner.* He ran a hand down his face to wipe it away.

'Did you hear what I said?' Rulf was waiting, watching him.

He dared to look up. 'What? Oh, yes. Of course.'

'No, you didn't, you were staring at your boots like you'd seen a ghost. I said that we might risk a hunk of bread and cheese before we venture out.'

The whispers were fading. 'Good idea.'

'And then, my friend, we'll have the whole day to enjoy ourselves.'

What was wrong with him? He'd been friends with William and Simon for years and he'd never wanted to touch them. So why Rulf? Why now?

'Thomas, you're like a maid with no ears this morning. Make haste.' Rulf hovered by the open door and glanced at him curiously.

He had to pull himself together. He cast around and said the first thing that came into his head. 'God's teeth, I'm hungry.'

His appetite lasted until he saw the food their landlady brought. The bread was dark and hard, and the cheese scarcely much softer, showing signs of blue mould. He nibbled at it, marvelling at how Rulf could eat such food with enthusiasm. Picking up the last crumbs with a moistened finger, Rulf wiped the corners of his mouth and led them into the fresh air.

Outside, the street was crammed and filled with cries from sellers shouting their wares. Passing open-fronted shops displaying everything from leatherware to candles, Thomas kept sight of Rulf's bright blue tunic bobbing ahead, making his way through the crowds until he found himself in the town square.

Traders were everywhere, haphazardly laying their goods wherever they could find a space. Cattle, goats and sheep wandered as their handlers tried to herd them into pens on the green in the middle. He could hardly hear himself think against the din of squawking fowl and drovers' cries. A ringing bell on a leading pony announced the arrival of a pack train some twenty ponies long, each beast attached by a rope to the one in front, their panniers filled with fine silks and goods from eastern countries. As they passed, the heady aromas of exotic spices fought against the stench of dung, human sweat and the stinking open drains running down the middle of the street.

Thomas picked his way through, craning for a sight of Rulf. A thick-set man turned his back to piss against the wall of the butcher's shop and someone rammed Thomas in the back. He spun around, his hand hovering over his purse, but it was only an old woman, dressed in rags with a willow basket hooked over one arm.

'Violets, sire, to bring good fortune to your lady.' She grinned a toothy grin and held out a bunch of wilting purple flowers. Her face was pale and pinched with hunger. 'Only a farthing.'

A farthing wasn't much, even for him. Thomas felt for his purse, but the crowd jostled him away, closing in until she was lost among the sea of brown and grey tunics. Looking over the heads, he saw Rulf standing by the water trough on the green, next to the pillory. He cut a striking figure with the sunlight playing on his cheeks and highlighting his hair.

Thomas shoved his way towards him. 'What a crush! This is how a market should be. The day I went to Holdesworthe with Rose, we had the place to ourselves and I couldn't wait to leave,' he said.

Rulf laughed. 'While you were still snoring this morning, I was in the yard talking to the innkeeper. He said that this is the first proper market since the Pestilence and the first time his inn's been full and taken money for over a year. He was down to his last few shillings and looking to pack up for he's a wife and mother to support.'

'Praise God, I was born a noble, but I wager by the end of tonight, he'll have more coins in his coffer than I have in mine,' said Thomas.

'Probably, but you have the status to do as you wish with yours. He doesn't. Look at them.' Rulf swept his arm around at the crowds. 'The people are celebrating their freedom, we all are, and who can blame us? For over a year, we've been fleeing for our lives or shut in our homes, too afraid to go out. Last spring, we'd never heard of the Pestilence, and by last summer we were talking of nothing else. No one knew what it was or what to do, only that none of us was safe. Now it's gone. Shops are open again, traders are back and the people jostle shoulder to shoulder as usual. We're all thanking God to be back to normal, for we're the lucky ones. We survived.'

It was true, and his idea to go to Combe Hide had worked. Maybe not as he'd planned, but they had survived and now looked set to grow and prosper. He was proud of that. And once the harvest was in, he'd sell the spare grain and fleece at a huge profit, pay off his men, have money left for the estate and, most importantly, have coins for his fund.

'Enough of such talk, though,' Rulf added. 'We're here to enjoy ourselves and so we shall. Do you hear the pipers? I do believe there are troubadours in town; shall we take a look? Then I'll visit the barber for a proper shave and a haircut. I'm sure I've got lice from that mattress.' He scratched his head. 'It's hardly the right image for Father Rulf.'

Thomas wanted to say that he liked the dark stubble on Rulf's chin but stopped himself.

'You don't know how lucky you are being fair; your growth doesn't show like mine,' Rulf went on. 'You should grow a beard.'

Thomas blushed, but before he could think of an answer, the sound of raised voices drew both their attentions away from each other.

'What's all the shouting over there?' Thomas said, who was too short to see. 'It sounds like an argument.'

'There's certainly trouble of some kind,' Rulf agreed. 'Come on! This could be interesting.'

He elbowed his way to the front of the large crowd, Thomas following in his wake until they arrived at a butcher's shop, where a barrel-chested man in a bloodied leather apron stood blocking the doorway. In front of him was a shorter man, who, by the look of his fine jupon with gold buttons on the sleeves, was of high status.

'Don't you raise your fist at me, butcher! I'm Gregory du Pont from the town authorities.' The man nodded to the crowd. 'I've had many a complaint about you and your rancid meat.'

'Who reported me? There's nothing wrong with my meat! Smell it!' The butcher thrust a slab of meat under Gregory du Pont's nose. 'Go on. You'll find no maggots there.'

'That's what you show us, but it's not the same meat when we get it home!' shouted a merchant. A rumble of assent came from the crowd. 'Your cheating ways give our town a bad name and affect trade!'

'Make way! Mind yer backs!' The crowd parted for two men hauling a hurdle, which they dropped at du Pont's feet. 'The hurdle as requested, sire.'

'You'll not drag me through the streets on that!' The butcher backed into his shop.

'I'll wager we will, you cheating cur!' Two men from the crowd pushed up their sleeves and stepped forward.

'There'll be a brawl if that Gregory doesn't do something,' Rulf remarked. 'My money's on the butcher.'

'Silence, all of you!' du Pont shouted. 'Your constant ravings make my head beat like a drum. The town has to keep its good name or we'll lose traders. Butcher, your shop's filthy. I can smell it from here and your meat is not to the required standards. You display fresh meat for sale but what you sell is bad. You'll be tied to the hurdle and dragged through the streets to the pillory and pieces of rotten meat will be tied around your neck. You'll stay there until sunrise tomorrow, and let that be a lesson to you. And if you don't mend your ways, I'll have the keys to your shop. Men!'

Rulf's eyes sparkled with excitement. 'This is more entertaining than the wrestlers! Let's see him in the pillory and look out for rotten veg to throw.'

Thomas loved this fun side of Rulf. He bit back a grin at the idea of what Peter would think of his priest if he could see him now.

At the pillory, du Pont fussed at the men securing the butcher's head and arms through a wooden bar, then nodded in satisfaction and stepped away. The merchant in the fine cotehardie hurled the first cabbage and others, including Rulf, quickly followed.

Thomas threw a mouldy wedge of bread, but wasn't sorry when it fell short. He'd never really liked the pillories. Someone threw an egg hitting the butcher on the nose in a sticky explosion of yellow and white, and the crowd roared with laughter. When they'd thrown everything they had, the fun was over and they melted away to find new entertainment.

'Well, that was fun,' Rulf said. 'Did you see me get him with that mouldy pear? Now, I'm off to the barber! What will you do?'

'I shall take a look at the corn merchants and see what prices they're charging. I'll meet you outside the barber-surgeon later.' He watched Rulf walk away until his blue tunic was lost amongst the throng, then looked away, the heat rising to his cheeks. Had anyone noticed him staring?

Nobody seemed to have done. Everyone was bustling around, busy on their own errands, and Thomas headed off to see the corn merchants, intending to talk to them and make a few contacts for his own grain.

As he wandered from merchant to merchant, his heart fell further and further to the floor. There was too much food and no one to buy it. The prices were so low he wondered how they were making any money. If they weren't, how was he supposed to? All those acres he'd ploughed, the tilling, the sowing and the harvesting, all for nothing.

The midday bell rang across the town and Thomas returned to the barber's shop. There was no sign of Rulf, so he leaned against the wall and waited.

'What you do think? A decent cut?' Rulf stepped out of the shop and stood before him, running his fingers through very little hair.

Thomas forced his thoughts to the present. 'I think you look like a priest without a cassock.'

'I think it's rather becoming. What's the matter with you? You look like you lost a shilling and found a penny.'

'I got it wrong. All that talk of nobles selling land and nothing being grown, I thought I was being clever. I thought that if I was the only one with grain to sell, I could charge high prices.'

'Sounds reasonable,' said Rulf. 'Why can't you?'

'Walk around the stalls and you'll see why. As Rose so nicely put it at Holdesworthe market, most of the people are dead and buried in the pits, so there's no one to buy it. I should have realised, but how was I to know how many had died? I'll end up with barns full of grain that I can't sell, and I won't be able to pay the men who will probably riot, and I'll end up rotting in Lyndeford Gaol as a bankrupt.'

'Of course you won't. And at least we'll have a lot of bread this winter.'

'This is no time for jests. Don't you understand? I'm a useless lord without a penny to my name. And we won't have a lot of bread, because I don't have a mill.' Thomas scuffed his boot through the dirt.

Rulf joined him against the wall. 'Then I suggest Peter stops work on the church and repairs the mill.'

'Don't you think I haven't thought of that? You're not listening to me: *I have no money.*'

'Is that all? Then, my young friend, worry no more.' Rulf threw an arm around his shoulder and bent his head close, lowering his voice to a more conspiratorial tone.

'There are ways to get money, but before I get to business, I've got a fancy to take an ale or two and watch the dancing. Come, I think it's this way.'

Thomas stared at Rulf's disappearing back, fighting to slow the pounding of his heart. People shoved into him, knocking him in the shoulder, and the pieman's calls went over his head as he followed the mesmerising blue tunic into the crowds.

Standing, watching the dancers, Rulf hummed to the fiddlers, his foot tapping in time as he drank his ale. Occasionally, he glanced over his shoulder to a group of men gathered in the corner. 'Now's a good time,' he whispered in Thomas's ear, a mischievous gleam in his eyes. 'Trust me and say nothing. Give me a moment and then follow.'

Thomas kept a discrete distance. When Rulf stopped at one of the dice tables, he hung back, unsure. Rulf was a fool if he thought he could gamble his way to money.

A young peasant lad was losing. When he was down to his last few farthings, Rulf stepped forward. 'Move over, lad, before you lose the lot.'

'Yes, sire.' The lad scooped up his remaining coins and scrambled out of his seat.

Rulf rubbed his hands together and took the newly vacated stool. Judging by his opponent's coarse clothes, Thomas reckoned he was a trader of some sort.

'You throw first, a penny a throw?' Rulf laid a pile of silver pennies on the table.

He lost the first six throws. The merchant's mouth twisted into a smile. 'Shall we up the stakes to two pennies?' he suggested, sliding two silver coins across the table.

Rulf nodded. 'Maybe that will change my fortune.'

It didn't. Rulf continued to lose, and Thomas inched forward. Rulf was already down over two shillings; he should walk away. He tried to catch Rulf's eye, but Rulf was too busy watching the dice.

The merchant's pile of coins continued to grow. With each throw, Rulf became visibly more agitated.

'We'll raise the stakes,' he said, slapping the table. 'I need to recover my losses, or I'll receive a sharp tongue from my lady wife tonight and little else!'

The crowd laughed. The merchant picked up a silver shilling. 'Too much for you?'

Don't do it, walk away, Thomas begged silently, but Rulf went to his purse and placed a pile of shillings on the table.

'Make it two.'

Thomas groaned as mounting excitement rippled through the crowd. He could barely watch. Rulf won with two fives but lost the next two rounds. What was he doing?

When Rulf picked up the dice again, Thomas held his breath. If Rulf lost this round, he'd drag him away before he gambled everything.

A six and a four. The crowd pushed forward. The merchant rolled the dice. A six and a two.

Rulf smiled and swept the coins towards him. More people stopped to watch. It seemed Rulf's fortunes had turned. He won the next round and most of the rounds after that, until the merchant was down to his last two shillings.

'Let's finish.' Rulf smiled. 'I don't want to leave you with nothing.'

The merchant shook his head. 'I'll play to the end. My fortune's turning; I can feel it.'

He rolled the dice. A four and a three. The crowd groaned. It was a poor score. Rulf picked up the dice, and Thomas dug his nails into the palms of his hands.

Two fives. The crowd cheered, and Thomas heaved a sigh of relief. Rulf stood and began scooping his winnings into his purse. The merchant leaned forward and slapped his hand over Rulf's and glared into his eyes.

A man in a leather jerkin nudged Thomas in the ribs. 'There'll be a fight. Sixpence says the merchant wins. His mates are in the crowd.'

'I'll not wager,' said Thomas.

'I will,' said a voice behind him.

Thomas waved at Rulf and mouthed *Walk away*, but Rulf just smiled.

'Double everything on the table, win or lose,' said the merchant, his stare fixed on Rulf.

The crowd gasped.

'I couldn't.' Rulf withdrew his hand. 'Stop now, while you still have a few shillings left.'

'Double or nothing, and my horse and wagon and goods. Damn it, you owe me the chance to win my losses back!'

'Rulf, don't!' Thomas pleaded.

Rulf looked across and held up his hand. 'What are your goods?' he said to the merchant, his voice calm and flat.

'Spices, silks and wines from the east. Worth a lot of money.'

Rulf rubbed his chin, considering. 'No, no I couldn't. It wouldn't be fair.'

The merchant leaned closer. 'You have to give me a chance. It's the rules. If I win, you pay me what my goods are worth. If you win, you take the lot.'

Rulf considered for a moment and tipped the remaining coins into his purse. He pushed up his sleeves and sat down. 'One throw each, win or lose. You first.'

Thomas sagged, barely able to watch as the merchant picked up the dice, shook them and tossed them down. Two fives.

The man leaned back, smiling. 'You'll need two sixes to beat that.'

Thomas sensed the tension amongst the throng and held his breath. Rulf picked up the dice and slowly rubbed them. His eyes never leaving the merchant, he blew on his hands for good fortune. With a flick of his wrist, he threw the dice. They landed with a clatter and rolled across the table.

The crowd leaned forward, watching them roll.

The first die fell on a six.

Thomas leaned forward as well, hardly daring to move.

The second die poised, then tipped onto six.

The crowd cheered, and Thomas breathed again. Defeated, the merchant stared at the dice and slumped back in his seat. Excitement over, the crowd drifted away, and Thomas hastened to his friend.

'You won! I thought you'd lost the lot and my heart was in my mouth when you upped the stake! I don't know how you did it, but from then on, you didn't stop winning.'

'Be quiet!' Rulf grabbed Thomas's arm and marched him smartly away. 'Just smile and keep walking.'

The merchant's voice followed them across the square. 'You cheated! I don't know how, but God's blood, I'll be after you!'

Thomas turned around indignantly. 'He didn't cheat! It was skill —'

Rulf's fingers bit painfully through his sleeve. 'Be quiet and let's get out of here before he and his mates come after me,' he hissed. 'I've a tidy sum in my purse and every cutpurse and thief will soon know of it. Quick, we'll find the wagon and get back to the inn.'

Rulf seemed to know where he was going, and Thomas struggled to keep up as he pushed and shoved his way across the square to the far corner of the market. The crowds were thinner there, and Thomas could see a line of wagons with an assortment of asses and mules dozing in their traces.

'The traders' parking area. It must be one of those. Come on.' Rulf started forwards, then stopped and barred Thomas's way with his arm. 'Wait! There's someone standing by that wagon at the end.'

Thomas gulped, not daring to move for fear of drawing attention. 'Do you think he's with the dice player?'

'Could be.'

The man, whoever he was, was short and lean. It was difficult to be sure from that distance, but to Thomas, he looked like he'd seen many summers.

'He doesn't look like a villein or cutpurse to me,' Thomas whispered. 'And if he is, he wouldn't be standing there.'

Rulf turned and flashed a smile, starting Thomas's heart pounding in a way that had nothing to do with the threat of violence. 'I just love your logical mind. But he could be a lookout and have accomplices hiding.'

Thomas didn't like the sound of that. He had never been any good at fighting. 'We don't even know if that is your wagon.'

'I'd wager it is. The merchant said there were wine and spices, and that wagon's the only one with barrels and jars.'

'We could leave it,' Thomas ventured. 'I mean, you've already got the coins.'

Rulf turned, the smile gone. 'Are you *mad*? I worked hard for that, and it's worth a lot of money. No, we'll take a look, but be ready. Keep a sharp eye for anyone lurking.'

Thomas swallowed. His idea of fun at the market didn't include looking for villeins, much less getting into a fight. 'What if there is?'

'Then we run. Now come on.'

Sweat broke out on Thomas's forehead as he and Rulf walked towards the wagon. Every shadow seemed to conceal an assailant, and he tried not to look at the man who was watching them.

As they neared the end of the line, the man stepped forward. Thomas tensed, but the man did no more than bow low.

'Pardon, sires, my name is Jorge.'

He had a thin greying beard, and his hair was long and as neglected as the brown ragged tunic he wore. He looked more like a beggar than a cutpurse, and Thomas wanted to laugh with relief.

Rulf started to board the wagon, but the man stepped in front of him. 'Pardon, sire, but I'm a Flemish weaver with a wife and many hungry children. We were forced to leave our home because of the wars. I bribed passage on a boat set for England, but it cost me everything I owned. We've been travelling ever since looking for a place to settle. You look like noblemen. Do either of you have need of a good worker?'

'A Flemish weaver, you say?' Rulf glanced at Thomas.

'The best, sire.' Jorge straightened up proudly.

'If you're seeking to settle and work, we might be able to help you. What say you, Thomas?'

Thomas smiled. Flemish weavers were the best, and Jorge could make a huge difference to the quality of the scarlet cloth. 'Yes. I need a weaver.'

Jorge's face lit up. 'God bless you, my lord!' He clasped his hands together, looked skywards and crossed himself. 'I'll not let you down.'

Rulf stepped forward. 'Let me introduce myself. I'm Rulf de Beauchamp, and my friend here is Lord Thomas de Chiddleigh. It's on his manor you'll be working.'

Jorge nodded. 'Where is this manor?'

'Combe Hide,' Rulf answered. 'It's a short day's ride, and we've this wagon that needs driving.'

Jorge beamed. 'Then I'm your man, sire.'

'There is one thing I should explain; I'm not *sire*. I'm Father Rulf.'

Jorge looked him up and down and shook his head. 'You English are a strange people, Father, but no matter. My family and I are ready to travel when you are.'

Rulf smiled broadly. 'Then let's be off!'

He and Thomas rode side by side out of Okewolde. Behind them, Jorge drove Rulf's newly acquired wagon. Sitting beside him was his wife and eldest son, with two younger sons and a daughter perched on bales of silk amongst the barrels of wine and jars of spices at the back.

'Not just a weaver, but a *Flemish* weaver; they're the best,' said Rulf. 'And I've a purse bulging with coins which I shall give to you, my friend. All in all, a successful day, I think.'

'I couldn't take that money,' Thomas protested. 'It's yours. You won it fair and square.'

Rulf burst out laughing. 'Of course I didn't! I cheated for you, and I want you to have it. Father Rulf can hardly have ill-gotten gains on his conscience, can he?'

Thomas was speechless. A priest? *Cheating*? 'How did you do it?'

Rulf smiled, reached into his tunic and held up two dice. 'I looked for a table using the same size and colour dice as mine and bided my time. Once the merchant thought I was a bad player, I encouraged the stakes to rise. When it was my turn, I switched the dice. These are weighted and only land on sixes.'

'I didn't see you do it.'

'You weren't supposed to. It's a little trick I learned in the inns of Oxford. It's easy once know how. And no, I'll not show you; it's best you don't know.' Rulf tossed the dice up, caught them one-handed and tucked them away again. 'Now, I'm tired. Let's get home.'

CHAPTER 35

As they turned into the yard, Thomas was so tired he couldn't remember most of the journey and was sure he must have been asleep in the saddle. All he wanted to do was to pull off his boots, flop onto his mattress and sleep forever. Combe Hide now seemed a veritable palace after the near-sleepless night he'd spent in that inn.

Reining his horse to a halt, he heard a loud voice coming from the barn. 'We're not taking no orders from a maid! Are we, men?'

Rulf raised his eyebrows and dismounted as Rose's voice wafted out on the breeze.

'I told you to start stacking the sheaves from that side!'

'And I told you, we're putting them over there!' the first voice said, louder now. 'What do you know about it? This is men's work.'

'I'm the reeve, and you'll do as I say.'

Thomas groaned and slid to the ground. He should have realised Rose would throw her weight around with her new title. By the sound of it, she was holding her own, which didn't surprise him. He could imagine her standing with her hands on her hips and her eyes glaring beneath her skewed coif.

'I've been doing this since before you were born,' the man retorted. 'Go back to the fields with the women where you belong.'

'You wait until Lord Thomas hears about this.'

He was already hearing it and wishing he wasn't.

'I'll wait alright, and until I hear different, I take my orders from the bailiff and no maid. Now get out of my way. Reeve indeed!'

The men's laughter carried across the yard as Rose stormed out of the barn. Scarlet-faced, she ripped her coif from her head and flung it to the ground. Her shoulders sagged and she covered her face with her hands.

'I think she's crying,' Rulf commented in a low voice.

That was absurd. 'Rose never cries.'

'She is now. You made her reeve. You'll have to find a way to appease both sides, and I don't envy you.'

He didn't envy himself.

Annie hurried out of the forge, clutching a bunch of greenery. 'Ah, my lord, you're back. Father Rulf.' She bobbed a neat curtsy. 'Thomas, I need a word before I take this moss to Josef. He's cut his leg on a scythe and there's blood everywhere.'

'Can't it wait?' He'd only just got back and already problems were piling around him.

'I'd rather speak now, my lord.' Annie's face was set, she wasn't about to be deterred.

'Pleased to be home?' said Rulf as an aside.

'Overjoyed.' Thomas turned back to Annie. 'At least let me see to my horse first.'

'I'll wait. I'll fetch you some of my herbal water, Father, I'm sure you'd like to soak your feet after your long ride.'

'Anything for a headache?' Thomas called after her.

'I'll find something,' she called over her shoulder.

And what about herbal water for my feet? But he couldn't be bothered to say it. Father Rulf got everything.

Thomas lingered over seeing to Henry. If he took long enough, Annie might get tired of waiting and Rose would be gone. He gave Henry a final pat and left the stables. Now he could now take off his boots and fall onto his mattress.

But Rose was leaning against the barn wall and glaring at Annie, who was waiting by the trough looking daggers back at her. His heart sank. Before he was within four paces, Annie accosted him.

'Did you tell Rose she was in charge of my dye shed? Only that's what she's telling folks. You may be the lord but I won't have it, Thomas. Your Mama and I worked hard all those years to make that red dye, as well you know. It was her life's work. I owe it to her to make sure it's done right, and so do you.'

Rose marched across. 'I knew you couldn't wait to tell tales about me! You already showed me how to make the dye.'

Annie shook the herbs in Rose's face. 'They're not tales, and I only showed you part of the dye making. You don't know how to use the secret ingredient; only I know that! And I'll not have you coming into my shed throwing your weight around. Who do you think you are?'

'I'm a reeve, that's who I am,' said Rose, lifting her chin. 'Lord Thomas said so. Didn't you, Thomas?'

Any moment now, they would scratch each other's eyes out, and he'd happily let them do it. Out of the corner of his eye, he saw Rulf cover his mouth, his blue eyes dancing with amusement.

'I said you could run the cloth sales if Annie didn't mind—' Thomas began.

'Well, I *do* mind. I'm not—'

'Forgive me for interrupting.' Rulf slipped between the two women, his hands loosely joined at his chest in a priestly fashion. 'As a priest, I have little knowledge of such matters, but it seems to me that God has blessed us.'

Thomas never stopped marvelling at how quickly Rulf switched to his other self. It was hard to believe that this was the same man who had thrown a cabbage at the butcher and cheated at dice.

Rulf continued in a controlled mellow voice. 'On the one hand, we have Annie, the only person in the shire who knows the secret of the coveted red dye. The good Lord has given us Jorge—' he indicated the wagon— 'a Flemish weaver who will teach us how to make the best cloth in the shire.' He turned to Rose. 'And we have Rose, with her organising and numeracy skills. And of course, we have our bailiff, Simon, who keeps the estate running and is known and respected among all. The good Lord said that we should live in harmony.' Rulf paused in the manner of all priests, his hidden accusation making his audience squirm with guilt.

Thomas frowned. Did He? The monks never mentioned anything like that.

'Instead of fighting amongst ourselves, we should work together, each respecting the other's status, skills and knowledge. That way, we shall repay God for His blessings and reap our just reward.' Rulf's voice had taken on that singing lilt of a priest and he glanced to the heavens. Thomas wouldn't have been surprised to see him put his hands together and say a prayer.

Annie was the first to speak. 'You're right, Father. We shouldn't argue,' she said. 'But Rose can't tell me what to do in my dye shed.'

'And what do you say, Rose?' said Rulf.

'As you say, Father, but I'm a proper reeve now. I'll say what dye is made and how much, but I suppose Annie could run the making of it.'

Rulf gave half a smile and inclined his head. 'And my Lord Thomas, what do you think?'

Thomas thought they should swap roles, since Rulf was making a much better job of being a lord than he was. 'I think we should all get on with it.'

'Good. Then perhaps Rose and Annie should speak to Simon and the three of you make yourselves known to Jorge.' Rulf threw them one of his most benevolent smiles. 'And now I shall retire to soak my feet in your excellent herbal water.' Holding the stone jar, he inclined his head to Annie. 'I wish you all Godspeed.' He made the sign of the cross and turned to leave. Passing Thomas, he gave him half a smile and winked.

'Well, my lord?' said Annie.

'Well, what? You heard what Father Rulf said.'

'But you are the lord. We want you to tell us what you think. I wouldn't want any misunderstanding,' said Rose, eyeing Annie.

'What I think is that one of you is old enough to know better and the other forgets who she is. Now stop squabbling and get back to work. I've enough on my mind without worrying about you two. Jorge, leave the wagon there and go with Rose; she'll show you your plot. Rose, when you've done that, go and find Simon. Introduce him to Jorge and then the four of you get together. And now, I'm going to remove my boots and rest my aching bones, and I don't want to hear any more from either of you.'

The women's faces paled. Thomas had no idea where his newfound strength had come from, but it felt good.

Annie sniffed. 'My lord.'

The two of them skulked out of the yard followed by a bemused Jorge and his family.

Clap, clap, clap.

'It's about time you showed some fighting spirit,' said Simon, sauntering from behind the forge. 'We need to talk.'

'Not you as well. My head's got a thousand hammers inside and I want my bed. Can't we speak tomorrow?'

'No, now. Rose has been throwing her weight around, telling everyone she's a reeve. Annie's not the only one who's upset; the men are furious.'

'I know, I heard them.'

'Don't get me wrong,' Simon added. 'Rose does a good job and I like working with her, but it's not as if she's a proper reeve, is it? I've tried speaking to her but she said something about a pact. You need to take her in hand or the men will be rioting.'

'Actually, I did make Rose a reeve,' Thomas said. 'I know I should have told you, but I didn't know she'd go telling everyone, did I?'

'What did you think she was going to do? You're an ass. Whoever heard of a woman reeve?'

'Well, it's too late to undo it now,' Thomas answered. 'And why shouldn't she be a reeve? She does the job well enough; better than a lot of men.'

Simon raised his eyebrows to the heavens. 'She's a maid. If it gets known, and it will, we'll be the laughing stock of the shire. Tell her she's reeve to the women only.'

How dare Simon tell him what to do? He wasn't a boy to be scolded by his bailiff. He was the lord, and he was too tired for this. 'No, I won't. If making Rose a reeve was a mistake, so be it, but I'll honour my decision as a lord should. You are my bailiff. Tell the men to accept it.'

'I'll tell them, but that doesn't mean it will happen,' said Simon. 'And you tell that young maid to stop ordering everyone around as if she's Lady of the Manor.'

'Anything, just sort it.' God, he wished he'd never made the damned pact.

'And where have you been? Disappearing off with the priest for two days.'

'We went to Okewolde market, and it's a good job we did. There's too much food and grain for sale with no one to buy it. The prices are half what they should be. I'm going to have a barn full of grain and no money to pay the men.'

'So that's what's given you a boars head. I happen to know there's no working mill in Holdesworthe,' Simon said. 'When we get our mill working, we'll be the only ones for miles around who can grind and have flour to sell, and that means coins in your coffer. Stop tying yourself in knots. You worry too much, that's your trouble.'

Yes, he did. He had a lot to worry about, more than Simon could ever guess. 'You're my bailiff. I need that mill working.'

Simon pressed his mouth into a tight line. 'I've just said I will! God's bones, I can't work miracles; I've only got a dozen or so men. You should take more responsibility. You're the one who made Rose a reeve, and then you bring back another family, which is good, but you expect me to sort them out. Like him.' Simon pointed to Gee, who was skulking around the outside of the house. 'You! What are doing? Go back to your work! He's always around here. Why don't you deal with things for a change?'

'I will if you let me. You said I was to ride my lands and leave everything to you and Will. Which is it?' He'd never raised his voice to Simon before. It felt surprisingly good.

Simon's face went rigid, and his hands gripped his belt as they stared each other down, then he turned and walked abruptly away.

Damn! This was his own doing. He should have thought more about his estate and spent less time playing chess with Rulf. He wished he'd never met — no, he didn't. He ran a hand through his hair and sighed. He'd lost William, he was shouting at Simon, and God only knew what he felt about Rulf.

What was happening to him? He needed to think and there was only one place to do that.

Sitting on his favourite stone by the river, Thomas stared at the water. A dragonfly darted up and down the bank, guarding its territory. The dragonfly knew how to keep its life in order. Why couldn't he do the same?

Rulf was a close friend, that was all. There was nothing wrong with caring for someone, even if he was a man. But what about that lurch in his stomach every time he thought of him or saw his smile? He'd never felt it with anyone before. He'd touched him and wanted to hold him, and that wasn't normal.

God, he was confused. If only there was someone he could talk to, but there was only Simon and he'd laugh.

Maybe he should talk to a priest? He'd not been to confessional since the Pestilence; he needed to go. If he confessed, no one would ever know and the priest would absolve his sins. He'd do his penance and his soul would be cleansed. And after that, he'd be able to see Rulf in a new light, man to man with no sinful thoughts.

Tomorrow. He'd do it tomorrow.

The next morning, Thomas rode to Holdesworthe with the sun on his face, singing to himself. After he'd seen the priest, he would treat himself to a duck pie and then have a quiet ride home to see how the harvest was coming along. He might even take his chess set and see Rulf.

Leaving Henry at the stables behind the inn, he walked briskly to the church, where he removed his hat and went in. What was it about a church? He felt cleansed for just being there. The priest smiled in greeting and led him to the confession booth and Thomas began to talk.

Later, much later, he stepped out of St Brideswell's church in a daze, feeling as though the priest had plunged a sword through his heart. He wandered down the main street, passing the pie shop without a glance, and soon found himself outside the inn where he'd left Henry. He paid the innkeeper, not bothering to wait for his change, got on Henry, and headed for home.

The priest had listened and given him absolution. His penance was severe and he welcomed that; he could cope with a week on his knees praying three times a day. It was what came after that he hadn't been prepared for. The priest had told him to sit back down, for he had something more to say. In a low and serious voice that was thick with censure, he'd said Thomas was at the tipping point of becoming a disgusting sodomite.

A sodomite. The worst sin against God from which there was no going back.

Thomas was weak, the priest had said, and would always be a target for the devil's work. He must be on guard for the rest of his life if he was to save himself or his soul would be cast into the flames of eternal hell.

The priest had been disgusted; his voice quietly harsh as he warned against the evils of sodomy. The only way to stop the Devil's temptation, he had said, was to pray.

Pray, and never be alone with Rulf again.

CHAPTER 36

Rose scuttled into the orchard and hid behind the hedge until the ox and cart passed along the lane. The men were going to the barn and hadn't seen her. She sighed with relief and immediately hated herself. She was a reeve who was hiding from the men because she couldn't take any more of their teasing.

It was so unfair. If she'd been a lad or the Lady of the Manor, they would obey her without question. She should have known that calling herself reeve wouldn't be enough, but she'd been so thrilled when Thomas agreed. Like a headstrong filly, she'd jumped into her role without stopping to think.

Now she was powerless and humiliated and didn't know what to do about it.

Simon had told her to leave the men's work to him and to stick to organising the women. She had protested, but secretly, his orders had come as a relief. It was the coward's way out, but it was better to succeed as a reeve to some of the workers than to be ridiculed by all.

She peered over the hedge. The lane was empty, the rumble of the cartwheels gone. The men would take a while unloading. She could get to Jorge's place and see how he was getting on with the looms before they returned. At least he was prepared to work with her.

Gathering up her skirts, she stepped from behind the hedge and walked briskly up the lane to Jorge's half-built cottage.

Thomas should have helped her deal with the men. He had the authority, but he'd done nothing. Something had upset his world, and she'd love to know what it was. A week or so ago, he was whistling and happier than a bee in clover, but since his return from Okewolde three days ago, he'd hardly spoken. He was either lost in his charts or walking around with his head down, when he was around at all. Most days he disappeared, and no one knew where he went.

She couldn't even tempt him with a game of chess. If anyone had asked her opinion, she would have said that he was maudlin after a woman. After checking on the looms, she'd go and see Annie; that one might know what was behind it.

Jorge wasn't at home when Rose arrived, but she saw two looms stacked in the corner of a half-finished wall. They were the usual rectangular wooden frame on a sturdy wooden base, but a yard wide and double the height; twice the size she'd ever seen. The downward warp strings were more closely strung together, and – unlike the looms she was used to – the strings were not weighted at the bottom with stones, but fixed to a bar.

No wonder the Flemish were famous for their cloth! With so many strings and tighter tension, any cloth woven on these would be finer than anything they could make. Rose stared at the looms, her quick mind already seeing the possibilities.

Next to the looms was a basket full of smoothly carved weft pieces used to weave the thread in and out between the warp strings. She picked one up, turning it over in her hands. It was the size and shape of a long plum and sat comfortably in her palm. The women could certainly work quicker using these. It was a shame Jorge wasn't there to demonstrate, but she'd speak to him as soon as the harvest was gathered.

Leaving the cottage, Rose checked the lane for any signs of the wagon, then hurried to Annie's dye shed. When she entered it, she nearly tripped over the large pile of wood on the floor, and there was a tun barrel in the corner that hadn't been there last time. A mix of musky herbs and sweet-smelling flowers filled the small linhay.

Ducking and dodging her way past numerous baskets filled with greenery that hung from the ceiling, she went further in. Bowls of all shapes and sizes jostled with an assortment of wooden spoons and rags for space on the shelves. On the floor, earthenware jars stood shoulder to shoulder like knights ready to charge into battle.

It was an impressive sight.

Annie was in the corner, stacking thick hazel poles used for stirring. 'Rose, hail! I've got everything prepared to start the red dye, and I've two lasses ready to help me. The lads are going to dig up the first madder roots after the harvest, so there's not much for you to do.'

Rose pursed her lips. Annie couldn't go around thinking she was running this little enterprise on her own, no matter what they'd agreed, but she had to be careful. She still didn't know what to do with the feather moss.

'You have been busy,' she said, wandering around, inspecting this and that. Peering into a bowl of white powder, she sniffed and quickly recoiled. She had no idea what it was or what it was used for, but it stank like rotting meat. 'I've been to Jorge's place and seen the first looms. You should see them. I didn't think it was possible to have so many warps. We'll make the finest cloth anyone's ever seen.'

Annie came out of her corner and wiped her hands on her apron. 'I look forward to that. It'll make all this effort worthwhile and bring in the coffers, which is what Thomas needs.'

That was exactly the opening Rose needed. 'Have you noticed how Thomas has changed since the market? If it were anyone else, I'd say he was maudlin after a woman.'

Annie laughed. 'That's absurd! He was only there a day!'

'He hasn't said anything to you, then?'

'No, and if he had, I wouldn't gossip about it to you or anyone else. He needs time to grow into his role, that's all, and he did come back to a load of trouble.'

Rose straightened her shoulders under Annie's rather pointed look. 'It wasn't all my fault, and if I was Lady of the Manor, the men wouldn't have challenged me.'

Annie put a stone jar firmly on the bench. 'You can get that idea straight out of your head. Thomas is highborn and you're not. Instead of dreaming about him, you should be thinking about settling down with one of your own kind. Jarin's a nice lad, or Lief the miller's son. He'd be ideal for you.' She fiddled with her headdress, stabbing the pins into the side of the fabric.

'I don't want to get wed,' Rose said. 'I'm not ready.'

'Not ready!' Annie exclaimed. 'You're fifteen summers. Soon you'll be too old. Don't you want a husband and children? Most maids do.'

'You didn't, and I'm not most maids.'

'It wasn't that I didn't want to, it—things just didn't work out that way for me, that's all. And anyway, I'm a healer. Healers don't have time for a husband and children, but you do.'

She might be the healer one day, although she couldn't see herself in the role. But if – no, not *if*; *when* – Thomas married, for the sake of begetting an heir if nothing else, would he keep her as reeve? When the estate grew and prospered, she might not be needed. What would she do then?

Lief was fair-looking in a rustic sort of way, and a miller's wife was highly respected, but she didn't want to be a miller's wife. The whole point of coming here was to get away from that.

Lady of the Manor. She hadn't been serious when she'd said it to Annie, but now the words were out there ...*Lady of the Manor*. She rolled the title around her head and liked the way it sounded.

But she was a commoner and Thomas was a lord. Annie was right; such a match was impossible. She might as well wish to marry a prince.

Smiling at her own foolishness, Rose stepped out of the dye shed and started down the still mercifully empty lane, heading for home.

CHAPTER 37

Thomas got up and rubbed his sore knees. For the past two weeks he'd prayed as the priest had commanded him to, but it wasn't helping. If anything, it was making him feel worse. He glanced longingly towards his chess set and thought about asking Rose for a game, but his heart wasn't in it and the set remained in its box.

When he thought about Rulf, which he did often, he was racked with guilt. When he didn't think about him, he felt empty, as though a part of him was missing. He was living in an endless spiral of torment, and it was driving him mad. He couldn't sleep for longing. He couldn't eat for feeling sick, and he couldn't think without his conscience nagging him. God's teeth, how much longer could he go on like this?

Rose came in, closed the door behind her with her foot and dumped a basket of blackberries and rose hips on the table. 'These will dry down nicely,' she said, popping a blackberry into her mouth. 'Want one?' She held out a blackberry.

Thomas shook his head. 'No.'

'They're very good.' She pushed it under his nose. 'I know you like blackberries.'

He shoved her hand away. 'I said I don't want one!'

'Don't get vexed with me; I'm only trying to cheer you up. You've been that miserable these past weeks.' Rose popped the berry into her mouth. 'What's the matter with you?'

'Nothing's the matter. I'm thinking, that's all.' Thomas slumped back and idly picked up a spoon from the table.

'What about?' Rose pulled up a stool, a trickle of dark juice running from the side of her mouth. She wiped it off with her finger.

'Nothing that concerns you,' he said, twirling the spoon between his fingers.

'Well, I've something that concerns you. I've seen the new looms and they're bigger and better than you can imagine.' Rose jumped off her stool and stood holding her shawl. 'I'll show you if you like.'

'Later. I'm not in the mood.'

'Oh, come on. You'll feel better for a walk up to Jorge's place.'

Rose's cheerfulness irritated him. He didn't want to feel better. Someone who had sinned so grievously, in thought if not in deed, deserved to feel like this, and he flung the spoon down on the table. 'Stop telling me what to do! You're always telling folks what to do. I should never have made you reeve.'

Rose put her hands on her hips. 'I'm a good reeve and you know it! And you should have supported me instead of hiding your head.'

The truth hurt. Thomas stood up, grabbed his hat and rammed it on his head. 'I'm going out for some peace and quiet.' In two strides, he had his hand on the latch.

'And I suppose teaching me to read and write is another mad idea! You haven't done that either!' Rose hurled the words at his retreating back.

Outside, Thomas kicked a stone angrily across the yard. With hindsight, the pact was a bad idea, but it was too late to back out now and he knew it. Swiping the hat from his head, he held it as though his life depended on it and marched across the yard. Splashing through the ford, he turned left and glanced up the lane for a forbidden sight of the black cassock.

Nothing. The lane was empty.

Unconsciously, he found himself walking up the hill towards the cave. He pictured Rulf inside, warming his hands over the fire or sitting on the floor, his legs outstretched. The image sent his pulse racing.

Think of something else. He tried conjugating a few Latin verbs, but that didn't help. In the privacy of the trees, he knelt down and prayed.

Dear God, I have sinned and done my penance and yet he still fills my mind. Help me to forget him…

The problem was that he didn't want to forget him. Maybe that was why his prayers went unanswered. It wasn't enough to confess your sins; you had to genuinely repent if you expected God to forgive you.

He didn't know how long he stayed there, but when he removed his hands, the tears had dried and his lips tasted salty. He wiped his face with his kerchief and hauled himself up.

God wasn't listening. With bowed head, he began the walk back down the hill. He had only gone a short way when he heard Rulf's voice from somewhere behind him and his heart was sent rolling in somersaults.

'Thomas! Wait! I've been looking for you!'

He stopped and glanced up the hill, poised on the threshold between right and wrong. He wanted to run to

Rulf, but the priest's words rang in his ears like the warning toll of a bell.

Summoning every ounce of willpower, he didn't look around. Pray Rulf didn't run after him.

Pray he did, because if Rulf instigated a meeting, then it wouldn't be his fault. He strained for the sound of hurried steps, longing for the feel of Rulf's hand on his arm. But there were no steps and no hand. With a sigh, he kept walking.

Rulf must realise he was avoiding him. He hadn't been to the cave or attended Mass since his confession with the priest. Sooner or later, Rulf was going to invite him to his cave to discuss the charts or have a game of chess, and then what would he do? Would he be strong enough to say no? How would he explain it if he did? God help him, would he always feel like this? If he did, Rulf's departure in the spring could be his salvation.

His salvation, and his damnation.

At the bottom of the hill, for something to do, he went to the fields to watch the last day of the harvest.

As the autumn sky faded to evening gold, the men threw down their scythes for the final time and the women stacked the last stooks. Dirty and tired, they formed a circle around Annie as she bound the last sheaf. God had been kind and sent good weather for them to finish. That night, clouds came over, the swallows disappeared, and rain drenched the fields.

Two days later, all the stooks were stored in the barn and ready for threshing. A sense of calm returned to the estate, and people smiled again. The harvest was in and there were still the gleanings to look forward to when the peasants put their geese on the cornfields to fatten on fallen grains, and women and children followed behind collecting any grain the geese missed.

Thomas stood by the open doors to the barn and breathed in the musky smell of wheat, oats and barley. The barn was stacked from floor to ceiling. It was so full that the last sheaves were packed tight to the entrance, and it had taken four men to do it. All of it waiting to be turned into ale and flour.

If Simon was right about Holdesworthe not having a working mill, the flour would be worth a tidy sum. He'd have money to pay the men and have coins left over. He could be out of here in a year or two. The thought brought a rare smile to his face.

Jarin struggled passed with a cart laden with stones. Behind him came Peter, carrying an armful of shovels. 'M'lord, I know it's good to be building the mill, but what about Father Rulf's church? It's not right, him praying on his knees in all weathers with no roof over his head.'

Thomas doubted if Rulf did much of that. When he prayed, he'd do it in the dry of his cave. 'Father Rulf understands,' he said. The image brought a pang and a hint of temptation.

'I'm asking, m'lord, for permission to take Jarin and to work on the church. One day a week, when I'm not needed in my forge.'

Peter's voice faded as Thomas glanced around. Everything was peaceful. The women were going about their daily tasks until the midday bell when the corn threshing would start, and the men were either up at the mill or clearing ditches. He wasn't needed.

Why shouldn't he go and see Rulf and enjoy a harmless game of chess? Rulf was a close friend; of course he cared and thought about him. There was no harm in that. And how was he to know if that priest had the voice of God anyway? He could have been like Rulf and just treating the priesthood as a job.

He looked up at the line of trees on the hill. He couldn't avoid Rulf forever. The voice of temptation whispered in his ear. He could top up his flagon, pick up his chess set and be at the cave by the first quarter. What harm would it do?

'M'lord?' Peter hitched the shovels and fidgeted with the weight of them.

Oh...Peter. What had he wanted again? 'I don't mind, but check with Simon first.'

Peter's face split into a grin. 'Thank ye, m'lord, thank ye. I have to say I didn't think ye'd see it that way. When the church is finished, me and Jarin'll start on the priest's cottage.' He shifted the shovels again, balancing them on his shoulder. 'One last thing, m'lord. Can we have pannage rights, and if so, how much do ye want? Only I've a nice couple of sows needs fattening, and them woods is right full of acorns.'

Thomas didn't have a clue, although Rose would know. It seemed mean to charge the peasants to roam their swine in his woods for acorns that hadn't cost him anything, but it was what lords did, and every penny counted.

'Sort it out with Simon, he's the bailiff.'

Before Peter had turned the corner, Thomas had filled his flagon, put his chess set in his bag and was on his way to Rulf's cave feeling ridiculously nervous. Damn the priest. If his soul went to hell, so be it; he was in hell anyway.

As he walked along the gorse path he had followed so many times before, a bush snagged his sleeve.

'Damn muxy stuff!' He yanked his arm free, leaving a small tear in his clothes. He'd bring a billhook with him next time.

'I couldn't agree more, although the flowers make a passable drink if you can avoid the thorns to pick them.' Rulf stood in front him, his arms open in welcome, a twinkle in his eyes and a broad smile on his face. 'I've been waiting.'

Three little words.

Rulf's gaze penetrated through him as though drinking in his very soul, holding him captive in those vivid blue eyes. *He knew*.

'You've been avoiding me,' Rulf went on, a flicker of humour in his face. 'I thought I'd offended in some way.'

'I had to be seen around the harvesting. It was my duty.'

'Ah, that. Well, it's good to see you. Come, I've found something I think you'll find interesting.'

Thomas followed him. It felt the same, and yet something had changed between them.

In the dim light of the cave, Rulf held out his hand. In the palm was a small crinkled brown ball.

God, he had beautiful hands. 'That's just an oak apple.'

'Not *just* an oak apple, my friend.' Rulf held it delicately up to the light.

Thomas drew in a sharp breath as his eyes were drawn, not to the oak apple, but to Rulf's smooth skin and his handsome face outlined against the light. The priest was right. He shouldn't be here, but he couldn't leave, not now.

'This is ink,' Rulf said. 'I'll show you how to make it, but first, we'll need more oak apples and I know where to find them. Bring your bag.'

He led the way through mature oaks that shadowed smaller hazel, holly and dogwood, and brambles sprawling in thick mounds of tangled strands across their path. As he brushed past, Thomas kept his hands firmly inside his surcoat.

'Along here are young oaks,' said Rulf. 'They're the ones we want.'

The very sound of his voice made Thomas's heart sing. Later, lying on his mattress, he would admonish himself for such thoughts but for now, he would glory in them. He continued to follow, his boots crunching on thousands of fallen acorns, just as Peter as said.

Rulf stopped in a clearing. 'This is the place. There are hundreds of oak apples here. Ideally, they should be taken at the end of winter, but if you need ink now, we can do something with these.' He twisted one off a branch and studied it. 'I can never tell if the grub inside has left, but as I understand it, the tree tries to kill the grub by making a poison and it's that which makes the ink. That's why it's the dark oak apples we want.'

Thomas started to pick them, acutely aware that Rulf was watching.

'You remind me of a statue of a Greek god I once saw,' Rulf said suddenly. 'You're beautiful. Don't ever change.'

Thomas's hand poised in mid-air and he blushed. He felt a depth of delight that he refused to understand. 'I don't know what to say,' he said, keeping his eyes focused on the branch, his hand trembling.

'Forgive me; I've embarrassed you. I was trying to tell you that you are special...and more than a friend.' Rulf's words hung in the air as he reached forward and gently traced the side of Thomas's face with his finger.

Ripples tingled down Thomas's cheek and through his entire body as his heart seemed to stop in his chest. He didn't know what to do or say, only that he wanted Rulf to touch him again.

'I think you feel as I do?' said Rulf. There was the barest hesitancy in his voice.

Thomas was out of his depth, but his body was stirring in response to a hitherto unknown physical and emotional need. A demanding, delicious sinful desire that was hard to deny.

'How can we be more than friends? You're a priest. You've taken the vow of celibacy. You're not allowed to desire a woman, and especially not—' Thomas coloured— 'me.'

'I am a man before I am a priest.'

Slowly, Thomas turned to face him, taking in every inch of Rulf's face. 'I've had feelings for a long time, but it's a sin.' He lowered his eyes, ashamed.

Rulf took Thomas's chin between his hands and looked deeply into his eyes. 'Is it so wrong? The church tells us so, but how can such feelings be sinful? Love is God's gift. A beautiful thing to be nurtured and cherished, whether it be between man and woman or man and man.'

Was this love? Thomas only knew that everything around him was full of joy as though lit by a thousand candles, his heart dancing.

Shyly, he laid his hand over Rulf's. 'How long have you felt like this?'

Rulf's mouth turned, hinting at a smile. 'Since the first day we met and you pretended to like my disgusting wine.' He chuckled. 'I didn't dare say, though; you'd have run a mile.'

Thomas smiled. 'Yes, I would. I suppose I realised when we were at the inn.' He lowered his face to stare at his boots.

'I know,' said Rulf quietly. 'I wasn't asleep. God knows it took all my self-will not to open my eyes, but if I'd responded, you'd have fled the room overcome with guilt and shame, never to look me in the eye again. I heard you bring up your dinner in the piss holes and saw the torture on your face the next day. Believe me, I suffered that torture with you, but I was too afraid of losing you to speak. I could see it in your eyes, but I had to let you decide. Today, when you came along the path and I saw the way you looked at me, I knew you had.' Rulf smiled, the familiar creases at the corners of his eyes.

Thomas backed away a little, desire warring with piety. 'But it's a sin. Our souls will be condemned to eternal hell.'

'Will they? It's what we're told, but there's no proof, any more than there's proof of heaven or hell. Are you willing to take the risk?'

Was he? He couldn't think of the right response, but one ugly piece of knowledge was lurking in the front of his mind. 'If anyone finds out, they'll hang us.'

'They'd do more than that to us. When we're Father Rulf and Lord Thomas, no one must ever know. We shall have to be on our guard at all times. This is between us, Rulf and Thomas.' Rulf leaned forward and kissed him lightly on the lips.

Thomas's blood surged with the heat of spiced wine. He'd never known such inner force. It was a thing of wonder, the birth of something beyond his comprehension. He reached out and stroked Rulf's face as Rulf placed his hand over his and held it to his lips.

How could something be wrong when it felt so right? Others had no mercy on such relationships, but his feelings were too wonderful and compelling for him to do anything but willingly surrender to them.

CHAPTER 38

The cotehardie strained against Thomas's chest. He fiddled with the laces and ran a hand inside the collar that was too warm in the evening sun. He couldn't remember the last time he'd worn it. He sniffed the scent of Annie's thyme water on his wrists. A little strong, next time he'd used fewer drops.

Today was no ordinary day. Today, he had to address his people, who were gathering in the yard for the presentation of the corn doll. This time, no nerves teased his stomach and no dry mouth strangled his words. He felt nothing but confidence and elation. Was that what love did to you? It was a strange and heady mix, and he rather liked it.

Love is a beautiful thing, to be nurtured and cherished, Rulf had said. And it was beautiful. For the first time in his life, Thomas felt invincible, as though he could dance on water or reach up and touch the moon.

He looked across the yard that was framed by standing torches, the flames sending purple shadows across the faces there. His nose twitched with the rich smell of roasting hog on the spit, making his stomach groan with anticipation. No Rulf yet. He'd wait.

You don't believe all that Pagan superstition, do you? Rulf had said, his tone slightly mocking. Of course he didn't

– he was a man of science and facts – but the peasants did, he had argued. Presenting the corn doll was a yearly ritual, and the harvest festival wouldn't be the same without it. Anyway, it didn't hurt anyone.

Not that this harvest festival was typical. The ceremony was taking place in the yard, and instead of presiding in a grand hall, he was standing outside the door to his house. He didn't have a high table, let alone a grand hall.

Still no Rulf.

His nerves started twisting his stomach in sickening knots. Rulf was never late.

I'll give a harvest blessing, but the church doesn't approve of the old customs and neither do I, he'd said, smiling. They both knew he was only coming for the spit roast.

Eleanor was hovering excitedly nearby, the corn doll clutched closely to her chest. As was the custom, she had made the doll out of the last sheaf of wheat gathered from the field, and no one was allowed to see it until she presented it to the Lord of the Manor.

Thomas smiled. He liked Eleanor with her unfailingly cheerful manner, and she worked hard making baskets and rope. She deserved the honour.

He cast his eye over the yard again. Folks were shuffling their feet and glancing impatiently at the barrels of ale. A child began to cry. The mother rubbed its back and rocked it. He strained to see over their heads but still no sign of Rulf.

He wanted Rulf to see him being self-assured when he spoke. He wanted Rulf to be proud of him. He'd wait a few more moments.

Maybe Rulf wasn't coming. What if— Thomas swallowed, his spirits falling to his boots— what if what had happened between them had been Rulf's way of saying farewell? Maybe he'd gone back to Oxford early.

No, Rulf wouldn't do that to him. He loved him. He'd said so last night.

The crowd went quiet. He couldn't wait any longer. Stepping forward, Thomas cleared his throat and raised his voice.

'My people, God has blessed us with a good harvest. Who presents the corn doll to guard over our grain for the dark months to come and ensure good fertility in the spring?'

Blushing, Eleanor came forward, curtsied and offered the corn doll. It was small, no larger than his hand and in the shape of a poppet doll. Eleanor had plaited a ring of wheat for a face and hair and woven a cone for a kirtle and tied a red ribbon between the two. It was a simple piece but made with care and so typical of Eleanor.

Thomas inclined his head and with due solemnity held up the corn doll for all to see. 'Eleanor, place this doll in the barn to guard the grain.'

As he turned from her, he saw Rulf standing at the back of the crowd. Once again, he felt that jump in his heart and warmth spread across his face. He mustn't give anything away, though. Smiling, he returned the doll to Eleanor's outstretched hands.

'My lord, are you ready for the blessing of the harvest?' Rulf stepped forward, his face still and innocent. Rulf was a good player, good at pretending like nothing was different.

'I am.'

Rulf gave his blessing and looked directly at him. 'I believe, my lord, that we are now ready for the festivities to commence,' he said with a respectful nod.

Thomas felt an urge to giggle but took his cue from Rulf and inclined his head again. 'Fiddlers, begin the music! Open the barrels! Let us celebrate our good fortune!' His voice rang out amid cheers and a rush towards the barrels. At last, his people could enjoy what they'd truly come for.

'I thought you weren't coming,' he said to Rulf in a low voice. 'I feared that yesterday was your farewell and you'd left for Oxford.' It sounded ridiculous now.

'I dozed off.' Rulf smiled and nodded to Janet and Peter as they walked past, then lowered his voice to barely more than a whisper. 'I could never just leave you, you must know that. But each day, the church grows more corrupt. There's important work to be done if their power is to be curtailed. I like the new hairstyle and cotehardie by the way.' Rulf turned away and in that simple movement, became Father Rulf amongst his flock once more. 'Annie! I must congratulate you on your excellent herbal water, it did my feet the world of good…'

Rulf liked his new look. A whoop threatened to burst from Thomas's mouth. He wanted to dance on air and shout from the rooftops, but he must control himself. He forced his mouth from a beaming smile to a dignified line, placed his hands behind his back and squashed the urge to whistle as he strolled amongst his people.

While the men jostled for space at the barrels and the women crowded around the trestles of food, Rose remained seated on the wall with her eyes firmly fixed on Thomas. He had changed from dour to all smiles, and she didn't understand why.

This morning, he'd been whistling and humming to himself when he came up to her.

'I beg pardon for the way I spoke the other day,' he'd said. 'You're a good reeve and I should have made your position known. I'll honour our pact and we'll start your lessons to read and write.' Then he'd smiled at her in that beguiling way of his. 'I was wondering, would you cut my hair?' He'd run his hand through his long fair strands. Strands that she envied. 'I thought cut square to the shoulder in the latest fashion, what do you think?'

Since when had Thomas bothered with fashion? But she had nodded, sat him on a stool and reached for the scissors. Running her hands through his hair had made her tingle, and she'd had an overwhelming impulse to kiss his neck.

There was a woman behind this change, she was sure of it. Men, particularly men like Thomas, didn't smarten their dress or think about their hair unless they were trying to impress someone. Maybe he had met a noblewoman at Okewolde market. She couldn't imagine how; he'd been with Father Rulf at the time, and was hardly likely to think of such matters in the company of a priest.

She watched Thomas parade amongst the throng, acknowledging curtsies and bows with a refined nod, the red jewel on his shoulder sparkling in the torchlight. He looked like a lord. Worse, he was acting like one. If he carried on like this, he would attract a noble lady, if he hadn't already, and she could forget any ideas of advancement, let alone being the Lady of the Manor.

Her heart lurched. Was she the reason for this change? He had given her a charming smile when she'd finished his hair.

She continued watching Thomas mingle amongst his people, walking with his hands behind his back and with his head held high. Maybe he was looking for her. She slipped to the ground, straightened her kirtle, pushed stray curls under her headdress and sauntered across the yard in his direction.

'My lord, forgive me,' she said, standing close by his shoulder, 'but are you joining the first circle of dancers? It is expected.' She lowered her eyes demurely and bobbed a curtsy. She didn't know why she was being so formal, but it felt right.

'Then I had better do so. I wouldn't want to disappoint. May I?' He offered her his arm in lordly style.

Her heart fluttered, and as he led her to the dancers, she tilted her chin and was his Lady of the Manor for a glorious, heart-stopping moment.

Her joy didn't last long. As soon as the dance was over, Thomas led her to Annie and with a bow removed himself from her company. The message was clear: he'd done his duty, and he hadn't been seeking her as a companion for the evening.

Rose nibbled her thumbnail, watching him parade around like a peacock, her eyes narrowed.

Who was this woman? More importantly, what was she going to do about it?

CHAPTER 39

'I don't see why she needs to read and write.' Maria protested, yanking a blue thread from her sewing box. 'That's for nobles and clergy.'

'Then Mama's efforts on your lessons were wasted,' Thomas answered. 'It's a beautiful art, and I praise anyone who wishes to learn. Rose, let's go outside where we'll have no audience.'

Rose followed him, lifting her skirts like a lady, and shot Maria a triumphant look behind Thomas's back on the way out. Whoever Thomas's woman was, she could make herself just as attractive, and now she was to be alone with him.

They sat on a pair of up-turned pails in a corner of the yard. Thomas scratched some lines in the dirt with a stick. He had scholar's hands, smooth and pale.

'What does it say?' she asked.

'R-O-S-E, Rose. Now you try.'

Frowning with concentration, she copied the letters. What magic! She'd drawn a few lines with a stick and she could write her name. How pretty it looked.

'Show me more,' she said.

Thomas wrote more letters. Every time he leaned forward to scratch them into the dirt, she made sure to lean forward too. If only she'd known she was having her first lesson today, she'd have worn her other tunic, the one which was a little tighter and lower in the front.

But no matter how close she leaned, how much she smiled or tried to catch his eye, he didn't so much as look at her. God's bones, he was hard work. You only had to lower your eyes to most lads and they'd be all over you.

'My wrist is aching and see how my lines shake.' She looked up through her lashes. 'Can you help me?'

Thomas covered her hand with his, and together they scratched out a firm 'B' in the dirt, but there was no turning of his head and no looking deeply into her eyes as he was supposed to do. When they'd finished, he simply removed his hand and told her to try again on her own.

She bit her lip. What more could she do?

'El's ringing the midday bell. I must go,' Thomas said, standing to leave a little too quickly. 'Keep practising; you're doing well.'

She'd have sworn that was relief on his face. 'Can we have another lesson tomorrow? I'm enjoying it, and you're such a good teacher.' Maybe a bit of flattery would work.

'I'm making ink with Father Rulf this afternoon and we may not finish today. I'll let you know.'

Not flattery then. Maybe she was wasting her time. Rose picked up the stick and wrote her name again, but without Thomas, it wasn't so much fun. She gave an approving nod to her work anyway and left it for others to see.

She was running out of time. Once Thomas had coins in his coffer, he might start thinking of marrying this woman who seemed to have turned his head. If that happened, she might as well give up.

'Eleanor's in the house waiting for you to make mead.' Annie came across the yard, carrying a bowl of sheep's milk. 'I hope you haven't forgotten.'

'No, of course not,' Rose lied. With a last proud look at her name, she hurried to the house.

Inside, Eleanor was happily spinning with her drop spindle, something all the women should be doing if they were to have wool to weave. Rose made a mental note to remind the women to keep carding and spinning the fleece.

'The honey and water we m-mixed before harvest is bubbling all on its own, so c-can we make m-mead now?' said Eleanor, her face lit with anticipation.

Rose dipped a finger into a pail of fermenting honey and water and licked her finger, grimacing at the raw taste. 'We need a cup, honey and some pails of water. Did you pick the apples and pears as I told you?'

'Two baskets, one of each and three pails of water from the river, and I've built the fire to heat the embers,' Eleanor announced proudly.

They poured the honey and water into a large iron pot, and Rose marked the level with a piece of charcoal. Eleanor chopped some fruit, tied it in a rag and dropped it into the pot, then added a cup of honey and had the honour of stirring it. Together, they hoisted the heavy pot onto a hook over the fire for the liquid to boil.

There were three pails of honey and water and only one fire. It was going to be a long afternoon, but Rose had to admit that life was never boring with Eleanor. Like a child, she lived in the moment with no ambitions or worries about the future.

Some people would call it God's judgment. Rose thought it was more of a blessing. Eleanor never had to worry about how to make men take her seriously, or being married to a man she didn't love.

Eleanor found her Table game and started to lay it out. Rose had never played it before, but if Eleanor could play it, she must be able to learn. After all, she could play chess and write her name.

The game was a square board painted with different coloured triangles, two dice and wooden discs for each player. The idea, Eleanor said, was to chase each other's discs around the board until the winner captured them.

To her surprise, Rose found herself enjoying it a lot more than she'd expected. Why didn't Thomas play this? It was much more fun than chess. She might suggest it, but it was probably too easy for him, and she didn't want him to think her childish.

They played until the liquid had boiled down to the mark, then Eleanor skimmed off the foam and squeezed the fruit pulp between two spoons as Rose had showed her. Using a piece of Maria's old kirtle, they strained the liquid into a pail to cool, ready to pour into a barrel later. They'd leave the top of the barrel off until after the fruit picking in a few weeks, then Eleanor would seal it.

They had just finished pouring the last pail when Simon came in for the evening.

'God's teeth, that smells good! Can I try some?'

'Rose says we have t-to wait until next spring before we c-can drink it,' Eleanor answered.

'So keep your mucky fingers out of it!' Rose slapped Simon's hand, which had been inching toward the pail. 'That's the mead done, so I'm off to make sure the women are spinning.' She untied her apron and replaced her coif.

Eleanor giggled. 'You said the women spinning. They'll get dizzy.'

'You know what I mean. Spinning the fleece, and stop twirling round and round like that or you'll be the dizzy one.' Rose pushed her coils under her coif and straightened her skirts. She'd truly enjoyed her afternoon with Eleanor, but she did have to check on the women.

And if God was good, she would meet Thomas coming home.

CHAPTER 40

Thomas marched up the hill, the billhook safely tied to his belt, humming. It was a week since he and Rulf had picked oak apples, but he'd been so busy with the harvest festival and teaching Rose to scratch letters in the dirt that this was the first opportunity to be with him on his own.

Not that Rulf hadn't haunted every moment of his days and nights. He had, and while outwardly dealing with everyday matters, his inner self was consumed with that first magical moment of awareness.

Rulf had said that love was a beautiful thing, and it was indeed. It had crept up behind Thomas, innocently and silently, burying itself with deep and exquisite pain.

If this was sinful, then God was truly cruel.

'Thomas! At last! Two days since the harvest festival and I've been waiting for you.' Rulf stepped from the entrance to his cave and embraced Thomas in a warm hug. 'The haircut suits you and I thought the cotehardie set off your slender frame very well. You should wear it more often. And—' Rulf delicately sniffed Thomas's wrist— 'thyme water, if I'm not mistaken. Ask Annie for some mint balm wash as well. It's wonderfully refreshing in hot weather.' His lips brushed Thomas's wrist before letting go.

'Now, my friend, to business. If these oak apples are not to shrivel like old maids before our eyes, we must get to work.' Rulf flashed him a smile. 'I have bowls and two stones to crush the apples to a fine powder.'

They needed no words to intrude during their work, but occasionally their eyes met and they exchanged a smile. It was enough to be there, together, and free from their barrier to the world.

'That should do it. Next, we add water or wine. Dare I risk some of my elder or nettle wine or is it too raw, even for ink?' said Rulf.

'Let's make some of each, then we'll know.'

'That's what I love about you: your logical mind is a marvel. Both it is. Then we'll leave it for a few days. At that point, we should add green vitriol. I don't have any, but I've seen iron used. It gives the ink a reddish tint. I take it my lord doesn't object?'

The creases dancing at the sides of Rulf's eyes left his face and tripped across Thomas's heart. 'Providing I can write with it, I don't care what colour it is,' he said with a grin.

'Just as well, because I scraped some rust off a few scraps of old iron in Peter's forge. We'll also need a cloth for straining and a dozen eggs for thickening next time you come.'

'A dozen!' Thomas echoed. 'I want to write with it, not use it as glue!'

'Some of the eggs are for me. Don't look like that; it's a long way up and down that hill.' Rulf stretched, his fingertips just touching the top wall. His sleeves slipped back to his shoulders, revealing arms covered with fine dark hairs.

Shyly, Thomas laid his hand on Rulf's arm. The hair was so silky, the arm so firm and masculine. He couldn't resist running a finger softly over the surface.

Rulf placed his hand over his, held it to his lips. 'God, Thomas, I wish you weren't so beautiful. You distract me with your wiles, but our knowledge of each other is fresh. Let's allow it to mature and develop like a fine wine.' Rulf held his eyes for a moment, then looked away. 'Remove your boots if you want and take your ease; I'm about to create a sumptuous meal.' He lifted the lid off a pot hanging over the fire and breathed in. 'Hare, wild garlic, spices from my acquired winnings and carrots. The carrots are a gift from Janet.'

'You've been poaching hare on my land! I could put you in the stocks for that.' Thomas grinned as he wrestled with his boots.

'If my dish doesn't please my lord, then I shall gladly take my penance.' Rulf's eyes glinted with the all too familiar twinkle.

'Do you get many gifts from Janet?' Thomas discarded his boots, sat on the floor and wriggled his toes in delight. His boots were good quality, but just a fraction too small across the toes.

'Not just from Janet, you'd be surprised. Peter made me a hammer, I get herbs and tonics from Annie, bowls of potage, all sorts. Jorge's wife gave me some wool the other day, although I've no idea what I'm going to do with it. All in exchange for a personal prayer. They believe my prayers are more likely to be listened to.'

'And are they?'

Rulf shrugged. 'I doubt it, but faith is a powerful thing. If they believe it, who am I to disappoint them?'

Who indeed? It didn't matter. Nothing mattered but being there. Thomas leaned back against the wall, wrapped in utter contentment.

Watching Rulf fussing over his dish, Thomas's thoughts drifted until he arrived back to the same unanswered issue. 'Rulf, can I ask you something?'

'Anything, although I don't promise to have an answer.' Rulf dipped a spoon into the pot, took a sip and frowned. 'A little more garlic. What is it you want to know?'

'When I arrived home at the time of the Pestilence, Mama sent me away. I told you that, remember?'

Rulf nodded and added a handful of crushed wild garlic to the pot.

Thomas hesitated. Was he about to betray a secret? But how could he be when he didn't know what the secret was? 'Mama said that certain knowledge might come my way, and if it did, I was to forgive her. And that they did their best at the time.'

Rulf glanced over his shoulder. 'Intriguing. Have you any idea what she meant?'

Thomas shook his head. 'No, and it's been bothering me ever since. I'm sure Annie knows, but she won't tell me. Rose and Annie are friends, and I was wondering about asking Rose to see if she could find out. Do you think I should?'

Rulf's face was one of pure disbelief as he turned, the spoon poised halfway to his mouth. 'Rose is the last person you should confide in.'

'Why?'

Rulf sat down beside him. 'My dear young friend, are you blind? Rose is smitten with you. She looks at you like a devoted puppy; you must have noticed. If I didn't know you better, I'd be jealous. If you take her into your confidence, she'll take it as encouragement. A maid's fancy, no doubt, but until it passes, you should be wary of her. A woman scorned can make a dangerous enemy.'

Thomas blinked. Rose could be difficult, headstrong and with fiery moods, but he'd never thought of her as dangerous, let alone an enemy. 'What should I do?'

'Stay out of her way and keep her busy. She's clever and capable. I'll wager she loves a challenge. Find her something new to do, that's my advice.' Rulf smiled for a moment then shook his head. 'If Rose had been born a noble, she would have made an ideal Lady of the Manor for you. She'd willingly have taken over managing the estate, and you'd be free as a bird.'

'How can you talk about me marrying? What about us?'

'Don't look so shocked. It will make no difference to us. Noble marriages are nothing but a convenience. You're the last Chiddleigh, so you need an heir, and a good dowry from a wealthy bride would give you coins.'

'But I don't have a mansion or wealth to attract a rich bride—'

'What about my winnings from the dice game?'

'Most of it went on paying the men, and Simon's taking the rest to rebuild the mill.' Thomas bit his lip and searched Rulf's face. 'It shouldn't be more than a year or two before the estate prospers, and then we can go to Oxford together. I mean...you won't be leaving in the spring now, will you?'

Rulf got up and busied himself with his cooking. 'That pot needs a stir, or it'll burn.'

'Rulf? You won't, will you?'

'Spring is a long way off, my friend. As to your Mama's little conundrum, I should forget it. All families have secrets, and most are best left that way. Now, to eat. Wait until you taste this!' Rulf turned with a flourish, presenting his pot like a precious gift.

Thomas took a spoonful of the hare stew. It tasted as good as it smelt. 'This is wonderful. You must make it again.'

Rulf laughed. 'You could be in for a long wait. Have you any idea how hard it is to catch a hare?'

Thomas laughed too, his fears allayed. Looking at Rulf now, his eyes shining in the firelight as they sat sharing a meal, it was impossible to ever think he would leave.

CHAPTER 41

'Rose! I've been looking for you, have you got a moment?'

'Thomas, hail! You're quite a stranger these days,' Rose said, dropping apples into the basket at her feet and patting her coif. Why did he always catch her when she was dirty and dishevelled?

'Yes, well, busy. You know how it is.' He stood a few feet away from her, not quite looking at her. It was a little disconcerting.

'What do you want?' she said, as though she had all day. In truth, there were still another dozen apple trees to pick and not many women to do it. She should have put fewer women on spinning and weaving, but the cloth sales were only a few weeks away at the end of October, and Annie was giving her earache nagging for more cloth.

'I've got a job for you,' Thomas said.

'...Oh.' She tried to hide the disappointment in her voice. What a nerve, putting more on to her when he couldn't even honour his promise of teaching her to read and write. 'I was hoping we could work on my letters. We haven't done that for a week or two. As for taking on another task, I'm busy enough as it is what with apple picking, helping Annie in the dye shed, the weaving and everything else. I can't do it all. You'll have to ask someone else.' She reached up for more apples. Why were the best ones always at the top?

'Wait until you hear what it is. I think you'll like it.'

Curious now, she turned. 'What?'

Thomas reached inside his surcoat and brought out a small roll of parchment. 'This is a list of words for you to practise writing with a stick—'

'I thought you said it was a job.'

'—because I want you to help Simon write the records for the estate. He doesn't like doing it. He always says he's too busy, and I know I can trust you to see it gets done.'

Me? But that's a job for the bailiff and the lord or...' A flutter rippled through her. Could he mean...no, of course, he couldn't. Then why this? She hardly dared look at him.

'The lady of the manor, I know. It's a responsible job, but I'm sure you're up to it.' He smiled at her and held out the scroll. 'You'll do it?'

Do it? Of course she'd do it, even if it meant staying up all night to finish her work and never sleeping properly again. She took the parchment and unfurled it. There was a list of a dozen words written in a reddish black ink, but she only understood one: *grain*.

'You want me to practise writing these words with a stick in the dirt? I don't even know what they mean.' This wasn't what she thought. She'd imagined herself seated at the table using a proper quill with Thomas beside her.

'They're words you'll use in the records. Simon will tell you what they mean, and you'll soon get to recognise them when you scribe the accounts.'

'Practise on my own?' Rose looked at him over the scroll. 'Don't you want to be with me to make sure I'm doing it right?' She looked up through her eyelashes and got no response, but then, if he was thinking of her in that way, he'd be discrete.

'You don't need me,' he said, readjusting his surcoat. 'Just copy them until you can do them easily.'

'And when I can, will you let me use a quill and show me proper writing? I want to write a letter.' *Like a lady*, she thought.

'This is proper writing. When you can do these, I'll give you another list to learn. You need a lot of words before you can put them together in a sentence and write that letter of yours. Who do you want to write to, anyway?'

There wasn't anybody. No one she knew could read, and she'd never heard of sentences, but a letter was proper writing. Something that ladies did.

She shrugged. 'I don't know, but I might do one day.'

'Yes, I suppose you might.' His mouth turned up in a faint smile, making her heart soar.

A Lady of the Manor wrote letters and did the accounts. He must mean it!

'I'll learn these as quickly as I can and start helping Simon,' she said. 'I won't let you down.'

'I know.' Thomas helped himself to an apple from her basket and took a crisp bite. 'I've got to be going. Let me know when you need more words,' he called back over his shoulder. Before he'd gone more than a few paces, he began to whistle.

Watching his slim frame walk away, Rose clutched the list of words to her bosom.

Her and Thomas. She could hardly believe it.

CHAPTER 42

January 1350

'God's bones, it's nearly sunset! That's your fault, keeping me talking about Aristarchus. You should have stopped me.' Thomas scrambled to his feet and searched round for his mantle and bag.

'Once you get going on your favourite philosopher and his phases of the moon, no one could stop you.' Rulf leaned back against the wall of the cave, his hands behind his head, watching Thomas with an amused smile. 'What's the hurry?'

'It's the 17th of January, Wassailing Day, and I have to give the toast. Everyone will be waiting for me. Dear Lord, where's my hat?'

'It's here.' Rulf held out a lazy hand, Thomas's green felt hat dangling from his fingers. 'I can't believe someone who is so enthralled with Aristarchus can believe in such pagan nonsense.'

Thomas rammed the hat on his head, fastened the gold shoulder buckle of his mantle and threw his bag over one shoulder. 'I don't, but the peasants do. Anyway, it's tradition and there's no harm in it.'

'I wouldn't know. I've never been to one.' Rulf settled back down, wriggling his toes in the warmth of the embers.

'Then come with me.'

'No, I'm fine here. If I go, the peasants will only start pestering me for prayers and blessings.'

'The hog's been roasting on the spit all afternoon and there's warmed cider laced with spices and honey.'

Rulf raised his head and scrambled to his feet. 'I'll get my cassock.'

Thomas smiled. He'd known that would work.

They left the cave together. At the end of the path, they turned down the hill towards the yard where the smell of roasting hog and herbs drifted in the air, and smudges of yellow marked a circle of flaming torches waiting for their lord.

'You never told me, how is the situation with Rose? Has she lost interest in you?' said Rulf using his staff to pick his way. 'Watch out for this patch; it's frozen and slippery from last night's rain.'

Thomas trod carefully. The lush green grass of summer had long changed to a dirty brown and was lying flat as though sleeping through the dark months. The bare trees looked like dark skeletons, their backs turned against the prevailing wind, their branches stretched forward like beggars seeking alms.

'I think so. She's certainly making a good job of the records and learns her lists much quicker than I thought she would. She's changed, though. Instead of slumping down on her stool, she sits gently, arranging her skirts and with her hands held in her lap, like Maria. She's walking differently too. No more marching across the yard with her coif askew, she uses short steps with her head held high. It's quite amusing, but I can't imagine why she's doing it.'

'Who knows what goes on in a woman's mind? They're odd creatures. She's probably trying to live up to her status of record-keeper. Remember how she behaved when you made her reeve?' Rulf stopped and rested on his staff. 'Why worry? You're free of her now.' He sniffed the air. 'That hog roast smells good, come on, my belly's rumbling.'

Rulf was right. Although Rose still sought him out, and there was something about the way she looked at him which was disturbing, but—no, he shook his head. He was being a nuddlejade; Rose was long over her silly maid's fancy. She hadn't mentioned playing chess for months.

'God's bones, it's cold. I hate this weather.' Thomas pulled his mantle close around his chest.

'I think we're in for some snow. Better to have it early and then the tracks will be clear for travelling in the spring.'

Thomas's heart gave an unpleasant jolt. 'Why should that bother you?'

Rulf stopped and turned to face him. Thomas didn't like the seriousness in his eyes and a cold chill ran down his spine. 'You are staying, aren't you?'

Rulf's eyes softened, his face sagging as though falling against its will. Casting a glance down the hill, he reached out and stroked Thomas's face.

'How can I leave now?' he whispered.

It was exactly what Thomas wanted to hear, and tenderly, he covered Rulf's hand with his. 'You can't. You love me too much.' He raised Rulf's hand and brushed his lips against the sweet-scented skin.

'I know, and God, I wish that I didn't.' Rulf paused, his eyes melting into Thomas's. 'This is dangerous, someone might see us.' He removed his hand and hid it in the folds of his cassock. 'Come, my lord, the spit roast is calling,' he said, his back disappearing into the failing light.

When they arrived in the yard, the waiting crowd turned towards them as their muffled voices hushed. Rulf stood back, his hands neatly folded across his chest, and Thomas took his place in front of the house. His people shuffled into a semi-circle before him as he poured a cup of cider. Holding it high, he called, 'Waes hael!'

'Drinc hael!' the crowd responded, raising their cups with a cheer. Janet passed a large bowl of warm cider to the first person, who refilled their cup and passed the bowl to the next and around the group in turn until returning to Janet.

'Are the Wassail King and Queen ready to lead us to the orchard?' Thomas's voice rang clear in the still air.

'Ready, my lord!' and 'I'm ready!' Jarin's and Eleanor's voices rang out from the front of the group.

'Then take us to the King of the trees!' Thomas lifted his cup in one final salute as Jarin and Eleanor, each wearing a crown of greenery, held up their torches and led the procession towards the orchard. The people followed, shouting, cheering and banging pots and pans in a discord of ear-splitting din.

Thomas joined Rulf, who had his hands over his ears. 'What on earth are they doing that for?' he shouted as they trailed behind the crowd.

'They're making as much noise as they can to awaken the sleeping tree spirits and frighten off any evil demons who might be lurking in the branches,' Thomas answered. 'Have you really never seen a Wassailing?'

'On my father's estate with my uncle the bishop? Are you jesting? The church discourages such events.'

Standing a little way back, they watched as the noise subsided and the group formed a circle around the largest tree in the orchard, the light of the flaming torches rippling through the branches.

'I see what you mean about Rose,' Rulf whispered. 'If she lifted her chin any higher, she'd fall over her own feet.'

'And she's wearing the maiden's headdress, loose over her head, instead of her usual coif. What's she up to?'

Rulf stroked his chin and chuckled. 'Maybe she's not over her fancy for you. Could be she's practising for when you pop the question.'

'This is no jesting matter.'

'Who's jesting? You said yourself that she's doing the records and if she at least tries to look like a noble, you could do worse. You should think about it.'

He didn't want to think about it. He had Rulf, but Rulf couldn't give him an heir. He pushed the thought away.

In the silence, the people's faces glowed pink and purple in the shadows as Eleanor stepped forward.

'What's happening now?' asked Rulf.

'The Wassail Queen is putting a piece of wassail – that's bread soaked in warmed cider – into the branches. It's her gift to the tree spirits to keep the health of the trees in the hope of a bountiful harvest in the autumn. Everyone will sing in a moment,' he said.

Eleanor returned to her place and a reverent disharmony of voices filled the air.

> *'Apple tree, apple tree, we all come to wassail thee,*
> *Bear this year and next to bloom and blow,*
> *Hat fulls, cap fulls, three cornered sack fulls…'*

Thomas swallowed. It was stupid, but it always moved him, and he coughed to cover it. 'Well, that's it. Now they'll go to the King pear tree and then the King damson.'

'Interesting. But don't you think it's a little sad that after all these centuries of the Church's teachings, the common masses still believe in such folly?'

'Of course I do, but think of it as a celebration, like May Day. And—' Thomas just stopped himself from taking Rulf's arm in time— 'there's still the hog roast to come.'

Rulf smiled at him. 'So there is. And as lord and priest we can safely assume our positions as first in the queue.'

In the safety of darkness, he held Thomas's elbow and steered him back towards the tantalising aroma of the spit.

CHAPTER 43

The Journal of Lord Thomas de Chiddleigh

February 1350

During these past months, I have longed to share my love, to be seen with him openly and proudly, but we are condemned to secrecy. It is hard to bear. Since I cannot share my feelings, I express them in words.

It is dangerous even to write of such things, and so I scribe in Greek for fear my words will be read and our secret exposed. When I am finished, I shall seal my work with wax and secure it at the bottom of my chest. One day, when our faces are lined and our hair is grey, we shall read it together over a goblet of wine and we shall smile and rejoice in our lasting love.

Love! What a joyous gift it is. I feel goodwill for everyone and everything. I walk with my feet on the path of heaven, my heart sings like a lark, and in these dark months, I see colour where others see grey, and I bask in warmth even though the ground sparkles with frost.

I now understand what moved the great poets to write of passion, for I feel what they must have felt when they wrote of souls entwined.

When I am with him, my heart and mind are consumed. When we are apart, I carry his image, from his entrancing blue eyes to the small mole on the back of his neck. Every inch of him is beautiful and is mine.

Knowing I am worthy of such love has given me a belief in myself I never thought possible. I revel in the knowledge that he will remain here until we leave together and begin a new life in Oxford, he with his work and me, at last, to study. We shall not have to wait too long, for the barn has grain, work on the mill is progressing and soon we shall be selling flour to everyone within twenty miles. Our wool and cloth sold well at the sales last October, enabling me to pay off the dues to my people and add coins to my coffer chest. Reading my charts, and with God's blessing, all bodes well for the future.

Simon has built a stone step bridge over the river, which is good for all of us, and his dwelling is complete enough for him to move in next month.

Rose has done nothing about moving out. I assume she will live with Annie when the time comes. She continues to act as a noble, and her manner makes me uncomfortable. Despite keeping my distance, she seeks me out at every opportunity and tries to act demurely. I find it quite amusing since there is nothing demure about Rose.

I am disappointed that her maid's fancy has not passed. Knowing what it is to be in love, I pity her. Unrequited love must be the cruellest love of all. If only she knew how much I love another!

Should the time come, God forbid, when my lover and I are condemned, I will never renounce him, for I am not ashamed of my feelings. On the contrary, I rejoice in them. I know who I am, and there is no going back.

More than that, I am a just and fair lord, and that swells my heart with pride, for I have kept my promise to Mama and proved I am not weak.

At last, things go my way and I have never been happier or more at peace.

—*Lord Thomas de Chiddleigh of Combe Hide*

CHAPTER 44

April 1350

Thomas sang loud and clear as he walked along the dry path to Rulf's cave. It was good to be on the other side of the dark months, and spring that year had arrived in a glorious spray of white and pink blossom. The wild daffodils bobbed their heads in a scatter of pale yellow amongst the lush green grass, wafting their scent across the fields. High above, the swallows announced their return in twittering arcs of black arrows.

Life was good. Bending down to pass through the low entrance of the cave, he raised his flagon with a flourish. 'What a beautiful day! It makes me glad to be alive.'

Rulf was standing in the centre of the cave by the hearth, examining his fingernails. He didn't answer. He didn't even look up.

Thomas dropped his arm to his side. 'Rulf? What is it? Are you ailing? Shall I go and fetch Annie?'

'I'm not ailing.' The reply was too deliberate, too calm. Rulf lifted his gaze, his eyes deep and troubled. 'Sit down, my friend. We must talk.' He sat down on the bench, staring at his hands, and Thomas joined him. 'The tracks are clear, and there's no further talk of Pestilence. Travel is possible again.'

A cold, sickening feeling crawled up Thomas's spine. It was spring, glorious spring and his future had arrived too soon.

Gathering his fears, he herded them into a safe corner of his mind where they wouldn't be visible on his face.

'You said you wouldn't go.' He strove for a calm, neutral tone, one fitting a lord and the man he so desperately wanted to be.

Rulf slowly raised his head. 'I know I did. But while I sit here, the church's corruption continues and grows day by day. John Wycliffe needs support, and I have the Bible translation to continue. I promised my friends that I would return.'

'You promised me that you wouldn't.' He groped for something, *anything* to stop this as his heart squeezed tighter and tighter. 'What about me? Don't I matter? What am I supposed to do without you?'

Rulf's eyes flashed. 'Of course you matter! Don't you think I haven't had sleepless nights over this?' He leaned closer and, with an oh-so-delectable touch, caressed Thomas's chin. 'And you don't have to do without me. Come with me.'

Thomas drew back in surprise. 'Come with you? To Oxford?'

'Yes! Think of it; the city of all learning. It's where you've always wanted to go. More than that, it's where you belong. I'll introduce you to men with minds that will dazzle you. Men who question the rule of the church.' He paused and looked deeply into Thomas's eyes. 'And men like us.'

Rulf's touch was gone, replaced with a sting that burned the backs of Thomas's eyes. He didn't want to hear this, any of it. He wanted to cover his ears, to turn back time to this morning and blissful ignorance. He bowed his head and stared at the ground, empty inside.

'Thomas, I want — no, I *need* you to come with me.' Rulf was looking at him through those beautiful long dark lashes as he had so many times, but he couldn't bear to see them.

Rulf stood up, running his fingers through his hair, then paced the room, the soft tread of his feet the only sound. At last, he stopped, leaned down and gripped Thomas's shoulders firmly. 'Look at me.'

Thomas lifted his head and saw his own tortured soul reflected back at him. They'd been united in something beautiful, and now it was being ripped apart like an old rag.

'I love you, and I don't want to live without you. You know that, don't you? But I must go.'

He could feel Rulf's urgent fingers clasping the linen of his tunic. Not a lover's clasp but a desperate, pleading hold.

'I thought you were happy here,' he said. His world was crumbling, and he was powerless to stop it, but he had to try. If he didn't, the thought of what might have happened would torment him for the rest of his days.

'I am happy, but don't you see? The church must be stopped. While I'm here, others are continuing John Wycliffe's work. I have to be a part of that. Besides you, it's all I have.'

The silence stretched between them until Rulf released him. Thomas watched his lover take a deep breath, pain twisting Rulf's handsome face into something ugly. Part of him wanted to make this easier on Rulf, and another part of him wanted to make it impossible. Neither part could win, so he sat between reality and hope, silent.

'As I watched the tracks dry and the trees come into blossom, I worried about what I should do. I almost prayed for rain to delay my decision.' Rulf laughed hollowly, even though it wasn't funny. 'Should I stay and be with you, who means everything to me? Or should I go to the man who needs me? Either way, I lose.' Rulf turned his head away, the imprint of his hands still warm on Thomas's shoulders.

He should have seen the change in Rulf. Should have realised his torment. If he had, maybe he could have persuaded him to stay, but he had been too wrapped up in his own bubble of euphoria. Now it was too late.

'I need you too,' he said quietly.

'I know you do, but the problem isn't just my work with John Wycliffe. Every time I hear a confession or give the Mass, I'm cheating the very folks who have faith in me. I can't pretend any more. Even I have a conscience.' His mouth quirked into the dry smile that Thomas loved so much.

Rulf bent before him, his eyes piercing through Thomas, his hands back on his shoulders. 'I'm begging you, please come with me.' He ran a finger gently down the side of Thomas's cheek, just as he had when he'd declared his love in the woods. 'It's the only way for us to be together. You mean everything to me, and I don't want to go without you.' He half whispered the last words, letting them hang in the air with the promise of unfulfilled dreams.

Thomas swallowed but couldn't speak.

'In Oxford, there are others like us. We would still need to be discrete, but we'd be together. You'd be free of this place, as you've always wanted. Think of it. You and me, forever. Say you'll come.' Rulf spoke quickly now, his eyes compelling.

Rulf and Oxford, the two most important things in his life. How he ached for them. How he longed to say *Yes!* and laugh with him and be safe in his arms, but he couldn't.

'I can't. I don't have enough money.'

Rulf frowned. 'What about the wool sales? You did very well there.'

'Yes, I did, but there's still the mill to finish. And Simon wants to build corn driers and there are always repairs to do. I don't have enough.'

Rulf threw up his hands. 'Damn the muxy corn driers! And what do you need money for? I can earn enough for both of us, and I'll contact my family – assuming they survived the Pestilence – and get my allowance again.'

He was wrenched in two as he heard the desperation in Rulf's voice and saw the hope in his eyes. He'd give anything to ease his pain, but there was nothing he could do. If he went now, taking money from Rulf, what would that make him?

No more than a sodomite whore, as the priest had predicted he would be. It would sour the very beauty of what they had.

'Rulf, I want to live with you but I can't live off you. It wouldn't be right. We're better than that, and I want to study. It wouldn't be enough to just be in Oxford; I want to be a part of it, to hold my own as a learned scholar. And there's my duty to my people.' How calm his words sounded while his world was caught in the whirlwind of a storm.

'Your duty to your people? Do you think your people give a damn about you? What about your duty to me?'

That wasn't a duty. It was a desire, one coupled with a deep heart-wrenching certainty that without Rulf, he was nothing. A tear trickled down his cheek and he watched it fall to splash on his boots.

'Thomas, the longer we stay here, the more likely it is that we'll end up giving ourselves away. If anyone so much as suspected the truth, the authorities would cut off our balls and hang us from the nearest gallows.'

He was well aware of that. 'No one's found us out yet. Why should they find out now?'

'A careless look between us, an unguarded moment like that smile you gave me in front of Gee, who knows? But sooner or later, someone will catch us. Then what?'

'Can't you wait another year? We could be more careful, and I'll have a good supply of cloth by then. One more good harvest and I'll have enough in my coffer to pay my way and leave others to run the estate. You can throw off your priest's cassock if you want, and I can leave with my head held high instead of slinking away in the darkness like a coward.'

Rulf ran a hand down his face and returned to his seat. 'And supposing it's a poor crop? What if something goes wrong with the dye and Annie and Rose don't produce the red cloth? Am I supposed to stay for another year and another whilst you wait for a good harvest and repair your precious mill?'

'I can't live off you like a paid whore. I—'

'God's blood! If that's what you think of me, you might as well go back to your people now and do your damned duty. Wait for your precious crops to grow and for your mill to be built. And while you're doing it, why don't you marry some woman and get an heir as well?'

The thrust of Rulf's words cut him like a sword. He was losing him, and there was nothing he could do about it.

'I thought you loved me,' Rulf said very quietly.

The deepest cut of all. 'I do love you.'

Rulf leaned close. 'Then you know and I know that every day when you take your woman in your arms, you'll think of me and your heart will bleed.'

Thomas looked at him wretchedly. It was all too much. 'I need more time to think about this. I—'

'Then go back to your manor and leave me to pack my things. Those muxy, uneducated peasants obviously mean more to you than I do.' Rulf turned his back on him.

Thomas reached out and touched his shoulder. 'Rulf, please, I didn't mean—I do love you, you know that. Please, don't do this to me. Don't make me choose.'

Rulf shrugged him off. 'I said go!' His voice trembled but the strength of it resounded off the walls, echoing the darkness of the moment.

He was helpless. It couldn't end like this. Rulf would turn. He'd open his arms. Tell him he'd wait and they'd cry joyfully together.

Rulf didn't turn. He didn't open his arms.

It was over.

There was nothing he could do except wipe his eyes and take a last look at Rulf's back. Slowly, he picked up his bag and hitched it over his shoulder. At the entrance of the cave, he put a hand on the cold stone and glanced back for one last memory.

'Stay the night,' Rulf said softly.

His heart leapt. God, how he wanted to, but it wouldn't change anything and would only make the final parting harder.

'I should get back,' he said.

'You know you don't want to.' Rulf's voice was barely above a whisper and as he turned around, his eyes were wretched. 'Please stay, for me.'

One look at those eyes and he was lost. Dropping his bag to the floor Thomas walked into the outstretched arms of the man he loved.

Early the next morning, Thomas awoke and lazily stretched his hand across the mattress, expecting to feel the warmth of Rulf's body.

The mattress was cold and empty, and his guts twisted. 'Rulf?'

Nothing. Rulf had probably gone to fetch water and would be back soon. Thomas got to his feet, looked around and felt his heart turn to ice and then shatter.

There was no leather bag in the corner. No untidy pile of clothes on the floor. On the bench where Rulf carelessly tossed his priest's cloak was a screaming space.

Thomas turned again, seeing the log table where it had all started with that first game of chess. The jars of herbs were stacked at the back of the cave. Next to them, Rulf's baskets of berries huddled together. Under the shelf, where Rulf had once kept his boots, there was nothing.

Rulf had gone. Slipped away in the night, leaving nothing but a faint scent of rosemary.

Thomas squeezed his eyes tight, threw back his head and silently screamed. His knees gave way and he sobbed.

When he could cry no more, he groped for the table to get to his feet and his hands touched something cold. He reached out and gently picked up the astrolabe, turning it over in his hands. Rulf had been so excited when he showed it to him.

Next to it was a folded piece of parchment. He picked it up his hands trembling, then sat on the bench and began to read.

My dearest Thomas,

Forgive me. I have to go now because I cannot bear to see the pain etched on your face. Like the coward I am, I leave whilst you sleep. Pray don't think ill of me.

I understand your dilemma as I know you understand mine. If I stayed, I should grow to resent my situation, as I am certain that if you came with me at this time, you would resent yours. Either way, it would destroy us.

So, my dearest love, it is best for both of us that I go now whilst we have only cherished memories to relive when we are missing one another.

I leave you my most precious possession. Think of me when you use it. And when you watch the eclipse, know that I shall be watching the same sky and will be thinking of you.

I love you from the very depths of my soul and always will.
Godspeed.
Rulf

Thomas let the letter slip through his fingers and covered his face with his hands as if they could stem the pain that overwhelmed him.

How could he? The knowledge ripped through him like hot daggers and crumpling to his knees, he lifted his face to the heavens and wept.

At last, he picked himself up and dried his face. Folding the parchment, he kissed it before tucking it inside his tunic. It was a risk to keep it, but one he was willing to take. He ran his fingers gently over the astrolabe and placed it carefully in his bag. He would never use it.

He had no idea what he was going to do or how he was going to cope. Pausing at the entrance to the cave, he glanced back.

'Damn you to hell, Rulf,' he said in a choked voice, and ducked into the daylight.

CHAPTER 45

'Get off!' Rose pulled at the basket, but the gander could smell the scraps and wasn't about to give it up. She hated geese unless they were roasting on a spit. Their bills were like saws and once they grabbed you they didn't let go, as an old scar on her leg proved.

Thomas was in a black mood again. For the last two weeks, he had left the house early, saying nothing and not returning until dark. He had puffy rings under his eyes, and she knew he wasn't sleeping because she'd heard him creeping out in the middle of the night. At first, she'd thought nothing of it – everyone needed time to themselves now and again – but when it was happening three or four in a row — she was convinced he had a woman somewhere. Her wager was on that red-headed little vixen, Dorothea, who lived up the far end of the valley.

Desperate to know, she'd followed him one night. To her surprise, he hadn't gone any further than the middle of the yard, where he'd stood for ages staring at the stars. His shoulders had shaken at one point. If it hadn't been too impossible to imagine, she would have sworn he was crying.

She grabbed the goose by the neck and twisted viciously. Muxy men! Father Rulf had just upped and left recently as well. According to Thomas, God had called the good priest to go on a pilgrimage to Canterbury. When Rose had asked how long he'd be gone, Thomas had turned on her and demanded how the hell he was supposed to know. She hadn't mentioned Father Rulf after that.

Here they were, the May trees in blossom, and Thomas was behaving like a sow with an itchy arse. Simon said that it had been around this time of year that he'd found Lady Joan lying in the ashes of Court Barton. She could certainly understand that, but she doubted it was the reason. Thomas hadn't been like this last spring.

If it wasn't a woman, what was it?

The goose squawked and flapped his wings, catching her in the face. Rose gripped harder. The gander had chosen the wrong day for a fight. That morning, she had put on her best kirtle, dragged a bone comb through her hair and gone to find Thomas.

It had taken her some time, but she'd eventually found him sitting by the river, a look of utter despondency on his face. When she had asked him what was wrong and if she could help, his expression of disdain had cut her to the quick. She could still hear his words now.

'It's nothing to do with you. I've kept my side of the pact. It's about time you kept yours and moved out.'

Then he'd stalked off, leaving her confused and more than a little vexed.

Over the past six months, she'd learnt every one of the words on his numerous lists and proved she could keep the records. She had even behaved as a lady to show him that she wouldn't disgrace him even though she was common-born. She'd been a ready ear for him, often suggesting they play chess together even though she detested the game.

And all her efforts had got her precisely nowhere. What more did he want from her?

The goose stopped flapping, and Rose looked down at the suddenly limp bird. Dear God, she hadn't meant to kill it. She loosened her grip, and the gander fell to the ground in a lifeless pile of feathers. Feeling awful, she bent down to stroke him by way of apology.

As she did so, the gander shook his head, hissed furiously and lunged at her with a screech.

'Muxy goose!' she yelled and aimed a kick at it. Her basket slipped, spilling her scraps across the dirt. 'Now see what you've done!'

The goose, with a gleam in his eyes, began his feast. Now she had nothing for the swine. Men! Goose, human, it didn't matter; they were all the same. Fawning over you when they were after something, and then acting as though you didn't exist once they'd got what they wanted, like Thomas and his wretched records.

Maybe she was to blame. Maybe this was her punishment from God for denying William and attempting to overturn the natural order of things, to be put in the exact same position of wanting someone who had no interest in her. She thought she'd seen that hint in Thomas's eye, but she could have been mistaken. She'd been far less subtle about rejecting William, and he'd still believed she loved him.

She wasn't sure how Thomas felt about her anymore. Whatever game he was playing, she'd had enough.

Her arm was throbbing. She pushed up her sleeve and saw a line of red marks left by the gander's serrated bill.

'Vicious thing!' Annie hurried across the yard. 'I heard the commotion. Did he get you?' She took hold of Rose's arm and peered closely. 'Nettle lotion will sort that out. Come to my room.'

That was all she needed; Annie fussing around with her lotions and potions. She sighed and followed.

Annie's room was little more than a small stone barn at the back of the forge. Shelves covered all walls from floor to ceiling, crammed with jars and baskets of every size and description, and bunches of flowers and herbs dangled from the ceiling. It had a musty smell, but it felt homely. There was a crude chair and sheepskin in one corner, and a stool, chest and thick straw mattress in the other.

Once Rose's arm had been suitably dabbed with nettle lotion, Annie poured them a clover tonic and sat in her chair while Rose took the stool. 'That gander's the same every spring, moody and irritable,' said Annie.

'A bit like Thomas, then. It's a shame you've nothing for ill temper,' said Rose.

'Oh, I have. I gave Thomas a jar of nettle and egg white to drink – he's not sleeping, you know – and also some chamomile tonic to soothe his mind.'

'Didn't work, did they?' said Rose, sipping her drink.

'I don't think he took them; he was just as troubled a week later. I tried talking to him, but he said there was nothing to talk about.' Annie sipped her drink thoughtfully. 'Of course, Thomas has always been sensitive, and he's got a lot of responsibility on his shoulders. He'll sort himself out.'

'I wish he'd hurry up,' Rose muttered. 'I'm tired of his moods. I don't know where I am with him. Ma always said that men didn't know what was good for them, and that they couldn't see what was under their noses without a woman to show them.'

'There's wisdom in that. Want some more tonic?'

Rose frowned. There was wisdom in it. Instead of waiting for Thomas to make the first move, maybe she should throw a few hints of her own.

Annie clutched her cup between her hands and snuggled into her fleece-covered chair. 'It's good to put my feet up and sit a while. I've been on the go since dawn and it's past the first quarter. I'm thirty-five summers, and my bones are letting me know. I'm glad I've taught you the red dye. When the good Lord takes me, you'll be the only person who knows the recipe. I'll trust you to keep it that way until you pass it on to your daughter.'

If she had anything to do with it, her daughter would be a lady and she'd find someone else to make the dye. She'd never thought about Annie getting old, but now she looked at her, she could see the grey streaks in her dark hair, the slight sallowness of her skin and the lines running from her nose to each side of her mouth. 'You're not getting old. There are years in you.'

Annie smiled wryly. 'I was pretty in my day. The best dancer in the village. No lass could turn a reel like me. I used to love all the celebrations; saints' days, May Day, the harvest and Christmas, never missed them. I was young and silly then.' Annie stared into her cup, sadness clouding her face. 'Lady Joan always put on a good spread and hired good pipers. The older men huddled around the barrels and the younger ones danced with the maids. They were good times.' She drained her cup and shook her head, dabbing the corners of her eyes with her apron. 'Listen to me, getting all maudlin. I'll be needing some of my St John's Wort tonic if I keep on like this. I see Simon's nearly finished his cottage, so I suppose you'll have to move out soon. You're welcome to share with me. It would be nice to have a bit of company.'

Rose glanced around the small room. Could she live here? Where else could she go?

'I'd like that, but just until I get my own place.'

'Then you best make yourself known to one of the lads before they're all taken. You're not getting any younger either, you know. Now, I must get on. Elsa is near her time and I promised I'd look in and give her some borage tonic. It's her first, and she'll need all the courage she can get.'

'I've tasks to do, too,' said Rose, getting to her feet. That was only partly true; she only had one pressing task, and that was to find Thomas.

CHAPTER 46

In the last of the moonlight, Thomas was again wandering the hills above his home. Four weeks had passed since Rulf left, and it felt like a lifetime. Sometimes he wept during these walks. Other times, he cursed Rulf for awakening feelings he didn't know he had, only to abandon him to them in pain and confusion.

He wasn't sleeping, and he had a favourite spot to go to when he couldn't stand to toss and turn any longer. He was there now; leaning against the giant oak tree, as he always did. It was peaceful and he had a clear view of the night sky.

If he looked down the hill, he could see the grey shadowy outlines of his home, where he was Lord de Chiddleigh. If he looked up the hill through the gorse and trees, he could see Rulf's cave, where once he was loved. He was standing between the two, which seemed fitting, since he belonged in neither.

His heart and soul had been ripped out of him. What was he supposed to do now? He'd kept returning to the cave for days after Rulf's departure. It had been comforting in a painful sort of way; he'd always hoped to find Rulf sitting there with that wry smile on his face. *I couldn't leave you. I had to come back,* he'd say, his blue eyes twinkling.

But the cave was always empty. After a week, he had stopped torturing himself and hadn't gone back since. He would never forget Rulf, but he had to rejoin the real world sometime and at least act as if he'd forgotten.

Rulf had been good at acting.

The sun was rising now, outlining the tops of the hills. Below, he could see a figure crossing the yard, a pail in each hand. By her brisk, no-nonsense manner, it had to be Rose. He'd been sharp with her, but she was tough. Soon, she'd move out and leave him in peace.

He turned as he did at that time every day and began his slow walk down the hill and along the river to his favourite rock. He'd rejoin the human race tomorrow.

Sitting by the water, he watched the brown trout camouflaged against the stones, just an occasional flick of their tail giving them away. They didn't have a care in the world. Did they feel pain?

Why did Rulf have to go? He'd said he loved him, but it was clear that he'd loved his work more. Damn John Wycliffe! He hurled a stone into the water and watched it sink.

Their relationship had been a glorious, bittersweet experience that was now driving him to his knees. God's blood, he had to forget, but how could he? How, when he wanted to relive and savour each past moment like a dagger prodding an open wound, cutting deeper and deeper so he could wallow in the pain.

Where was Rulf now? Sitting comfortably in an inn jesting with fellow travellers? Or was he dragging his feet along a dusty track feeling as miserable as he was? Either way, he prayed God would keep him safe.

The ancient poets had written that time was a great healer. He prayed they were right, for this was worse than any ailment. Even wise Annie didn't have a lotion for a broken heart.

He tossed another stone into the water and watched the trout dart away in an indignant swirl of grit and sand.

What was it Rulf had said? *Why don't you marry some woman and get an heir?* He'd been angry at the time, but what else was there left for him to do? Getting a wife wasn't as mad as it sounded.

Could he lie with a woman, knowing what he was? If he did, by the time he had a son, he'd have enough in his coffers to leave this place and he'd have done his duty. There would be nothing to stop him from going after Rulf.

He snapped a piece of grass and chewed the end. Would Rulf still be in Oxford? What if he'd forgotten him, or worse, found someone else? He couldn't bear that. Rulf would always haunt him, wherever he went. That was his penance from God for committing such a sin.

One year, that's all he had asked. Rulf could have waited, *should* have waited, but the man was selfish. It had only ever been about Rulf; what Rulf wanted, what Rulf needed. He couldn't recall a single time when Rulf had abandoned his plans to fall in with one of his ideas, yet the man had taken his capitulation for granted.

He had to face the truth: Rulf was never coming back, and maybe he was better off without him.

He threw away the grass and brushed himself down.

It was time to move on.

Gathering the loose folds of his surcoat, Thomas headed upstream towards the mill. The work had progressed so much that he almost didn't recognise the place. The overgrown path was cut wide enough for an ox and cart and piles of large timbers and stones lined the verges. The regular kerchunk of axes on wood, handcarts squeaking for lack of goose fat, and the rhythmic tap, tap, tap of mallets on stone filled the air.

The path ended in a wide turning circle. Behind crude wooden scaffolding, the mill walls towered above him, looking solid and determined. The place was a hive of activity, the men barely pausing to lower their hoods as they passed. Simon must have every man and boy working up there.

'Don't drop that, you cloth head!' Simon shouted from somewhere behind the mill.

Thomas found him with a group of men by the huge waterwheel, straining under the weight of a long, thick pole. They manoeuvred one end to the wheel axle and, bracing themselves, took the weight of the pole on their shoulders. Peter and Jarin were beneath the wheel, hammering wooden pegs to hold the pole in place.

'Beg pardon, my lord, we're trying to connect this shaft to the wheel axle,' said Simon, his head bent to his shoulder. Red-faced and contorted, he reminded Thomas of those wretched caged monkeys in the markets. For a moment, it made him want to laugh.

'Peter, make haste, damn you! We can't hold this for long!' Simon shouted through gritted teeth.

'Keep your hat on! I'm hammering as fast as I can! Jarin, hold the muxy peg still, can't ye? And mind my thumb, ye numbskull!'

Thomas allowed himself a smile. It wasn't so bad to be back.

With the shaft in place, the men crawled from under the wheel, wiping the sweat off their faces and rubbing their hands on their hose.

'Not sorry to see that done.' Simon nodded. Turning away from the men, he came closer to Thomas and lowered his voice. 'What in God's name has been the matter with you? I feared you had evil spirits in your head. Gossip was that you had scrofula and were planning to travel to London to seek a touch from the King to cure you.'

Thomas stiffened. He should have expected this. 'A bad tooth, nothing more. But that was enough to drive me out of my wits and put a mood on me worse than a cur with fleas. I'm well now.'

'And the tooth?' Simon raised his eyebrows.

Thomas shrugged. 'I pulled it out. What does the shaft do?'

'It connects the waterwheel to a system of gears and cogs that turn the two grinding stones. What really ailed you?'

'I told you, a rotten tooth. Now are you going to show me the mill or not?'

The pursed lips and raised eyebrows told him that Simon didn't believe one word.

'If you say so. This way, my lord.'

Inside the walls was a maze of huge wooden cogs and gears and driving poles. The miller, Josef, stepped forward and proudly began explaining the name and purpose of each piece in enthusiastic detail.

'Lief, show Lord Thomas the part you made.' Josef pushed his son forward.

Thomas did his best to pay attention, but the lad's voice faded into dreams of Rulf. Rulf was probably sitting by the roadside, biting into an apple stolen in an illicit raid on an orchard. It was the sort of thing he would do.

'My lord?' Josef had a foot on the bottom of a vertical ladder leading to the next floor. 'Would you like to see the hopper and chute where the grain goes?'

Thomas jolted back. He didn't like ladders and liked heights even less. The mill was suddenly suffocating; too much noise, too many people and too many questions.

'Another time, perhaps, but you've done well. You too, Lief. I must go; I've just remembered that there's something I have to see to.'

Before he could make his escape, Peter stepped forward. 'Before ye go, my lord, when will Father Rulf be back? Or are we getting a new priest? I mean, I went to all that trouble to build him a church, and then he ups and leaves. And now we have to trudge over six miles to Holdesworthe for Mass and confessions. It's a long way and folks are wondering.'

'I don't know when he'll be back or if we're getting a new priest. I'll let you know when I do.' Walking briskly, Thomas ignored their puzzled faces and pretended not to hear Simon call after him. The first steps back to reality had been harder than he thought.

He branched off the main path. A little way along on his left was Rulf's round cob cottage. He remembered Peter building it during the dark months. The walls were two feet thick and built of mud, dung and straw and trampled firm by men's feet. They were built in layers a yard high, leaving each layer to settle for weeks before putting on the next. It had been a painfully slow process.

He could see Rulf leaning back against the wall of his cave and hear him saying that he hoped the cottage would never be finished. *He liked his cave.* He'd waved nonchalantly. *I'm comfortable at home, wherever that was, life is good.* Rulf was a rebel in every sense, but his casual dismissal of Peter's hard work left a slightly bitter taste in Thomas's mouth that had never been there before.

Turning the bend in the path, he saw Rose and groaned.

'Thomas!' she called, hurrying towards him. 'I was beginning to think you were avoiding me.'

He'd been avoiding everyone. A glance to left and right confirmed there was nowhere to go. 'No, I've been thinking, that's all. I need to make haste.' He made to step past her, but she moved with him, blocking his way.

'Thinking about what?'

'Nothing much; just the future and things.'

The future? Rose's heart beat a little faster. Now was her chance. Possibly her only chance. Her Ma's voice echoed in her head. *Men need telling. They never say what they think. There are times when you have to do it for them.*

Dare she? Lasses weren't usually so bold about such matters, but Thomas had had months to make the first move.

'What about the future?' She tilted her head shyly and smiled. She mustn't rush this. She had to bide her time and let him come to his own conclusions.

'The estate.' He tried to walk on but she stood firm, ignoring his sigh.

'Only I wondered if that future you're thinking about concerns me?' When he didn't answer, she pressed on. 'I know it would be unusual, but these are unusual times and neither of us is getting any younger.' That should be enough to encourage him. She dropped her gaze demurely for added effect. Her heart squeezing the breath out of her, she waited, ready for her moment. Now he would step forward, ask her to be his lady, take her in his arms and kiss her, just as she'd imagined many times.

'What do you mean unusual?'

He wasn't supposed to say that. 'I assumed...well, you being a lord, you'll need an heir. You have no Lady of the Manor, and when you asked me to do the records I thought...I mean…' The words died on her lips as she saw the look of realisation creep over his face, followed swiftly by shock and horror.

Every bone in her body from her feet to her fingertips turned to stone. She'd got it horribly, horribly wrong. He wasn't shy. He was appalled at the idea. She bit her lip and felt the heat of embarrassment melt her bones and burn her face. 'I just—what I meant was—'

'Dear God, Rose! I knew you had a maid's fancy for me, but you, Lady of the Manor? Seriously?'

She swallowed hard. She'd never felt so humiliated in her life. If God had come down and taken her there and then, she'd have welcomed him with open arms.

Thomas shook his head. 'I can't believe you truly thought—Rulf warned me and Annie mentioned something ages ago, but I didn't think you were serious.' He half-turned away and ran a hand through his hair. 'That's why you've been copying Maria. You've been practising being Lady of the Manor.' His mouth turned up at the corners, and to her shame, he began to laugh..

'I have not!' she lied. Why had she opened her big mouth?

'I've seen you copying how she eats and sits, and crossing the yard with your head in the air carrying two stinking slop pails in your hands for the swine.' He was laughing openly at her now, and she felt anger mix with the humiliation.

'You can laugh, but you're not much of a catch. You're poor as a church mouse, you've no proper manor house and no social contacts. Who else is going to have you?'

'No one, and right now I don't care. I'm sorry, Rose. I shouldn't laugh, but come on, you must see the funny side of it. You trailing after me like a lost pup thinking…'

There was no funny side to it. Her efforts, her foolish notions and her dreams of grandeur all melted in a pool of mortification around her feet, then rose and grew into a furious cloud of tattered pride.

'How dare you? You led me to believe you liked me! You were quick enough to see me last autumn when you wanted your accounts done, and what a task that turned out to be. Simon had neglected the records for months and it took me weeks to catch up. And when I wanted more words to learn, all I got from you was another list. You talked about me keeping my side of the pact, but what about you? I haven't had a proper writing lesson in months, and you still haven't told me what a sentence is!' She stopped just short of stamping her foot, glaring at him with her arms folded. It wasn't much, but gestures and anger were all she had left to salvage her pride.

Thomas opened his palms. 'I will explain when you're ready. You need to know about punctuation, conjugation of verbs and prepositions first.'

He stood before her, so calm and reasonable. She wanted to run at him, her hands flailing, her nails clawing his face until he felt as belittled as she did.

'Don't try to confuse me with your fancy words! I'll learn your punctuations and prepo—popper—what you said! I'm not stupid, even if I am common.' She stood as tall as she could.

'I know you're not stupid, but parchment is precious and I can't afford to waste it. We'll start the lessons again when the ground's soft enough to scratch, I promise.'

'So I'm a waste now, am I? And I'm sick of scratching the ground! I want to write properly, like a lady.' She hadn't meant to say those last words but it was too late.

Thomas thinned his lips a tight white line. 'What's the point? I'm never going to marry you and you're never going to be a lady. You'll never need to write a letter.'

There it was – her future thrown at her feet. 'Well, don't worry; I wouldn't marry you now if you were the last man in the shire! And you can find yourself another reeve, for I'll not be doing the records.' Gathering her skirts, and with as much dignity as she could muster, she swept past him.

He'd soon miss her and regret his mistake. Fighting the tears lodged in her throat, she ran down the path; not like a lady, but like the common peasant she was and would always be.

CHAPTER 47

The following morning, Thomas watched Rose drag the last of her belongings out of the house and winced as she banged the door hard behind him. He'd offered to help, but she'd looked at him with such disdain that he'd decided it was better to keep his head down and his mouth shut.

He could have been kinder yesterday, but she'd caught him off guard and he didn't like having things sprung on him, especially something as preposterous as that. He still couldn't believe that she'd thought the two of them would—well, no matter. She was gone, so that was one problem solved and, he smiled to himself, she wouldn't give up being his reeve either, not when she liked it so much.

He glanced around the empty room. It was very quiet. Idly, he drew an isosceles triangle on the table with his finger. For all his good intentions, there was little for him to do. The men who weren't building the mill were harrowing the fields for sowing, trudging up and down the lines, dragging wide wooden rakes behind them as the sharp nails scratched the ground in grooves. He'd been to check on their progress earlier and watched the children scampering after them picking up stones. Gee had been there, barking orders and waving his stick trying to supervise them.

There was no avoiding it: he needed someone to fill the void left by Rulf. Not romantically – no one could do that – but if his relationship with Rulf had taught him one thing, it was that life was too short to waste. Who could he talk to? Simon was busy, everybody was busy. There was one person…

With a new sense of purpose, Thomas filled his flagon and helped himself to a hunk of cheese and a couple of wrinkled apples from Janet's store. Whistling, he went to the stables, grabbed the tack and saddled Henry.

Moments later, he was cantering along the valley, passing his peasants' hovels with a nod and a wave to anyone who happened to see him. At the top of the valley, where the track met High Drovers Road, he shortened his reins, pointed Henry north, and dug in his heels.

Henry's hooves pounded the ground, and as the wind rushed through Thomas's hair, his troubles were whisked away in clouds of dust. This was what he needed: to get away and see new sights. He leaned forward, urging Henry on until the horse was blowing and covered in white flecks of sweat.

Thomas stopped, letting the horse recover, then turned his face to the wind and breathed in deeply. The cool spring air slid down the back of his throat like a cleansing tonic. If only he could untie the shackles of his title and feel like this forever. He'd go where he pleased, stop at an inn or lie under a tree letting the sun soak his face without a care in the world.

He'd come close to those feelings when he'd been with Rulf, but Rulf had abandoned him. Sighing at what might have been, he loosened his reins and let his horse stretch his neck and amble forward at his own pace.

What he'd give to turn back the days and be sitting on a riverbank again, his fishing pole cut from a nearby hazel, innocently whiling away the day with William as they'd done so often as boys. It felt like another lifetime.

But that was the crux of the matter. He was no longer a boy. Time flies, as Brother Luke had been so fond of saying. It flew in more ways than one, for the sun was already nearing midday and if he didn't find what he was looking for soon, he'd be spending the night under the stars with an empty belly.

Using the sun as a guide, he continued northwards. He'd only been so far north once before and that had been with Simon, a few years ago. He had a vague memory of seeing the old bailiff's house perched high amid a criss-cross of ancient stone walls. Scanning the landscape, he could see no walls; only a few Blackface ewes who lifted their heads at his approach and bounded away, bleating for their lambs to follow.

The land was larger and wilder than he remembered with miles of rough grazing stretching as far as the eye could see. The few trees bent against the prevailing south-westerly winds, their deformed branches stretched out like the hands of wizened old men.

The wildness was peaceful with nothing but the soft sound of Henry's hooves and buzzards mewing high above. He started humming then stopped. That was the tune Rulf had always hummed when contemplating his next move on the chessboard. God's bones, would he ever find peace?

'Hail, stranger!'

Thomas jumped. A man was walking towards him. He couldn't quite make out the figure, but his heart lurched and his mind soared. As the man drew closer, Thomas's excitement fell to his boots. For a moment he had thought...

William stopped a few paces away, his fist clenched around the staff of his crook. He held his stare, his ruddy face tanned with the weather-beaten look of old leather.

Looking down from the height of his horse, Thomas stared back. Coming to find his old friend suddenly didn't seem like such a good idea.

For a long time, neither spoke nor moved, then William bowed low with an exaggerated flourish. 'My lord. What brings you to these parts?'

'I came to see you,' Thomas said, his voice tight and high.

'Then I'm at your disposal, my lord.'

Thomas fidgeted in his saddle. 'Will, I...'

This was impossible. He couldn't talk to him like this. He slid from his horse, took a deep breath and looked William in the eye. 'I've come to beg pardon. I've no wish to be at odds with you.' Trembling, he offered his hand forward. He needed William to take it. He needed a friend.

William's eyes roved from Thomas's face to his outstretched hand and back again. His back stiffened and he squared his shoulders.

Thomas inched his hand a little further forward. William didn't move. Thomas's arm was starting to ache and he was feeling a little foolish when William stepped forward, his crook falling to the ground with a clatter. He lifted his arm and Thomas closed his eyes, preparing for the blow.

A large rough hand grasped his elbow. 'I accept, my lord.'

He opened his eyes to William's grinning face and breathed again. With a grin of his own, he placed his other hand firmly over William's, hand to elbow, in the gesture of true friendship. They gripped harder and their grins grew until they burst into laughter.

'I thought you were going to hit me,' said Thomas.

William chuckled. 'For a moment, so did I! But it doesn't do to fall out over a lass. Tell me, how is the troublesome Rose?'

'She's well and troublesome as ever. Will, I swear by God Himself and the Blessed Virgin that I never had an eye for her.'

William placed his hand on Thomas's shoulder. 'Don't look so worried. It's of no matter now. Come, you look weary. We'll go home, have an ale and Iswolde will find us food.' He slapped him manfully on the back.

'Who's Iswolde?' said Thomas as he fell into step next to William.

'Iswolde is my wife.'

The merchant's daughter who William had had his eye on? No, she couldn't be. No woman of such standing would marry a head shepherd and live in a wild place such as this. Thomas didn't like to probe, so he let William talk about the sheep and the lambing until they reached the house on the hill.

It was the same old bailiff's house that Thomas had been looking for, but he hardly recognised it. No longer a ruin of stones amongst bracken and thistles, the grey stone house now stood solid against the elements. A neat fence lined the front with a wattle gate and stone path leading across a large square yard to a solid wooden door. On one side grew a young rowan tree, planted to ward off evil spirits, and on the other was a pile of logs, bundles of brushwood and an axe lying on a chopping block. Two openings with their wooden shutters pinned back peered out from beneath a bracken and grass thatch that hung low like an overgrown fringe.

'Welcome to my humble home, my lord. Boy! Come and see to Lord Thomas's horse. Iswolde! We have company.' William opened his gate and stood proudly aside allowing Thomas to pass through.

A young lad scurried from nowhere, lowered his hood and took Henry around the back of the house. William had done well for himself to have a servant; even Thomas didn't have one of those.

'I've set up tenter poles for sheep and goat skins.' William indicated half a dozen square frames made from hazel, with skins attached by leather throngs, stripped and stretched for drying. 'I'll get good belts and bags from those, and I've a contact at the Saturday market at the port,' he added.

Where William saw leather, Thomas saw parchment. He made a mental note to speak to Simon when he got back. For the first time in weeks, he felt like his old self with no shadow peering over his shoulder.

'And this is the last of the dried bracken.' William indicated an untidy heap of brown foliage in the corner. He tapped the side of his nose. 'Bedding for the goats and it gets the embers going, Pa taught me that in his forge. I'll harvest more come autumn; there's plenty more where that came from.' He laughed.

William had a right to be proud; he'd accomplished so much and with only one arm. Thomas didn't know why he was surprised; William had always been the positive, confident one. While he always analysed from every angle before making a decision, William jumped straight in and got on with it. Maybe he should be more like that.

The door opened and a tall, slender young woman hurried out, pinning her coif as she came.

'Iswolde, Lord Thomas has come to see us.' William stood a little straighter and puffed out his chest.

Iswolde dipped a curtsy, lowering her eyes demurely. 'My lord.'

'God be with you,' said Thomas. 'I'm pleased to be welcomed to your home.'

Iswolde blushed, her hands clasping and unclasping her apron. She didn't look like a merchant's wife. Her hands were rough from work and her clothes too plain.

'Come on in. Iswolde, some food and drink for our lord. I've a small alehouse at the back where I brew my own. Izzy gathers the wild grains for me. Sit down by the hearth and take off your boots if you've a mind.' William pulled a crude chair covered with a sheepskin close to the hearth, then joined Iswolde at the other end of the room.

Thomas dutifully sat but kept his boots on. He had a hole in his hose, something he'd meant to ask Eleanor to darn.

'I thought you said you'd never let Lord Thomas darken our threshold?' Iswolde whispered, unfortunately loudly enough for Thomas to hear. He picked up a stick and poked the embers, pretending not to listen. 'I don't know what I'm going to give him. There's little in the stores and it's too early for anything from the garden.'

'What about the pot over the fire?'

'I can't give him that! There's mutton in it – the lord's mutton – that we're not supposed to have.' Frantically, Iswolde rummaged through a collection of baskets.

Thomas hid a smile. He'd rather have liked some mutton.

'Ah, yes, I see. Well, there must be some bread, and what about that cheese? Ye make a fair cheese,' said William.

'I was saving that cheese. There's a few wrinkled apples left.' Iswolde plunged her hands into a barrel on the floor.

'If ye was saving the cheese, I can think of no better time for it.'

That was the old William, the one Thomas knew. He gazed around with a prickle of envy. The house was one room, like his own, but smaller and was graced with an air of warmth and welcome. The room was clean and orderly with grasses on the floor. A central hearth glowed red, sending a thin trickle of smoke through a louvred opening in the thatch above. The iron pot bubbling over the hearth gave off a tantalising smell of meat and herbs that made his stomach rumble. Bunches of dried herbs and flowers hung from the beams, adding a background musk to a homely atmosphere.

William raised his voice. 'Ale! It's a bit rough; I drink faster than it can brew!' Ceremoniously, he carried over a flagon and two wooden cups, then dragged over a crude wooden chair for himself, readjusted the fleece on top of it and poured the ale.

Iswolde bobbed a curtsy and laid out platters of bread and cheese on the table, pushing the bundles of nettle and nettle twine to one side.

'If I'd known you were coming, Izzy would have cooked something more fitting,' said William.

'Anything is welcome, thank you. Your Ma used to give us food like this when we went fishing; bread and cheese wrapped in a piece of sacking that always had grits of black in it from the forge.'

'Aye, I remember. We could go fishing tomorrow. There's a stream nearby, but the sea's only three hours' ride. I haven't been that way since before the dark months. It'd be good to go again.'

Iswolde hovered nervously by the door. 'Prithee, my lord. I've fowl to see to.' She dipped a curtsy and quickly escaped.

'You've done well,' said Thomas, choking on the raw ale.

'I worked hard. But all this—' William swept his hand around the room— 'is Izzy's doing. She's a fine wench.' Sitting back amongst his fleece, he was the epitome of a contented man at ease in his own skin.

'I envy you. Where did you find her?'

'I had my eye on a merchant's daughter. Skin as fair as milk she had. I was doing well but even with my fine clothes and putting on a noble voice, I was aiming too high. Her Pa heard me cursing at the dice tables, said I was common and told me to keep away. I wasn't good enough for his daughter, he made that quite clear. A few weeks later, I was at the market and got talking to a codman selling leatherware. I told him I was a head shepherd and his ears pricked up. He said we could strike a deal and introduced me to his daughter Izzy. I liked the look of her and we got wed. I've been supplying hides to him ever since. Only taking what's my due,' he added quickly.

Thomas shrugged. If William wanted to take a few hides now and then, he didn't mind. It was a small price to pay for his friendship.

'I've been blessed and I'm thankful.' William poured himself another ale. 'And how are you? Has God blessed you?'

Thomas twisted the cup in his hands, wondering how to answer.

'Yes and no,' he said eventually, 'but I'm fine.'

'We're alike, you and I,' said William offering the flagon. Thomas shook his head, his throat still burning after only one sip. The ale reminded him of Rulf's wine, which was almost as bad.

'I mean,' William continued, 'we both had big ideas, me to be a smithy as my Grandpa Will and Pa wanted, and you to go to some place of learning. Neither of us managed it. I lost an arm in the wars and no matter what Pa said, I'd never have been a smithy. And your brother Richard died at Crecy, leaving you to be the lord. None of us expected that, although many weren't sorry.'

'But you've broken your shackles and I haven't,' said Thomas.

William frowned. 'The estate's doing well, isn't it? And you're a lord, so why so maudlin?'

What could he say? That he was a heartbroken wreck, struggling to forget his male lover? Hardly! William wouldn't sympathise with that. He might even report him. He could be honest and admit that he didn't want to be a lord but somehow, that seemed ungrateful.

'You're at peace with your life. That's more than I am.'

William raised his eyebrows and rubbed the back of his neck. 'If you're that unhappy, you should do what I did—'

'How can I? I can't just walk off. I've duties and responsibilities. It's different for me.'

William leaned forward, resting his arms on his knees. 'I know you can't, but you can make it better for yourself. Take a wife. I recommend it, especially on a cold night.' He leaned back with a glint in his eye and smiled.

Thomas knew alright, but not in the way William would ever imagine.

'I thought it was a lord's duty to get an heir,' William added. 'Isn't that what all you nobles want?'

'Where am I going to meet a lady? I've no contacts, and even if I did manage to ingratiate myself into society,

I've no money and not even a hall to entertain. Without those, no one would take me seriously.'

'Why marry a lady? She'd be no good for you anyway. Do what I did: find a lass who gives you what you need.' William chuckled. 'I cursed your name before, but I soon came to see that losing Rose was the best thing to happen to me. She didn't want to come here, and she'd have made my life hell because of it. And a merchant's daughter wouldn't feed stray lambs and card fleece, but Izzy's different. She was born a few leagues from here. Her kin's still there, two of them are my shepherds. She cooks, sews, spins, weaves, dries the skins, milks the sheep and goats, tends the garden and looks after me, all without a word of complaint. What more can a man want?' He studied Thomas. 'What do you want to do?'

Go to Oxford and be a physician, maybe find Rulf. 'Have more time for my charts and study—'

William sat up and slapped his thigh. 'There you are then! It's simple. Find yourself a capable, solid lass who can manage things for you, then you can play with your charts. Many Ladies of the Manor cover for their absent Lords, I don't have to tell you that. And grow a beard, the lasses like it, I don't know why you keep shaving it off.'

Thomas felt his smooth chin. He wished!

'And dress like a lord,' William added. 'Find a lass who can think for herself and manage your workers. You don't want a silly little cloth head.'

Their eyes met, and both their faces split into mischievous grins. Thomas shook his head. 'No, I couldn't,' he said.

'God's teeth, why not? She's perfect.' William slapped his thigh again and laughed. 'She's not the prettiest filly in the field, but she's wide, and you want a lass who's wide.'

'Wide?' Thomas echoed.

William nodded knowingly. 'Broad hips for birthing, slip them out easy. Many a lass dies on the birthing bed; you don't want yours to be one of them. I mean, you need an heir.'

William made it sound like he was looking over a horse. 'What would folks say?'

'Why care what folks say? You're the lord! Just do it, and if folks gossip, put them in their place. That's what lords do and what peasants expect.' William leaned forward, his voice excited. 'Listen, when you get back, put it to her. I know Rose; she's always had ideas above herself. She'll jump at it.'

Rose. Could he? Could he really? Thomas bit his lip. 'She won't. Yesterday, she as good as asked me to marry her and I laughed in her face. Now she's not speaking to me and refuses to be my reeve.' He risked another sip of ale and immediately wished he hadn't.

William roared with laughter. 'So you haven't been hankering after her!' He slumped back in the chair, still smirking. 'There was me thinking it was you, and all along it was her! If that doesn't beat all! Come on, I want the whole story.'

Thomas sighed and told William of all the times Rose had followed him, of her hints that were so obvious to him now, and of their pact. 'You see how it is. How can I ask her now?'

'Easy. Start by begging her pardon. Tell her you've spent a lot of time thinking; she'll believe that. Tell her she was right and you were wrong. It doesn't hurt to let women think they're right once in a while, otherwise they get moody and start nagging. Then tell her what a wonderful Lady of the Manor she would be. Women like flattery; it makes them feel important.' William nodded with the air of an expert. 'Trust me, she'll agree.'

Maybe she would. She could take over running the estate, and he'd have all day to work on his charts and to do as he pleased. She'd give him an heir, although he didn't like to think too much about that side of things, and later he could go to Oxford. It would be one in the eye for Rulf if he did.

The more he thought about it, the more tempting it sounded. Slowly, a smile spread across his face. 'You're right. I'll do it. Thanks.'

'Any time, my friend.' William grinned mischievously. 'Now, let me pour you another ale.'

CHAPTER 48

Rose rearranged the baskets yet again. She missed being a reeve and was itching to know what was going on but she wouldn't ask; she had her pride.

Thomas had come home two days ago from wherever he'd taken himself off to, and he hadn't said a word.

Neither had she. He'd laughed at her; she wasn't going to be the one to break the silence. It was up to him to make the first move.

She shoved the last basket under the shelf and glanced across the room. Something was on Thomas's mind; she could tell by the way he was pacing and idly peering into jars. Occasionally, she caught him looking at her as though he was considering something.

He must have noticed the women idle in the yard and seen eggs left in the boxes and the dirty swine pens. He was missing her, that's what it was, and he was summoning up the courage to ask her to be his reeve again. If he didn't do it soon, she'd have to swallow her pride and ask him. She'd worked hard for that position; it had been foolish to throw it away in a fit of pique.

'Sit down, Rose,' Thomas said, carrying two stools across to the hearth.

Finally. She hid a smile and sat next to him, waiting. He was twiddling his thumbs; a sure sign he was fumbling for words. He always dithered when he had something to say.

At last, he cleared his throat and stared at the ground. 'I came to say that you were right and we should beg pardon,' he mumbled, his words bumping into each other as they tumbled off his tongue. 'And I'd like you to be my Lady of the Manor.'

She hadn't expected that! What had suddenly got him to that? For the first time in her life, she had no idea what to say.

With more conviction, he looked her in the eye. 'I said, I would like you to be my wife.'

Her heart quickened. She could already feel the smooth silk on her skin and the weight of a jewel at her throat. But if he thought she'd jump at his bidding when it suited him he had another think coming.

'You've got a nerve! You said I wasn't good enough for you. I'm just a mere miller's maid, remember?'

'I was wrong. You surprised me the other day, but when I thought about it, I realised that I need a wife who I can trust to run things.'

She knew it! He'd be lost without her.

'I'm sure there are such noble ladies – Mama was one of them – but where am I going to meet one? I'm not known to society, and even if I was, look at this place.' He swept an arm around the room. 'It's hardly fitting for a daughter of high birth.'

'You could build it up.' Wait, should she have said that? She didn't want him to change his mind.

'I don't have the money for that, and it's time I was married. As my lady, you'd have to dress appropriately for saints' days and celebrations, but there'll be no jewels or surplus coins to waste, no invitations to banquets. You keep the records, so you know my situation. Anyway, I don't suppose such frivolous trappings matter to you.'

What a fool he was. Of course it mattered. Those frivolous trappings were the very things that made a lady different; the peasants would never take her seriously dressed in a rough woollen tunic. She couldn't wait to feel a figure-hugging kirtle and run her fingers along fitted sleeves with actual buttons. She'd never had buttons; they were a new idea for the rich. And she would have them, because she kept the records, and it would be the easiest thing in the world to find a few coins for a silk kirtle or two.

'Well?' he said.

It occurred to her that Thomas needed her more than she needed him. She knew exactly what he needed her for: an heir.

'You want a lot from me. If I agree—' (of course she'd agree; hadn't she been dreaming about it for months?) 'the marriage will be on equal terms. I'll not be under your control any more than I would another man, just because you're the lord.'

Thomas looked genuinely shocked. 'I wouldn't dream of controlling you! You would have your responsibilities and I would have mine.'

Deliberately, Rose paused and tilted her head to one side. 'Are you sure? I wouldn't want to embarrass you.'

'You won't embarrass me. It's not as if we're going to be entertaining or going anywhere,' he added.

She let that pass because her mind was racing. Their fortunes lay in wool and red cloth. She'd get the women spinning and weaving night and day. She'd instruct the men to plant more madder for red dye and have more maids to help Annie. Over the dark months, she'd have men and boys digging more drainage ditches on the water meadows to give grazing for more sheep, and they could build mud banks to make trout ponds by the side of the river. The coins would flow in, enough for kirtles, furs and jewellery. She'd hire a reeve – no, two reeves – to take her place and she'd persuade Thomas to build a grand hall where she'd throw extravagant banquets with minstrels and dancing, and she'd mix with the highest nobles in the shire.

'The wedding will have to wait until after haymaking,' Thomas continued. 'I'll tell Peter to finish the church and ask the priest at Holdesworthe to come here, since Ru— since we have no priest of our own. I'll write an announcement for the church door giving three weeks' notice of the marriage; and that reminds me, I need more tenter frames to dry skins for parchments. You can see Simon about that.'

He was talking about their marriage and thinking about parchments. Parchments! Some sign of tenderness would have been nice, but she was under no illusion of romance. This was a purely calculated arrangement with no affection on his side, although she hoped to change that in time.

What sort of lover would he be? She had no experience in that area, but many a lass had been only too ready to gossip about her fumblings in the hay. She'd wager she was wiser than he was about such matters. After all, what could a former boy scholar who'd grown up surrounded by monks possibly know of love and matters of the marriage bed?

'You'll have to win the peasants to the idea.' She was already calling her own kind *the peasants* as though she was no longer one of them. Well, soon she wouldn't be.

How good it would be to be on the other side, secure and respected. 'They may not accept me, and I'll not have a repeat of when I was reeve.'

'My people—'

'*Our* people,' she corrected him.

He grinned in that boyish way of his. '*Our* people will accept it because I will tell them to.'

Poor naïve Thomas, believing such a thing. Folks wouldn't accept it, any more than she would have done.

Let folks tut behind their hands. They were peasants, and she would soon be the Lady of the Manor.

CHAPTER 49

'Marry *her!* Now I know you've lost your wits!' Maria threw her stitching onto her mattress. 'God's teeth, Thomas, she's a miller's maid! She's no land or wealth and no connections to society. How am I going to find a husband? She's— she's nothing. You can't!' She glared daggers at Rose, who was sitting on the other side of the hearth.

'You can say what you like. I am going to marry Rose and she will be my lady, so you'd better get used to it,' said Thomas, matching Maria's glare. 'Don't you think of anyone but yourself?'

'I'm thinking of both of us. You'll be a laughing stock and I'll never get a husband. Look at her, sitting there like a cat with the cream.' Maria turned to Rose. 'Oh, I see it all now. *Let's play chess, Thomas. Teach me to read and write, Thomas.* You've been planning this for months, and he's too much of a nuddlejade to see it! What did you do to him? Put a peasants' concoction in his ale to addle his mind?'

'How dare you!' Rose snapped. 'I didn't know Thomas was going to ask me, and I may not have lands or wealth, but at least I can run this place instead of sitting around like a useless cloth head!'

'I am not useless! I help Eleanor make twine and I spin. ..sometimes,' Maria admitted. 'Ladies of high birth don't dig ditches or gather hay, unlike some of us.'

Rose took to her feet and strolled to the barrel at the end of the room. Turning, she smiled sweetly. 'Shall we have an ale to celebrate?' She paused for effect before adding, 'Sister?' It was fun watching Maria's face turn from pale to puce.

'Sister! You're no sister of mine—'

'I like a wedding,' Eleanor piped up. 'You'll be Lady Rose. Shall I c-curtsy to you?'

'No, you shan't!' Maria snapped. 'Be quiet, El; you don't understand.'

'I was only asking. You c-can wear a new kirtle on your wedding day, Rose, and I'll m-make a flower ring for your hair.'

'If she's having a new kirtle, then I'm having one too.' Maria said. 'It's the least you can do, Thomas.'

'I can't afford any new kirtles. Rose can borrow one of yours for the wedding. You don't mind, do you, Rose?'

She drew herself up. 'Yes, I do mind! I'd rather walk into church in my tunic than wear one of her castoffs.'

Maria snorted. 'I shouldn't worry. I've only got two, and neither of them would fit.'

'We c-can all have new silk kirtles. I'll m-make them for us,' said Eleanor. 'We still have the silks and c-cloths Father Rulf brought back from the m-market.'

'El, I love you!' Maria threw herself across the room and kissed Eleanor on both cheeks. 'And I shall have first choice, because Rose will have pale blue.'

'I can choose my own colour,' Rose said, bristling.

Maria sighed. 'You see what you're marrying, Thomas? Rose, noble maidens wear pale blue on their wedding day for purity. Don't you know anything?'

Rose clenched her fists behind her back and bit her tongue. She wouldn't give Maria the satisfaction, and ladies didn't show their emotions. Or did they? 'I would have chosen blue in any case, since it's my favourite colour.'

'With no Father Rulf, who's going to marry you? Don't tell me you're going to do that handfasting thing the peasants do. I couldn't bear it.' Maria shuddered dramatically, sitting back on her mattress.

'The priest from Holdesworthe will conduct the service in our church,' said Thomas.

'It hasn't got a proper roof. What if it rains?' Maria picked up her bone needle and the discarded work but made no move to resume her sewing.

'Then we'll get wet, won't we? It's no good complaining, Maria; I'm marrying Rose and that's an end to it. And you'd better sew quickly, El, because the wedding will be in July. You have four weeks.' Thomas snatched his hat and let the door slam behind him.

Standing outside the door, he struggled to calm his furious breathing. Rose had really held her own. Calling Maria *sister*; he chuckled to himself, then put on his hat and strode towards the forge. Better get it over with.

Annie and Peter were both inside and looked surprised at his entrance.

'I'm glad you're both here, for I've some good news to share.' With his hands behind his back, he glanced from one to the other. 'I'm taking a wife,' he announced.

'Well, that's a surprise!' Annie said. 'And not before time.'

'That's why ye've been so quiet of late and slipping off on your own. Lasses do that to a man. At least, our kind of lasses do.' Peter crossed his arms and leaned against the wall. 'Don't know about your kind.'

'Who is she?' asked Annie.

'Rose.'

'*Rose?*' Peter and Annie echoed simultaneously.

Thomas smiled, enjoying their astonishment. 'Yes. Rose.'

'But you can't! She's a miller's lass. Folks won't accept her, and what about Maria? Rose will be above her in rank. Have you thought of that?' Annie's reaction was exactly what he had been expecting, and William had been right: he didn't need to care about it.

'She's right, m'lord,' Peter said. 'Best to think again. Ye'd do better choosing one of yer own.'

'I don't want one of my own. Rose is perfect. I thought you'd be glad to hear I'm getting married..'

'We are, but *Rose*? Thomas, don't be hasty. I'll give you some chamomile, it'll soothe your mind and help you think about this.' Annie scrambled to her feet with an agility that belied her years and headed for her shed.

Thomas caught her by the arms. 'I don't need your chamomile. I've already asked her, and she's accepted me. The wedding is in July.'

The embers in Peter's forge crackled as the pair looked at him in silent disbelief. He had nothing more to say, and he wasn't interested in hearing their objections. He was sick of his people telling him what to do.

He was the lord, and this was his new beginning.

CHAPTER 50

July 1350

'M-Maria, sit still! I c-can't braid the ribbon in your hair if you keep m-moving.' Eleanor pulled out the ribbon with a sigh and began again.

'The braids are even, aren't they? They have to be or the coils will look different.' Maria sat with her hands in her lap, her mouth in an impatient pout.

'Yes, but you m-must stop fidgeting.'

Rose watched from her stool, her composure hiding the knots that her stomach was twisting itself into. With all the fuss Maria was making, anyone would think that she was the one getting married this morning.

Annie bustled through the door in a new blue kirtle and cream linen surcoat. She'd pinned her hair and wore a matching cream veil in place of her usual fitted coif, one end thrown loosely over her shoulder in the manner of an unmarried woman.

Rose had never seen her look so lovely. She pushed her fingers through her own wiry curls and smoothed the pale blue silk of her wedding kirtle. It felt tight, and the close-fitted sleeves she had dreamt of were irritating her. It wasn't Eleanor's fault – she'd made the kirtle beautifully – it was just that she had never worn anything so fitted. How ladies wore them all day and still managed to breathe was beyond her.

'I've brought some rose water for your hair.' Annie put an earthenware pot on the table.

'Not there! I'm laying out my custards.' Janet examined the shallow bowls, holding each one up and giving it a shake. 'They haven't set, and I don't know what I'm going to do.'

'I'll put them outside on the cool stones to set,' Annie said. 'They'll be fine.'

'I've some honeyed berries to go with them,' said Janet, bustling back and forth to the table with platters of hedgerow leaves, bowls of primrose, violet and marigold petals, loaves of bread and rounds of goats and sheep's cheese. 'All this food has to go outside on the trestles, and the men still haven't rolled out the barrels of ale, and Thomas said to use a casket of Father Rulf's wine. There's so much to do, and where are those dozy lasses who are supposed to be helping me?' She stood back, regarding the table with dismay and wringing the life out of her apron as she spoke. 'Did you see the hog roast as you came in? Were the boys turning the spit and keeping the embers hot? I'd best go and check; if they stop turning, one side will burn and the other will be raw.'

'Stop fussing. Everything will be well.' Annie picked up the last bowls of custard. 'Now go and get changed, and while you're about it, drink some of my clover tonic to calm you.'

'It's the lord's wedding and I want it to be right.' Janet hurried over to the trestle, but Annie stopped her with a firm hand.

'I'll see to it, now go. We haven't got long. Will and Iswolde are at the forge with Peter, and he's already poured a second jug of ale. Tell him I said he's not to drink too much before we set off for the church. You

know how loud he gets with an ale or two inside him.'
Annie manoeuvred Janet to the door. When the other woman was safely outside, she let out a long sigh, sending an escaped wisp of hair floating up over her veil. 'You look pretty Rose. That pale blue suits you.'

'What do you think of me?' Maria jumped up and slowly twirled, holding out the rich yellow folds of her kirtle. 'I'm wearing the purple amethyst that Mama gave me. Look.' She held out the sparkling jewel on a gold chain at her throat. 'Doesn't it go well? What jewellery are you wearing, Rose?'

She didn't have any jewellery, as Maria well knew. 'I'm still thinking about it.'

'I shouldn't think too long. We'll be leaving soon.' Maria swept back to her seat with a flourish. 'A shame your hair's so short and curly or you could have had braids in the latest fashion, like mine.' She patted her newly-braided hair, smirking.

Rose bit her tongue. If she wasn't about to be a lady, she'd have crossed the floor and wiped that smug smile off Maria's pretty little face. As it was, all she could do was hold her hands tightly together in her lap and feign indifference. Behaving like a lady was more difficult than she'd thought.

'Rose looks beautiful as she is. With a ring of roses on her head, she won't need braids or jewellery,' Annie said, placing a protective hand on Rose's shoulder.

'She's sitting very still for someone who's getting married,' Maria retorted. I've never known her so quiet. I expect she's practising being the lady she isn't.'

'I am here, you know!' Rose protested. She wasn't practising – well, alright, she was – it was having to hold her stomach in that was killing her, and all because the damn kirtle showed every bulge. It wouldn't have mattered so much if Maria hadn't cut such an elegant figure. There were no bulges in her kirtle.

'She's just nervous, aren't you, Rose? It's quite natural. You wait until it's your turn, Maria.' Annie gave Rose's shoulder a reassuring squeeze.

'At least I shall marry into my own kind.'

Rose dug her nails into the palms of her hands. She was doing the right thing in marrying Thomas, she was. It would all work out. If she told herself enough times, she might even come to believe it.

'El, let's take a look at you. Give us a twirl,' said Annie.

Eleanor duly twirled, her eyes shining, her rosy cheeks flushed. 'I p-picked the p-pink silk because it's so p-pretty.' She ran over to Rose and hugged her. 'It's so exciting and you look beautiful. You'll be one of us and c-can sit with M-Maria and me.'

'No, she can't,' Maria muttered just loud enough for Rose to hear. For once, Rose was in complete agreement; she could think of nothing worse than being forced to sit with Maria for every meal.

'Maria, El, you'd better set off for the church. Put your boots on and you'll need your mantels; there's a fresh breeze and it looks like rain,' said Annie. 'I'll walk up with Rose after.'

'I'm not wearing boots,' Maria protested. 'I shall wear my leather shoes with the punched holes on the top.'

'Then they'll spoil, for the paths are muddy and full of puddles after the rain,' Annie said. 'It hasn't stopped in weeks. The hay's ruined and what isn't black will rot in the stacks before the dark months are out. Then what'll—'

'*What'll we feed the ewes?* Yes, I know. That's all anyone's been saying lately.' Maria thrust an angry foot into a boot.

'It's the ewes that give us the wool that brings in the coins.' Rose couldn't keep quiet any longer. She'd heard whisperings amongst some folks that the bad weather was an ill omen, and Thomas was already praying for a good harvest to make up for it.

'C-come on, M-Maria!' Eleanor bounced over to the door and held it open. Looking at her, Rose felt a warm rush of affection. At least there was one person who truly wished her joy. 'I'm so excited; I c-can't wait to get there!'

'You're the only one,' Maria muttered. 'I'm coming.' She made a show of getting up, threw a fur-lined mantle around her shoulders and stamping out.

'She'll never accept me, will she?' said Rose. 'The women used to respect and talk to me but ever since Thomas announced our wedding, they've turned their backs. I'm not sure where I belong anymore.'

She'd been dreaming about this day for so long and thought she'd be excited but all she felt was nerves and doubts. She should never have started this. Hot needles pricked the backs of her eyes and she had a strong urge to bury her face on Annie's shoulder and cry.

'They're jealous, that's all. It's not easy to step out of your own kind. I should know; I was friends with Lady Joan and folks talked about me something wicked. But you have Thomas and people will soon get used to it. You'll see.'

'I'm not a cloth head, Annie. Thomas doesn't want a real lady; he wants an unpaid reeve who will give him an heir.' She sniffed and resisted the urge to wipe her nose on her sleeve.

'There's more to being a lady than wearing fine clothes and jewellery. Many ladies run the estates while their lords are away. You're better at running things than he is, and you both know that.'

'I do. I just wish he...' Rose's voice trailed away and she looked at Annie.

'You're fond of him, aren't you?'

She nodded, fighting her tears.

'This is the way nobles do things. Marriage is for the benefit of both sides. If you like or love each other, that's wonderful, but it's not necessary. I'm sure Thomas will come to care for you in time.'

She hoped Annie was right, but she was in no position to expect it. After all, she had wanted to marry him and get a better life, and now she had. A common lass like her should be grateful.

'He hasn't even put on a good feast. He said he can't afford it.' Rose dabbed the corners of her eyes delicately with her kerchief. 'I know he's tight with his purse strings, but God's teeth, Annie, it's my wedding.'

'He's just worried, what with the hay and everything. Now, get your boots. I'll pin your flower ring onto your hair and once you get to the church, you'll feel better.'

It would take more than a ring of roses to do that.

As soon as Annie had finished her ministrations and Rose stepped outside, the wind blew cold around her ears. The moor was hidden beneath a thick cloak of dark cloud and drops of rain hit her cheek. Was this another ill omen? Shivering, she pulled her mantle close.

By the time she and Annie had walked the hill to the church, the hem of her kirtle was mud-stained, her mantle damp, and she'd wager that her hair had frizzed into tight curls. It always did that in the rain. Trust Peter to build a church on top of a hill, fool of a man that he was.

She stopped to scrape her boots clean on the grass and straightened the kirtle that still threatened to strangle her. Could she truly be the Lady of the Manor?

Well, she was about to find out.

Glancing at Annie, she took a deep breath and stepped into the clearing where a crowd had gathered in front of the church.

Keeping her chin high and a smile on her face, she walked slowly taking small steps like a lady. The men removed their caps as she passed, and the women bobbed a curtsy. Was it respect, or were they keeping her sweet because she was the lady?

Hoping to see Thomas, she looked over at the church, but it wasn't Thomas she saw, it was William. She stopped short and couldn't help but gasp. He looked more handsome than the last time she saw him, standing tall in his fur-trimmed mantle clasped together at the front with a wide gold double-ring brooch in place of cheaper ties. Underneath, he wore a cream tunic and a fine houppelande with long slits down each side that hung in rich blue folds to below his knees. He looked noble, there was no other word for it, and she couldn't deny the flutter that swept through her.

Standing next to him was a woman. She must be Iswolde; Annie had told her about William's wife. She was taller and thinner than she was and pretty in an ordinary sort of way with her dark hair braided in loops behind her ears, like Maria's. Her linen green kirtle was fine enough, and the leather belt with a gold buckle shone with quality.

Rose's eyes roved over Iswolde's fine blue surcoat showing under a darker blue mantle made of the finest cloth and folded her own poorer one closely around her.

Iswolde had her hand on William's arm, and they were laughing. They looked happy, and Rose couldn't take her eyes off her. The woman must have sensed her staring, for she glanced across and dipped a curtsy. As she rose, a large gold pendant glistened in her cleavage.

Rose's hand went to her bare throat. It wouldn't have taken much for Thomas to give her even a simple bead chain to wear. Didn't he care if his lady was humiliated?

Knowing him, the thought had never crossed his mind.

Annie nodded encouragingly and nudged her forward. A few women stood in tight circles, and she noticed one or two of them glancing over their shoulders before turning back, their heads bowed. They were gossiping about her, probably noticing that she wore no jewellery. What did that say about how the lord saw his lady?

She wanted to hide and never set eyes on any of them again. Gone was the little miller's girl who could run home and snuggle into the warmth and safety of her Pa's arms. She was all grown up and on her own.

She could have been standing next to William with a gold pendant around her neck right now, if she hadn't been so determined to better herself. Or she could have married Leif, the miller's son. He'd given her the eye more than once, and milling was a life she knew, whereas this—no! She had got what she wanted. Jewels or not, affection or not, she would be the lady.

God, the butterflies were back.

Annie was craning her neck, searching the faces. 'There's Thomas, coming round the back of the church with Father Marcus. Doesn't he look handsome in his feathered hat? Are you ready?' She adjusted the flower ring on Rose's head and fussed with the folds of her kirtle. 'You look lovely and every inch a lady,' she said with a nod of approval.

Rose's nerves eased the tiniest bit. God knew she needed approval from someone who wasn't Eleanor. Her legs were as weak as a newborn lamb's. What was she doing here?

Thomas was waiting with the priest in front of the church door, dressed in his best cotehardie, a gold and jewelled buckle on his fur-lined mantle sparkling in the light. As they approached, he turned to face her, his expression blank and pale. Was he having doubts too?

It didn't matter if he was; it was too late for both of them. There was no going back.

The crowd fell silent and all eyes turned to her. She swallowed, gathered her skirts, raised her chin and stepped forward.

For good or ill, her lord was waiting.

Standing next to Thomas, she was in such an agony of mental turmoil that she could barely hear the priest's words. She was sure the congregation could see her trembling. She stole a glance to her right. Thomas was standing tall, looking handsome and staring ahead.

'Lord Thomas de Chiddleigh, wilt thou take Rose Miller, here present, for thy lawful wife, according to the rite of our Holy Mother the Church?'

'I will,' Thomas answered clearly.

The priest turned to her. 'Rose Miller, wilt thou take Lord Thomas de Chiddleigh, here present, for thy lawful husband, according to the rite of our Holy Mother the Church?'

Rose swallowed in a dry throat. 'I will.'

Thomas took her right hand in his, and the priest sprinkled them with holy water before blessing the ring.

'Let us pray. Bless, O Lord…'

The words floated over her until she felt Thomas slide a gold band onto her finger.

'With this ring, I thee wed and I plight unto thee my troth,' said Thomas, smiling at her.

She stared at the ring. It was really happening. In turn, she placed a matching gold band on Thomas's finger. 'With this ring, I thee wed and I plight unto thee my troth.'

After all her months of plotting, they had finally made their vows. She had rehearsed this moment in her mind many times, but now she was wondering if she'd just made the biggest mistake of her life.

The priest opened the church doors and led them inside for the nuptial Mass.

Walking beside her husband, she had no choice but to leave Rose Miller at the threshold and step forward as Lady de Chiddleigh, Lady of the Manor.

'Pipers! Fiddlers! Play your tunes! Boys, open the barrels; maids, carve the spit roast! This is my wedding, and we shall make merry!' Thomas stood proudly before his people and lifted his goblet high in the light of the torches, his face bright to the rousing cheers.

He waited until the voices faded and the crowd had wandered away, then he drained his goblet in one gulp. He needed that, and he needed another and probably another after that. The service had gone well, although Father Marcus was a bit dour, and now he, Thomas, was a married lord as his people expected him to be.

He glanced at Rose, who was being led to the food tables by Annie. Rose would run the estate well, no doubt about that, and with God's blessing, she would give him a son, but was this really what he wanted?

He held out his goblet for a boy to refill it. He'd made the decision and now it was all about the future, building his estate, making it profitable, and finally going to Oxford.

Would Rulf still be there? Thomas pursed his lips, angry with himself. It wouldn't matter if he was. He was a married man; he didn't need Rulf anymore, especially not after the craven way he had deserted him.

So why did he feel like he was acting in a mummers' play, waiting to remove his mask?

A ring of dancers was gathering in the centre of the yard. Annie caught his eye and inclined her head towards Rose. She was right, he should lead the dance with his lady.

Draining his third goblet of wine, he wiped his mouth and walked towards his wife. Inclining his head in respect, he offered her his hand. With a smile, Rose placed her hand in his. It was the first time they had touched as a married couple. He put on his happy groom's face and led his wife to the circle of dancers.

He felt nothing at all.

CHAPTER 51

Rose woke to her first morning as Lady of the Manor and she didn't feel any different. Gently, she pulled back a corner of the sacking curtain providing privacy to her and Thomas's room and peeked out.

Maria and Eleanor were still asleep. Thomas was seated at the trestle. A candle in a wooden holder gave a glimmer of light to his left, an inkpot was placed to his right and a line of goose quills was laid neatly in a line before him. She could hear the scratching of the quill as his hand scurried across the parchment.

Last night was the first time she'd lain with a man, and she'd been nervous she would disappoint him. She needn't have worried; it had all been over so quickly that she wondered what all the fuss was about. Maybe Thomas would improve with practice. Knowing Maria and Eleanor were on the other side of the sacking hadn't helped but she had plans for those two.

Rose started to dress herself. She had no lady's maid and no chance of one; Thomas had made that very clear. *Maids cost coins,* he had said when she'd asked. Well, give her time, and that would change as well.

Slipping the smock over her head, she pulled on her woollen stockings, tying them above her knee with tapes, then wriggled into a fitted green kirtle. Apart from her wedding kirtle, it was the only one she had. Eleanor had promised to sew another one for her, but she had enough to do making twine to tie the corn stooks for the coming harvest. Pray God, August would be hot and dry or the grains would mould after the recent wet weeks and there would be little to reap.

Tying her knife and purse to her belt, Rose reached for her drop spindle and hesitated. Did ladies spin? Maria never wore one, but the women needed all the wool they could get to weave. Besides, she wasn't a typical lady, and who would dare criticise the Lady of the Manor? She tied it on, then pinned her veil in place. A married woman's veil now, one that draped over her head with the ends wrapped around her neck and felt like it was strangling her until she tugged it looser.

Checking herself from head to toe, she was finally ready to face her first day as Lady of the Manor.

She ducked through the sacking and sauntered over to Thomas.

'What are you doing?' she asked.

'Working.' He dipped the end of his quill into the inkpot and continued writing, not even lifting his head to acknowledge her.

She peered over his shoulder and wondered whether to mention her writing lessons, but decided against it. The parchment was covered in triangles and numbers that meant nothing to her. 'Is it to do with your charts?'

His hand poised over the parchment, and he sighed. 'No, it's not, but I need to concentrate. Don't you have things to do?'

Was that all he had to say to his wife on the morning after their marriage? No term of endearment, no smile, not even a *good morning*? Even if this was a marriage of convenience she'd expected he'd show her a little more courtesy, if only out of basic good manners. 'Of course I do, but I thought it would be nice to talk for a while. It is our first morning as husband and wife.' Her hand hovered above his shoulder, but didn't quite dare make contact.

Thomas put down his quill and turned to face her with an annoyed expression. 'Rose, I'm sorry if you feel I was harsh, but I do need to get on with this. We'll sit and talk later.' Then he turned back, picked up his quill and continued his scratching.

She wasn't wanted. It was just another day.

First on her list was to check that Peter had made the nails and crooks for repairing the thatch roof. Gathering up her skirts and tiptoeing around the puddles as daintily as she could, crossed the yard to the forge. The door was ajar, and she heard Peter and Annie talking as she drew nearer.

'I never believed Thomas would go through with it, and Rose was having doubts,' Annie was saying. 'He'll never mix with society now, not once they know he's married a miller's maid. And what will happen to Maria? How's she going to find a husband? Has he thought of that?'

''Tis selfish of him. I thought he had demons in his head and he'd change his mind. Ye're a healer, Annie. Is his mind addled?'

Was that what everyone was saying; that Thomas had only married her because he'd lost his wits? If so, the situation was worse than she'd thought.

'I don't think so, but he has been very quiet of late. Too quiet, I would say. I'd a mind he had the black devil's dog on his shoulders but he denied it. I offered him my chamomile tonic to soothe his thoughts, but he wouldn't take it. Then he came out with this mad idea.'

There was a silence as though Annie was thinking. Rose was afraid to hear more but couldn't resist listening and edged nearer.

'I felt sorry for her,' Annie added. 'Thomas didn't even give her a marriage brooch to confirm her new status, and she has no jewellery of her own.'

Rose had never heard of a marriage brooch, but now she had, she was determined that those records would provide her with a gold ornament or two to wear with the new kirtles that Thomas was going to pay for.

'For Thomas's sake, I suppose I should support Rose. Folks don't want her as their lady and they could make life difficult for both of them. The women look up to me and I'll try to bring them around, but if Rose gets above herself like she did when she was reeve, it won't be easy. You could help. The men respect you. Talk to them and squash any bad talk.'

Peter didn't reply, but his face must have spoken for him, because Annie added, 'Don't look like that! Think about it. I best hasten; I've angelica to pick and willow bark to cut and it's a devil to peel. Folk'll be needing cures for their coughs and stiff joints come the cold months.'

'If ye're by the river, give Gee a message from me. Tell him to find Jarin – he'll be in the woods cutting logs for the embers – and say that he's to come back quick if he wants a go at shoeing. The lad's been asking to try for a while, and happen he's ready.'

'I feel sorry for that lad. I'd like to see him get away from Gee. Couldn't you take him on as an apprentice? He could have Will's old bed. I don't know much about smithy work, but he seems to have a knack for it from what I've seen.'

'Aye, he's good enough, but who's going to pay his way? I can't learn him for nothing.'

'I know, but you could do with a trained lad now Will's gone. Well, I'd better be about my business.'

'And I'd best get on too. Simon wants more shovels for digging the ditches.'

Rose heard the solid ring of Peter's hammer on iron and Annie's footsteps heading for the door. Hastily, she sidled around the corner out of sight.

As soon as Annie had gone, Rose hurried back to the forge and promptly tripped over a pail of mutton fat that was outside.

'Damn muxy thing!' She rubbed her leg as a deep ache buried its way into the bone. Hitching up her skirts, she spat on her hand and rubbed in the spit to bring out the colours, then glanced around guiltily. Fortune was with her; there was nobody to see the new Lady of the Manor behaving like a peasant.

Peter thrust his head over the door. 'Oh, it's ye. How long have ye been standing there?'

Hastily dropping her skirts, she lifted her chin and looked him straight in the eye. 'I haven't been standing here; I tripped over this pail. What's it doing here?'

Peter shrugged. ''Tis a forge. I use it to dip the iron or it rusts.'

'Yes, well, I came to see if you've finished the nails and crooks for the thatching,' she said.

'I will when I've done the shovels.' He ducked back into the darkness of the forge.

No *my lady* from him. She felt horribly conspicuous standing alone in the yard and dressed up in her fine kirtle. As Rose the reeve, she'd known exactly what to do. As Lady Rose of the Manor, she was lost.

Her gaze fell on the fowl, and she had an irresistible urge to collect the eggs. It was a job she'd been doing since she could walk, and she still got the same thrill every time she picked up newly laid eggs from the straw. Awkwardly, she smoothed her silk kirtle. Like so many things, collecting eggs was a thing of the past.

But she was the same Rose underneath all her finery, and there was still work to be done. Wiping her hands together, she marched briskly across the yard, then remembered who she was. She raised her chin, delicately lifted her hem out of the mud and continued as the Lady of the Manor towards the fields and her workers.

CHAPTER 52

September 1350

'Look at those stooks! I don't think we've ever had such a good harvest. Another day or two and we'll have it safely in.' Thomas beamed, his enthusiasm oozing from every pore as he and Rose stood watching the workers gathering the harvest. 'Praise God! We'll celebrate well; a roasted hog, even a ewe, and two – no, three – barrels of cider.'

His fervour annoyed her. 'I'm surprised you can afford it when you can't afford a maid for me.'

'Give me a chance; we've only been married two months. I promise that your maid will be top of my list when the coins come in from the sales of surplus grain.' He frowned for a moment. 'After Michaelmas and the men are paid, of course, and the dues are in, and the mill is finished. We'll talk about it then.'

He'd have forgotten by then. It was alright for him; she'd never seen him so happy, strutting around the place and far too absorbed in his work to notice her. If he had, he'd have known that it wasn't only the lack of a maid that was troubling her.

She wished he would touch her arm once in a while or smile lovingly, or do something – anything – to show her he cared. Even allowing for a man's blindness in such matters, couldn't he see how much she longed for just a token of affection?

Across the fields, the sound of her peasants' voices drifted towards her. They were singing as they worked.

Oats and barley, wheat and rye
Grow ripe and fat for us to scythe
To reap and tie in barns we store
Praise God His harvest evermore.

It was her favourite reaping song, one she'd sung at many harvests, and it brought tears to her eyes. At that moment, she would have swapped her title for the chance to be back working on the fields with her friends and feeling the sweat running down her aching back.

'I used to enjoy harvest time.' She dabbed her eyes with her kerchief. It was fine pink silk and embroidered by Eleanor as a wedding gift. It was too nice to use; her sleeve used to be good enough for her.

'And now you can look on as the Lady of the Manor with her lord, while others do the work for you.' Thomas smiled at her, as though she should be the happiest woman alive.

'That's just it. Being the lady isn't—'

'— isn't what you thought?' His eyes twinkled a little, making her feel small. 'Being the lord wasn't what I thought, either. You'll have to find your own way, like I did.'

'But you were born a noble. I wasn't. And *they*—' she nodded in the direction of the field— 'don't accept me. They laugh and talk about me behind my back. They did it when I was first made reeve as well, but I thought being the Lady of the Manor would be different.'

'Do they do what you tell them?' Thomas bit the end of a stalk and chewed it, his gaze fixed on the field now.

'Yes, but—'

'Then that's all that matters. I'm surprised you're bothered, a tough sort like you.'

'I do have feelings,' she said softly, but either he didn't hear her or pretended not to, for he didn't turn to her. She wasn't as tough as she'd thought, and it did bother her.

'They'll soon get used to you.' He glanced up at the sky. 'It's almost noon. I must get back to my work. And don't worry about how they treat you; just think of it as part of the job.'

Part of the job! She was surprised he didn't give her a manly slap on the back. 'You didn't tell me that when I said *yes*!' she shouted after him.

Thomas pursed his lips and kept walking. He sympathised with her, but he didn't know what she wanted from him.

No; that was a lie. He knew exactly what she wanted: his love. The one thing he couldn't give her.

He was trying to be a good husband. He made few demands on her, which suited him, and he left her free to run the estate. He'd assumed that was what she wanted; he hadn't reckoned on her loving him and expecting him to feel the same, so he'd retreated like a coward and feigned ignorance to her hints, but all that did was make her more vexed.

The sooner she was with child, the better. That would calm her down and they could both relax.

Two weeks later, Rose was on her way back to the house when she heard giggling behind the forge and couldn't resist taking a peek to see what was happening.

The redheaded maid, Dorothea, was parading up and down, a hand on her hip as she sashayed backwards and forwards with her nose stuck in the air, just like Rose and Janet had mocked Thomas all that time ago.

'Oh, Thomas!' Dorothea clasped her hands dramatically to her bosom. 'I'm your lady, and I'm so far up my own arse that I can't see where I'm going. And everywhere I walk, jewels and primroses fall out of my kirtle.'

As the screams of laughter rang in her ears, Rose gathered her skirts and fled to the safety of the house. Letting the door slam behind her, she ripped off her headdress and threw it on the floor.

'Don't slam the door!' Thomas said from the table. 'You made me blotch my work. It took me ages to do and now I'll have to do it again.' He reached for his pot of sand to soak up the ink.

'I hate being the lady!' Rose burst into tears.

Thomas sprinkled sand onto the parchment, shook the surplus onto the floor and examined the damage. 'It'll take some work but I should be able to save it.'

'Damn your parchment! God, you're the most selfish, unfeeling man I've ever met! You sit here all day, scratching away at your work, whatever that is, whilst I run your estate. You've no idea what I have to put with. Doesn't it bother you that the peasants spit behind my back? Don't you care that your wife is so upset?'

He looked up, astonished. 'Of course I care, but you knew it wouldn't be easy. And I'm not selfish. I let you do as you please and run the estate, and I do my work. That's what we agreed. What on earth do you have to cry about?'

He had no idea. 'They hate me and say things behind my back; wicked, cruel things. I can't do this on my own. I need you to talk to them, as their lord.'

'Peasants always moan about their lord and lady. It doesn't mean anything. They whine about us, and we complain they don't work hard enough. It's the way it is. And no, I can't speak to them; that would undermine your position.' Thomas twirled the quill between his hands. 'I don't want you to be upset, but the best thing is to ignore them. They'll soon get tired of it.'

That was the most ridiculous advice she'd ever heard in her life. 'I've tried, but it makes no difference. I'm beginning to wish I'd stayed as your reeve and we'd never married.'

'Do you?'

Was that a look of surprise or hurt? She softened a little. 'No, of course not, but I need your support. And maybe a hug now and then. Is that too much to ask?' Gently, she rested her hand on his shoulder.

'I'm sorry.' Thomas stared down at the quill, now still in his hands. 'I don't find that sort of thing easy.'

'I'm not a fool, Thomas. I know you didn't marry me for love, but I did think we'd be more together-like. Things don't feel any different to before we were married.' She lowered her eyes. 'I had hoped you might come to feel something for me.'

He smiled up at her then; not a lover's smile but a guilty, rueful smile. 'Maybe in time. We've not been married long, have we?'

'Yes, in time.' Even as she said the words, she no longer believed them.

It was as though Thomas was holding something back, something hidden beyond her reach, and if she walked out the door now, he would dip his quill into the ink and continue working, their conversation forgotten.

'Why don't you go and see Annie, share one of her tonics and have a woman-to-woman chat?' Thomas suggested. 'That'll cheer you up.'

It wasn't Annie she wanted, but Thomas was oblivious to her, lost in his world of figures and triangles. Sadly, she removed her hand. 'Maybe I will.'

After she left, Thomas stared for a long time at the closed door, then threw his quill across the table and cursed. All she wanted was a hug and a few caring words from her husband. It wasn't unreasonable, but if he showed her affection, he'd be giving her false hope. That wouldn't be fair to either of them.

It was different when he took her under the cover of darkness. That was expected of him, and he needed an heir. He felt nothing for her at all in that way, but better to let her think of him as cold than a liar.

He rescued his quill and looked guiltily at his charts. Maybe he had been neglecting her a little. He should do something to make her happy. He glanced around the room and smiled. Tomorrow, he'd tell Simon what he wanted him to do.

'That's how they are,' said Rose, sipping a cup of clover tonic and staring at a bunch of wild marguerite daisies hanging from the roof in Annie's linhay. 'They'll never accept me. I've tried talking to Thomas, but he was no help. I don't know what to do.'

'From the gossip I've heard, they think you've forgotten where you came from. They assumed that because you were one of them, you would use your influence to do something for them, and you haven't.' Annie refilled her cup.

Now that Annie said it, Rose realised she was right. It had never occurred to her before. 'Something to make their lives easier you mean?'

Annie nodded. 'Exactly. Now, if you can do that, you'd be the best Lady of the Manor to have ever lived.'

'Then I'll have to think of something, won't I?'

'You will.' And the two women raised their cups to her success.

That night, Rose lay on her mattress and thought about her conversation with Annie. She couldn't change the amount of work the peasants had to do, and she couldn't change how long they worked since they needed every daylight hour, and there wasn't enough surplus food to give anything away either. That left only one thing.

Pulling the cover up to her chin, she snuggled down and smiled, inwardly hugging herself with glee.

She'd give them something to talk about.

CHAPTER 53

Inside the house, Rose helped Thomas move the table to straddle across the threshold.

'That looks good.' Thomas straightened the edge of it. 'The peasants can queue up in the yard and come here to pay their dues. Will you and Simon be alright on your own? Michaelmas is a long day, and there are always arguments about payments.'

Rose tidied the scrolls into neat piles. 'We'll manage. Shouldn't you be going? It's a long ride to William's place, and you don't want to be riding at night,' she said.

'I won't be. The sun's barely up; there's no need for haste.' Thomas set two ink pots precisely in the centre of the table.

There was a great need for haste; the quicker he was out of there, the better. 'You never know, Henry might cast a shoe or something. You go, I can finish this.'

'He was only shod last week. Now, I've sharpened half a dozen quills. That should be enough, but there are some spares on the trestle, just in case. And the chest of coins is on the floor between you and Simon.'

'I know; I nearly tripped over the muxy thing. Now, stop fussing. Simon won't be long.' She put a firm hand on Thomas's back and held out his hat.

Ignoring it, he stood back to check everything was in order. 'I'll collect Will's dues while I'm there, and I'm going to speak to him about his business with Iswolde's father. I don't mind if he takes a few hides here and there or the odd joint of mutton, but judging by how well he's doing, he's taking more than that and we need to make some sort of arrangement.' He leaned forward and nudged the quills into a perfectly straight line.

'You mean you want to charge him. Are you thinking of parchments or coins?' God's bones, he was impossible to hurry. All the times she'd wanted him to sit down and talk with her, and the one time he chose to do so was the one time she wanted him to leave her alone. With a sigh, she put his hat on the table.

'Both. I'm always running short of parchment, and I don't want to stop my work. I'm scribing everything I learnt with the monks – Latin, Greek and Logics – and there's a lot of it.'

'What's logics?'

'Triangles, angles and numbers. They're important for calculating movements of the stars and interpreting charts, amongst other things.'

'I don't see why you have to write it all down when you have it in your head. What's the point?'

Thomas picked up his hat and twisted it in his hands. 'I want to refresh my mind, in case I want to study further. I mean, you never know.'

'You've been to school, what more is there to know? Now, if you'd said it was to teach our son, I could understand it.'

'You're not, are you?' His eyes dropped to her belly and the tone of excitement wasn't wasted on her.

She shook her head. 'No, not yet.' A bit more activity from him might help, she thought, but that was for another time. Simon would be here soon and she wanted Thomas gone.

'Oh,' His disappointment wasn't wasted either. 'Well, when the time comes, I certainly can teach our son. I'd like that.'

She was sure he would, and equally sure that he'd make a good teacher, but there wasn't time to discuss it further. She opened the door to a chilly autumnal blast that swirled the first brown leaves across the doorway. Outside, a queue of peasants stamped their feet, huddled in their hoods or with their shawls wrapped to their chins. Folks wanted to get on with the day's work, or they'd be toiling after dark.

'Here comes Simon. Tell Iswolde she's in my prayers; she must be close to her birthing.' She swallowed her envy with a smile. Maybe a child would bring her and Thomas closer together. 'Do you have Will's account scroll?'

Thomas patted his surcoat. 'Safely in my pocket.'

'Then I'll see you tomorrow. Have a safe journey and God's speed.' She didn't quite push him out the door but the moment he was outside she shut it firmly.

At last! Now all she had to do was deal with Simon.

It wasn't long before Simon inched his way around the table. 'I see we're all set to gather the dues,' he said. 'I saw Thomas heading for the stables. Isn't he joining us?' He eyed the two chairs with a slight frown.

'No, he's visiting Will about the hide business.'

Simon's face cleared. 'Good idea, hides are very profitable. It's good to see Thomas so engaged with estate matters. We've got you to thank for that.'

'We have?'

'Of course. Getting married makes a man, and he's obviously very fond of you.'

It wasn't obvious to her, but a small part of her bloomed a little at Simon's words. After all, Simon knew Thomas much better than she did. Maybe she'd just missed the signs. 'He is?'

'Yes, he was saying only the other day how much easier it is now that he can leave everything to you as the Lady of the Manor.'

Oh, that sort of fond. Why wasn't she surprised?

'You sit here,' she said, pulling out a chair. 'As each person comes to the table, you find the scroll, and I'll record and deal with the payments and dues.' She settled herself firmly in the left-hand chair.

'Wouldn't it be quicker if I record while you sort the coins?' Simon slipped into the chair next to her.

'I've never been on this side of the table before. I'm looking forward to taking money rather than handing it over.' That was true. She *was* looking forward to it, but not for that reason.

Simon shrugged. 'You'll be doing both, but if you say so.'

The first hurdle crossed, she smiled to herself and watched him reach for a scroll. Now for the tricky bit.

'Let's get started,' she said.

Opening the door her heart sank. The first in the queue was Cecily, who was about as sharp as a blunt nail. Rose would have to do what she could and hope she got away with it.

'Cecily, come forward.' She forced a smile onto her face and took her seat.

Cecily made her way unsteadily towards them. A thin grey shawl was wrapped around her shoulders, and two filthy feet showed through the broken straps of the wooden plattens on her feet.

'Cecily, here we are,' Simon ran a finger down the list of names. 'Labourer and unskilled spinning and weaving at one penny a day.' He nodded to Rose who picked up her quill. 'I see here that you only worked half the possible three hundred and thirteen days last year—'

'Look at these hands, sire.' Cecily held out clawed hands, scrawny with stick-like fingers, the backs a mesh of knotted blue veins. 'I'm old, I work best I can.'

'—making a total of one hundred and fifty-six pennies and one halfpenny, or thirteen shillings and one halfpenny,' Simon continued, taking no notice.

'I can't live off that for the next year! You're not going to deny an old woman, are you?' She leaned forward, her fetid breath coming in clouds through blackened teeth.

Simon reeled and placed a hand over his nose. 'Less the rent for your cottage at five shillings, making a total payment of eight shillings and one halfpenny. Ah, I nearly missed it,' his finger traced along the line. 'You also had pannage for one swine for two weeks at half a penny per day. Taking off the seven pence, you are owed seven shillings, five pennies and one halfpenny.' He sat back and glanced at Rose. 'Got that?'

Rose nodded, her quill scratching the entry in her records.

'Pannage indeed! One poor old swine eating acorns what God's given for free. May you be forgiven, charging an old maid.'

Rose cast a discrete eye at Simon, who was watching her. This could be difficult. If she could succeed with Cecily, he couldn't stop her, but she couldn't do that all the time he was checking what she did.

Thinking quickly, she drained the cup of ale in front of her. 'I'm sorry, Simon, could you get me another cup? My throat's as dry as a well in summer.' She coughed a few times for good effect.

'If you're going to drink that fast, I'll bring the jug,' he said, scraping back his chair and disappearing to the other end of the room.

As soon as his back was turned, Rose bent down to the chest and lifted one bag of silver shillings and another of pennies and half-pennies, then counted out the coins into neat piles.

'There we are.'

Cecily frowned. 'That's too much.'

God, Cecily was going to argue. She hadn't reckoned on that. Simon had filled the jug and was coming back. She didn't have long.

'No, it's right. Take it, there're others waiting.' She pushed the coins firmly across the table.

Simon was half way across the room.

'But bailiff said seven shillings five pence and one halfpenny. There's more like—' Cecily counted on her fingers— 'ten shillings or more here. I don't want no misunderstanding. I'm not being called a thief—'

Oh Lord, Simon was three paces away.

'No one's calling you a thief, Cecily. This is a gift from your lady. Now, quickly, put the coins in your purse. Everyone will get the same: an extra farthing per day for women, and one halfpenny extra for men.'

'Did you hear that?' Cecily turned and yelled behind her. 'She's given us more pennies! Farthing for women and a halfpenny a day for men.' She turned back beaming through the stumps of her teeth. 'God bless you, my lady! I always said you was a good 'un.' Scooping the coins into her purse, she pulled the strings tight and held it up for all to see. 'A present from our lady!' she announced before walking jauntily away.

Sly old hag; that Cecily knew every trick in the book. But Rose had looked after her own.

Now let them talk about her.

'Just a moment. You there! Come back!' Simon's voice boomed in her ear as he dumped the jug of ale in front of her, spilling a brown pool of ale that spread towards the scrolls.

Cursing him, she frantically mopped up the liquid with her kerchief. It had all been going so well.

Cecily stopped and a murmur rippled along the queue. Simon leaned over Rose's shoulder and peered at her accounts. 'The daily rate is two pennies for men and one penny for women, you know that. Why have you given her more? Thomas didn't say anything to me about that. Does he know?'

Simon's face was close to hers, his eyes wide in surprise or anger. The murmur was growing. Above it, she could hear Cecily's voice raised in querulous protest.

'I'm no thief! I told her, sire, I'm no thief! She gave it me!'

'Keep your voice down,' she hissed to Simon. She crossed the floor, smiling at the queue, and said, 'Wait there, all of you. You too, Cecily.'

She shut the door and turned to face Simon. 'You know how they've been to me. I had to do something to get them on my side, and they do struggle to live on what they're paid.'

'You should have asked Thomas. I don't like going behind his back.'

'Neither do I, but you know how mean he is. He'd never have agreed.' She lifted her chin. 'It's done now, and they all know about it. If you say there's been a mistake, they'll blame you and you'll demean both our positions.' She liked that new word, *demean.* It was a noble's word.

She could see Simon weighing up the situation. 'What about the King's law?'

'What King's law?'

'The one he declared that said no peasant was to be paid more than they earned before the Pestilence. *That* law.'

She'd never heard of such a thing. 'Well, I don't suppose he'll find out about us down here. What would happen if he did?' Rumour had it that the king had a temper. The thought of Lyndeford Gaol loomed in her mind with a shudder. Few survived long in there. Her Ma said that Peter had been sent there once for something he hadn't done, and he'd barely been alive when got out.

'Fines, maybe gaol. I don't know but it wouldn't be good. Honestly, Rose, you shouldn't have done it.'

'If you're waiting for me to beg pardon, you'll wait in vain.'

Simon sighed. 'You've told them now. I can't ask for the money back; the men will riot. But I don't like it. There's supposed to be trust between a lord and his bailiff. Promise me that you'll tell Thomas as soon as he gets home and make sure he knows I had nothing to do with it.'

He looked genuinely worried, and she knew it was only the queue of peasants outside that was keeping his temper down.

'Of course I'll tell Thomas. I was planning to anyway.' She smiled at him, feeling more like the lady than she had since the day she'd wed.

'Make sure you do,' he said, then pulled open the door and resumed his seat. 'Next!' he barked.

Rose sat back in her place and looked up to see the redhead, Dorothea, standing in front of her with her husband, Cedric. Cedric doffed his cap and Dorothea curtsied.

'My lady,' she said.

Rose smiled. 'Dorothea. It's been a good harvest, hasn't it?'

Dorothea swallowed, and Rose revelled in her discomfiture. She could read the girl's thoughts as plain as if they'd been written on her face. Ladies didn't converse with peasants like this.

'Yes, m'lady.'

'We managed to store a lot. Enough to keep us going through the dark months and into spring.' Rose never took her gaze off Dorothea's face. 'Do you like spring?'

'Y-yes, m'lady.'

'So do I. Spring always brings the promise of new life and new flowers, doesn't it? Bluebells, daffodils.' Rose's smile grew slightly wider. '*Primroses.*'

The look of sudden dread and horror that flashed across Dorothea's face was sweeter than any honey on Rose's tongue. An upstart Lady of the Manor was still a Lady and too high-ranked to upset.

'You may like to know, Dorothea, that other people aren't quite as fond of primroses as you seem to be,' she added. 'I'm sure you understand me.'

Dorothea bobbed another rapid curtsy. 'Yes, m'lady.'

'Good.' Rose bit back her smile and started counting out the coins. There'd be no mimicking today or tomorrow, she'd wager.

Now all she had to do was find a way to tell Thomas what she had done, and she had a feeling he wasn't going to like it.

CHAPTER 54

'How much?' Thomas choked on his drink.

His talk with William had gone better than he had expected, and he was looking forward to getting as many parchments as he could use and an agreed payment for hides. Payments he needed to finish the mill and to go towards his first year's fee of at least eighty pounds at the university. Life had been good.

The moment he'd arrived home from seeing William, Rose had helped him off with his boots, poured him some warm spiced wine and insisted he settle in his favourite chair by the hearth. It wasn't his birthdate, and he had thought it odd. Now he knew why, and his wine no longer tasted so good.

'How much?' he repeated.

'Only an extra halfpenny for men and a farthing for women,' she said, topping up his drink.

'What in God's name were you thinking of?'

'I had to do something. You said that after we were married, you'd make the peasants respect me and you didn't. When I asked for your help, all I got was a shrug and an order to find my own way. So I did.' She met his stare calmly, unashamed. 'It's not much.'

'It is when you add it up over a year. God's teeth, I'll have nothing left. Do you realise you've just cost me all the extra coins I'd negotiated with William? You can't do things like that without talking to me first. You're the lady, not the lord, and whoever heard of raising peasants' wages? I'm sure it's against the law.' An annoying little voice was starting to whisper that he should have listened to her, should have kept his word, but he'd been busy with his work. Besides, with the amount she talked, he couldn't be expected to listen to everything she said. 'Did Simon know?'

'No, it was all my idea. Simon had nothing to do with it. I'd already made the first payment before he realised.'

'You planned this, didn't you? And come to think of it, it was your idea that I should visit William. *It would be nice to see Will again,* you said. *Think, if you can get him to expand his hide business, you'll have all those extra groats coming your way.* You're a cunning wench.' A lot more cunning than he had realised, despite her smaller brain. 'What you did was wrong, Rose.'

'I know I should have asked you, but I was desperate. I didn't know what else to do.'

He would have said *no* all right. He still couldn't believe that she had paid the peasants more than they were due. What kind of lady was she?

'And are the peasants now on your side?' he demanded, with just a hint of sarcasm.

'Oh, yes. I've had nothing but smiles and curtsies ever since.' Rose topped up his wine and shuffled closer, looking up at him through her lashes. 'Forgive me?'

If she thought feminine wiles would help, she was going to be disappointed. 'Forgiveness doesn't come into this. You deceived me, and there's nothing I can do about it now, as you well know.'

'Typical! I try to make peace, and you stick your nose up and refuse to accept it.' Rose got up, ruffling her skirts straight. 'Well, that's the last time I beg pardon from you!'

'Good, because that means you won't be such an ass again!' He snatched his hat off the bench and stalked out, slamming the door furiously behind him.

Less than a heartbeat later, Rose pulled it open again. 'Haven't you forgotten something?'

He turned, half angry, half bemused. She was leaning against the doorpost, holding his boots with a mischievous smile on her face. 'You'd have trouble walking across the yard in your hose and you've a hole, I can see your big toe.'

He glanced down at his feet, and Rose giggled.

'There's no point getting vexed with each other. Come back in, and I'll darn that hole for you. I don't know what you'd do without me,' she said.

Infuriatingly, neither did he.

They sat in silence as he watched her bone needle weaving in and out of the threads of his hose. Secretly, he admired her cleverness. If she'd been a boy and a noble, she'd have made a fine scholar. Next time, he'd pay more attention, he vowed.

'There! Good as new.' Rose bit the thread off with her teeth and gave him back the hose. 'Am I forgiven?' she said, as he pulled the hose tight and tied them to his waistband.

He wasn't sure about that, but the deed was done, and there was nothing he could do to change it. 'I suppose so but promise me you won't do anything like that again.' He straightened his linen shirt and pulled on his boots.

'I promise, but I was desperate. The peasants will work harder now that they like me.'

'Maybe. Anyway, come with me. I've something for you. Get your cloak.'

'Something for me? Oh, Thomas!'

He wasn't sure that she deserved what he had in mind, but it was impossible to hold a grudge when her face lit up with childlike excitement like that. For all her headstrong ways, Rose was a young lass who loved him. He knew how it felt to love someone.

'Shoes or boots?' she said.

'Boots. We're going by the river.'

Leading the way, he brushed past the overhanging gorse bush and walked on another hundred yards before stopping. Across the river and standing beyond a narrow stone-pack bridge was Simon's house. Built in the same style as his childhood home, it had a neat wattle fence along the front, a straight stone path leading to a wooden front door and two welcoming openings on either side with wooden shutters. A thick head of golden thatch hung almost to the ground.

'Why have we stopped here?' she asked.

'Look to your right. What do you see?'

'Father Rulf's empty cottage. I hope you're not suggesting we move in here, because if you are, you have another think coming!'

Thomas smiled, delighted by her indignant response. Now he had outwitted her for a change.

'Not us, but it would be perfect for Maria and El—'

'Oh, Thomas!' she squealed. 'I love you!'

Before he could stop her, she had her arms around his neck and was hugging him. He hadn't bargained on such a reaction. She was almost crying, and then she looked up and kissed him.

'Think, with them gone, we can sit together by the fire of an evening. And—' she purred— 'we won't have to wait until dark or need the sacking partition anymore.'

Oh Lord, he hadn't thought of that.

She ran a finger down the side of his cheek and he was back in the woods with Rulf, seeing his smile, hearing his voice and feeling the touch of his hand on his face.

He knocked her hand away, and guilt jabbed him at the sight of her hurt expression. It wasn't her fault he was so wicked. He brought her fingers to his lips, pushed all memories into the recesses of his mind and slammed the lid.

'Have you told Maria?' she asked.

'Not yet. I thought we'd do it together.'

'I can't wait,' she said with a wicked smile.

Maria threw down her stitching and ran to him. 'Oh, Thomas! Do you mean it?'

For a second time that day, a woman flung her arms around him, although Maria was different. At least she would never expect anything from him but brotherly affection.

'Of course I do, and you can have your meals here if you wish.' He looked over Maria's shoulder and saw Rose's smirk change to disapproval. He shrugged at her furious shake of her head. 'They've got to eat somewhere. You can't expect Maria to cook, and they won't stay long for meals. Will you?' he asked rather pointedly.

'Are you jesting?' said Maria. 'When we've our own place with no one bossing us around?' She glared at Rose before extricating herself from Thomas and turning her attention on Eleanor. 'Think, El, we'll be free to do as we like!'

Eleanor clapped her hands and laughed delightedly. 'We can dance and sing all evening!'

'We can and we will.'

Rose was happy and Maria was happy. Women, it seemed to him, were easily pleased once you worked out what it was they wanted.

The day had ended better than it had started. Pulling a parchment towards him, Thomas picked up his quill and returned to his work.

CHAPTER 55

It was two weeks before Christmas. Rose ambled towards the last peasant dwelling, pulling her cloak close around her frozen ears. The sun was no more than a milky halo behind a pale sky, and the wind was biting with the promise of colder days to come. She looked for a stone to rest but couldn't see one and leaned against a hedge instead. She was so tired these days.

Looking down at her belly, she placed a gentle hand on the curve. It seemed impossible that another life was growing in there. A June birth, Annie had said, and promptly given her lavender lotion to rub onto her growing bump to ease the birth pains.

Rose tried not to think about that. No matter how much Annie reassured her that not all births were long and painful, she'd heard grim tales of women bleeding to death. She'd never forgotten the day when she was picking daisies to make a chain for her Ma and heard screams coming from inside Matilda's house. She'd covered her ears and ran all the way home. *She's having her first,* Ma had explained. *All women have to go through it. It's God's will whether they survive or He takes them on the birthing bed.*

God's will or not, Rose had vowed there and then she'd never go through that but, like most women, here she was.

She'd known in October when Thomas and Simon had been due to ride to Exeter to register the red cloth with the Guild. She'd only missed one monthly course, but she knew. She hadn't said anything at the time because she wanted to go with them. She'd never been to a city and longed to see the new cathedral and parade the streets as a lady. If Thomas had known she was with child, he might have forbidden it.

To her disappointment, he'd forbidden it anyway, telling her to stay behind and run the estate.

He and Simon had returned in high spirits a week later, flourishing the Guild seal. It had been an exciting moment and an excuse to open a cask of Father Rulf's wine, for the seal guaranteed the quality of their cloth and allowed them to sell in towns as well as markets. Thomas had registered the red cloth as *Chiddleigh Scarlet*. That had made Annie cry. She'd said it was what Lady Joan had called it, and she should have lived to see it.

A few weeks later, Rose and Annie had waved off the wagons loaded with red cloth for the Okewolde Wool Fayre and had waited anxiously for news of the sales. A lot of work and money had been invested in the cloth; it had to sell well.

They needn't have worried. The Belgian merchants had fallen over themselves to buy the Chiddleigh Scarlet, and at top prices too. Thomas's purse was full and, encouraged by the profits, he had bought more blackface sheep from the northern shires and ordered an extra field to be planted with madder to make more red dye for more cloth. Annie had remarked they would need every plant they could get to keep up with the ever-growing flock of sheep, and maybe Thomas would like to contribute to the urine supply because the way things were going, they wouldn't have enough to fix the dye.

Rose smiled to herself. Typical Annie. Gathering her cloak around her, she turned back towards home. Her daily exercise was over, and she was looking forward to putting her feet up with a cup of ale.

On the first day of December, she had told Thomas she was with child. She had expected delight, but the clear relief she'd seen on his face had been a disappointment. Then he'd beamed at her, and her heart had swelled. Maybe he'd just been anxious that she wouldn't be able to produce an heir although he hadn't been exactly proactive in that area himself.

'It's the best news!' he had said, opening his arms to her for the first time. 'You must look after yourself. I trust you've seen Annie and will do everything she says. No more rushing around. You've my son to think about now.'

Dear, impossible Thomas. No kisses or endearing words. She should have been vexed, even a little hurt, but she had long come to realise that he wasn't that sort of a husband.

And if he didn't exactly lavish attention on her, she had nothing worse to reproach him with than the lack of affection. He never beat her or spoke roughly to her. She had made him happy, and that was all that mattered.

Now, with God's blessing, she would survive the birth and give Thomas a healthy son.

CHAPTER 56

30 June 1351

Outside the house, Annie plunged a pile of bloodied cloths into a pail of water, wiped her brow and looked up to see Thomas ambling into the yard.

'Thomas!' She stretched up, hearing her spine crackle pleasantly as she eased the kinks out of it. 'You look as tired as I feel.'

'I've been walking most of the night. I didn't know what else to do.' Thomas hastened forward, staring at the closed door that led into the house. 'Is-is everything alright?'

His stomach gave another wrench to add to the twisted knots he had been suffering since Rose's first birthing pains had started. His future depended on the next few moments, and he could read nothing in Annie's face except complete exhaustion.

'Everything is well. Rose is resting, but mother and child are both healthy; praise God and St Margaret.' Annie looked skywards and crossed herself.

'Praise God indeed!' He ran a hand over his face, weak and giddy with relief. He could never love Rose as a man should love a woman, but she was a superb wife, running the estate and leaving him to do the important work, such as his charts.

'Is it a son?' He barely dared ask because that was the crux of the matter. Only a son could set him free.

'Yes, a healthy boy. Go in and see. You can have a few moments while I sort the swaddling and warm some rose and chamomile tincture for Rose. Go on!' Annie opened the door and pushed him through.

Inside the darkened room, the pungent smell of herbs filled the room. Candles flickered on the table, on the trestle and beside the new bed he'd had made especially for the birthing. Removing his hat and clasping it to his chest, he walked quietly towards the end of the room where Rose was lying with her head sunk into plump feather cushions.

As he drew nearer, she opened her eyes and smiled.

'Thomas, I'm so glad. Come and see.' She patted the fur covers and stretched out her hand to him.

As he took it and sat beside her, he could see damp traces of sweat in her hair, her face pale and strained, but as she lowered her eyes to the newborn child lying by her side, they shone with motherly pride.

'Your son,' she said, 'just as you wanted.'

He followed her gaze. The boy had wisps of fair hair and long lashes. His eyes were light brown and his cheeks flushed a healthy pink. He couldn't help it, his eyes welled.

His son. The innocent key to his future.

'You can pick him up if you want,' said Rose.

He did want. He wanted to feel him, touch him, breathe in the smell of him, look into his eyes and marvel at the miracle he had helped to create.

She picked up the child and gently placed him in his arms. Fighting his tears of pride, Thomas took in every detail, from the perfectly formed hands and toes to the two miniature ears and the tiny button nose.

Gently, he stroked the boy's head. 'He's perfect,' he said, turning to her and smiling.

Rose touched his arm, and for the first time, he felt a connection.

'Thank you.' He swallowed. 'I shall name him James, after my grandfather.' He looked down at the child. 'And I shall make an estate for you to be proud of, little James.'

'Not just you, both of us,' she said, with a touch of her old spirit. 'Together, for James.'

Their eyes met in a magical moment.

And Thomas knew where he belonged, and it wasn't in Oxford.

CHAPTER 57

October 1351

'Ugh!' Thomas dropped the wooden spoon into his bowl and pushed it away. 'I don't know what Janet's done to these chickpeas, but there's a lot of spice in them. I'm sorry, Simon; you came here for a decent midday meal and this is what you get.' He took a good gulp of ale.

'It's a little strong,' Simon replied, 'but with a cup of ale, it's tolerable.'

Rose shrugged. 'She's using up Father Rulf's spices before they go stale. I like it.' To make her point, she wiped her bowl clean with her fingers.

'Well, I don't. I could taste nothing but ginger, and it's burnt my tongue,' said Thomas.

'Ginger's good for you; it cleanses the bad humours. You should eat it.' Rose pushed the bowl towards him.

'I'll take my chances with the humours.' He pushed it back. 'And tell Janet to stop putting spice into everything. I'd rather waste them. After all, they didn't cost anything.'

'Of course they did,' Rose said. 'Father Rulf must have paid for them, and spices are expensive.'

If only you knew. Thomas smiled to himself. How long ago it seemed now. For a fleeting moment, he wondered what Rulf was doing.

He glanced at James, asleep in his crib, and smiled with pride. What would Rulf say if he could see Thomas now, a married man with a son? He'd throw back his head and laugh in disbelief.

He missed their conversations more than he liked to admit. Rose was only too willing to sit and chat of an evening, but she wasn't educated, she didn't understand the stars, and her idea of a debate was to raise her voice and get vexed.

Sometimes, in the quiet of the night, he allowed himself to think about what might have been, but one look at James and he knew he'd made the right decision.

'I swear James grows bigger every day,' said Rose, giving the crib a gentle rock. 'And Thomas swears the boy watches him.'

'He does!' Thomas protested. 'And he understands every word I say as well.'

'Give him a chance, he's only four months old. Now, to business over a warm wine, before he wakes and screams the place down,' said Rose.

'Where's the maid?' said Thomas, reaching out and running a hand over James's hair.

'Busy weaving. The cloth sales are in a few weeks and I've every woman on the looms. Leave James be, will you; I'm enjoying the peace. Honestly, Simon, the way he fusses over him, anyone would think he was his mother.' Rose laughed. 'Now, is the millwheel mended and working?' She pushed the bowls to one side, poured warmed wine into three cups and handed them around.

Simon nodded. 'It is, and we've picked up trade from Holdesworthe and surrounding villages, though access is a problem. Folks have to come over the hill on nothing more than sheep tracks, which will be impassable come the dark months.'

'Then we'll build a road wide enough for carts. We can clear the ling and stones and make a route following the curve of the hill,' said Thomas, leaning on the table with his hands clasped before him.

'We'll need channels across the path, like the ones on Six Mile Hill, to stop the water rushing down and creating ruts.' Simon helped himself to another cup of wine, his enjoyment plain on his face.

'If we're going to all that trouble, we should build ovens to bake bread,' said Rose. 'Not just for our people, but for the folks coming to the mill.'

'That's a good idea,' Thomas agreed. 'And while we're on the subject of building, Rose and I have been discussing this place. We'd like to have an outside kitchen, like Mama had, and turn this room into a grand hall.'

Deep down, he wasn't sure about this. It would cost a fortune, but Rose wanted it, and he was learning that the way to a peaceful life was to let Rose have her way.

'And an upstairs chamber,' she interjected. 'Don't forget that.'

'An upstairs as well? You are getting ambitious. You'll be holding banquets next,' said Simon.

'We might,' Rose said, glancing at Thomas.

'It's all Rose's idea, but do we have the men to do it?' he said.

Simon stroked his beard thoughtfully. 'As far as general labourers go, yes, but you'll need to hire master carpenters and, assuming you intend to build in stone, stonemasons. It will take a long time and it won't be cheap.'

'Of course we'll use stone. It's Thomas's manorial seat; he needs a house reflecting his growing status. And

Maria still has to find a husband. There's enough in the coffers to make a start.'

Thomas nodded. 'I also need to show that James is a good prospect. I intend to arrange a good marriage into a titled family for him.'

Simon raised his eyebrows. 'You've changed your tune. Was a day when we couldn't get you to look at your purse, let alone open it. All you were interested in was your work. Are you still doing that, or have you finished?'

'It's finished, as far as it goes.' With a pang, Thomas glanced to his chest, where his scrolls lay neatly tied and untouched.

Rose laughed. 'One day, you can teach James, then I'll have two of you scratching out triangles.'

Thomas smiled. He was looking forward to that. He could see the pair of them leaning over the table as he explained the charts and taught his son Latin and Greek. Later, when James was older, they would sit together gazing at the night sky debating theories before James went to Oxford.

'He may not want to learn,' Simon said. 'I didn't.'

Of course James would want to learn; the boy was his son.

'First, I want my house,' said Rose, rising to refill the wine jug. 'We also talked about building a weaving barn where we could have all the looms together instead of scattered around the cottages. And the other thing to agree on is whether to build corn driers for the next harvest.'

'We can't do it all at once, but the corn driers are essential in case of a wet harvest—' Simon began.

'We've got visitors!' Rose interrupted, peering through the opening. 'Thomas? Are you expecting anyone?'

'No. We never get visitors. We've been here three years, and no one has come.'

'Well, they have now and judging by the outriders and banners, they're important.' Rose smoothed her kirtle and ran her hands through her hair. 'God's bones, I'm a mess! Where's my veil?'

Thomas went over and peered through the opening. A procession was entering the yard, led by two noblemen mounted on a matching pair of fine chestnut horses. Behind them came two outriders, one holding a yellow and red flag with a family crest in the centre, and the other, a red and yellow pennant. Bringing up the rear, two peasants were driving a horse and wagon.

'What do they want?' Thomas wondered.

'Lost, probably,' said Simon, joining him.

They watched the two men dismount. The taller, younger one nonchalantly removed his gauntlets whilst casting an eye around the yard. He nudged his older companion and said something, and the pair of them burst out laughing. Whoever they were, Thomas didn't like the look of them.

'I don't recognise the family crest.' He turned to Simon. 'Do you?'

'No, but they're high ranking. Look at those swords and the jewelled rings on their fingers and the size of that gold shoulder buckle!' Simon sighed. 'Wish I could afford one like that.'

So did he, but right now his mind was more about getting rid of them as fast as possible. Noble visits could last for days, and in the next day or two – if his calculations were correct – he would witness the most important event of his life: a total eclipse. It was a once-in-a-lifetime opportunity, and he didn't intend to miss a moment of it pandering to wealthy visitors.

Thomas reached for his hat and sighed. 'I'd better find out what they want.'

'You can't greet them looking like that. Your tunic's got stains down the front; give it here,' said Rose, holding out a hand.

He obliged and went to his chest, where he rummaged amongst his clothes and took out a jupon.

'No, not that; we haven't time to do the laces. Wear your blue tunic and put on the wide belt, the one with the gold buckle. Make haste! They'll be knocking on the door any moment,' said Rose from where she was wrestling with her veil.

It was pointless to argue, so he delved into his chest again while Rose scrunched the stained tunic into a ball and stuffed it behind some pots. She shoved the dirty bowls into the swine bucket and pushed it under the shelves before hastily spreading the floor rushes around with her foot.

'I told Agnes to change these yesterday; they're filthy. What will they make of us? We'll have to offer them food and drink, but God's teeth, what am I going to give them? We have Father Rulf's wine, I suppose and we can use the pewter goblets; if I can find them.'

Rummaging amongst an assortment of pots, bowls, odd piles of wool waiting to be spun and discarded candle ends, Rose found the goblets, blew out the cobwebs, and hastily wiped the insides with a corner of her surcoat.

'Stop panicking.' Thomas pulled his tunic over his head. 'I doubt they're looking for us; they're probably lost, like Simon said. I'll find out who they are, we'll give them a quick drink and send them on their way.' He tightened the buckle on his belt and walked over to the door.

His hand was poised on the latch when two firm raps came from the outside. Rose wiped her hands on the back of her kirtle, smoothed the folds, and after a final fiddle with her veil, nodded. Thomas fixed a smile on his face and opened the door.

In spite of the pride he took in his tunic and belt, the two men standing on his threshold made him feel like the scruffiest peasant on the estate. Their rich blue and green mantels were well-tailored and lined with expensive squirrel fur, their cream linen houppelandes gathered with belts studded with sapphires and emeralds, and their boots were made of the finest calf leather.

Thomas swallowed. 'sires, be welcome,' he said, bowing low.

The taller one nodded and removed his blue velvet hat, revealing red hair cut neatly to the shoulder. Thomas resisted the urge to flatten his own tangled mass.

'God keep you. I seek Lord Thomas de Chiddleigh,' said the taller one, eyeing him from top to toe.

Looking up at the imposing figure, Thomas wished he was taller and had worn his jupon.

'And may God keep you, sire. I am Lord Thomas. May I enquire who…' his voice trailed off as the man visibly stiffened, his green eyes narrowing to slits.

'Sir Percy de Gravesmire, Earl of Devonshire. This is my uncle, Sir Gorvenal.' He indicated the older, stouter man with a round ruddy complexion standing next to him.

The Earl of Devonshire! The most wealthy and influential person in the shire had come to see him, but why? The previous earl had been a cunning old man who was known as the Fox, and his son didn't look any more pleasant.

'I take it you do have servants to see to our horses?' The earl's narrow green eyes stared accusingly under arched red eyebrows.

No, he didn't. Well, not exactly; Jarin would be in the smithy, and he could do it. Before he had a chance to call for him, however, the earl dismissed the situation with a sigh and a wave of his gauntlets.

'I thought not. No matter, my men will see to it.' He clicked his fingers, and like two obedient hounds, two men were off the wagon and stood before their master with their heads bowed and their caps in their hands.

'Where are your stables?' The earl turned back.

'Behind the smithy, and we've plenty of hay and corn. Prithee, my Lord Courtesy—my lord, enter and take some wine.' Thomas stood back, wishing his grand hall was already built as he allowed his betters to go before him.

The earl and Sir Gorvenal left their swords by the door and stood in the middle of the room, the earl's eyes taking in everything from the central stone hearth to the shelves in one corner, the back wall littered with overflowing baskets to the barrels of wine and ale at one end, and finally, to the table in front of the open shutters.

He sniffed. 'I see you choose a humble life. But then, we can't all live in castles, can we?' He gave a few flicks of his gauntlet over Thomas's chair before taking his place at the head of the table.

Rose quickly brought the only other chair for the earl's uncle, who nodded his thanks with more geniality than his nephew had shown. Thomas grabbed a stool and sat at the opposite end, looking up at his visitors from his lowly seat.

'May I introduce my wife, Lady Rose?' he said, as Rose poured wine into the goblets before perching on the end of the bench. 'And this is Simon de Perceaux, my bailiff.'

The earl nodded, swilled the wine around his goblet, wrinkled his nose and ventured a sip.

'Surprisingly good,' he said, helping himself to a honeyed damson from a dish Rose had hastily set in front of him. 'But surely you've not come so low for this to be your manorial house?'

'We came here to escape the Pestilence.' Thomas tried to keep the defence out of his voice and failed. 'The original manor was destroyed by fire.' *Mama*. If he could have had one wish granted, it would be that his mother had lived to hold her grandson.

'Ah, and you didn't have the funds to return and rebuild?' A demeaning smile played about the earl's thin lips. 'These are trying times for us all. I understand.'

Thomas doubted if the earl understood much more than his own coffers, but knew better than to say so. Feeling decidedly uncomfortable, he wiped his hands down his hose and fidgeted with his belt, which, in his haste, he'd buckled too tightly. Sitting in his place at the head of his table was the most wealthy and important man in the shire. He could hardly demand an explanation for the man's presence, even though he was bursting his brains trying to work out what he could be doing there.

The earl finished his wine, held out his goblet for a nonexistent servant to refill it, then helped himself from the jug.

Thomas fumed. The earl was deliberately embarrassing him, playing with him as a fisherman reeling in a fish, but why? He glanced at Simon who shrugged and studied the ceiling.

The earl and his uncle politely commented on the recent good harvest and the state of the tracks. Thomas let Simon handle the small talk; he needed to think. Had the earl heard of the Chiddleigh Scarlet cloth? Did he want to strike a business deal, or was it the secret of the red dye he was after? He would never give him that, but the earl owned thousands of sheep across the shire. A business arrangement with him would be worth a lot of money. He could dye the earl's wool, maybe set up a partnership? Some said the earl had the ear of the king.

The king! Thomas's mind sped into action. His Chiddleigh Scarlet could end up on King Edward's back. Word would spread through the court. Nobles were fashion-conscious these days; it could become the latest fancy. He could earn a fortune, and there might even be a place for James in the royal court.

'Have you thought of rebuilding? A noble must have a grand hall. It indicates his status, and you can't entertain without one.' The earl replaced his goblet and folded his hands comfortably across his stomach. 'I was with Lord Sedworth only last week — are you acquainted with him?'

'No, but I intend to build — '

The earl smiled knowingly. 'No, I thought not. No matter, Lord Sedworth has built a new hall. It's quite magnificent. You really should see it; it would give you a few ideas.'

Thomas didn't care what Lord Sedworth had built. The longer the earl sat in his chair, the more he disliked him. Looking at the earl's foxy eyes and mean mouth and given his predecessor's reputation, perhaps going into business with him wasn't such a good idea.

Then again, the earl had influence everywhere. Influence enough to block Thomas's trade, turn the merchants against him, and maybe even persuade the guild to withdraw the seal. He'd be ruined. A shiver of dread ran up and down his spine. He needed to tread carefully; it would be foolish to cross swords with such a man.

Rose placed another bowl of honeyed damsons on the table and returned to he end of the bench. She held her head high, her face as regal as any princess, but her hands were clasping and unclasping restlessly in her lap. Pray God she wouldn't speak boldly and give away her birth. That would shame them both.

Thomas watched his visitors eating and drinking their way through his stores. If the earl didn't say what he wanted soon, there'd be no damsons or wine left for the dark months. Should he ask the reason for his visit? This house might be humble compared to the earl's estates and Lord Whatever's new hall, but it was his house, and he was still master of it. He ran a nervous hand around the back of his neck.

'Thomas? I said, would you like more wine?' The jug was poised in Rose's hand. He nodded. He had a feeling he might need it.

Rose refilled the jug from the barrel at the end of the room. In the lull, he watched a drop of wax slide down the side of the candle. The earl smiled over his goblet from the other end of the table, watching him like a hawk targeting a mouse.

Putting his goblet firmly back on the table, the earl leaned back. 'My steward was at the Okewolde fayre a few weeks back. He reported the sales of a new cloth, the Chiddleigh Scarlet. It seems the merchants paid high prices for it. It is yours, I believe.' He stretched out his legs in front of him, his hands resting over his belt.

Thomas's heart fluttered. So it *was* the cloth he was after. He sat up straight and lifted his chin. 'Indeed it is. I intend to expand my flocks, plant more madder, install more looms—' A sharp kick under the table stopped him. 'Just ideas, it's early days,' he said weakly, avoiding Simon's warning stare.

'I'm sure. I sent my man to the guild to trace your whereabouts. I've been looking for you. You'd better read these.' The earl held out his hand to Sir Gorvenal, who delved into a leather bag and produced three parchments.

Thomas wiped the sweat from his palms. If these were contracts, the earl must be keen.

'The Favian one first,' said the earl, his hand still waiting. 'You can see by the two red ribbons bound with the civil law notary's seal that it's a legal document.'

They *were* contracts! Thomas forced to turn his grin into a serious expression as he scanned it, checking the bottom for the earl's signature.

'I don't understand. This is signed Favian de Riddleham. Who is he? I don't know anyone by that name.'

'He is, or was, the Earl of Barcombe's nephew. Read the contract. It explains everything.' The earl held his hands across his lap and stared at the roof with an air of boredom.

Thomas pulled the candle close. As he read, his hopes melted into disbelief that gripped his stomach and turned his mind to ice.

He read it again. 'It says here that Mama – I mean, Lady Joan – sold all the Chiddleigh lands to this Favian de Riddleham, and that he leased them back to her on tenure. That was—' his gaze flicked up to the top of the parchment—

'on 12th August 1348, just before the Pestilence came to the manor. That can't be right. Why would she do that?'

'Who knows? But it's definitely her seal and all perfectly legal,' said the earl, examining the fingernails on his right hand.

1348. He'd been in Tavistoke at that time. He turned to Simon. 'Do you know anything about this?'

Simon shifted in his seat. "Not really. My father, Carac, was Lady Joan's bailiff; I had very little to do with it. I know she relied upon his advice for many things.' He hesitated and cleared his throat. 'I've never seen that particular document, but I have seen others.'

Thomas frowned. He felt like the only person in the room who didn't know the plot of the play. 'What others?'

Simon licked his lips. 'In the beginning of '48, not long after your father died, I remember Lady Joan showing my father a letter from my Lord Courtesy's father —' he glanced at the earl with a respectful nod — 'the then Earl of Devonshire, and also some contracts she'd found in your father's coffer.'

'Did you read the letter? What did it say?' Thomas's heart pounded as he edged forward on his seat. Was he finally about to discover what his mother had meant by certain facts becoming known?

Simon fidgeted with his sleeve. 'I did read it and — Thomas, there's no point in going over what it said now.'

'There's every point if it concerns me! What did the letter say?'

Simon bit his lip and sighed heavily. 'God's bones, I wish I'd never mentioned it. If you must know, the letter was written to your father after the earl returned from the wars in France.'

'And?' Thomas pressed.

'And it stated that your brother Richard fled the battlefield at Crecy against orders to advance. As a result of his cowardice—'

'No! Richard wouldn't have deserted. He was brave. His only dream was to be a knight, you know that.'

'I'm sorry, I only know what was in the letter. Because of Richard's cowardice, the earl denounced the Chiddleigh family as traitorous and reclaimed the Knights Fees lands that he'd previously given to your father.'

Thomas shook his head, baffled. The words *coward* and *Richard* didn't belong together; Richard had always been the bold, strong knight. All these years he'd believed in his brother; envied him, aspired to be like him, compared himself to him, when all the time he was nothing but a weak coward?

'There must be some mistake. Where's the proof?'

The earl looked Thomas straight in the eye. 'There was no mistake. My father was on the battlefield and saw Richard fleeing for the trees. He wasn't the only witness; I was on the hill watching the battle with King Edward and my Lords Norfolk and Halifax. We all saw your brother running away faster than a whipped cur, and the king was furious. After the battle, Richard's own men found him hiding in the bushes.'

'He probably fled because he was wounded.'

The earl raised his eyebrows. 'Do you doubt the word of your king?'

'No,' Thomas said hastily. He didn't need a charge of treason to add to his troubles. 'Was Richard alive when he was found?'

'If he was, his men probably killed him. It would be no more than he deserved. It's one thing for peasants to be craven brutes, but you expect more courage from a knight.'

Richard, cowering before his men? It wasn't a pretty image. 'That doesn't explain this Favian man, though.'

Simon cleared his throat, glancing to the earl for permission. 'There was more in the letter. The earl had written to the Earl of Barcombe, Favian's uncle, urging him to disassociate himself from the Chiddleigh family. The earl owned your Ashetyne lands; your father was only managing them.'

'We noble families of the highest ranks do well to keep favour with the king. Your mother's situation was unfortunate but there was nothing else my father could have done. You understand, of course?' The earl finished with his nails, looked up and smiled.

He understood perfectly. The higher ranks looked after themselves, courted favour with the king and never gave an ass's tail about anyone else.

'And the contracts?' he asked, keeping his voice as level as he could.

'From a money lender in Exeter. Sir John had been borrowing heavily for many years. He owed a great deal,' said Simon.

'Why didn't you tell me any of this? When we discussed our plans, you never mentioned Richard or the debts.'

'What was I supposed to say? Thomas, hail, God save you. The harvest's looking good this year, and work on the mill's progressing nicely. Oh, by the way, your brother was a coward and your father a penniless sot? Besides, the southern lands are too far off to be of any use to us here. I knew nothing about Favian whatshisname or the tenure; I swear on my soul I didn't. I only knew of the letter about Richard and that the debts existed. I assumed you did too.'

The earl coughed. 'It seems your bailiff knows more about your affairs than you do. Not a wise way to run an estate. I find it pays to know everything about everyone. There is also this.' He passed Thomas a second parchment.

Thomas was still reeling and turned to hide his trembling hands. Quickly, he scanned the parchment. 'This appears to be a promissory note signed by a Peyton de Riddleham and made to Percy de Gravesmire, Earl of Devonshire for the Chiddleigh lands.' He looked through the flickering candlelight to the earl's shadowy figure at the end of the table. 'That's you.'

The earl held his two hands together at the fingertips and nodded. 'Precisely.'

'I don't understand,' said Thomas. 'I thought Favian de Riddleham bought the lands.'

'He did. Favian bought the lands, allowing Lady Joan to clear her debts. He then, very generously in my opinion, leased them back to her. She would have done well to marry him; the Riddlehams own vast lands and have the wealth that comes with them. It would have solved her problem nicely.' The earl shot a smile down the length of the table. 'Regrettably, Favian died in the Pestilence and his estate went to his cousin, Peyton.' He leaned back and sighed dramatically. 'Peyton was a drunk and a gambler. Unfortunately, he wasn't as skilled at dice as he thought he was. It was during a game of hazard that I accepted that note, and with a throw of two fives, I acquired the Chiddleigh lands. I have the legal documents here.' He offered Thomas the third and final parchment.

Thomas took it and read it, his mind spinning. It was as the earl said; the sly man in front of him owned all the Chiddleigh lands to the north.

He had nothing left. James, his heir had nothing.

'My uncle keeps my accounts and has tallied the accrued monies owed for the tenure.' Sir Gorvenal again searched through his bag and produced a scroll tied with red ribbon which he passed to Thomas.

Slowly, Thomas unrolled the parchment, his eyes widening as he read down the long list of figures.

'You'll note the annual tenure has been due on Michaelmas Day since August 1348, when the original agreement between Lady Joan and Favian de Riddleham was signed.'

'The Pestilence stopped everything!' Thomas slapped the scroll angrily, his voice rising. 'The sums mentioned here are outrageous!'

The earl shrugged. 'Business is business, and the figures include the penalties and added interest for non-payments.' He flashed another smile down the table. 'That's why I'm here. To collect my dues.' The earl flicked an imaginary piece of dirt from his hose. 'But the northern land is of no use to me, so if you wish to discuss repurchasing it, I'm open to sensible offers.'

The sanctimonious devil. How he would like to wipe that smile off his evil, pinched little face, but that would only get him into more trouble and a cell in Lyndeford Gaol.

'If it's of no use to you, why don't you hand it back?' Thomas demanded. 'How do I know you haven't falsified these documents?'

'Why in God's name should I do that? The lands are all but worthless. Frankly, I shall be only too delighted to get rid of them, but business is business and a debt has to be paid.' The earl sat with his hands across his stomach, smiling at Thomas with the confidence of the victor.

It was checkmate. There was nothing Thomas could do. He glanced over to James – dear, innocent James – asleep in his crib and felt sick. He had failed his son before he'd even started.

'This is a shock. I need a moment to think,' said Thomas, and rose to his feet with as much composure as he could muster. He bowed to his guests, picked up his hat with a trembling hand, and walked out, closing the door behind him.

Leaning against the wall, he ran his hands down his face and let out a long sigh. Only this morning, he'd been on top of life's mountain with a glowing future spread out below him for himself and his child. Now, everything had slipped through his fingers so fast he could barely keep up.

Richard, the debts, losing his lands and so much money owed to the earl it would take every penny he possessed to repay it. Rose could forget about her new house, Maria would end up an old maid, and James's future looked as bleak as his own.

The door opened, and Simon came out to join him. 'Thomas? The earl is waiting for your answer. You'll have to pay him his dues, or he could take you to court.'

'You think I don't know that?'

'Can you pay?'

Thomas gave him a scathing look. 'What do you think? I might have enough to settle the debt, but there's no way I can buy back the lands. The man's as wily as a fox and insufferable. He's enjoying this.'

So many secrets. Was that what Mama had meant; the debts?

There was only one person who might be able to answer that question, and that was Annie. Thomas glanced at

Simon. 'Tell the earl that he'll have his answer by the end of the day, but I need to check some things first.'

Simon frowned. 'Check what?'

'Just do it, Simon.' His life might be in ruins, but he was still the lord. This time, he wouldn't be put off. Annie had known his Mama better than anybody, and it was time this secret was brought to light.

CHAPTER 58

'Annie! Annie, I need to speak to you!'

Annie heard Thomas's angry voice booming across the yard. Hastily, she spooned the last of the lotion into the jar, wiped her hands and hurried out of her linhay.

'Whatever's the matter? I was on my out. Eliza trod on a nail and needs some mugwort cream for her foot.'

'Eliza and her foot will have to wait,' Thomas snapped. 'We need to talk.'

'Not trouble I hope. We'd better go inside.' Without waiting for an answer, she led him into her linhay. Whatever had happened, by the look on Thomas's furious face, it must be bad. 'Sit down, have some clover tonic, and tell me what's got you so vexed,' she said, pulling an empty half-barrel from under the bench.

'I don't need to sit down, and I don't want your tonic. And I'm more than vexed; I'm shocked, I'm angry, I'm…' There were no more superlatives to describe it. He started pacing, and anxious for her pots, Annie patted the barrel.

'Sit down or you'll knock something over.'

Thomas didn't sit, but he did stop pacing. 'Do you know who's sitting in my chair at the head of my table right now? The Earl of Devonshire, that's who! And he just told me I don't own the house he's sitting in! More than that, I don't even own the lands we've been working for the last few years.' He flung himself onto the barrel, glaring at her.

'That can't be right,' she said.

'It is, and he's got the documents to prove it. Apparently, Mama sold the Chiddleigh lands to a Favian de Riddlecombe to clear my father's debts. Favian leased them back to her, but he died, leaving the tenure to his cousin who gambled it away to the earl, who's currently drinking my wine and telling me he owns everything I possess. But you knew all that already, didn't you?'

Good Lord, he was out of his mind! 'How was I supposed to know any of that? I have no dealings with the likes of an earl.'

'Mama would have told you.'

There it was again, secrets haunting her as they had for most of her life. Yes, Joan had told her things, and yes, there were things that Thomas didn't know, but that hadn't been one of them.

'She didn't and even if what the earl says is true, you've other lands,' she said.

'Oh no, I don't. There's a letter from the old Earl of Devonshire who was at the Battle of Crecy with Richard. All the talk of Richard dying in glory defending his king was lies. Richard was a coward who deserted his men. Can you believe it?' Thomas ran his fingers savagely through his hair. 'My big, brave brother! If it wasn't so tragic, it would be funny.' He laughed a maniacal laugh. 'Thanks to Richard, I've lost all my other lands too.'

He was bordering on hysterical. She poured a cup of clover tonic and thrust it at him.

'Drink this before you have a seizure.' Her eyes skipped along her shelves. Where had she put the silver cramp ring that protected against such fits? It wasn't on any of the shelves.

Thomas drank the clover tonic and slumped, looking utterly defeated.

'Thomas—' she began.

Don't you understand what this means? I've lost my estate. I've no home, nothing. nothing! We are all at the mercy of that...that devil's fox in there. And you've been keeping it all a secret from me. What else have you been keeping from me, Annie?'

Annie reached into her apron pocket for her kerchief and wiped her eyes. Crying wouldn't help either of them. 'On my immortal soul, I knew nothing about the lands or the debts. Your Mama never mentioned them. We talked, yes, but we talked about us, not estate business.'

His eyes were distant. He was too swept up in his own grief to be listening. 'Damn my brother! He was trouble as a boy and he's still causing trouble from the grave. He was an arrogant bully. To think I looked up to him all this time. What a fool I was.'

'How dare you speak of Richard like that! It's wicked to say such things.' She fought her tears and her voice softened. 'He looked so handsome on his white horse when he left for France.'

Such memories, wonderful memories but the moment had come; the moment she had always known would come. It wasn't the time and place she would have picked, but that was her own fault; she'd had plenty of times and places before when she could have told him. She felt weak and tired as she looked down at her hands. Once, on a festival long ago, they'd been smooth and beautiful and she'd been a maid with her whole life ahead of her, secure in the invincibility of youth. Now they were lined, showing all of her thirty-five summers.

Slowly, she lifted her head and looked with pity into Thomas's eyes. How could she add to the anguish she saw there? What good would it do after all these years?

But Thomas was demanding to know, and she had promised Joan that she would tell Thomas the truth one day. The day was now.

'You're right,' she said. 'There is something else.'

The smell of the linhay filled her nose, the distant sound of hammering rang from the forge, and someone was talking outside in the yard, but the words were lost to her. She'd carried this burden for so long. It would be a relief to finally set it down.

A tear trickled down her cheek. She brushed it away, raised her chin and looked straight into his eyes. 'Richard wasn't your brother.'

There it was, after all this time, laid out for him to see. She bowed her head and let the tears fall.

'Of course he was. Unless—' He went white, then set his jaw. 'No. No, Mama would never—'

'Not your mother. *Me.* I was Richard's mother.'

'*You*? You and Papa? No, my father was no saint, but he wasn't the kind of brute who'd betray his wife with a peasant maid.'

'You're right. He was many things, but he wasn't Richard's father.'

'Then who was?'

'A village lad.' She wouldn't tell him that Richard's father had been Sir John's cousin, Aldred of Combe Hide. She wouldn't tell him that Aldred had forced her. She could at least spare him that. 'Richard was *my* son and no matter what people said about him, I'm proud to have been his mother.'

Thomas stared at her in shock and bewilderment. 'I don't understand. Richard was the eldest son. How? You must have tricked Mama to save your shame. How? How did you do it?'

She could easily say that she'd switched Joan's stillborn child for her own and save Thomas further pain, but that would spin into more lies. She was tired of lying. 'I didn't trick her. She knew. She always knew.'

'I don't believe you! She'd have been denying my birthright as the heir and favoured son. She wouldn't have done that to me. She loved me.'

She felt his pain just as she had felt the pain of handing over her child. 'It wasn't like that. We were both no more than girls. Your Mama wasn't to know that she'd have a true son one day. And by the time you were born, it was too late; Richard was already your brother.'

'If you didn't trick her, then why did she do it?'

She could see him wrestling with the revelations. How she wished she could make this easier for him but she couldn't. 'Joan's first child was a difficult birthing and was stillborn.' She wiped her eyes. 'Your Mama was exhausted and slept,' she said simply. 'I feared for her life and stayed with her. My son, Richard, was two weeks old. I was holding him when your Papa came into the bedchamber. He saw me and assumed the baby was his.' She took a deep breath, fighting the memories that had haunted her ever since. 'He demanded I give him his son. I was a peasant and terrified of him. I couldn't tell him the boy was mine, born out of wedlock. The shame. He'd have thrown me and Peter off the estate. We'd have been paupers, begging for our food in the streets. I was trapped and frightened, so I did what all peasants must do: I obeyed my lord, and I gave him my son.'

It sounded so simple now, but it had been the worst moment of her life. She sobbed again, just as she had all those years ago.

'Then you did trick her! Mama believed Richard was hers, just like Papa did.'

'No! Joan knew her baby had died. Don't you see, it was too late? What would your father have done if he'd discovered our deception? Joan knew about my child, and she'd helped me to conceal it. She'd protected me. What would have happened to her? Your Papa could be a cruel man. She was as frightened as I was. We'd been through so much together, and we agreed it was best for both of us if she kept Richard as her own. All we had to do was keep it our secret.' Her voice softened and she stared at her hands in her lap. 'May God forgive me, I have paid for it every day of my life. Can you imagine how I felt every time I saw Richard? How I longed to hold him? And later, when you were born, the guilt every time I saw you.'

Slowly, like a candle flame growing and giving light, things became clear to him. 'That's why you were always with us. It wasn't to look after me, as Mama had said. You were there for Richard. It was always about Richard.'

'What could I have done? You've had a taste of the peasant life that first winter. How much worse would it have been without shelter or food. I know Peter can be a nuddlejade at times, but he's still my brother. I couldn't punish him for my sin.'

Thomas forced himself to look at her. She was hurting as much as he was. Rulf's face danced in front of him. Their fear of discovery had been no different to hers.

'You were in a difficult position. You were terrified of my Papa, of the shame, of people's condemnation and of being cast out or worse if your secret became known.'

He swallowed. 'I can sympathise with that better than you know. I forgive you but I cannot forgive Mama.'

He rose to his feet, feeling the bruising hurt like someone squeezing every drop of blood from his heart. Turning on his heel, he walked away.

He followed the river upstream, his mind trying to make sense of it all. Reaching his rock, he sat with his head in his hands staring into the deep dark stillness of the middle river.

The worst part was his Mama's treachery. Mama, the most important person in his life, whom he had loved and worshipped, had deceived him for his whole life. She'd known that he, not Richard, was the rightful heir, and yet she'd stood by and let his father despise him.

Had she felt guilty? If she had, she'd never shown it. Had she loved him? He'd thought she had, but was that just an act? She'd acted well enough with Richard.

The hurt gouged a hole in his very soul until there was nothing left. He bit his lip and dug his nails into his palms. He wouldn't cry. She wasn't worth his tears.

When he thought of the torment he'd gone through to keep his final vow to her to be a fair and just lord, all because he'd loved her and wanted to make her proud.

Tears burned his eyes and he bit harder. God, how he hated her! Heartfelt sobs worked their way from the depths until they burst out of his throat, and he cried until he was nothing but an empty shell.

Where did all this leave him? Was he still a lord? He no longer had an estate. At best, he could be a tenant farmer to the earl, toiling in the fields to keep from poverty and paying his dues every Michaelmas, lining up with his peasants, cap in hand. The thought brought bile to his throat.

And James. What would become of him? All the plans he'd had for him were gone. He could never afford to send him to the monks at Tavistoke, let alone Oxford. His son would never rub shoulders with the king. James would be a pauper, scratching a living with a failure for a father. Would his son hate him? He couldn't bear that.

He was alone, save for Rose. Good, reliable, and capable Rose. If they were to survive, the will and strength would have to come from her, for he had no stomach for it.

Wiping his face with his sleeve, he stared into the dark heavy water below. There was no dancing dragonfly today. He doubted there ever would be again.

'My young friend, you look as though you would like to jump in and drown. Trust me, it isn't deep enough.'

Thomas lifted his head towards the voice.

Standing on the path, not ten paces away, was Rulf.

CHAPTER 59

The birds stopped singing, the river stopped flowing and the scent of the bushes ceased to fill the air.

Rulf smiled. It was as though he had never left, and Thomas walked into his open arms and sank into their comfort.

Together, in silent union, Rulf stroked his hair. Thomas lifted his head and brushed Rulf's lips. As he did, the flame within him flickered and burst into life.

'Rulf, I—'

Rulf laid a finger against Thomas's lips. 'Later. Don't spoil the moment.'

Thomas drank in every inch of him: his sparkling eyes, the creases when he smiled, his long lashes, the very scent of him, all just as he remembered.

Rulf took his hand and led him to the rock. They sat swinging their legs over the edge of the river like two young boys, content in each other's company whilst a dragonfly darted backwards and forwards in an iridescent green streak along the water's edge.

'I've missed you,' said Rulf at last.

'And I you. I can't believe it's really you.'

Silence descended, but it was a comfortable silence. There was no need for words. Just being with Rulf was all he needed.

Finally, Rulf spoke. 'There were times on the road to Oxford when I nearly turned back.'

'I prayed you would. I'd go out and stare at the track every day, but you never came. In the end, I went to see William to make my peace.'

'How is he?'

It was surreal, talking so calmly of William so that anyone seeing him would never guess his inner turmoil. He wondered if Rulf would suggest they go to the cave. He'd like that.

'Doing well. He's married now and seeing him so content made me envious. When I returned, I took your advice.' Thomas cast an anxious glance sideways.

Rulf's eyes sparkled with amusement. 'I hope it was good advice. It isn't always.'

Thomas took a deep breath, keeping his eyes fixed on the water. 'I married Rose. I only did it to get an heir, and thank God, Rose gave me a son for I didn't relish going to her bed.' His words tumbled out.

Rulf threw back his head and laughed. 'Good for you! Another duty ticked off the list.'

'You don't mind? I feel like I've betrayed you.'

'If you'd said you preferred her touch to mine, I'd be most hurt. But you're a lord. Of course you had to get an heir.'

'I'd given up all thoughts of Oxford and believed myself a happily married man, but one thing I've learnt today is that things can change when you least expect them.'

Rulf squeezed his hand. 'If you tell yourself something for long enough, you end up believing your own deception, but true love will always find a way. We are powerless against it. That was why I had to come back.'

He chuckled. 'But enough of this. We're together now, and that's all that counts. What's your son called?'

'James. He's a healthy child with a loud voice when he's hungry. I'm very proud of him.'

'And so you should be. How's everything else? Was it a good harvest?'

'Yes, and the estate is now thriving, and I've plans—' No, he didn't, not anymore. The earlier events of the day crashed over him like a nightmare. 'Rulf, I had a visit today from the Earl of Devonshire.'

'That wily old fox? He'd sell his mother for an extra penny. Is that what troubles you?'

'That and other matters I'd rather not talk about. As you said, let's not spoil the moment.' He would never talk of them. He never wanted to think of his mother again. 'Why come back now?'

'I thought about returning many times, but you said you wouldn't join me until you could support yourself. I knew if I came back, I couldn't stay. I'd be opening old wounds and that wouldn't have been fair to either of us.'

'You could have written.' His words sounded petulant even as he said them.

'As, my young friend, could you. I suspect you didn't for the same reason as I: any correspondence in the wrong hands would be dangerous, and I saw little point in scribing about the weather.'

The same slight admonishment mixed with humour. Rulf hadn't changed a whit. Even if he had, Thomas wouldn't have cared.

'How are things at Oxford?'

'John Wycliffe is still there. I reunited with my friends and we continue our secret translation of the Bible. I'm under no illusion that things will change in my life, but someone must begin for others to follow. But enough of serious talk. Tomorrow is the eclipse. You hadn't forgotten?'

'Of course not! It's the most important day in the astral calendar, and I can't think of anyone I'd rather share the moment with.'

'It seemed a fitting moment. Tomorrow, we shall stand by that tor—' Rulf pointed to a group of jagged rocks outlined against the sky— 'and witness what many never do and never shall.'

'You'll stay here tonight, then?'

'I can't; my companions are camped at the tor. You must meet them. Their minds will astound you. Join us tonight. I promise you'll enjoy their company.'

'So, you're not alone?' Thomas swallowed his disappointment.

'I am and I'm not. You'll understand when you meet them. Tell me you'll come.'

How he wanted to. A whole evening with Rulf, and he'd waited so long to meet such learned men, but how could he? His place was with Rose and James, particularly after the events of the day. He supposed he could leave in *one of his sulks* as Rose called it, but that would mean lying to her, and he'd never done that.

'I must warn my people about the eclipse. If I don't, they'll be scared and panic. I was going to do it this morning, but the earl arrived.'

Rulf shook his head. 'You worry too much. Your people are peasants. They'll panic whatever you tell them.'

Whether it was being with Rulf again or the events of the day, he didn't know, but a surge of rebellion flooded through him. Rulf was right; why should he care about his people's fears? They weren't his anymore. He'd done his duty, and now it was time to think of himself.

'You're right, but I should warn Rose. She'll be as scared as the rest. If I make haste, I can be with you before dark.' The very daring of it thrilled him.

'Then make haste and bring a flagon or two of that excellent wine I procured from Okewolde, if you haven't drunk it all.' Rulf raised a playful eyebrow.

'The earl might have.' Thomas glanced around for curious eyes, saw none and kissed Rulf on the cheek. 'God's speed and praise God you're back.'

He ran along the path. Rulf was back! If he'd had wings he would have flown.

CHAPTER 60

Rose watched the door close behind Thomas. She didn't blame him for leaving; in fact, she wished she could do the same thing. As she understood it, Thomas was now a lord without lands, so what did that make her?

Without a word, Simon slammed his goblet on the table, making her jump. He grabbed his cap and marched to the door.

'Simon...' she said, but he ignored her and strode outside.

What was she supposed to do now, on her own with the earl sat at the head of the table like he owned the place, which it seemed he did. She dared not look up and kept her eyes fixed firmly on the table as silence shrouded the room.

What did a Lady of the Manor do in high company? Make conversation, she supposed, but about what? She knew nothing of the earl's life or the people he mixed with. The earl had already talked of the state of the tracks and the harvest, so those topics of discussion wouldn't work.

Nervously, she coughed and sipped the dregs from her goblet.

'More wine?' she ventured. She could do with some.

A smile played around the earl's lips. He drained his goblet in reply, then held it out along with the empty dish of honeyed dates. He'd probably realised that she wasn't of high birth; nobles had a way of knowing such things. She'd been brought up to believe that nobles were her betters and high-ranking nobles were men of honour and gallantry. That was a merry jest if ever she'd heard one. This earl was more cunning and odious than the beggars who feigned poverty in the streets. Unlike the beggars, though, she didn't know how to handle him.

At the barrel, she took her time filling the jug. Was there any more honeyed fruit? It was supposed to be for Thomas, but none of that mattered now. He probably wouldn't want to eat anyway, not after this.

The earl's eyes were burning a hole in her back as she searched through Janet's collection of bowls and jars. There must be something she could give him. Pray God he didn't intend to stay for an evening meal; she only had chickpeas and rabbit stew, hardly fit fare for an earl. If he did eat it, she wondered what he'd make of the spices in it. She hoped they burnt his mouth.

She found a clay jar of pears in honey syrup that would have to do and glanced over her shoulder at the door. What was taking Thomas so long?

Forcing a smile, she returned to the table. 'I'm sure Lord Thomas won't be long,' she said. 'Where are you travelling to?'

'We had hoped to stay the night here and rest our horses, but—' the earl gazed around the room with distaste—'I see you are not able to accommodate guests.'

Only on the floor, she thought.

The silence stretched and Rose felt her cheeks flame with embarrassment. As a miller's daughter, she'd give him the sharp end of her tongue and show him the door. As a lady, she didn't know what she should or shouldn't do.

Sir Gorvenal leaned forward, his round cheeks flushed with pink, almost like a maid's. 'It's of no matter, Percy. If we make haste, we still have time to reach Okewolde before dark, and we can travel on to Exeter tomorrow.'

He had a soft voice and kind eyes. He seemed like a nice man; she'd try talking to him. 'Do you have business in Exeter, Sir Gorvenal?'

'Indeed, my lady—'

'And we'll have even more if Lord Thomas returns and tells us whether he wants to buy his land back or not' the earl interrupted. 'I can get the contract drawn up in Exeter and settle this tedious little affair once and for all. Where is he, confound the man?' He stared at the closed door as if he could will Thomas to reappear.

Tedious little affair! It was their lives he was talking about. In an effort to keep a rein on her temper, Rose smiled at Sir Gorvenal.

'How is your lady wife, Sir Gorvenal?'

'Alas, there is no lady wife—'

'He was promised to the Lady Elizabeth, second daughter of Lord Runscombe of Somersetshire, but the Pestilence got her,' the earl said. 'The whole family died. They were of sickly blood.'

'I'm sorry. Pray God for her soul.' Rose crossed herself.

'It's of no matter. Neither of them had met, and last year I bought the entire Runscombe estate for a few pounds. It worked out better than the marriage contract, and Gorvenal here didn't end up with a horse for a wife.' The earl laughed. 'Ugly wench, she was. You had a lucky escape there, Uncle. Of course, it leaves Gorvenal in an unfortunate situation. He's only got a brace of running hounds to keep him company, and he's not getting any younger.'

Not trusting her tongue, and glad to be out of his company, Rose got up. 'With your permission, I'll go and find Lord Thomas.'

She opened the door and very nearly collided with Maria. For once, she was glad to see her.

'Is it true? Do we have noble visitors? Who are they? The whole place is buzzing with gossip.' Maria's face was flushed, her eyes wide with girlish excitement as she strained to see over Rose's shoulder. Behind her, Eleanor hopped up and down in a frenzy of excitement.

'Shh! Keep your voice down. The Earl of Devonshire, and his uncle, Sir Gorvenal, are here to see Thomas about business,' Rose whispered.

'The Earl of Devonshire!' Maria shook her skirts and adjusted her headdress. 'Introduce me.' she said, sweeping into the room with Eleanor following on her heels like an excited puppy. In the centre of the room, she dropped into a deep curtsy, keeping her head lowered with her eyes looking demurely through her lashes. 'My Lord Courtesy.'

Maria was wearing her best yellow kirtle and had her hair braided in loops behind her ears. Rose could imagine her panic as she'd changed and got Eleanor to braid the yellow strips in her hair.

Was there a correct, noble way to introduce someone? If there was, she didn't know it.

'Lord Courtesy, Sir Gorvenal, this is Lord Thomas's sister, Maria, and Eleanor...ah...' What should she call Eleanor?

'My companion,' Maria supplied. 'My lords, be welcome.'

Rose stood awkwardly to one side, watching with envy at how easily Maria took command of the situation.

The men inclined their heads. Sir Gorvenal's gaze roamed from the top of Maria's head down her fine silk kirtle to her red velvet slippers and up again. 'Mistress Maria, Mistress Eleanor, I bid you join us.' He indicated the space on the bench next to his chair.

Waiting until they were settled, he reached across for the jug. 'Some wine, Mistress Maria?' he asked. The man had hardly said a word since he'd arrived, but as soon as he'd clapped eyes on Maria, he was fawning all over her, twisting a gold ring with a large ruby stone around his little finger. There was no reason for Rose to stay, and she was only too happy to leave them in Maria's capable hands. This was one area in which Maria was definitely better than she was.

'I'll see if I can find Lord Thomas,' she said.

'Do; I'm anxious to leave,' said the earl without looking at her.

At least Maria would keep their guests entertained. Now all she had to do was find Thomas and see if they could find a way out of this mess.

CHAPTER 61

By the time Rose returned to the house, it was nearing the third quarter. She paused on the threshold to steel herself and went in.

'I can't find Lord Thomas anywhere,' she said brightly. 'I expect something urgent has called him away.'

The earl was leaning against the table now, the top of his head almost touching the beam, his velvet feathered hat and gauntlets in his hands.

'We can't wait any longer,' he said, adjusting his hat to a jaunty angle on his head. 'We need to make haste if we're to reach Okewolde before dark. Tell Lord Thomas that I'll return in a week to collect my dues and that I'll have a contract drawn up, should he wish to purchase the Chiddleigh lands. If he doesn't, he'll need to let me know his intentions. He's welcome to stay as a tenant, of course, but I'll need a decision one way or the other. Godspeed, my lady. Mistress Maria; Mistress Eleanor.' He nodded and, fastening his sword, ducked through the door.

'Alas, it seems I must take my leave,' said Sir Gorvenal, his eyes never leaving Maria's face. 'I look forward to our next meeting.'

'As do I, my lord.' Maria lowered her eyes coyly.

Rose shook her head. There was nothing coy about Maria.

'Godspeed, Mistress Eleanor.' Sir Gorvenal nodded politely.

'Godspeed.'

Sir Gorvenal retrieved his sword and gauntlets and stepped close to Rose. 'May I have a word, my lady?' he said quietly.

God's teeth, what now? Why couldn't he just go and leave her to her thoughts? 'Of course, my lord.'

Once they were outside, he closed the door behind them and lowered his voice. 'I'm aware it's too much to hope for, but may I ask if Mistress Maria is promised?' His eyes searched her face hopefully as he fumbled with his gauntlets.

Rose's mind raced. Could he seriously be interested? If so, at least something good would come of the day.

'No, my lord. I understand she was promised, but her future husband succumbed to the Pestilence.' It sounded better than Thomas hadn't bothered finding a husband for his sister.

An eager light came into Sir Gorvenal's eyes. 'Forgive me for being so forthright, but I've taken a liking to Mistress Maria. She's quite beguiling. Do you think Lord Thomas would consider a marriage contract between her and myself? I'm a wealthy man and keep a good house with reliable servants. I live quietly, hold the Sabbath, never gamble, and enjoy only a modest drink of wine. I've been seeking a wife for a while, but until now, I've met no one to my taste.' He twisted his hat awkwardly in his hands.

He sounded rather dull for Maria, who had always said that she wanted to wine, dine and dance, but he *was* a high-ranking noble and a wealthy one at that. In the circumstances, Maria couldn't hope to do better.

How were such matters conducted? It felt uncomfortable discussing Maria's future without her being present, much like people had assumed Rose would be happy to wed William. Thomas should be here instead of leaving everything to her as usual.

'Maria has no wealth. Maybe you should discuss it with Lord Thomas on your return next week?'

'Of course, but I am not seeking wealth or lands; I have sufficient. It would be an advantageous match since it would give the house of Chiddleigh a much-needed connection to the house of Gravesmire. I am only a third son, it's true, but given Lord Thomas's unfortunate circumstances—'

'Gorvenal! The horses are ready, make haste!'

'My young nephew, impatient as ever. I'll leave you to speak with Lord Thomas and pray for good news. Until next week, my lady, Godspeed.' He bowed and mounted his horse.

Well! She hadn't expected that, but then, she hadn't expected any of the events of that day. She watched her visitors canter out of the yard and, feeling totally exhausted, returned inside.

'Did you see how he looked at me? That soft voice and those eyes!' Maria burst out. 'Oh, Rose, I know he's not young, but I shall *die* if I don't see him again.' She clutched her hands dramatically to her bosom.

'Well, don't die just yet; he's coming back in a week. Now, please leave me. It's been quite a day and I'm exhausted.' Dismissing the girls with a nod, she closed the door behind them, turned around and leaned against it.

She could have told Maria of Sir Gorvenal's proposal, but she wasn't in the mood for her gushing outpourings. That would have to wait. She poured a full goblet of wine from the barrel and downed it in a single swallow. Wiping her mouth with the back of her hand, she poured another, then slipped off her boots and sank into her chair.

Sir Gorvenal could be the answer to Maria's prayers. That would be one problem solved. She poured another drink and picked up the scroll of monies owed. It was an enormous sum; no wonder Thomas was so outraged.

Figures rolled through her mind. The corn driers would have to wait, and she could forget extending the house for a while, but there was just enough to pay the outstanding dues. Unless Thomas had some money of his own that she didn't know about, there wasn't a hope of buying the lands, and she didn't know what they were going to do if he couldn't. Become tenant farmers, she supposed, although she couldn't see Thomas doing that.

And now there was the matter of Maria and Sir Gorvenal. Something she still couldn't believe, let alone talk about. What was she going to do?

And where was Thomas?

CHAPTER 62

Thomas threw open the door, then remembered the earl. Pulling his clothes straight, he went in, but the room was empty apart from Rose, who was sorting dried herbs at the trestle. She glanced up at him with cold eyes, her fingers thrusting into the mounds of herbs.

He knew that look. Rose was vexed with him for walking out, and he didn't blame her. Their marriage had taught him to keep his head down. She'd chide him soon enough.

'The earl and his uncle have gone then. Praise God, I missed him. Never have I met a more odious and arrogant man.' He tried the lighthearted approach and helped himself to a cup of wine. Rulf was back and the eclipse was due. It was a moment for celebration.

'You seem happy, considering what's happened. Where've you been?' she said, ramming sprigs of thyme into one basket and marjoram into another.

'By the river, thinking. Rose, listen to me. There's something you should know. I was going to tell you—'

Her hands paused clutching a bunch of thyme. 'I'm not sure I want to hear it.'

'Don't worry, it's nothing bad. It's very exciting. I was going to tell everyone at the third quarter bell, but what with the earl and everything, I forgot. Tomorrow is a really special day. There's going to be an eclipse sometime between first quarter and midday.' He filled the first flagon of wine and pushed the wooden stopper firmly into the top. He didn't want it spilling on the steep walk to the tor.

Rose rubbed a hand over her brow and dropped the herbs onto the trestle. 'I thought you were going to say…'

She looked relieved, but why? He'd never understand her.

'So what's an ellipse?' she asked, her voice sounding tired.

'*Eclipse.* An ellipse is an oval shape. It's when the moon passes in front of the sun. At least, I think it is. Some scholars say it's the other way around. It doesn't come very often, and when it does, it'll look like the sun's being eaten—'

'God save us! It's the devil's dragon swallowing the sun!' She crossed herself. 'It's an ill omen, and after today—Thomas, what are we going to do about the earl?'

He sighed. 'I don't know what we're going to do. We'll talk about it after tomorrow.' Speaking of it now would spoil everything.

'You're in a strange mood for someone who's lost everything.'

'I'm trying not to think about today. The eclipse is special, and I don't want anything spoiling it. It won't happen again in my lifetime. And I just told you, it's the moon moving across the sun. There is no dragon.'

'That's what you say, but Grandma Ellyn knew all about it because her grandma saw it. She said men fired arrows from their longbows to kill the dragon. They rang bells, banged pails, and hammered on doors to frighten it away.'

Thomas put the two flagons of wine on the table and stood opposite her. 'Rose, trust me, there's no dragon, and there's no need to ring the bell or bang pails. Tell the peasants that, will you? I have to go, and I'm relying on you to keep everyone calm.'

'Where're you going now? You can't leave me on my own with James! Supposing the dragon comes for him? They like babies, you know. And how am I going to stop folks being scared when I'm scared myself?' There was panic in her voice, and Rose didn't panic easily. 'And Thomas, we need to talk. Sir Gorvenal—'

'We can talk about all that when I get back. I'm sorry, but I'll never get another chance. I'll learn a lot from this.' He knew it wasn't fair to leave her, but for once, he was doing what he wanted, and not even Rose was going to stop him. He stuffed his charts and the astrolabe into his bag.

'You haven't said where you're going,' she said, eyeing the two flagons of wine.

He didn't think she'd come after him, but you never knew with her; she was capable of anything if she'd a mind. He'd die of shame if she followed him to the tor and found him with Rulf.

'Somewhere on High Drovers Road. It's high with a good view. I'll study the stars tonight, get a bit of sleep towards daylight and be ready for tomorrow.'

'On your own with two flagons of wine? You'll be so drunk you won't be able to see the sky, let alone the stars.'

There was something in the way she said it that made him uncomfortable. He avoided her eyes; she had a woman's way of knowing when he was lying. 'I'll be fine.' Slinging his bag over his shoulder, he grabbed the remaining flagon and headed for the door.

'I'll tell folks about this ellipse then shall I? But don't blame me if they've all fled when you get back or James has been eaten by the dragon!' She rose from her chair, her hands firm on the table.

'*Eclipse*. And don't worry, you'll be safe.' He lifted the latch and, with the tiniest pang of guilt, left her standing there.

'That's easy for you to say! I hope the muxy dragon gets you on that road!' she yelled after him.

Thomas paid her no mind. He was already thinking of Rulf waiting for him at the tor.

CHAPTER 63

A thin finger of blue-grey smoke dissolved into the inky night sky, and the smell of woodsmoke drifted down the moor, bringing the promise of warmth and something to fill Thomas's grumbling belly.

He hitched his bag further up his shoulder and stopped to catch his breath. It was a steep climb, but he'd nearly reached the tor. In spite of the crisp autumn chill in the air, he felt hot and clammy nervous excitement. In a hundred or so paces, he would meet some of the best minds in the kingdom, something he'd dreamed about since he was a boy. Not in a chamber full of expensive furniture smelling of beeswax, hidden deep somewhere amongst the wise old stones of Oxford, but here, beneath the stars on the top of the moor.

What should he speak of? He didn't want to sound like a nuddlejade. Who was that ancient Greek astronomer Brother Leviticus talked about? Aristarchus, that was it. He claimed to have calculated the distance from the earth to the sun using the phases of the moon, but Brother Leviticus had said he was wrong. That could make a good debate.

Thomas wiped his hands down the sides of his mantle. On the other hand, it might be better if he listened. He was educated compared to the rest of his people, but these were serious and studious men. Men who had probably forgotten more than he could ever hope to learn in a lifetime. Best not to open himself to ridicule.

Fifty paces.

He could hear voices and smell stewing meat and herbs. His mouth watered; he hadn't eaten since dawn. He nursed the flagon of wine between his arm and chest, its contents sloshing with every step.

Twenty paces.

Dark outlines appeared like shadow puppets against the yellow flames. Thomas wiped his brow with his sleeve. His heart was ringing in his chest like a bell, and his mouth was dry. He could hear the crackle of wood on the fire beneath men's voices and taste the smoke in the air.

Another twenty paces and the puppets were clothed in muted shades of night purples, their faces a patchwork of shadows. Two men were hunched beside the fire, another pair stood close by. He couldn't see Rulf.

His stomach stopped grumbling and started twisting itself in tight knots. He didn't want to walk in on his own. He'd wait until he saw Rulf.

One of the men stared towards him, nudged his companion and said something. Thomas saw him pick up a thick stick from near the fire and come towards him.

'Rulf!' His voice was barely a whisper.

Away from the light of the fire, the man seemed a giant, threatening and looming larger with every stride.

'Rulf!' Thomas repeated, louder this time. He retreated but felt the hard granite of a boulder at his back. The giant stopped a few paces away, his stick beating time in his palm.

'Hail!' Thomas squeaked. 'I'm Rulf's friend, Lord Thomas de Chiddleigh?' His name came out as a question as he stepped forward a pace and held out his trembling hands in supplication.

For a moment, the man didn't move, then his shoulders relaxed and his hands dropped to his sides, his mouth turning up into a broad smile. 'Why didn't you say? Be welcome, Rulf's friend. I'm Marcus and this is my friend, John.' He nodded to a shorter man behind him. 'Rulf's spoken a lot about you. Come, and if that flagon holds wine, you're even more welcome.' Marcus slapped Thomas manfully on the back, sending him staggering, and steered him towards the warmth of the fire.

'This is Lord Thomas, Rulf's friend we've heard so much about. Where is he by the way?' said Marcus.

'Taking a piss behind that tree. Be welcome, Thomas. I'm Philippe and this is my friend Athius.' Philippe had one arm draped around Athius's slender shoulder. Athius's dark elfin-like face glistened in the firelight. 'He hails from Greece, but he can't help it.'

'Hail, I—'

'Thomas! I feared you were lost and I'd never get to taste my wine.' Rulf appeared from behind the tree, beaming. Leaning close, he kissed him on the cheek.

Heat spread from the back of Thomas's neck as his eyes darted nervously to the other men. Rulf laughed.

'No need to be wary here,' he said, taking Thomas's hand and leading him to the fire. 'We are of like minds. Be seated.'

Thomas smiled nervously at the group around the fire and took his place.

'Now, my friend, open that flagon, and Marcus, fetch the bowls. That rabbit pot is torturing my empty belly,' said Rulf.

Thomas ate greedily. The food was so delicious that he was easily persuaded by Athius to take a second helping, after which he sat back with his cup of wine and surveyed Rulf's companions.

They were not as he'd expected. There were no robes, no long grey beards or learned faces. Most of them were not many summers older than him. Marcus's balding head glistened in the firelight as he bent to add more sticks. His ginger beard was trimmed to a point instead of being cut square in the usual manner. Was that the Oxford fashion? Thomas stroked his chin. He could finally feel a few bristles there, but they were so fair that they didn't show. John, who sat next to Marcus, looked to be the oldest; there was a grey tinge to his whiskers that the others lacked.

'Need a piss before I wet myself,' Marcus said. He rose and hurried to the tree.

'You're like a waterfall; you never stop going!' Philippe shouted after him, as the men burst into laughter.

Thomas smiled awkwardly. He'd never heard such crudity from noblemen and wasn't quite sure how to respond.

'You'll get used to them. It's all in jest.' Rulf rested his hand on Thomas's thigh, sending a pulse of excitement up his leg. Thomas tensed, embarrassed at such a public display. Even married couples didn't show such affection outside of their bed.

Rulf leaned close. 'Relax, my friend. Here, we are free from prying eyes condemning us to ridicule and the hangman's noose.'

Thomas nodded, but these men seemed so adult, as though hailing from another world. Athius put his arm around Philippe's shoulder, and Philippe responded with a kiss. Should he be more open, like them, and put his arm around Rulf?

He should say something. Not about Aristarchus; that topic of conversation seemed a bit pompous now.

'Rulf was sorely missed by everyone after he left,' he said. 'The priest from Holdesworthe took over, but he's a surly man.'

Philippe choked on his wine, spitting it in a shower of spots down his front as Athius and John burst out laughing.

'You didn't pull that one again, did you, Rulf?' said John.

Rulf shrugged and glanced nervously at Thomas.

'Hear this, Marcus! Rulf has been playing the priest again! Can you believe it?' said John, shaking his head.

'Not after Winchester. The townsfolk ran us out of town as I recall. Thought we'd never get out of there alive.' Marcus resumed his seat. 'You've got a nerve, Rulf, but then you always had.'

'Rulf?' Thomas looked at Rulf, feeling like the butt of a jest he didn't understand. 'What are they talking about?'

Rulf studied his drink and then looked straight at him. 'I'm not a priest. The cassock's a disguise I use sometimes. I wanted to tell you, but there was never a right time, and then I met your people; how could I say something after that?'

'The priest is one of Rulf's many faces,' said Athius, the curved tones of his accent hinting at warmer lands. 'He makes a good beggar too, particularly in a crowded market. Ladies can't resist that handsome face.'

'Only once, and we were desperate, remember? We'd lost all our money on cards.' Rulf's voice was flat, his eyes fixed on Thomas.

'Your pipe-player's the best.' Marcus turned to Thomas. 'Have you heard him? He plays a mean tune after a few ales.'

'No, I haven't.' Rulf not a priest? Playing the beggar? Who was this Rulf they were talking about? He turned to face him. 'You lied to me and my people. You gave Mass. You took their confessions!'

'You took confessions?' John was looking at Rulf in much the same way as he was. 'Using the cassock for safety's one thing, but hearing people's confessions is a step too far, even for you.'

'I had no choice if I didn't want to be found out!' Rulf snapped. His eyes softened as he turned back to Thomas. 'You know I never wanted to be your priest, but once I'd started, how could I stop?' He reached out and stroked Thomas's face, smiling. 'I thought if I told you the truth too soon, I would lose you. Forgive me?'

Rulf looked sorry and he sounded sorry, but he had lied to him, lied to his people. He'd violated his trust, he'd abandoned him, and now he was acting as though it was nothing.

'How did you get a cassock if you never took your vows?' Thomas asked.

'He stole it from a priest,' said John, poking the fire into life.

'He what?' Thomas's eyes widened in disbelief. 'Rulf, is that true?'

'It's not as bad as it sounds. I was sharing a room with this priest at an inn. He was a boring old man and snored like a hog.' Rulf chuckled at his own wit. 'I didn't get a wink of sleep. I was on my way own home, travelling alone, and he'd been bragging about how his cassock kept him safe on the roads and how folks in the villages gave him free bed and food. I'd seen the size of his purse, tight old cur.' Rulf drained his wine. 'Look, I'd only a shilling left, it's not safe alone on the roads and I'd a long way to go. I saw the cassock lying on the stool and thought, why not? He owed me that for keeping me awake. So I took it. I often wondered what happened when he woke to find he'd nothing to wear but his hose and boots.' He laughed.

'And I'll wager you took his purse too,' said Marcus.

Thomas wanted to laugh with the others, but he couldn't. There was something intrinsically wrong about stealing from a priest and, even worse, finding it humorous. Brother Leviticus and others from the monastery had been his friends. They dedicated their lives to God and helping others. They travelled to take alms to the poor and risked their lives to visit lepers outside of the town. It could have been one of them that Rulf had stolen from.

'You look appalled. I suppose I shouldn't have done it, but that old fart turned out to be right; no one challenges a priest.' Rulf took the flagon and poured himself another wine. 'This—' he swept his arm in an arc— 'is the real me. I hope it isn't too much of a shock.'

It was more than a shock, and as with everything, Rulf was trying to make light of it as though it was all some sort of jest. Who was this man he thought he knew?

'What about Oxford and your degree? You told me your uncle's a bishop and you were an acolyte. Were those lies too?'

'Not exactly. I was at Oxford, but I never took my degree.' Rulf was beginning to look a little uncomfortable now.

'Too busy in the inns,' said Philippe, helping himself to more wine.

'As were you!' Rulf retorted.

'And your work at Oxford and your uncle? Are they true?'

'Everything about John Wycliffe is true. And my uncle is a bishop, although I'm the last person he'd have as a priest. I'm the wild son. The embarrassment of the family they don't talk about.' His voice had taken a sincere note, as though he was beginning to see the gravity of what he had done.

Thomas felt sick to his stomach. The one thing that he'd been happy about was finding Rulf, and now the man he loved had turned out to be a stranger who delighted in lies and deceit. The hurt and the treachery built in his throat and finally erupted over his tongue.

'You lied to me! You let me think you were a priest when you were nothing but a mummer from your pretty blue eyes to your toes.'

'Come now, it's not so—'

'I loved you! And you said you loved me or was that another lie?'

'Of course not! I do love you—'

'Then why did you do it? Why did you never tell me the truth?'

'I didn't mean—' Rulf suddenly looked shaken. 'Thomas, I truly intended to tell you, but the timing was never right. I always hoped the day would come when you would see the real me.'

'And how in God's name was I supposed to do that when you spent all our time together pretending to be someone else? How easily you switched from pious priest to friend and lover! How well you knew your way around the inns and the dice table, but then you'd had plenty of practice, hadn't you?' Thomas shook his head. 'Life and people are just a merry jest to you, aren't they? I'll wager you've had many a laugh at my expense.'

'It wasn't like that.'

'Then what *was* it like, Rulf? I trusted you, and you've destroyed that. You cheated me and my people. Dear God, we all believed in you. You heard their confessions. I don't care what your precious John Wycliffe has to say about the church and its power; what you did was unforgivable, and one day you'll answer to God for it.' The words poured out of his mouth, he didn't know where they came from, maybe, deep down they had always been there.

Rulf took a long, deep breath. 'I don't blame you for being angry but—'

'How dare you blame me for anything after what you did! I trusted you and you betrayed me. You betrayed everyone you ever spoke to on this estate. How could I have been so blind?'

Oh, how he wished Philippe or one of the others would laugh, slap him on the back and tell him it was all a bad jest, but one look at the embarrassed faces around the fire was enough to tell him that they wouldn't.

'You should have told me.'

'I never found the right moment.' Rulf's once dazzling blue eyes were dark as he grappled to explain.

'God's piss, Rulf. We had plenty of moments together.'

'Yes, but...I didn't want to hurt you.'

Thomas gave a bitter laugh. 'Too late!'

They were both silent. He stared into Rulf's face. The face of a liar and a cheat who had scant regard for anyone. He couldn't bear to look at it, couldn't bear to be near it. He got to his feet.

'Thomas, I'm sorry. Please—' Rulf caught hold of his sleeve. 'You can't leave. I need you.'

Thomas looked down at the face that had once been so beautiful and was now ugly. 'It's always you, isn't it? *You* needed me to stay that night. *You* wanted to go to town. *You* slithered away like a snake that night because you didn't want to say goodbye. You betrayed me, but you think I can't leave because you need me to stay.' Thomas kicked out at the fire, sending a shower of sparks into the night air. 'Well, what about what *I* need? I don't know who you are anymore, and I'm not sure I want to.' He picked up his bag, slung it over his shoulder and turned his back for home.

Rulf's steps crunched on the path behind him, but he didn't look back. A hand landed on his shoulder and spun him around.

'Please, Thomas, I'm begging you! You can't just walk away from me like this.'

'Why not?' Thomas knocked Rulf's hand aside. '*You* did!'

'Thomas! Wait! I'm sorry, I'm begging you. What about the eclipse? At least stay for that and we can talk.' Rulf sounded desperate, but it was too late. He never wanted to hear that voice again.

'I'll never lie to you again, I swear! I'll find a way to make it up to you. I'll even burn the cassock if that's what you want, just please don't go.'

Thomas paused on the path, just long enough to give Rulf the same vain hope that his former lover had once tormented him with.

'Goodbye, Rulf,' he said coldly.

He walked on and this time he didn't cry.

CHAPTER 64

Thomas didn't know where he was going, nor did he care. He just knew that he had to get as far away as possible. It seemed ridiculous now that he had thought in terms of learned discussions with those men. They must have thought him a right fool to have believed Rulf. God's blood, he wished he'd never met him.

His eyes misted over, and he wiped them, furious at himself. He wouldn't cry. Rulf wasn't worth it, and damn him for coming back into his life and stirring up emotions he had all but forgotten. He had a wife and a son. He was content. He didn't need Rulf.

Thomas skirted around the orchards and climbed the hill, driving himself to the top without stopping. Without thinking, he took the sheep track to the cave, stopped by the entrance and looked down to the yard below. It was quiet. Everyone was indoors for the night, but he wasn't ready to go home.

He glanced at the entrance to the cave. Why not? Rulf was nothing to him now. The cave was just another hole in the rocks.

Inside, nothing had changed. The makeshift table and the bench, where they had played chess so many times, were still in the same place. In the round stone hearth were the ashes from that night they'd spent together.

He dropped his bag in its usual place by the wall. God, he was tired. Tired of lies, tired of being disappointed, tired of being angry and sad. Just tired.

Laying down, he curled into a ball and squeezed his eyes tight shut and pushing the day's events into the far corners of his mind, he drifted into an exhausted sleep.

He awoke to a thin shaft of light coming in through the entrance. For a moment, he expected Rulf to walk in, then everything that had happened the day before tumbled into his mind: the earl, the scrolls, Simon, Annie, his Mama and Rulf. It was as if every secret in his life, every lie and deception, had come together on that one day like the lines on his charts. Well, damn them all.

He stretched and got to his feet, aware of a gnawing pain in his stomach and a burning thirst in his mouth. He went to the jars at the back where Rulf had kept beans and grain, but the mice had beaten him to it long ago. In a basket, he found a couple of wrinkled apples. One was rotten and the other showed small teeth marks. Thomas cut them off, wandered outside and took a bite. The fruit tasted soft and a little sour, and tingled on his tongue, but it was better than nothing.

Below, his people were going about their daily work, and he stood watching them. He would have to go back to Rose and James to face his future, whatever that might be, but that was for tomorrow. Today, this one last day of freedom, was going to be his.

Tossing the apple down the hillside, he went back into the cave. There was work to be done before the eclipse. Nothing and nobody could spoil that.

He removed the astrolabe from his bag and put it back on the table where Rulf had left it for him, then spread his charts over the floor and checked his calculations again. The eclipse could happen at any moment. He went outside and stared up at the sky.

Almost without him noticing, the birds stopped singing, and an eerie calm settled over the land as he watched the horizon turn from hazy blue to grey. The air chilled, and in moments, day became night.

In reverence, Thomas raised his eyes to the heavens. Slowly, the smallest dark indent formed on the edge of the sun. Below, he heard his people screaming, banging on doors and beating pots. He couldn't help them now. He watched in awe as the crest grew and showed black, as though the sun truly was being eaten. For a moment, he wondered if Rose and his people were firing arrows at the dragon.

He stood in silent wonder watching the blackness swallow the sun. His eyes burned but he couldn't look away. The dark disc slid slowly across the sun until it turned black with a halo of yellow, orange and red flaring out like the tongue of a dragon.

Spellbound, Thomas swallowed a lump in his throat and knelt in homage. Never had he felt so insignificant as he stared at the black disc continue its journey, slowly releasing the brightness of the sun behind it. The dark sky gave way to blue as the air warmed and the birds resumed their song.

The moment was over, and the sun was shining as though nothing had happened.

Thomas remained on his knees and prayed. This was a moment to be shared with others. He gazed up at the tor and wished for a fleeting moment that he was there with the men.

He wasn't ready to go home. He wanted to sit and savour the miracle over and over. He remained on the hill, motionless as the sun reached midday and slowly slipped towards the third quarter.

Familiar steps sounded on the path. He didn't look up.

'I thought I'd find you here.' Rulf stopped a few paces away. 'May I?' He indicated a rock next to Thomas.

The lurch in his heart had no right to be there, but he didn't turn. He shrugged and kept his focus on a pair of buzzards soaring in high lazy circles above the valley. As Rulf sat, Thomas caught a whiff of the familiar thyme water.

'Did you see it?' Rulf asked.

'Yes.' How he longed to turn and look at him, but he had his pride and kept his eyes on the buzzards.

'Wasn't it magnificent? It didn't last as long as I thought, though. Philippe reckoned —'

'I don't care what Philippe reckoned. Why are you here?' Thomas turned then and was shocked at how vulnerable Rulf looked. His troubled eyes were framed with dark rings, and his shoulders hung down. In a strange way, it made him more real. Thomas suppressed the urge to hold and comfort him, instead staring at him in a way that made him feel as though he were no more than a statue.

Rulf shifted beside him. 'I did what you asked. I burnt the cassock.'

'I didn't ask you to do that.'

'I thought you'd want me to. And look, I've got my dice.' Rulf held out his hand. 'I'll never use them again, I swear.' In one swift throw, he hurled them over the hillside.

Hating himself, Thomas wanted to forgive Rulf and feel his arms around him, but he couldn't. Not just like that.

'I understand how you feel,' Rulf said. 'What can I do to make it up to you?'

'You have no idea how I feel. You deceived me and my people, and worst of all, you cheated God. There's nothing you can do.' He spoke as harshly as he could, knowing that if Rulf took him in his arms, he'd be lost. A small traitorous part of him hoped that he would.

Rulf got up, shifting his feet. 'It's a long and treacherous journey back to Oxford, and the daylight is shortening by the week. The others have already left for Okewolde and I'm joining them there. We're staying overnight at the inn. We'll buy provisions in the morning. John likes his food.' Rulf tried a jest, but Thomas didn't respond. 'We're leaving by the midday bell,' he added.

The buzzards were higher now, just black specks disappearing in and out of the clouds.

'We're taking the road east to Portsmouth and then the main drovers' road north to Oxford. You can't miss it.' Rulf's voice was contrite now, hoping.

The silence stretched between them.

'I thought I'd say, you know, in case…'

Thomas resisted looking at him. 'I'm not the boy I was when I met you. I've grown up, and I know you for what you are. You're selfish, a liar, and a taker.' *But God help me, I still want you.* 'I have my life here with Rose and James. So go back to Oxford, Rulf. Just go.' The words choked in his throat.

'If that's what you want, then I will. But Thomas, you're standing at a fork in life's path. One way leads to happiness; the other to a lifetime of regret. If you swallow your pride and go right, you'll be true to yourself. But if you go left, you'll be denying who you are and letting our love slip through your fingers, and the memory of today will haunt you for the rest of your life.'

He heard the crunch of Rulf's boots as he turned to leave. 'I love you, Thomas, and I always will. Choose wisely.'

Then Rulf's steps faded along the path and out of his life.

Wise or not, he had chosen his path. Rulf was right about being haunted; he already was. He sat watching the buzzards until they dwindled to black dots on the horizon. Then he rose, dusted himself down and went inside the cave. Carefully, he rolled up his charts and tucked them into his bag. He looked at the astrolabe, hesitated, then picked it up and shoved it to the bottom of his bag.

As he left the cave, he didn't look back. Instead, he walked forward to his unknown future with Rose and James.

CHAPTER 65

Thomas rested his head in his hand and pushed the potage around the bowl with his wooden spoon. Without moving, he cast his eyes through the open shutters. The sun had almost disappeared below the top of the moor. Rulf would be at the inn by now, sitting around a table with the others enjoying an ale. He could hear their lively exchanges. John's deep voice telling a jest and Rulf's laughter.

Rose put down the carrot she was chopping and studied her husband. She'd seen him moody before and knew when he wanted to be left alone, but she'd never seen him quite like this. His eyes had been dead since he got home a short while ago. She had a feeling she knew why, and that worried her. He worried her.

She had expected him to burst through the door, full of excitement about the eclipse. She'd braced herself to listen to his endless theories and strings of words she didn't understand, but he'd hardly spoken at all, just sitting and staring out of that window in one of his dreams.

'Aren't you going to eat that? You know I don't like waste,' she said, returning to her carrot.

Thomas pushed the bowl away with a sigh. So, it had already come to this. The Lady of the Manor, chopping her own carrots. Although Rose looked far more at home in her tunic and apron than she ever had in a silk kirtle.

He scraped back his chair, went to the opening, crossed his arms and stared at the tor that was almost invisible in the darkening sky. The camp would be silent now, the fire nothing but ashes. Grey and dead like his future.

'Thomas, I need to talk to you about Maria,' Rose said.

Her words hung like a fog in the back of his mind, buzzing there like a particularly annoying bee. He heard the knife slam on the table, but he didn't turn round.

Rose gritted her teeth. She knew he wasn't listening. He could likely walk out that door and she wouldn't see him until morning. He'd done that before, more than once.

'Thomas, Sir Gorvenal has asked for Maria's hand in marriage. He seems a nice man, he keeps a good house and has a quiet life, although I'm sure Maria will soon change that!' She waited for a smile or some reaction, but Thomas didn't say anything. Didn't even turn around. 'I explained she has no wealth, but he said it didn't matter. Maria's sixteen summers and at her age, it's a good offer. She's quite besotted with him. What do you think?'

Rose's voice floated behind him. Rulf and the others would be going to bed soon, in preparation for the hard day's ride they had ahead of them in the morning. Tomorrow, after breakfast, they'd buy provisions. Rulf would go straight to the wine merchant. Thomas smiled at the thought.

'Whatever you think best. You're a woman, you know how to manage these things better than I do,' he said.

God's teeth, he wasn't going to pass this on to her as well. 'Like I manage everything else around here? Like I managed the earl, not to mention your people and the eclipse when you weren't here? This proposal is the one good thing that has happened, and you don't even care! You're the lord, she's your sister, you make the decision.'

Thomas turned his head enough to glance at her over his shoulder. 'You've spoken to her?'

'No, of course not; I was waiting for you. Sir Gorvenal will be bringing a marriage contract when he returns with the earl next week, and he'll expect an answer. Think of it, Maria could be Lady Gravesmire. It wouldn't do us any harm. You never know, the earl might consider...'

Her voice washed over him and he returned to his dreaming. Tomorrow at midday, the horses would be saddled, standing at the tying post. Phillipe, Marcus, John and Athius would return, their arms laden with provisions, and a beaming Rulf would be strapping flagons of wine to his horse.

'Thomas, this is important. Stop staring out of that window and listen to me!'

'I am listening, and I told you it wasn't a dragon and I was right.'

The horses would be laden, and the group ready to leave. Rulf would be glancing up the road, his face shining at every sound of a horse, expecting it to be him.

'I'm not talking about the muxy dragon. I was scared and I hid with James under the table, not that you care. Where were you anyway?'

God's bones, she was in a mood. With an exaggerated effort, he turned around. 'I went to High Drovers Road to see the eclipse, like I told you.'

'On your own?' She stepped from behind the table and stood opposite him.

What made her ask that? 'Yes, of course on my own.'

Was it the innocent look on his face, or the disappointment she felt, knowing he was lying? She, who loved him, would do anything for him, and this was how he treated her. Whatever it was, the fury boiled inside her.

'Don't you dare lie to me! Do you think so little of me that you think you can lie as if I don't matter? I'm your wife, although you seem to prefer the company of men!' She shut her mouth with a snap. She hadn't meant for the truth to come out that way.

'How dare you!' His voice matched hers as they glared at each other.

'I dare because I saw you. You and Father Rulf. Don't try and deny it; I went looking for you after you left me with the earl. I went to the river and I saw you with him.'

And God how she wished that she hadn't. If she'd waited with the earl, she would never have known, would never have seen her hopes of Thomas's love for her die before her eyes.

'I didn't believe it at first but then...' She could barely bring herself to say the words. '...then, you held hands and you kissed. You never kissed me. Have you any idea how much I longed for that? You and him, it's...it's *evil*. Bad enough you'd sin like that, but to do it with a priest!' Her cheeks were flaming, her voice rising. She was lashing out, hurting him as he had hurt her. 'May God forgive you. Such sin and wickedness; I've heard about men like you—'

'Men like what, Rose? Tell me, what are men like us?' His jaw was set as he stood tense before her.

'Sodomites!' She shouted the word in his face. 'That's what! The most wicked and sinful men in the eyes of God. No wonder you never came to my bed. I thought it was my fault, that I'd done something wrong; when all the while you were pining for him every night! You and him together. It's horrible, I can't bear to think of it.' She couldn't look at him and turned away.

'Then don't. Because you don't know what you're talking about.'

'I know that I love you, but you're too blind to see it.' She could have lived with that, love in marriage was too often a matter of chance, but to know he was giving himself to another, and Father Rulf... 'Don't tell me you love him. There's no such thing between men; it's unnatural.'

Thomas leaned close, his eyes piercing hers with a passion she'd never seen before. 'Yes, I do love him, and he loves me. And don't you dare try to make me feel guilty about not wanting you as a woman. You were only too happy to marry me to get a title. I've given you a respect and status that you would never have found on your own, *Lady* Rose.'

'And I've given you an heir and the freedom to draw your stupid triangles!'

They glared at each other, both breathing heavily, neither of them flinching even when the shutter banged on its hinges.

At last, Thomas took a stool, sat down and patted the one next to him.

'Sit down. Shouting won't change anything.' He rested his head in his hands. 'My God, you must hate me. I never asked to love him, but I can't help it.' His eyes filled with tears; his voice small. 'I know it's wrong, but it feels so right. I don't expect you to forgive me, but can you at least understand what a love like that feels like?'

Yes, she could. Oh God, she could.

'When I'm with him, it's like I'm free and I know who I am. When I'm here—' he swept his arm around the room— 'it's like I'm chained and living a lie.'

He looked at her then. In his eyes, she saw not the contrition or repentance that she'd hoped for but love and torment.

'I've always loathed being the lord, that's no secret. All I ever wanted was to study at Oxford. I had dreams of mixing with the best minds in the land. Last night I nearly did. Rulf and his friends were camped by the tor to watch the eclipse. But Rulf and I quarrelled, and I left. I spent the night in the cave and watched the eclipse from there. I heard the banging pots down below.' He smiled dryly. 'I thought I was settled with you and James, but yesterday when I saw Rulf again it all came back, and now I don't know anymore.' He hung his head.

It didn't absolve him of his sin, but this was the real Thomas, the one she'd never known. Seeing him so defeated, she could only imagine how difficult it must have been to keep his love a secret while being tied to a life he didn't want. In that respect, they were very alike.

'We all have our dreams and try to think of ways to make them come true,' she said.

'The good Lord knows who I am and how I've sinned. It's why He sent the earl. It's His punishment. I'll never go to Oxford, and you don't have to worry about Rulf. He left today. I'll never see him again.' His voice broke and he sobbed into his hands.

He really did love Rulf. And wasn't she more fortunate? He might have broken her heart, but not intentionally, and she had got the life she wanted. Apart from James, he never would. He was a beaten man.

How she wanted to go to him, to hold him and take away his torment, but it would only make the next moments harder. She leaned close and put her hand on his arm.

'I don't pretend to understand the love between two men. It is a sin, but I don't hate you. I love you. The way you looked at Rulf when you walked into his arms reminded me of my Ma and Pa. That's what shocked me the most; I know love when I see it.'

It was because of that she was about to do what she was. What she'd known she would do from the moment she saw them together. She would like to have taken his face between her hands and held him the way Father Rulf had, but she wouldn't. It wasn't her he wanted. It had never been her, and it never would be.

Thomas's eyes were wet with tears as he raised his head. 'Forgive me,' he said.

Rose slipped off her stool to kneel in front of him and took his hands in hers. 'It's God who has to forgive you, not me. I fear for you, but my lips are sealed.'

Thomas nodded and stared over her shoulder through the opening at the night sky. 'I suppose we'll be tenant farmers to the earl,' he said. 'Will we cope?'

She would, she was born a commoner, but he wouldn't. Toiling on the land day after day, going hungry in the dark months and having to bow to the earl and his bailiff? He would hate it. And what if someone else had seen Thomas and Rulf and the truth came out? She didn't care about Rulf – it was obvious that he'd corrupted Thomas – but Thomas would be hanged. What about James when he grew up and discovered the truth? And he would; there would be plenty of gloating folks only too willing to tell him.

The smallest part, held desperately within her, had prayed it wouldn't come to this. Later, she was sure that she would hate herself, but right now, she was the only one who could set them free.

Quietly, she laid a hand on his shoulder and followed his gaze to the tor. 'Does he mean that much to you?'

'He means everything.' Thomas didn't look at her. She didn't need to see the truth in his eyes; she could hear it only too well in his voice.

'Then go to him,' she said, in a cracking voice that she barely recognised as her own.

'It's too late.'

'It's never too late.'

He turned to her with quiet hope on his face. 'What about the earl? And James?'

'You leave the earl to me. We'll soon be family. James will be fine, and you'll be back to visit us.'

'And you? Will you be fine?'

'I'll manage. Don't I always?' she said brightly but her eyes welled with tears as inside she wept. 'Now go.' *Go before I lose my courage.*

They smiled in a silent shared understanding, and for the first and last time, she felt a true bond between them.

She watched him pack a few things into a bag. Then he stood, forlorn, with the bag hanging from his hand before slowly going to the door. With his hand poised on the latch, he turned. 'Thank you,' he said. 'Thank you for everything.'

As she watched him hurry towards the stables, she put a hand to her cheek where he'd kissed her and let her tears fall.

'May God have mercy on your soul, and mine for helping you,' she whispered, crossing herself.

Thomas rode out of the yard and onto the lane, then stopped. He glanced back at the house they'd all built, at Peter's forge, the barn and the yard. In a strange way, he would miss it. He looked high to the hills and the fields they'd ploughed and harvested.

Rose was standing in the doorway. As she'd always said, what would he do without her? He could never love her, but he would always be grateful to her.

He raised a hand in farewell, then turned and rode to his new life.

CHAPTER 66

August 1352

In the shade of the tree, Thomas ran a hand inside the collar of his jupon. It felt hot and awkward, like him. He couldn't remember the last time he'd worn one. Life at Oxford was more casual, and he wasn't used to large gatherings like this.

In front of the Earl of Devonshire's private church, the most important nobles of the shire clustered in their bright silks, like exotic blooms on a green carpet. The odd shrill laugh pierced his ears as he hovered on the fringes, scanning the crowd for a familiar face. He didn't know any of them, and even though it was Maria's wedding, he was beginning to wish he hadn't come.

His feet ached; it had been a long and tiring journey. What wouldn't he give to sit down, take off his boots and rub his toes, but there was no chance of that until after the wedding festivities.

He glanced at the church. Even from back here, Maria looked radiant, her face shining as she greeted each guest with a warm welcome.

Sir Gorvenal bent his head to hers, his cheeks flushed, his eyes never leaving her face. Thomas smiled. The man was clearly besotted with her.

Rose appeared in an emerald green kirtle, threading her way between the groups. He smiled. Still the same

Rose with the same wild curls. Behind her came a maid with a small child clutching her hand.

James. How he'd grown! He was walking now. The boy had fair hair, like his, and was watching everything as he passed, a sure sign of a sharp mind.

'That's my boy, James,' Thomas said to his companion, his chest visibly swelling. 'I won't be a moment.'

He left the shade of the trees and walked towards Rose as she emerged through the sea of people, flitting from one to the other like the dragonfly he had loved to watch.

She caught sight of him as he approached and stretched out her hands in greeting. 'Thomas! God keep you. I thought you weren't coming. Maria was frantic and calling you every name you can imagine. What a hot day!' She fanned herself with her hand.

She had lost a little weight and seemed taller as she held herself elegantly before him. 'Rose, hail. It's good to see you. My horse cast a shoe and we had to walk the last miles.'

'You're here now, that's what matters.' She cast a glance over his shoulder. 'No Father Rulf?'

'No. He gave up the priesthood.'

'You're still...friends, though?' Her eyes searched his face as she waited for his answer.

He gave it, choosing his words very carefully. 'I shall always have a regard for him, but we're not as we were.'

When they had arrived at Oxford, Rulf swore he had changed. He wanted to study, he had said, and to resume his translation of the bible. For a few weeks, he had. He'd attended lectures and applied himself. They'd been happy together, and Thomas had enjoyed helping Rulf with his studies.

One night, Rulf had come home very late and very drunk. When Thomas had spoken about it the next morning, Rulf had protested that it was only one night of fun, just once a week; that wasn't too much ask, was it? And no, Thomas had supposed it wasn't.

But one night quickly turned into two and then three. Rulf stopped attending lectures, saying they were boring and anyway, Thomas could help him catch up. More disappointed than angry, Thomas had helped him, and every time he did, Rulf had promised faithfully that he would stay out of the inns and return to his studies.

Then one afternoon, Thomas had been late for a lecture and taken a shortcut along a back lane. As he passed an inn, he'd heard a raucous laugh and a voice he knew only too well. With a sinking heart, he'd stopped and looked in through the open door. Rulf had been sitting in the corner playing dice. Philippe, John, Marcus and Athius were standing behind him, their faces glowing in the candlelight, just as they had around the campfire.

Rulf threw the dice across the table. Two sixes. His opponent sighed and pushed a large pile of coins towards him. Rulf raised a flagon of wine and laughed. 'Another time, my friend, when you've recovered your losses.'

At that point, something inside of Thomas had snapped. He had given Rulf chance after chance, and the man had squandered every single one of them. He was never going to change.

'Rulf had radical views against the church,' he said to Rose. 'He was working with others in secret. It was only a matter of time before the church authorities got to hear about it.'

'I had no idea. How did they find out?'

Thomas shrugged, but inside he was smiling. 'Who can say? An anonymous message perhaps? Rulf left town in rather a hurry and won't be returning for a long while.'

'Does that mean you're coming home?' There was hope playing in her eyes, although she was doing her best to hide it.

He shook his head. 'No. I shall finish my studies and—' he glanced over his shoulder at the young man waiting for him under the trees— 'there's Michael, you see. My new friend.'

Rose followed his gaze, and her shoulders sagged almost imperceptibly. 'Yes. Of course.' She smiled a little too brightly. 'Did you hear the service?'

'Yes, we arrived just as it was starting and stood at the rear. You look well.'

And she did. Her cheeks flushed a healthy pink, there was a ready smile on her lips, and she was dressed in the finest emerald silk with silver daisies embroidered on the sleeves. A gold and green pendant sparkled in the sun at her throat.

'As do you. Oxford suits you. Put on a little weight though.' She patted his stomach.

He smiled sheepishly, conscious of the laces straining across his chest.

'Too much sitting down and easy living,' she playfully chided him.

That was true, and he did miss his morning walks on the moors with the fresh smell of the ling and the sight of the mist clinging to the valleys. But Oxford had its own wise charm with ancient yellow stone buildings standing shoulder to shoulder along the narrow streets of the city. And on the quarters of each day, a cacophony of bells rang across the towers as scholars clutched parchments and hurried to their lessons.

He loved to walk those streets and touch the walls, knowing that centuries of wisdom and knowledge were etched into the fabric of their stones.

'Maria hasn't run you too ragged in her preparations?' he said.

'Of course she has, and I wouldn't have expected anything less. But you must meet James.' Rose waved her maid forward. 'He's just started walking and thank goodness, for he's too big to carry. Not that I do much of that in public,' she added. 'James, come and meet your Papa.'

Papa sounded strange. What did a father say to his young son whom he hadn't seen for nearly a year? The maid coaxed the reluctant child forward and he stood half-hidden behind her skirts, staring wide-eyed at Thomas.

'James, I'm your Papa.' Thomas crouched and went to take the boy's hands, but James twisted away and buried his head in the maid's skirts.

Embarrassed, Thomas stood up, not sure what to do. He had imagined a joyful smile, even a laugh from his son, and he'd looked forward to scooping him up in his arms, feeling the boy wriggle in delight as he held him close. It had never occurred to him that the boy would be scared of him.

'He'll get used to you,' Rose said. 'All children are shy of strangers.'

The word *stranger* sat uncomfortably, but that was the price of being an absentee father. He smiled in a vain attempt to hide his disappointment.

'I suppose that's what I am. I should have thought.' He looked down at James and offered his hand again, but the child stayed within the safety of the skirts, sucking his thumb and eyeing him warily.

Rose waved the maid away and leaned close. 'The earl didn't want James to come. He said he didn't want tiresome children cluttering up the place, but Maria insisted and what Maria wants, Maria gets. Sir Gorvenal dotes on her, and she had him in the palm of her hand before they were even wed.'

'I can believe that. She looks happy though.'

'Oh, believe me, she is. She attends every banquet and social occasion, dressed in only the finest fashions. She's become quite the talk of society.'

'I'm pleased for her, it's what she always wanted. Is Annie here?' asked Thomas, stealing another glance at James, who was now ignoring him in favour of a large beetle that was crawling over the ground.

'Somewhere.' Rose scanned the crowd of people. 'She's probably with Eleanor. El is Maria's official companion now and will live with her and Sir Gorvenal on his estate. You should see his house! The grand hall alone is twice the size of your old manor house, and there are so many silver and gold dishes on display, I lost count. El wanted Annie to come to the wedding, and Annie didn't want to disappoint her. Mind you, she's not happy having to wear a kirtle but it's appearances, isn't it?'

'Since when were you bothered about appearances?' said Thomas.

Rose tinkled a laugh and delicately held a hand to her throat. 'Oh, I'm a proper lady now. Maria's been giving me lessons over the dark months, would you believe it? I can walk, talk, eat and dance like any highborn. Imagine that; and me, a miller's lass!' She leaned close and whispered behind her hand. 'What would these folks think if they knew?' She laughed delightedly. 'It's all a load of nonsense of course, but nobles live by these rules, God knows why.'

Rose was so vibrant, so refined, she even held herself as a lady. And to think he'd agonised for weeks after he left as to how she would cope. He should have known better; Rose was a survivor.

'Where are the wagons?' she said. 'There's the earl, in the turquoise cotehardie with gold buttons, strutting across the lawn. I swear it gets shorter every time I see him and have you noticed the length of his pointed shoes? Maria says it's the fashion and all nobles are wearing them, although how they walk in them is beyond me.' She giggled behind her hand. 'Listen to me, gossiping like an old maid! Did you receive my letter?'

'Yes, and the contracts. I couldn't believe it when I saw them. How did you get the earl to waive all debts and sell the Chiddleigh land for so little?'

Rose shook her head and patted him on the arm. 'Really, Thomas, for a clever man, you can be so naïve. The earl could hardly have Lord de Chiddleigh, his brother by marriage, as his tenant farmer, could he? Once Maria understood the situation, she said as much to Sir Gorvenal and dropped a few more words here and there. If word got out – and Maria would have made sure that it did – the earl would never have lived down the scandal.' She paused for breath and glanced around. 'Where is the bridal wagon? It still hasn't arrived. I hope it won't be long; it's so hot, and I've been standing all morning.' She fanned herself again.

'What news of the estate?' he asked.

Rose's letter had been expansive about the contracts, but sparse on details, and some time had passed since then. He had no interest in coming back to Combe Hide, but he still wanted to know how his people fared.

'Oh, the estate! Simon has big plans. He wants to build an inn on High Drovers Road with a brew house and stables at the back. We see a lot of travellers and wagons on that road coming and going to the port at Plymouth and the Okewolde fayres. An inn could be very profitable. He's even talking about having a forge and a wheelwright up there. Peter says he won't move his forge, but that's Peter for you. You could tell him grass was green and he'd insist it was red just to be contrary.' Rose leaned in close and lowered her voice. 'Gee died. Found in a drunken stupor and he never woke up. I shouldn't speak ill of the dead—' she crossed herself— 'but I'm not sorry. Anyway, Jarin's got the cottage now and is Peter's apprentice. I'm paying his way, but everyone needs a helping hand to better themselves, don't they?'

Thomas nodded. Rose was managing beautifully, just like she'd said she would. He was pleased, of course, but it would have been nice if she'd needed his advice on something. But then, he had nothing really to complain about. He had the life he wanted.

'And after this wedding, the builders are coming. I'm so excited! The whole of the house is to be a hall with bedchambers above and an outside kitchen at the back, just as we planned. It's Maria's present to me for arranging her marriage, and because she says she couldn't bear to have her sister living a moment longer in such a place.' Rose leaned close again and whispered. 'Sir Gorvenal is most generous, you understand. But listen to me chattering on! Come and greet the happy couple.' Daintily, she lifted one corner of her skirt and led the way through the guests to the church entrance.

'Thomas!' Maria beamed at him. 'Praise God, you came, and don't you look well? Oxford suits you. I'm not surprised, though; you were never happier than when you had a quill in your hand or charts to study. I'll wager you're the cleverest there.' She trilled a laugh.

'I wouldn't say that.' Thomas shifted his feet modestly. 'But I've met some very interesting people. Men of great learning who think —'

'Yes, enough of all that dry scholarly talk. This is a day for celebration!' Rose cut in. 'Doesn't Maria look beautiful?'

She did. He had never seen her look so pretty. Her cheeks blushed pink, her eyes sparkled with joy, and her dark hair, flowing long to her waist, gleamed like the purest jet. She was dressed in a pale blue kirtle of the finest silk, heavily embroidered in gold thread and studded with pearls and sapphires. On her head, she wore a ringlet of honeysuckle and forget-me-nots. She was more than beautiful, she was radiant, but he didn't know how to say it. How did a man compliment a bride?

'I like your dress,' he said.

Maria burst out laughing. 'Dearest Thomas, and so you should.' She leant forward. 'It cost Gorvenal a fortune, but when I saw the fabric, I just had to have it. And look!' She held out her gold pendant, tilting it so the sunlight played across the facets of the sapphire. 'Gorvenal's wedding present to me. Isn't it quite the loveliest thing you ever saw?' She giggled. 'I can't wait to show Lady Halifax. She'll be green with envy!'

Thomas smiled. Sir Gorvenal wasn't the earl Maria had always said she'd marry, but it was obvious that he would make her very happy.

'I wish the wagons would hurry up,' said Rose, looking anxiously around.

'The earl is furious, but I don't mind.' Maria smiled up at her new husband with real affection. 'Nothing is going to spoil our day, is it, Gorvenal?'

Sir Gorvenal beamed at her proudly. 'Nothing, my dear. This day shall be perfect, just like you. But if you'll permit me to tear myself away, I want a word with Lord Thomas for a moment.' His voice changed to a serious tone. 'Over here, away from prying ears.'

Curious, Thomas followed him around the side of the church, where they were unobserved.

Sir Gorvenal raised himself to his full height and cleared his throat. 'I'm a man of few words, so I'll come straight to it. I've been hearing things about you. Tongues are wagging and I'm not surprised.'

Had he discovered the truth about his relationship with Rulf? But how could he? Thomas could already feel the blood draining from his face, the hangman's rope being placed around his neck. 'I don't know what you've heard, but I'm sure—'

'Come, you must know! Everyone's talking about it.'

There was nowhere to run, and Michael was out of sight. Nervously, Thomas swallowed. 'I'm not sure what you mean.'

'This cloth of yours—'

'The *cloth*?' Relief blazed through him like the sun and he had to steady himself with a hand on the wall. 'You want to talk about the cloth?'

'Of course. What did you think I meant?'

'Nothing!' It had been a stupid thought; the act of a guilty conscience. If his sin really had found him out, he'd have known it the second he showed his face.

'Are you feeling alright?' Sir Gorvenal peered at him. 'You look a little pale.'

'It's just the heat and the journey. You were saying?'

'Yes, now look, I don't have to tell you how well it sold at the fayre last year. But Percy and I have been talking, and we think you could do better. You need to expand, and now you are family, we can help you do that. Do you see what I'm saying?' His eyes shone out from his round jovial face.

Thomas's mind was already leaping with possibilities. 'Are you suggesting we go into business together?' he said, trying to contain his excitement.

'Exactly! I propose a three-way partnership. The earl has thousands of sheep spread over the shire and royal connections, you have the red dye, and I will manage the negotiations with the merchants and dealers, look after the figures, that sort of thing. What do you say?' Sir Gorvenal beamed at him, his hands resting on his rounded belly.

Such a venture could be worth a fortune, but he and the Earl of Devonshire in business together? He trusted the man about as far as he could throw him, but Sir Gorvenal would hold the balance of power and he seemed genuine enough. Rose liked him, and he trusted her judgement. He'd be a fool to turn down such a proposal.

'I like the idea,' he said, fighting to keep the grin off his face.

Sir Gorvenal beamed wider. 'I thought you would. I said to my nephew that you'd know a good deal when you saw one. Of course, we'd need new dyeing sheds and weavers to cope with the extra work but that can be discussed later. So, we have an agreement?'

'We do.'

'Good man!' Sir Gorvenal slapped him on the back so heartily that Thomas nearly fell to his knees. 'I'll have the papers drawn up and the three of us can get together to sign them.'

'The four of us. I want Lady Rose to be included.'

'Really?' Sir Gorvenal frowned. 'I'm not sure Percy will agree to have a woman involved.'

'I live mostly in Oxford, and Lady Rose handles all my affairs. She'll be the one dealing with this, not me. If Lady Rose isn't included in the contract, then there will be no contract.'

Sir Gorvenal shrugged. 'If it's what you want.'

'I do.' He couldn't wait to tell Rose, she'd be thrilled.

'Then it's agreed. I'll contact the notary and—'

'Prithee, my lord, the wedding wagon has arrived,' a young page interrupted. 'You're wanted at the front of the church.'

'Tell them I'm coming.' Sir Gorvenal turned to Thomas. 'My wife is waiting, and what a fortunate cur I am. Come, we've finished here and at last the feast! I can't tell you how my belly's rumbling. Maria has all sorts of entertainments organised; troubadours, minstrels, mummers performing a play, acrobats and dancing.' He lowered his voice. 'I haven't danced in years, but do you know, I'm quite looking forward to it.'

A driver dressed in the Gravesmire family colours of red and yellow sat on a high seat of the wedding wagon, which was decorated with white roses and honeysuckle with seats covered in the finest fox fur. It was pulled by an immaculate white horse, his mane and tail braided with red and yellow ribbons.

Maria sat smiling and waving to the crowds and looking every inch the Lady Gravesmire. With a proud smile, Sir Gorvenal climbed up to join her. The groom flicked the reins, and the wagon rolled forward to a chorus of cheers.

'They make a handsome couple,' said a voice at his shoulder.

Annie looked strange in her fitted kirtle, he nearly didn't recognise her. 'Annie and Eleanor, Gods health. Yes, they do,' he said, watching the wagon disappear around the bend.

'M-Maria looks so p-pretty,' said Eleanor.

'She does, and so do you.' He was learning.

Eleanor smiled and held out her pink skirt. 'It's new and my favourite c-colour. M-Maria gave me this.' She twirled her hand in front of him, showing off a silver bracelet.

'I hope Sir Gorvenal is as rich as he looks,' Annie said. 'The way Maria is spending his money, he'll need to be.'

'I'm to be M-Maria's c-companion and we're going to live in Sir Gorvenal's big house.' Eleanor pointed vaguely into the distance behind her. 'Over there.'

'I'm sure you'll be very happy,' said Thomas.

Annie smiled at her. 'El, why don't you get in the next wagon? I'll join you a moment.'

Eleanor nodded and skipped to the line of waiting wagons.

'She's been so excited about this wedding, and what with Maria having everyone running this way and that, you can imagine how these last weeks have been!' Annie fanned herself. 'Tell me, how's Oxford? You look well.'

'So everyone has been telling me. Oxford is everything I dreamed it would be and more.'

He wanted to tell her about Rulf being out of his life. He wanted to tell her about Michael, a gentle man with a generous heart, but he couldn't. Instead, he said. 'I've made new friends and I'm enjoying my studies.'

Annie smiled. 'I'm glad. It's what you always wanted, and you deserve it.'

They stood in silence, watching the most important guests climb into the wagons.

'There's no need for you to worry,' Annie went on. 'Rose is quite happy, you know.'

'I know.'

'And Thomas, I'm glad you know the truth. I should have had the courage to tell you years ago.' Annie rested her hand on his arm and her eyes were a little moist as she looked up at him. 'You have a thriving estate and one day, James will take over. Your Mama would be very proud. You should be very proud. You couldn't have done more.'

He felt a little choked. 'I did my best. The past is behind us; it's the future we have to look to.'

'That's all any of us can do.' She dabbed her eyes with her kerchief. 'Look at me getting all maudlin. It's a wedding!'

They watched the wagons pull away until only one was left. Eleanor turned around and waved frantically.

'I'd better go. Are you coming with us in the wagon? It's a mile to the earl's house.'

Thomas glanced over his shoulder. His feet were sore, but Michael was waiting in the shadows under the tree. 'No, I'll walk.'

Annie smiled. 'Of course.'

Had she guessed? It wouldn't surprise him. Maybe it came with being a healer, but Annie had always struck him as being wiser than most.

He and Michael watched the last wagon turn the corner and disappear through the wide avenue of elm trees.

'There go my people. They don't need me now,' said Thomas.

'They will, from time to time,' Michael said. 'But come! Let us enjoy the festivities and then tomorrow, home to Oxford where we belong.'

Thomas smiled at him. 'Yes, home to Oxford.'

And together, they walked down the lane.

Look out for the third book in the Chiddleigh Saga that continues their story

Printed in Dunstable, United Kingdom